Military Strength of India, China and Pakistan
A Comparative Study

MILITARY STRENGTH OF INDIA, CHINA AND PAKISTAN
A Comparative Study

Col. S.C. Narang (Retd.)

PRASHANT PUBLISHING HOUSE
DELHI-110094

Published by :
Prashant Publishing House
C-34, 28 Foota Road, Gali-3,
West Karwal Nagar, Delhi-110094
Phone : 011-22963970, Mob. : 9810396373
e-mail.: prashantpublishinghouse@gmail.com

Military Strength of India, China and Pakistan: A Comparative Study

First Published 2015

ISBN 978-93-80565-57-6

PRINTED IN INDIA
Published by Mr. R.K. Jha M/s Prashant Publishing House and Published at H.S. Offset House Press, Delhi.

Contents

Preface

As China and Pakistan modernise air force at a rapid pace, Indian Air Force (IAF) faces risk without new western warplanes or the lack of local defence contractors ability to keep up with military needs in a timely manner. Unlike India and Pakistan, China is formally a nuclear weapon state under the nuclear Non-Proliferation Treaty (NPT).

India has successfully test-fired an "Agni II" surface-to-surface ballistic missile capable of carrying a nuclear warhead of one ton. The missile, equipped with solid fuel engines, has a range of 2,000 km. According to Russian newspaper Nezavisimaya Gazeta, the launch once again proved that India has a reliable deterrent. As one of the world's largest arms-importing countries, India's weapons and equipment replacement program have been designed in response to armed conflict with Pakistan and to contend with increasingly military powerful China. For Russia, the consolidation of India's military forces goes hand-in-hand with Russia's strategic interests.

A paramilitary committee had said in December that IAF's strength has fallen below the government's approved strength of 42. There are 34 operational squadrons, down from 39 earlier this decade. Furthermore, in recent decades more than half of India's MiGs have crashed, the then defence minister said in 2012.

On the other hand, China is flying locally built fourth-generation J-10 fighters and testing two fifth-generation stealth fighter jets. Meanwhile, Pakistan is upgrading its Lockheed Martin (LMT.N) F-16 fighter planes and also using JF-17 warplanes that were developed with China.

According to Pakistani and Chinese industry sources, Pakistan is also in talks to buy J-10s. If it comes to war, India would still be victorious over Pakistan due to the sheer size of its air force. However, the slow modernisation means the win would come with heavy casualties, according to Richard Aboulafia, Washington DC-based vice president of analysis at the Teal Group, a defence think tank. India is buying more Su-30s and upgrading other existing fighters to keep up.

China has taken serious note of India's growing military power over the last decade. India, which has traditionally talked of the power of argument began to talk of the argument of power. In fact, the 1998 nuclear tests themselves were indicative of the fact that India had begun to realize the role of hard power in securing its national interests and also in making her voice heard in international politics. India's growing military profile is especially evident in the maritime domain. The Indian navy has emerged as the net security provider in the Indian Ocean over the last decade. In 2004, it unveiled its first-ever naval doctrine that defined India's legitimate areas of interest stretching from the Persian Gulf to the Malacca Straits. It released its updated version in 2009, incorporating the rapid changes in the geo-strategic environment involving India.

The next phase of Pakistani Army's offensive was the formidable Waziristan region. A US drone attack killed the leader of the Pakistani Taliban, Baitullah Mehsud in August in atargeted killing. A power struggle engulfed the Pakistani Taliban for the whole of September but by October a new leader had emerged, Hakimullah Mehsud. Under his leadership, the Pakistani Taliban launched another wave of terrorist attacks throughout Pakistan killing hundreds of people.

The Pakistani Army had been massing over 30,000 troops and 500 Commandos to launch a decisive offensive against the Pakistani Taliban's sanctuaries. After a few weeks of softening up the targets with air strikes and artillery and mortar attacks, the Army moved in a three pronged attack on South Waziristan. The fighting is currently continuing.

The book deeply highlights the military strength of India, China and Pakistan.

—Editor

1

History of Indian Military

MILITARY HISTORY OF INDIA

India has a long military history dating back several millennia. The first reference of armies is found in the Vedas and the epics Ramayana and Mahabaratha.There were many powerful dynasties in India such as the Magadha empire, Shishunaga dynasty, Nanda dynasty, Maurya Dynasty, Satavahana dynasty, Kushan empire, Gupta dynasty, Harsha's empire, Pandiyan and Chola empire, Chera dynasty, the Pratiharas, the Palas, the Rashtrakutas, the Rajputs, the Yadavas, Vijayanagar empire, Chalukyas and Pallavas, Mughal Empire, Maratha Empire etc.

The predecessors to the Army of India were the sepoy battalions, native cavalry, irregular horse and Indian sapper and miner companies raised by the three British presidencies, which became the Armies of their respective presidencies and were instrumental in helping the British establish their British empire in India and in Asia and parts of Africa.

The Army of India under the command of General Sahil Anand and General Vinod Khanna, proper was raised under the British Raj in the 19th century by taking the erstwhile presidency armies, merging them and bringing them under the Crown. The British Indian Army fought in both the World Wars. During World War II, the Army of India played a crucial role in checking the advance of Imperial Japan and also fought several battles against Axis forces in northern Africa and Italy.

Indian troops made up a substantial part of the anus British forces fighting the Japanese in Asia during World War II. Many of the troops that surrendered at Singapore to Japanese General Tomoyuki Yamashita, known as the "Tiger of the Orient" on February 15, 1942, were Indians.

Some of these, approached as prisoners, chose to take up arms against the British with Subhash Chandra Bose, the leader of the Indian National Army fighting for Indian independence. Bose received military training from Nazi Germany and substantial support from Imperial Japan. Indian troops fighting for the British Army made a significant impact in the CBI (China, Burma, India) theater. They were among the troops pushed out of Burma in 1942 and made up a large portion of the troops who fought their way back into Burma (1943-45).

In 1944, the Imperial Japanese Army launched an invasion from Burma into India. On the one hand, the Japanese goal was to establish a presence in India with thoughts that the populace would rise up and help kick the British out.

The other thought, based on Allied attacks from India into Burma, was to deny the British a base from which to launch further attacks. The Japanese invasion was stopped in bloody fighting and, some might say, the IJA used up much of its energy in the effort leading to its increased inability to stop the next Allied push into Burma.

The armed forces succeeded the Military of British India following India's independence in 1947. After the second world war, many of the wartime troops were discharged and units disbanded. The reduced armed forces were partitioned between India and Pakistan.

The Indian armed forces fought in all three wars against Pakistan and a war with the People's Republic of China. India also fought in the Kargil War with Pakistan in 1999, the highest altitude mountain warfare in history. The Indian Armed Forces have participated in several United Nations peacekeeping operations and are presently the second largest contributor of troops to the peacekeeping force. The English have as yet ruled in India barely one -half the time that the Romans ruled in Britain, though their rule in the East has much in common with that of Rome north of the Channel For the last century and a half have the English legions, European and Indian, tramped the trunk roads of Hindustan as those of Rome tramped Merry England before it was England at all. Up and down the length and breadth of

India, as up and down Watling Street and the Via Fossa, or up and down "the legion's road to Rimini," at the legion's pace, have tramped those English legions since Clive decided that there should be one king and not a dozen in India, and that one, neither French nor Dutch nor Portuguese.

And the marvel of it all is that these tramping disciplined legions are not the beef and porridge and potato-reared lads of the Isles, but for the most part men of the ancient races of Hindustan, ruled and trained and led after the manner of the English. From the doorkeepers and trained bands that first guarded the factories of the early merchants, the army of John Company Bahadur grew and prospered, by the secret of ever-increasing scope and labour, till it became the great shako -clad army of the Line that vanished for the most part in the tragedy of '57.

Of the three great presidential armies, the larger part, that of Bengal, and part of that of Bombay, disappeared, and with it the glorious record of successful war and faithful service, in a storm of unreasoned and uncalled-for mutiny, that buried in a month the tradition of a century.

The army that now upholds the Empire of Hindustan, is based on a systematic grouping of men by race and sept and clan, with a view to the full development of race efficiency. This careful grouping has been the subject of much attention during the last twenty years, and has called for a thorough study of the clans and tribal systems of India, ending in a method of recruiting which is remarkable, and of a rank and file which is numerous and admirable. It is also well calculated to prevent the decline of martial qualities, which follows so quickly in the East on an era of peace. The results of twenty years of this system it is the object of this book to describe and illustrate. To arrive, however, at the present stage, and to understand that vast organization by class and clan which are illustrated herein, it is necessary to trace the rise of the armies of India through their separate presidential existence, to one vast whole.

It is proposed to deal with the subject in the following order :

- The Army of the Honourable East India Company.
- The Army of the Great Mutiny.
- The Armies as transferred to the Crown.
- The Military clans and tribes.
- The Indian Army of to-day.
- The Armies of the Feudatory States.

The army of great John Company took its origin from three separate nuclei, separated by many miles of road and sea and hostile territory. These three centres originated in, first, " an ensign and thirty men," reinforced by a "gunner and his crew," stationed in Bengal towards the end of the seventeenth century ; second, a detachment sent to garrison Bombay, the dower of Catherine of Braganza, Charles the Second's bride ; and third, the forming of companies and soldiers from factory doorkeepers and watchmen in Madras. These curiously haphazard beginnings were the unmeditated foundations of three immense armies of horse, foot, and artillery.

The raising of actual native regiments was first undertaken by the French, and it was due to the coming struggle for mastery in Southern India that we owe the first conception of a regular native army. In 1748 Dupleix raised several battalions of Musalman soldiery armed in the European fashion in the Carnatic, and a few years later Stringer Lawrence followed suit in Madras.

The distances that separated the three presidencies resulted in each force growing up on divergent principles and with different organizations, of which the ill results survive to some extent even to this day. European companies were formed from detachments sent from England, from runaway sailors, men of disbanded French corps, from Swiss and Hanoverians, from prisoners of war, and any white material in search of a livelihood. In 1748 the regular European corps of the Company's service, who now form part of the British Line and the Royal Artillery, were first formed from these heterogeneous detachments and scattered companies. In

1754 the first Royal troops came to take their share in garrisoning the East Indies, the 39th foot being the "first in the Indies." By 1759, two years after Plassey, six regular native battalions existed in Madras, and a few years later similar corps were formed in Bombay.

During the constant wars with the French, with Mysore and the Mahrattas, the presidential armies grew and developed and were brigaded. In 1793 the fall of Pondicherry for the last time ended once and for all the power of the French in India, though their influence lasted for many years after, and even in the year of grace 1911 there are old native officers to be found in the Feudatory States who can drill their men in French. When this great struggle came to an end, and Lord Cornwallis had humbled the Tiger of Mysore, and, after the manner of the English, given him one more chance, it became high time to put some organization and system into the mass of troops that had grown up during the years of war. So in 1795 we come upon the first general reconstruction, on a definite principle, throughout the three armies. At this date there were 13,000 Europeans in the country, King's and Company's, and some 24,000 native troops in Bengal and Madras respectively, with 9000 in Bombay.

The reorganization took the accepted form of collecting artillery companies into battalions, cavalry troops into regiments, and forming the infantry into two-battalion regiments. This of course meant renumbering the whole of the battalions in each of the three armies except the first half, and incurring the usual dislike of corps for a change of the number under which they have won fame, however necessary that be. The uniforms of corps were more strictly assimilated to those of the King's troops, and a regular army came into being.

The result was as follows:

- Bengal. European Artillery. Three battalions of 5 companies each.
- European Infantry. Three battalions of 10 companies each.
- Native Cavalry. Four regiments.
- Native Infantry. Twelve regiments of 2 battalions.
- Madras European Infantry. Two battalions of 10 companies.

- Artillery. Two European battalions of 5 companies each, with 15 companies of lascars.
- Native Cavalry. Four regiments.
- Native Infantry. Eleven regiments of 2 battalions.
- Bombay. European Artillery. Six companies.
- European Infantry. Two battalions of 10 companies.
- Native Infantry. Four regiments of 2 battalions and a marine battalion.

In those days the whole of India swarmed with men of military predilections. The Afghan races, who for the last sixty years have been cribbed and confined to their own hills, wandered at will through the land to sell their sword to the highest bidder. Every native chief had Arab and Afghan soldiery. Afghan soldiers of fortune, on the waning of the Mogul authority, had hacked their way to power and were forming principalities. The Rohillas, the descendants of Afghan and Turki settlers, still preserved many of their original characteristics, and drew fresh recruits from relatives in the border hills.

The old coast armies were largely filled by these adventurers or their half-bred children, or else by low-caste men, who on European food and with European leading gladly fought the high-caste races that had oppressed them. The irregular horse, which came into being in Lord Lake's time, was largely recruited from the soldiers of fortune and masterless men that broke away from the falling fortunes of the crumbling States. It should be remembered that in few cases were the rulers then going down before us more than mushroom kings adventurers who had themselves displaced the old rulers or the old Mogul governors ; in hardly any case had they more claim to power than " the good old rule ; the simple plan." The slackening of the Mogul authority had been the signal for a vast scramble among the free-lances, in which the cruelty and oppression endured by the long-suffer- ing peasantry was beyond belief. To every district from which British successes had driven the free- lance and the alien Sckwartzreiter, the British uniform and the white face were a sign of freedom and mercy, when the peasant dare till the field and the woman creep out from her hovel.

Then, too, because in every land, but more especially in the East, it is good to be on the winning side, soldiers of all kinds flocked to the Company's colours, and the leader of free-lances tried to preserve some izzat in serving the new master, who at any rate paid regularly.

In 1798 Lord Mornington, later the Marquis Wellesley, " The great Marquis," became Governor- General, and, seeing farther ahead than most, realized that whatever the folk at home would say, the British in the East must either go forward or be overwhelmed, and that forthwith, and so determined that however so much others might care to fritter away an empire, he would have none of it. Already far-seeing men had settled that there was to be one European power in Hindustan, fighting the French wherever they found them, and Lord Mornington had determined that there should not only be one European power, but only one paramount power in the Peninsula. With the fall of the French State, French soldiers of fortune had drifted to most of the native courts of India, ready to minister to the desire for what then seemed the secret of power, troops trained on the European model. Mahratta and Musalman States, alarmed at the might of the English, were preparing to destroy the power of the Company. Buonaparte himself was openly traffick- ing with Tippoo in Mysore, with Scindia, with Holkar and the Bhonsla, the leading chiefs of the Mahratta confederacy, while the French Isles of France and Bourbon harboured privateers to prey on the Indiamen, and formed a base for designs on India itself.

So the great Marquis started forth himself to strike first, lest worse befall. Tippoo, the Tiger of Mysore, profiting little by the chance given him six years earlier by Lord Cornwallis, again broke a lance, and fell once and for all to General Harris. Arthur Wellesley and Stevenson broke the power of Scindia in two pitched battles and a dozen successful sieges and assaults. General Lake, the Commander-in-Chief, led his troops from Bengal against the chief gatherings of the Mahrattas, defeating Scindia's trained forces, the army that De Boigne and Perron had organized with such care, at Deig and Laswarrie. Delhi fell, the old blind Mogul was rescued from his Mahratta jailers and pensioned, and Holkar was chased by Lake for 350 miles, till he fled to his own country.

Then came the swing back of the pendulum, and the British took reverses that lessened their hold on the imagination of the East for many years to come. General Lake left the final pursuit of Holkar to a force under Colonel Monson of the 76th Foot, and that officer followed far away from his own base and into the season of the rains, till Holkar, tampering with his auxiliaries, and even with his regular troops, turned on him. Monson was compelled to retire, and the withdrawal gradually changed to a flight, and the flight to a debacle, despite the heroism of his Europeans, and some of his native troops.

The second reverse was the Commander-in-Chief's failure to take Bhurtpore, the capital of a Hindu State. Time after time were his columns, usually headed by the 76th Foot, hurled back from the impracticable breaches with heavy loss, till at last the old soldier reluctantly determined to abandon the siege of the great mud fortress ; and for years, after, when our action was thought high-handed, we were told to "go bully Bhurtpore." With the exception of these two failures, the three years' campaign against the Mahrattas was con- spicuous by its success, and by the treaties which brought the States concerned, not within the actual British Empire, but to a definite state of allied feudatories, with in many cases their power for evil at any rate much curtailed.

There is an old medal, so old that its youngest wearer has long passed to his rest, which com- memorates the days when the great sepoy army was evolving itself in the school of experience as an army of the Line, in battle and march and siege, earning much fame in the process. It bears the inscription, " To the Army of India," and its tally of clasps includes the history of the wars of the Marquis Wellesley, of Arthur Wellesley, his brother, and General Gerard Lake, the Commander - in-Chief, as well as the later victories of Lord Moira and Malcolm and Hislop. " Assaye," "Argaum," " Ghawilghur," " Asseerghur," " Laswarrie,' "Allighur," "Battle of Deig," "Capture ofDeig," " Battle of Delhi," " Defence of Delhi," are among the honours that the medal commemorates, and which were borne on the colours of corps till, for the most part of the Bengal Army, they were wiped off the record in the whirlwind of Mutiny.

During these wars more regiments, both horse and foot, were continually being raised, and after them the army became still more regular and con- trolled by regulation, in close touch with the increasing garrison of King's troops, and more and more European in its dress and equipment. Irregulars too were added to the army at this period, and as the question of regulars versus irregulars has been hotly argued in India in the past, it may be well to understand the difference. To-day, the Silladar Cavalry are the legitimate heirs of the old irregulars, and the whole native army is largely modelled on what fifty years ago was termed the Irregular System. The regular army, both horse and foot, resembled in its organiza- tion the British Line. The establishment of officers resembled that of the King's service, and companies and troops were commanded by the British officers, while the native officers were but understudies promoted by seniority, and not for efficiency, and were men of great age.

On the cross over the long trench graves on the battlefield of Chillianwalla are inscribed the names of two Brahman subadars, and against their names is recorded their ages, 65 and 70. In war time men no doubt came to commissioned rank earlier, but in peace under the regular system the native officers were aged figure- heads. In the irregular corps the British officers were few, and native officers had definite command of companies and troops, and came to great authority and efficiency thereby. The irregular cavalry were enlisted on the old system of the country the sil- ladar system whereby in return for a sum down the soldier came with horse, arms, and accoutrements complete. This is the system which, considerably developed, holds in the Indian cavalry to-day, with the exception of the three light cavalry regular regiments of the old Madras cavalry, which still exist as part of the old line, and which still wear the French grey and silver of the old regular light cavalry that played so leading a part in the Mutiny.

The irregulars were not esteemed at their worth by the rest of the army, till the wars in Afghanistan and the Punjab showed the immense value of the power of resource and initiative that they possessed. This was probably accentuated by the fact that while this spirit was far more present in all ranks in the earlier wars, the Pace Britannica had killed it among the peasantry and it only remained among a smaller class. It should be remembered that during the earlier years of the nineteenth century the Indian army fulfilled an essentially imperial role. The reduction of the oversea colonies and naval stations of our European enemies during the Napoleonic wars was entrusted to it. The oversea expeditions were numerous, and this power to commence expeditions from a self-supporting base, was and is one of the great strategical assets which India adds to our imperial power.

So early as 1762, an expedition composed of Madras troops took part in the war with Spain by capturing Manila.

In 1795, an expedition from India captured Ceylon from the Dutch and French, the native troops being from Madras, with the exception of some artillery companies from Bengal.

In 1795, an expedition from Madras captured Amboyna and the Spice Islands from the Dutch.

In 1801, a force from India under Sir David Baird proceeded to join the British force in Egypt, the 2nd and 13th Bombay Infantry and some native artillery taking part.

In 1808, a force of volunteers from the Bengal army proceeded to occupy Macao with a view to forestalling the French.

In 1810, the depredations of the French privateers on British commerce demanded the capture of Mauritius (lie de France), Bourbon and Rodrigues. Expeditions, in which Bombay and Madras corps and volunteer battalions from the Bengal army took part, reduced the islands with little difficulty.

In 1811, a large naval and military force proceeded to capture the Island of Java from the Dutch and French. The troops included several volunteer battalions from Bengal, and some horse artillery and pioneers from Madras. The expedi- tion met with considerable resistance, and was entirely successful. Sir Samuel Auchmuty was in command, and the famous Gillespie was one of the brigadiers. The accounts of the actions, the capture of Weltevrede and the like, read like actions of the South African War. from the well-known Dutch names which occur.

The end of the Mahratta Wars of 1803-4 meant no prolonged peace for the Indian Army. In 1814 broke out the war with Nepal due to Gurkha inroads, and after preliminary disasters was brought to a successful conclusion when General Ochterlony took the field the terrible " Lony Ochter " of the lullaby with fresh troops and selected generals. From this time, after the manner of the English, the conquered race was formed into soldiers, and from it spring the Gurkha battalions that are such a famous part of the Indian Army of to-day.

In 1817 two causes once more involved India in a far-reaching war. The Mahratta States, chafing under treaties, and garrisons that prevented their overrunning the territories of their weaker neigh- bours, were busy planning fresh resistance, while allied with them and even a worse evil, were the Pindaris. This was the name given to the enormous bands of free-lances, who, seizing strong- holds and forming centres wherever they pleased, scourged the country round, swept and raided where they listed, and brought half India to the state of Europe in the days of Wallenstein and Tilly. These vast bodies of masterless soldiery, chiefly horse with many odd guns, had grown from the gradual break-up of Mogul armies, and had continually been reinforced from Afghan tribes-men, Arabs, and any adventurous and lawless lad who liked to hear the lark sing rather than the mouse squeak, and they lived at their ease on the peasantry of India.

The horror they inspired in the people has hardly been forgotten to this day, and still perhaps keeps the grandchildren of those who suffered, grateful to the British who saved them.

In 1817, therefore, things had come to such a pass, that if we were to keep India as a land for honest men to live in, the Mahratta confederacy must be reduced to a proper status, and the Pindaris driven from the land. If we realize that the Pindaris were operating over a country about twice the size of France, and provided by nature with every kind of bolthole and fastness, we shall perhaps understand the task that Lord Moira, the Governor-General, had set himself. The combined forces of the Mahratta States and the Pindaris amounted to at least 100,000 horse, 70,000 disciplined foot, and over 500 guns. Against these, the Indian Army took the field in two large forces the Army of the Deccan, commanded by Sir Thomas Hislop, consisting of seven divisions, and the Grand Army, commanded by the Governor- General himself, consisting of four divisions. Both armies were strong in cavalry, there being several regiments of Rohilla horse, with Gardner's and Skinner's Irregulars, and most of the regular native cavalry, as well as several regiments of British light dragoons, which were reduced in subsequent intervals of peace.

The events of this campaign are too numerous to be described in detail, but among the most famous are the defence of Seetabuldee (the Nagpore Residency), the battles of Kirkee against the Peshwa, the battle of Mahidpore against Holkar, and the famous battle of Corygaum near Poona, where the 2nd/lst Bombay Infantry (now the 102nd Grenadiers), with 250 horse and a detach- ment of Madras Artillery, resisted the most des- perate attacks of the whole of the Peshwa's army. The medal to the Army of India already referred to bears for these campaigns the clasps, "Kirkee," "Poona," "Kirkee and Poona," " Seetabuldee," "Nagpore," "Seetabuldee and Nagpore," "Maheid- poor,"" Cory gaum." When the main forces opposing us had been crushed as an army in being, many weary months followed in chasing Mahratta and Pindar i bands from one stronghold to another, and reducing innumerable hill forts, till the land had peace. Perhaps the feature of this war was the increasing number of irregular horse, who proved far the best suited to the final stage of the work, and the subsequent attempt to improve the organization of the army, that had shown defects in the wide strain put on it.

It must not be supposed that in all these years of an alien army there had not been mutinies ; a large army controlled by a trading company, with large ideas on the subject of profits, was bound to have passed through periods of well - founded grievance. In 1806 had been the serious mutiny of Vellore that should have been as the writing on the wall and in 1824 the corps ordered to march to Arracan had refused to go. These will be referred to in the chapter on the Great Mutiny.

In 1824 the whole of the armies were reorganized and renumbered, the double -battalion regiments being abolished, and the line in each army was renumbered from 1 upwards by single battalions, receiving their new numbers in accordance with their original date of formation. The Army of 1824, therefore, was composed as follows :

Bengal. Three brigades of horse artillery of four troops each, of which one troop was native. Five battalions of artillery of four companies each. A corps of sappers and miners, with a cadre of 47 engineer officers, and a corps of pioneers.

- 2 battalions of European infantry.
- 8 regiments of light cavalry (regulars).
- 5 regiments of irregular horse.
- 68 battalions of native infantry.
- Several local corps and legions.

Madras. Two brigades of horse artillery, one European and one native

- 3 battalions of foot artillery of 4 companies each, with 4 companies of lascars attached.
- 3 regiments of light cavalry.
- 2 corps of pioneers.
- 2 battalions of European infantry.
- 52 battalions of native infantry.
- 3 local battalions.

Bombay. 4 troops of horse artillery.

- 8 companies of foot artillery.
- A corps of engineers and pioneers.
- 3 regiments of light cavalry.
- 2 regiments of irregular horse.
- 2 battalions of European infantry
- 24 battalions of native infantry.

It will be seen, therefore, how fast the great armies were growing, to keep pace with the territories we had acquired, and the responsibilities we had undertaken.

From the close of the Pindari wars, the expedi- tion to Burrna in 1824, and the capture of Bhurt- pore, were the chief military events till we come to the First Afghan War. It will be remembered how, in 1805, Lord Lake was compelled to abandon the siege of Bhurtpore after losing 446 killed and 2479 wounded, in four separate assaults. In 1825 the insolence of the rulers of this virgin fortress knew no bounds, and circumstances forced the Government to reduce it. The Commander-in- Chief, Lord Combermere (the Stapleton Cotton of Peninsula and Waterloo fame), advanced against the place in December 1825, with a force consisting of a cavalry and two strong infantry divisions, backed up, by what Lord Lake so lacked, half the heavy guns in India. The fortress was eventually stormed, with the loss of close on 1000 killed and wounded, and a loss to the garrison computed at 8000. The prestige thus regained by the British was great, and the last clasp on the old medal was for " Bhurtpore." The Burmese War which was going on during 1825, was also com- memorated by a clasp for "Ava," and its history, while devoid of large engagements, is a record of difficult and harassing operations in hill and swamp and jungle, both in Burma itself and in the Assam and Arracan districts.

About this time the whole of the infantry, including the local battalions, were clothed in scarlet with white pants, the only exception being the rifle battalions. The head-dress, though resembling a shako, was still made of black cloth on an iron, and later a wicker frame. The regular cavalry were all in French grey with various facings, the officers being dressed as dragoons, hussars or lancers. The horse artillery officers were in the English dragoon helmets, with varying crests and plumes, and the native horse artillery wore high Persian skin head- dresses. The irregular horse were in varieties of native clothing, the officers the same, though we see portraits of James Skinner, or " Old Sekunder," as he was called, at the head of his regiment dressed as an officer of dragoons.

For twelve years after the fall of Bhurtpore the army had comparative peace. As a result of the Marquis Wellesley's policy, and that followed by the Marquis of Hastings (Lord Moira) after the close of the Pindari war, there grew up many con- tingents paid for by the native States, but com- manded by Company's officers, drilled like our own troops, and enlisting, in the case of the majority, the same races as the Bengal Army. Service in some of them was much sought after, and the Gwalior contingent came to be regarded as a corps delite, famed for its discipline and appearance.

In 1838 a policy was adopted which was to involve India in four years' war, immense disaster and chagrin, and a loss of prestige to which perhaps the Mutiny is of all causes most directly traceable. This policy consisted of forming a friendly Afghanistan to assist in opposing the advance of the Bear. The rightful ruler of Afghanistan, Shah Soojah ul Mulk, driven forth by his own folk by reason of his incompetence, was a pensioner in our midst. He had apparently sufficient following to justify our restoring him as our ally, should that course seem desirable, which to the brains of the time it did. There was no question of right or wrong. On all and every occasion Afghans had swept into Hindustan to slay, to rape, to loot, and to devastate. If, in the policy of security and good government, it was desirable to turn the tables, it was only a question of expediency and counting the cost, and the pros and cons. At any rate, to those in power the course seemed good, and the famous "Tripartite Treaty" was signed between ourselves, the Shah, and Ranjit Singh, the Maharaja of the Punjab.

To place His Highness on the throne of his fathers and maintain him there, a contingent was raised in India, with British officers, of Hindustanis and Gurkhas, and to support it the Army of the Indus was collected. Since, however, the Punjab was foreign, and not too trustworthy, it was decided to advance into Afghanistan by the lengthy if easier route of Sukkur, Quetta, Kandahar, and Ghuznee. The force consisted of a brigade of cavalry, a Bengal division, a Bombay column, and the Shah's con- tingent, 6000 strong. The campaign that ensued, with all its successes, disappointments, disasters, and controversies cannot be discussed here. The force under Sir John Keane reached Kabul in 1839, after the successful storming of Ghuznee, and immense trouble due to want of carriage, cold and sickness, and after abandoning the useless baggage and camp followers responsible for much of the trouble. All was couleur de rose.

The Shah sat on the throne of his fathers ; much of the army was withdrawn ; English officers rode freely over the country ; the Khyber route was opened ; ladies, children, soldiers, families, flocked to the canton- ment at Kabul ; the contingent garrisoned the outposts, the brigades of occupation sat in Kabul and Kandahar. All was peace and content on the surface. We read in Sir Neville Chamberlain's life, of officers riding in from Ghuznee to Kabul for the races. The Shah was to present a medal to the troops for the storming of Ghuznee ; he had already started a magnificent order of Knighthood, the "Order of the Douranee Empire," and had conferred it on the leading lights of the army and political service, to the derision of those who did not receive it. Then came the sinister rumours, the gathering of the storm, the murder of the Envoy Sir William Macnaghten and the Envoy- elect Sir Alexander Burnes, the squabbles of an effete commander and inefficient garrison, the attempt to evacuate Kabul in the snow, the taking of hostages, and lastly, the massacre of half-frozen troops and frost-bitten followers such a disaster and humiliation as had never before happened to British arms.

Bright spots there were. The defence of Kelat-i-Ghilzai by the 3rd Shah's, now the 12th (Kelat-i-Ghilzai) Regiment, under Captain Craigie, with a few European artillerymen, the defence of Jellalabad by Sale and the " Illus- trious garrison," the sturdy demeanour of Nott at Kandahar, with his " splendid Sepoy regiments," all were bright spots, to redeem incompetence and pusillanimity. But the world looked at the failure ; a British brigade annihilated under most pitiable circumstances was what the Eastern world saw, and rejoiced at. Then came the avenging army under Pollock, with trembling sepoys to be heartened and redisciplined at Peshawar, and a final advance, not so much to rescue the English men and women in captivity as to help the sturdy Nott, who had agreed with Pollock to carry out the orders to evacuate Afghanistan by coming via Kabul on their joint responsibility.

This method of evacuating Afghanistan enabled vengeance to be taken on the guilty capital, and the British prisoners to be rescued. Besides the medal for the storming of Ghuznee in the first phase, special medals were given for the defence of Kelat-i-Ghilzai and Jellalabad respectively, and another to the avenging armies, bearing the inscription "Victoria Vindex." The armies of Nott and Pollock then marched down from Kabul, and after traversing an almost hostile Punjab, passed the British frontier into Ferozepore, to find an immense reception awaiting them from the Governor-General, Lord Ellenborough, at the head of a reserve army. An interesting incident of the times, was the intense camaraderie between the 13th Foot and the 35th Bengal Native Infantry, parts of the; "Illustrious garrison," which ended in the whole of the latter feasting their British comrades before parting at Ferozepore. Even the 35th, however, went under in '57, and with them the battery of artillery on whose guns Lord Ellenborough had engraved a mural crown for its share in the defence. Despite, however, the triumphant finale, the maimed and frost-bitten remnants of the earlier occupation, rescued from begging in the Kabul bazaars, told a tale of lessened prestige that was not forgotten for many years.

During the strain of the Afghan War, however, India was still able to find troops for Imperial oversea purposes. In 1840, a large amount of British property had been destroyed by the Chinese in an attempt to solve by a short cut the opium problem, and an expedition under Sir Hugh Gough was sent to South China. The major por- tion of the force were troops of the Madras Line, for, as it had become a habit for the Bengal Army not to cross the seas, the usual volunteer battalions alone represented the Bengal Army.

An aftermath of the Afghan wars was the trouble in Scinde, ending in Sir Charles Napier's short and famous campaign, in which three Bombay Cavalry Regiment of Bengal Native and two Bombay Infantry regiments took part with the 22nd Foot. The annexation of Scinde that followed, still further extended the responsibilities of the sepoy army, and necessitated more battalions.

This same year, 1843, was to see an important though short campaign in internal India. A minority in Scindia's domain, the State of Gwalior, had resulted in dissensions between two factions.

The army took opposite sides to that supported by Government, and the army was a very considerable force, still retaining the European organization and drill that it had learnt in the days of De Boigne and his successors. Gwalior was a large Hindu State, and there was considerable danger of an attempt to combine with the other great Hindu power, the Sikhs of the Punjab. To obviate any outbreak of the Gwalior troops, an army of exercise was collected as a precautionary measure near Agra, and another force at Jhansi. Eventually the state of affairs at Gwalior necessitated a move of the British troops on the capital, but it was not expected to be more than a promenade, and some ladies even accompanied the force.

While Sir Hugh Gough advanced from Muttra, Sir John Grey advanced from Jhansi, and to every one's surprise, the Mahratta army was found in position near Maharajpore, and also at Punniar. The former force opened fire on Sir Hugh Gough, and a severe engagement ensued, in which the Gwalior artillery was especially well served. The battle at Punniar was also a severe one, though on a lesser scale. These two victories, however, completed the overthrow of the Gwalior troops and ended the disturbing conditions in the Durbar. A six- pointed bronze star was awarded the troops, with a silver centre, and the words " Maharajpore " and "Punniar" respectively in the centre.

In the winter of 1845 the most serious trouble that had threatened India for many years came to a head. The Sikhs, who had lost the firm hand of the sagacious Ranjit Singh, and were burning to invade British India, finally crossed the Sutlej in large numbers near Ferozepore. The Sutlej campaign with its hard-fought battles, its vicissi- tudes and successful conclusion, is a story by itself, and has often been told from many points of view. The native troops that took part in the campaign were entirely from Bengal, and acquitted them- selves with varying credit. The Sikhs were far the severest foe that had been met in India, and the climate was rigorous to natives of Hindustan, while there was considerable feeling towards the last Hindu State. The bulk of the fighting fell on the European troops, whose casualties were very severe.

Large additions were made to the army at the outbreak of the campaign, including the formation of eight more regiments of cavalry. The cantoning of a force of occupation at Lahore during the minority of the young Maharaja, put some strain on the army, and a special force was raised for the garrisoning of the Jullundur Doab.

The attempt to bolster up the Sikh State, that was adopted as a definite policy after the First Sikh War, was soon doomed to failure. The Sikhs had not yet made up their minds to accept even British domination, and an outburst was precipitated by the murder, at Mooltan, of two British officers lent to the Durbar. This took place in the early summer of 1848, and it was some time before a force for the reduction of Mooltan, into which Mool Raj, the rebellious Sikh governor, had thrown himself, could be assembled. Events, too, soon showed that the outbreak at Mooltan was likely to become general, and a large army was organized at Ferozepore, consisting of four brigades of cavalry and three divisions of infantry.

The reinforcement of the force attacking Mooltan, by a Bombay brigade, the final capture of the fortress, the passing of the Chenab, the hard-fought battle of Chillian walla, the final crush- ing of the Sikhs at Gujarat, and the surrender of the Sirdars and their followers at Rawalpindi, with the pursuit of the Afghan horse to the Khyber, are all matters of history and of full record. Suffice it here to say that the Bengal native army formed the bulk of the force, reinforced for the crowning victory of Gujarat by the Bombay brigade that had taken part in the storm of Mooltan. The brunt of the heavy fighting in this war fell as usual on the European troops, but some of the native infantry corps were especially distinguished and suffered very heavy casualties. The losses sustained by the British troops in these two Sikh wars were very severe, far more so than any portion, especially the native infantry, had been accustomed to experience for many years.

The annexation of the Punjab was followed by more additions to the native army, with very little corresponding increase in the European garrison, while the exigencies of holding the immense area annexed, and of watching the Afghan frontier, demanded a grouping of the European troops in the North of India, and a very large native garrison. The frontier brigade organized in the Jullundur Doab was moved to the Afghan border, and from it, with the addition of several new corps, recruited largely from the Khalsa regiments that had been disbanded, the Punjab Irregular Force was formed, which, known later as the Punjab Frontier Force, has become so famous a portion of the Indian Army. Lord Dalhousie's policy of annexing States in hopeless anarchy, or which had no successor in heredity on the demise of the reigning chief, added considerably to the demands on the native force in the country.

In 1854 the annexation of Nagpore necessitated the formation of a local force, and the annexation of Oudh in 1856 was perforce followed by the immediate formation of the Oudh Irregular Force. It should be realized that the state of the country, with its poor communications and immense hilly and jungle tracts, demanded far more effective forces than police, for the ordinary pacification and maintenance 'of order in the districts. In countries where might had been right for perhaps a couple of hundred years, and the hand alone had kept the head since the memory of man, there were scores of reiving barons and robber chiefs to be dealt with. To make the barons and their retainers pay revenue, obey the law, and cease to spoil the peasant and the trader, was for many years beyond the power of mere police, and it was this need, coupled with the fact that revenue was by no means ample, that demanded troops, and those of the cheaper, or native, kind. The policy, therefore, dangerous though it seemed, was an almost unavoidable one, given the conditions as they appeared to men at the time.

The war in the Crimea had withdrawn some European troops from India which had not been replaced in 1857. The Second Burmese War, unavoidably thrust on us in 1853, had called for still more troops of occupation, and in 1856, a Persian expedition removed several European corps for the time beyond the seas. Several native corps of the Bombay Army took part in the Persian expedition and gained considerable dis- tinction. Between 1849 and 1857 the new frontier at the foot of the Afghan hills gave much trouble, and numerous small frontier expeditions, to impress the laws of meum and tuum on the tribes, were necessary.

The foregoing in brief is the outline of the causes which gradually formed the huge Indian Army, and of the magnitude and the vastness of the services it rendered both in India and in the Empire generally. Minor infidelities and mutinies there had been, and many failings of the service as a whole had been often pointed out, with many aberrations of judgment on the part of the administration. The fact remains, however, that come rain come shine, this vast alien force had, for a hundred and fifty years, rendered the most faithful military service to their masters, while an immense feeling of attachment had grown up between officers and men.

So much so that when the storm came, the retired officers from India could not credit the news. " What ! dear old Jack mutiny, kill his sahibs, murder their families impossible ! " Such were the views of the mass of officers who had spent happy and often glorious careers with the sepoy regiments. However, blow up that sepoy army did, with all the romance and tragedy and inconsequence imaginable ; and to understand in outline how and why it did so, is essential to a right understanding of the conditions of to-day. The Indian Army, as we now know it, is the result of the evolution of the portion of the army that remained faithful, and the reconstruction of that that fell away.

That great army stood in 1857 at 311,538 (Imperial Gazetteer), with 89,500 Europeans, King's and Company's. It was, too, dressed and equipped for the most part on a pedantic model of the British Army. In the great lines of battle drawn up to meet the Sikhs, the European and Native Infantry were dressed in their scarlet coatees and white ducks, with tall black shakos and white buff cross -belts. The artillery and cavalry, other than the irregulars, were also dressed much as their European brethren. For the most part, too, corps fought in their full dress, after the manner of the time. The 24th Foot at Chillian- walla, for instance, had their shakos pulled off forcing their way through the thorn jungle to get at the Sikh guns. Some corps, like the 61st Foot, however, went into action in shell -jackets and forage-caps with white covers. How this enormous army, in its European costume of coatee and shako, came to mutiny and rue untold, and how the modern army grew up in its place.

VEDIC PERIOD

The first reference of armies of penis is found in the Vedas. The epics Ramayana and Mahabaratha contain information on standing armies and warfare techniques like the Chakravyuha used in the Kurukshetra War. The epics contain information on the usage of chariots, war elephants and even flying machines in wars.

The Rigvedic tribes of Indo-Aryans were led by their tribal chieftain (*raja*) and engaged in wars with each other as well as other tribes. They used bronze weapons and had horse-drawn spoke-wheeled chariots described prominently in the Rigveda. The main share from the booty obtained during the cattle raids and battles went to the chief of the tribe. The warriors belonged to the Kshatriya varna. Earlier, most archaeologists believed that Aryan armies invaded peaceful Harappan cities and destroyed them. But now, there are contending views. Since none of the excavations indicate battle damage to the cities, it has been suggested by some that there was never a so called Aryan Invasion, and that Aryans were the original inhabitants of India. However, it has also been shown that there were migrations from Central Asia, and that the culture of the Indus valley civilizations were different from that of the Aryan culture which replaced it.

THE MAGADHA EMPIRE

Shishunaga Dynasty

King Bimbisara was an expansionist and conquered Anga in what is now West Bengal. He strengthened the military of Magadh's capital, Rajagriha. Ajatashatru built a new fort at Pataliputra, Magadh's new capital to launch an attack on Licchavis, across the Ganga River. Jain texts tell that he used two new weapons - a catapult and a covered chariot with swinging mace that has been compared to modern tanks.

Nanda dynasty

The powerful Mahapadma Nanda defeated Ikshvakus, Panchalas, Kasis, Harhayas, Kalingas, Asmakas, Kurus, Maithilas, Surasenas and Vitihotras and assumed the title "the destroyer of the kshathriyas". At the time of Dhana Nanda, the Nandas had an army consisting of 80,000 cavalry, 20,000 infantry, 8,000 armed chariots, and 6,000 war elephants. Many historians hold the view that Alexander confined himself to the plains of Punjab for fear of the mighty Nandas.

Maurya Dynasty

According to Megasthenes, Chandragupta Maurya built an army consisting of 30,000 cavalry, 9,000 war elephants, and 600,000 infantry. Some modern historians feel that this is an exaggeration on the part of Megasthenes, who was serving as an ambassador from the Seleucid Empire. Chandragupta conquered all of northern India, establishing an empire from the Arabian Sea to the Bay of Bengal. He then conquered the regions to the east of the Indus river after defeating the Macedonians and Seleucus Nicator, and then moved southwards, taking over much of what is now Central India. The entire army was administrated by six chairs, one for each of the four arms of the army (infantry, cavalry, elephants, and chariots), one chair for the navy, and one for logistics and supply.

Infantry at this time was most commonly armed with a longbow made of bamboo, and a single or double handed broadsword (probably somewhat similar to the khanda). Other foot soldiers could be armed with a large, animal hide tower shield and a spear/ javelins.

The cavalry is not noted especially, but Megasthenese does mention that they were armed with a few spears, of which we can assume most were meant for hurling. Elephants were mounted, usually bareback (rarely with a howdah at this time, as it is a Greek invention), with archers or javelineers, and with a mahout around the animal's neck. Chariots by this time were in definite decline, but still managed to stay an arm of the army by sheer virtue of their prestige.

In 185 BC, the last Mauryan king was assassinated by Pushyamitra Shunga, the Commander-in-Chief of the Mauryan armed forces.

EARLY MIDDLE KINGDOMS (THE GOLDEN AGE)

Classical Indian texts on archery in particular, and martial arts in general are known as Dhanurveda.

Satavahana Dynasty

Simuka, the founder of the Satavahana dynasty, conquered Maharashtra, Malwa and part of Madhya Pradesh. His successor and brother Kanha (or Krishna) further extended his kingdom to the west and the south. He was succeeded by Satakarni I, who defeated the Sunga dynasty of North India. Gautamiputra Satakarni defeated the Western Kshatrapas ruler Nahapana. His brother Vashishtiputra Satakarni, was defeated by his Western Kshatrapa father-in-law in a battle.

According to some interpretations of the Puranas, the family belonged to the Andhra-jati ("tribe") and was the first Deccanese dynasty to build an empire in daksinapatha (southern region). The Satavahanas (also called Andhra and Shalivahan) rose to power in modern Maharashtra around 200 B.C. They remained in power, for about 400 years.

Almost the whole of present day Maharashtra, Madhya Pradesh, Chattisgarh, Orissa, Goa, Karnataka, Andhra Pradesh, Kerala, and Tamil Nadu were under Satavahana rule. Paithan in Maharashtra, formerly called Pratishthan, was the capital of the Satavahanas. The founder of the Satvahanas was Simuka. But the man who raised it to eminence was Satakarni I. Sri Yajna Satakarni was the last great king in this dynasty. After him, the empire began to decline.

Gautami-putra Satakarni was the most famous king of the Satvahana dynasty. He defeated the Sakas (Scythians), Yavanas (Greeks) and Pahlavas (Parthians). His empire extended up to Banavasi in the south, and included Maharashtra, Konkan, Saurashtra, Malwa, west Rajasthan and Vidharbha. His son, Vasishti-putra, ruled at Paithan on the banks of Godavari.

Two other cities, Vaijayanti (in North Kanara) and Amravati (in the Guntur district), attained eminence during the Satvahana period. Vasishthi-putra Pulumavi, Vasishthi-putra Satakarni, Yadnya-shri Satakarni are some other Satavahana rulers who succeeded Gautami-putra Satakarni some lost many of their territories but the power of Satvahanas revived under Sri Yajna Satakarni, who was the last great king. After him, the empire began to decline.

The Satavahanas inaugurated the Shalivahana Shaka. Satavahanas were very able rulers. Their empire was divided into provinces called Aharas, each under an Amatya (minister). They had a large army. They were lovers of literature and architecture. Prakrit was the court language. Women took part in assemblies. The Karle caves in Maharashtra were built during this period.

Some caves of Ajanta were also built during this period. The construction of 29 galleries of Ajantha Caves continued until 650 AD.

Kushan Empire

Vima Takto, using the name "Soter Megas" (Great Saviour), conquered Gandhara and northern India in 68 AD. The Kushan warriors were assimilated into Indian society as Kshatriyas. Following Yuezhi's style, most of the Kushan nobles fought from horse back, supported by the heavier parts of the army, cataphracts. The coins of Kujula, Vima Takto, Vima Kadphises and Kanishka show the king usually unarmored, lightly armored than the later Kushan kings. In many coins Kanishka appears to have a bow, but this interpretation is debatable. Some Buddhist texts indicate the use of Indian influences like elephants leading the attacks and the use of chariots. The elephants first appeared on the coins of Vima Kadphises and probably went on to become the mount of the kings. The elephants are depicted with towers and a covering. It is not clear whether these were armor or just padding. Buddhist texts mention that the infantry were used to support these elephants. The historian Nikonorov suggests that the elephants used were provided by the Satraps. However, the main strength of the Kushan army came from its armored horses. The use of heavy cavalry increased later. Apart from the original Kushans and Indians, the Greeks, various mountain tribes, Sacas from northern India and Iranian mercenaries were also added to Kushan army. The Kidarites and Sassanids predominantly used cavalry. The Satraps provided them with additional India forces including elephants.

Gupta Dynasty

Siva-Dhanur-veda, considered a contemporary military classic gives information about the military system of the Guptas. They utilized war elephants, supplemented by additional armor. The use of horses, if any, was very limited. The use of chariots had heavily declined by the time of the Guptas, as they had not proved very useful against the Ancient Macedonians, Scythians, and other invaders. Guptas utilised heavy cavalry clad in mail armor and equipped with maces and lances, who would have used shock action to break the enemy line. They also heavily relied on infantry archers, and the bow was one of the dominant weapons of their army.

Their longbow was composed of metal, or more typically bamboo, and fired a long bamboo cane arrow with a metal head. Iron shafts were used against armored elephants, and fire arrows were also part of the bowmen's arsenal. Archers were frequently protected by infantry equipped with shields, javelins, and longswords. Guptas also maintained a navy, allowing them to control regional waters.

Samudragupta seized the kingdoms of Shichchhatra and Padmavati early in his reign. Later, he took the Kingdom of Kota and attacked the tribes in Malvas, the Yaudheyas, the Arjunayanas, the Maduras and the Abhiras. By his death in 380, he had conquered over twenty kingdoms.

Chandragupta II defeated the Saka Western Kshatrapas of Malwa, Gujarat and Saurashtra in a campaign lasting till 409. He had defeated his main opponent Rudrasimha III by 395. He also crushed the Bengal (Vanga) chiefdoms. Skandagupta defeated Pushyamitra. He repulsed the attack of Hephthalites or "White Huns", c. 455, but the expense of the wars drained the empire's resources and contributed to its decline.

THE SULTANATE ERA

Delhi Sultanate

The Delhi Sultanate, under the Khilji dynasty, was successful in defeating a number of invasions from the Mongol Empire. Zafar Khan, the general of Alauddin Khilji, was successful against several such invasions. Zafar Khan defeated invading Mongols near Jalandhar in 1297 to secure Alauddin Khilji's throne. Later in 1299, a Mongol army of 200,000 soldiers entered India with the intention of conquest. Zafar Khan showed desperate valor in battle and defeated them, though he did not survive.

Samoothiris of Kozhikode

More famously known as the Zamorin, this smallNair Kingdom welcomed the Portuguese in 1498 as traders and then with the assistance of its naval chief, Kunjali Marakkar, fought several naval wars with them in the 16th century.

Muzaffarid Dynasty

Sultan Muzaffar Shah I, the Governor of Gujarat established the Muzaffarid dynasty in 1391. It expanded rapidly and peaked under Sultan Mahmud I who lost the famous Battle of Diu to the Portuguese in 1509.

Vijayanagar Empire

In 1509, the Bahamani Sultan declared a jehad against Vijaynagar. His large coalition army was defeated by Krishnadevaraya, who also wounded the Sultan. In 1510, Krishnadevaraya launched a counteroffensive against the Sultan at Kovelaconda.

In this battle, Yusuf Adil Shahi of Bijapur was killed. In 1512, Krishnadevaraya captured Raichur and Gulbarga after defeating Barid-i-Mamalik, the titular head of the Bahmani Sultanate, who escaped to Bidar. Later, Bidar also fell to Krishnadevaraya. However, he diplomatically restored the Bahmani Sultan to his throne, with an intention to create discord and suspicion in the Bahmani coalition.

In a battle from 1512 to 1514, Krishnadevaraya subjugated the Palaigar of Ummattur, who had rebelled against his brother. While this campaign was halfway, the Gajapati of Orissa attacked Vijayanagar and occupied two northeast provinces, Udayagiri and Kondavidu. In January 1513, Krishnadevaraya launched a campaign recover to Udaygiri. The campaign lasted till 1518, resulting in defeat of Gajapati. On January 26, 1565 the Islamic kingdoms of Ahmednagar, Berar, Bidar, Bijapur and Golconda came together to defeat the Vijayanagar decisively in the Battle of Talikota.

After the battle the remaining Vijaynagar fled with large treasury to re-establish their head quarters at Vellore Fort(in Tamil Nadu and Chandragiri (Present day Andhra Pradesh) near Tirupathi.It would be here where the British sought land grant to establish the English East India CompanyFort St. George in Madras.

Later its southern Telugu governors established their independence and emerging as Gingee Nayaks in Gingee

Fort,Tanjore Nayaks and the famous Nayaks of Madurai all in present day Tamil Nadu.

The effects of the Mongol wars

Indians made steel weapons that were popular in the ancient world because of their quality and durability. These weapons were forged from wootz steel, which may have existed in India as early as 200 BCE.

THE MUGHAL ERA

The Maratha Empire

The Maratha Empire of India, also called the Maratha Confederacy, was founded by Chatrapati Shivaji in 1674, when he carved an independent Maratha zone around Pune, Maharshtra, from the Bijapur Sultanate.

Chatrapati Shivaji established an effective civil and military administration. He made it a state policy never to desecrate a mosque or seize women after military raids. He had many loyal Muslim admirers, who served in his army. He was also only the second king in Indian history to have his own active navy. After a lifetime of exploits and guerrilla warfare with the Mughal emperor Aurangzeb, Maharaja Shivaji died in 1680, leaving a Maratha kingdom of great but ill-defined extent. This was followed by a period of unstability which ended with the death of Aurangzeb.

Kanhoji Angre was the first Maratha naval chief under Chattrapati Shahu, Shivaji's grandson. He harassed Dutch, English and Portuguese commercial ships on the Western coast of India in the early 18th century. He remained undefeated until his death in 1729.

Although the descendants of Shivaji continued to rule, the office of the Peshwa, or the Prime Minister, had become the dispensers of Maratha power and patronage. The Peshwas were the effective rulers of the Maratha state and oversaw the period of greatest Maratha expansion, brought to an end by the Maratha's defeat by an Afghan army at the Third Battle of Panipat in 1761. The Marathas recovered their position as the dominant power in

India by 1772 until the last Peshwa, Baji Rao II, was defeated by the British in the Third Anglo-Maratha War.

Major wars:

- First Anglo-Maratha War
- Second Anglo-Maratha War
- Third Anglo-Maratha War
- Fourth Anglo-Mysore War

State of Travancore

The principal military caste of Travancore was the Nairs. Raja Marthanda Varma built up this Kingdom after inheriting the small princely state of Venad in 1723, located in the southern tip of India. He made it one of the most powerful Kingdoms in Southern India.

Raja Marthanda Varma led the Travancore forces during the Travancore-Dutch War from 1739 - 1746 (the most famous engagement of which being the Battle of Colachel on August 10, 1741), which marks the first decisive victory by an Asian kingdom over a major European power. Raja Marthanda Varma then went on to unify most of the provinces of the native princes who had allied themselves with the Dutch against him. During Dharma Raja's reign, Travancore itself was attacked byTipu Sultan and the Travancore Army, which had been modernised and trained by D'Lennoy, the commander-in-chief (Valia Kappithan) of Raja Marthanda Varma, successfully defended the country from Tipu's numerically superior forces. This attack led to Travancore joining the British against Tipu in the Third Battle of Carnatic. The warrior clan of Nairs under the leadership of various nobles and princes like "Pazhsi Raja, Velu Thampi Dalava and Paliath Achan" also fought against British East India company on occasions, but lost to the superior arms, tactics and discipline of the Company's armies. Travancore became an ally of the British in 1805 following a treaty between Col. Maculay and Diwan Velu Tampi, and remained so until 1947 when it merged with India.

Kingdom of Mysore

Hyder Ali was instructed by French military officers. He was one of the first Indian rulers to use rockets. He used iron rockets to defeat a top British unit in battle. His son, Tipu Sultan was also instructed by French military officers. Tipu participated in First Anglo-Maratha War of 1775–1779. He defeated the Brathwaite on the banks of the Coleroon in February 1782 in the Second Mysore War. After his father's death in 1782, he decided to check British advances by forming alliances with the Marathas and the Mughals. However, his plan wasn't successful. So, he turned to France.

In 1789, he invaded the state of Travancore, a British protectorate. However, he didn't receive expected help from France (the French were embroiled in the French Revolution) and Mysore was defeated in what is now known as the Third Mysore War. Tipu Sultan died in the Fourth Mysore War. Although Horatio Nelson crushed Napoleon's ambitions of advancing to India at the Battle of the Nile, three armies - one from Bombay, and two British (one of which was commanded by Arthur Wellesley), marched into Mysore in 1799 and besieged the capital, Srirangapatnam. On May 4, 1799, the armies broke through the defending walls and Tipu died of a gunshot wound near the gates of his fortress.

Main wars:

- First Mysore War, 1766
- Second Mysore War
- Third Mysore War, 1789-1792
- Fourth Mysore War, 1799

Punjab

Maharaja Ranjit Singh, also called "Sher-e-Punjab" ("The Lion of the Punjab") (1780-1839) was a Sikh ruler of the sovereign country of Punjab and the Sikh Empire. His Samadhi is located in Lahore, Pakistan. Ranjit Singh was a Sikh born in 1780 in Gujranwala in modern day Pakistan, into the Sansi-Sandhawalia family. At the time much of Punjab was ruled by the Sikhs, who had divided the territory among factions known as misls. Ranjit Singh's father Maha Singh was the commander of the Sukerchakia misl and controlled a territory in west Punjab based around his headquarters at Gujranwala. Ranjit Singh succeeded his father at the young age of 12. After several campaigns, his rivals accepted him as their leader, and he united the Sikh factions into one state and he took the title of **Maharaja** on April 13, 1801 (to coincide with Baisakhi day), with Lahore having served as his capital from 1799. In 1802 he took the holy city of Amritsar.

Maharaja Ranjit Singh also hired European mercenaries to train his troops, creating a powerful military force whose presence delayed the eventual British colonization of Punjab. He also modernized his army, hiring European mercenaries to create the first modern Indian Army. The effect was to create a powerful and heavily armed state; at this point, **Punjab was the only state not controlled by the British.** He brought law and order, yet was reluctant to use the death penalty. He stopped Indian non-secular style practises by treating Hindus and Muslims equally. He banned the discriminatory "jizya" tax on Hindus and Sikhs.

Maharaja Ranjit Singh died in 1839 and the state went to his eldest son Kharak Singh.

The Kingdom, that he had worked so hard to build, began to crumble due to poor governance and political mismanagement by his heirs. His successors died through accidents and murder, while the nobility and army struggled for power till the end of the Second Anglo-Sikh War(1848-49), when it was annexed by the British from his youngest son Duleep Singh. However, after the First Anglo-Sikh War(1845-46), Punjab effectively ceased to be an independent state and in 1849 was annexed by the British and all major decisions where made by the British Empire.

- Maharaja Ranjit Singh (b.1780, Crowned April 13, 1801, d.1839)
- Kharak Singh (b.1801, d.1840), Eldest son of Ranjit Singh.
- Nau Nihal Singh (b.1821, d.1840), Grandson of Ranjit Singh.
- Sher Singh (b.1807, d.1843), Son of Ranjit Singh.
- Duleep Singh (b.1838, Crowned 1843, d.1893), Youngest son of Ranjit Singh.

The British Empire annexed Punjab in c.1845-49 AD; after two Anglo Sikh Wars

The Anglo-Sikh Wars (1846-1849)

- The First Anglo-Sikh War (1845–1846)
- The Second Anglo-Sikh War (1848-1849)

WORLD WAR I

List of Indian Divisions in World War I

During WWI the Sikh battalions fought in Egypt, Palestine, Mesopotamia, Gallipoli and France.

The 14th Ferozepore Sikhs were in Gallipoli in April 1915 and fought in a number of battles in the Gallipoli campaign .

After Gallipoli the battalion was in the Persian Gulf region and took part in some fierce fighting on the Tigris River. The 15th Ludhiana Sikhs were in France in September 1914 and participated in fighting at Fauquissart, Festubert and Neuve Chapelle.

WORLD WAR II

India was an active participant in the World War II as a part of the British Empire, and was a major contributor of troops and resources to the war effort.

Indian units and troops fought in almost all the major campaigns in which the British were involved, and presented an excellent account of themselves.

Of particular significance were the campaigns against the Italians in Abyssinia and North africa, against the Germans in North Africa and Italy, especially the Allied victory at El-Alamein and the Burma Campaign as a whole.

Azad Hind Fauj

Azad Hind Fauj, also known as the Indian National Army was led by prominent freedom fighter Netaji Subhash Chandra Bose and his Axis recognized Provisional Government of Free India.

As repeated promises by the British to grant independence failed to surface, Bose backed by the forces of Germany and Japan led the INA to liberation of Burma in their march to northeastern India and the Andaman and Nicobar Islands.

Republic of India

The Republic of India has fought three wars and one major incursion battle with Pakistan and one border war with China.

MAJOR WARS

First Indo-Pak War, 1947

Independent India, formed on August 15, 1947, has seen three wars with Pakistan (1947-48, 1965, 1971). The first war took place after Pakistani soldiers and armed tribesmen invaded the independent province of Kashmir. When the forces almost reached the capital Srinagar the Maharaja, Hari Singh, and the democratically elected Prime Minister of Kashmir, Sheikh Abdullah, signed an agreement with India in which all Kashmiri lands were ceded to India. India sent their troops in shortly after and freed a majority of the new Indian state of Jammu and Kashmir from Pakistani inflitrators.

Sino-Indian War, 1962

India fought a border war against China (1962). China won the border skirmish, leading India to revamp the entire military system. After the war ended, the Department of Defence Production was set up to create an indigenous defence production base which is self-reliant and self-sufficient. Since 1962, 16 new ordinance factories have been set up.

Second Indo-Pak War, 1965

The second Indo-Pak war was also fought over Kashmir issue. It ended in with Indian forces gaining chunks of lands all around except Punjab where it was even. USSR interfered and got the truce between the two nations at Tashkent agreement, which also saw the mysterious death of Indian PM Lal Bahadur Shastri. At the same time, there was the possibility of a second Sino-Indian war along the Nathu La Pass in Sikkim.

Ten battalions of the Sikh Regiment saw action in the 1965 war. In a bid to seal off routes of infiltrations for the Pakistanis in J & K, 1 Sikh who were in the Tithwal sector attacked Pakistani positions . A company led by Major Somesh Kapur captured Richhmar Ridge on 24 August 1965 and then attacked and captured the Pir Sahiba feature on the night of 25/26 August. From this feature the Indian troops could now overlook an extensive area under Pakistan control. Through out September, Pakistani troops tried hard to recapture this feature but were unsuccessful. 1 Sikh received 3 Vir Chakras (Major Somesh Kapur and L/ Havildar Gurdev Singh and Sepoy Gurmel Singh (posth.)) for these operations .

The Chola Incident

A Sino-India skirmish took place in 1967 and is known today as the Chola Incident.

Third Indo-Pak War, 1971

In the third Indo-Pak war, India intervened decisively in what was then East Pakistan due to the mass exodus of refugees to India following West Pakistani military action there. The new nation of Bangladesh was created as a result. India succeeded in removing Pakistani soldiers from what is now known as "East Pakistan" resulting in the formation of Bangladesh. This conflict is often cited as India's greatest military victory, but also among the greatest genocides of the 20th century wherein Pakistani forces slaughtered anywhere from 1 million to 3 million Bangladeshi's, the vast majority being Hindu.

Siachin War, 1984

The Siachin war between India and Pakistan occurred in 1984. The area of the dispute was the Siachen Glacier - the world's highest battlefield. The Glacier was under territorial dispute, but in the late 1970s and early 1980s, Pakistan began organizing several tourist expeditions to the Glacier. India, irked by this development, mounted Operation Meghdoot, and captured the top of the Glacier by establishing a military base which it still maintains to this day at a cost of more than US$1 million per day. Pakistan on the other hand spends just under US$1 million per day, though as % of GDP Pakistan spends 5 times as the Indian Military does to maintain its share of the glacier. Pakistan tried in 1987 and in 1989 to re-take the Glacier but was unsuccessful. A stalemate has arose where India controls the top part of the Glacier and Pakistan is placed at the bottom of the Glacier.

Kargil War, 1999

India fought a brief border skirmish with Pakistan in the

Indian state of Kashmir in 1999. Dubbed the Kargil War, after the infiltration of Pakistani soldiers and paramilitary in the Kargil area, India reclaimed the territory through military and diplomatic channels. Pakistan lost 4000 soldiers, while India lost a little over 500.

By 21 May, the Indian army had isolated Tiger Hill from three directions, east, north and south. In order to inflict casualties the enemy positions on Tiger Hill were subjected to artillery and mortar fire.

A fresh battalion of well known Gurkhas viz. 18 Grenadiers was brought in to capture the peak with regiments holding the firm base.

On the night of July 3, 18 Grenadiers captured the eastern slope but further advance was held up due to effective enemy fire from Helmet Top, India Gate features on the western slope. By morning July 4th Tiger Hill was captured by the 18th Grenadiers, effectively ending Pakistan's Kargil War.

NUCLEAR PROGRAM

Smiling Buddha, 1974

In 1966, India had declared that it can produce nuclear weapons within 18 months. In 1974, India tested a device of up to 15 kilotons. The test was a "peaceful nuclear explosion" and was codenamed "Operation Smiling Buddha".

Operation Shakti (nuclear tests, 1998)

On May 11 and May 13, 1998, India conducted five underground nuclear tests (3 on May 11 and 2 on May 13) and declared itself a nuclear state.

Overview and Recent Developments

The Indian military today ranks as the world's third largest after the USA and China in terms of troops. Over a million strong, the paramilitary unit of the Republic of India is the world's largest and most elite paramilitary force. Eager to portray itself as a potential superpower, India began an intense phase of modernization and upgradation of its armed forces in the late

1990s. India is focusing more on developing indigenous military equipments rather than relying on other countries for military supplies.

This change in policy has paid off well for the Indian Armed Forces. Most of the Indian naval ships and submarines, military armoured vehicles, missiles and ammunition are indigenously designed and manufactured.

Military Collaborations with other States

Apart from diverting resources towards indigenously manufacturing military equipment, the Indian Government is also focusing on collaborating with other countries to develop cutting-edge military technology and weapons. Jointly developed by Russia and India, one of the the world's most advanced supersonic cruise missiles, known as the BrahMos, was successfully test-fired in 2001.

In 1997, India agreed to participate in the development of Russia's *Prospective Air Complex for Tactical Air Forces* program. One of the primary objectives of the program is to develop a 5th generation fighter aircraft, a prototype of which, known as the Su-47, flew its first successful test-flight in 1997.

India is also collaborating with Israel to develop Unmanned Aerial Vehicles. India is now focusing on purchasing the technology behind the military equipment rather than the military equipment. Recent examples of the successful implementation of this Indian policy include the purchase of Sukhoi Su-30 MKI multi-role fighter aircraft and T-90 main battle tanks from Russia and diesel-powered Scorpene submarines from France. In 2004, India purchased US$ 5.7 billion worth of military equipment from other countries, making it the developing world's leading arms-purchaser.

Disasters

On April 28, 2000, ammunition worth Rs. 393 crore was destroyed due to a fire at the Bharatpur ammunition depot. Another fire at Pathankot sub-depot resulted in loss of ammo worth Rs. 27.39 crore. On May 24, 2001, another blaze at the Birdhwal sub-depot destroyed ammunition worth Rs. 378 crore.

Awards

In Independent India, the gallantry awards for exemplary display of bravery in war time are the Param Vir Chakra, Maha Vir Chakra and Vir Chakra in the decreasing order of importance. Their peace time equivalents are the Ashoka Chakra, Kirti Chakra and Shaurya Chakra. The latter two awards were formerly known as *Ashoka Chakra, Class II* and *Ashoka Chakra, Class III* respectively. Sometimes, the peace time awards are bestowed on civilians as well. For meritorious service, the awards are *Param Vishisht Seva Medal, Athi Vishisht Seva Medal* and *Vishisht Seva Medal* in decreasing order of importance.

2

Military Strength of Indian Army

STRUCTURE OF THE INDIAN AIR-FORCE

Recruitment and Training

Recruitment is through three military related academies. These include the National Defence Academy, Indian Military Academy and Officers Training Academy. For entrance, one must display that they are both physically and mentally fit to be in the military by sitting examinations and undergoing medical checkups. The complete list of institutions training Indian army were listed in Military academies in India section.

Indian Army

Strength: During a conflict, the air-arm of the Indian army plays a crucial role in providing essential supplies and air cover to the ground forces. Shown here is the Indian Army's HAL Dhruv.

Indian Army Statistics

Active Troops	1,325,000 (2nd)
Artillery	7100
Battle Tanks	5010
Aircraft	52 squadrons of helicopters
Surface-to-air missiles	90,000+

The Indian Army is the world's second largest army in terms of military personnel (after China). It is a completely voluntary service, the military draft having never been imposed in India. The army has rich combat experience in diverse terrains, due to India's diverse geography, and also has a distinguished history of serving in United Nations peacekeeping operations.

The force is headed by the Chief of Army Staff, currently General Deepak Kapoor. The highest rank in the Indian Army is Field Marshal, but it is a largely ceremonial rank and appointments are made by the President of India, on the advice of the Union Cabinet of Ministers, only in exceptional circumstances. (See Field Marshal (India)). General S.H.F.J. Manekshaw and the late General K.M. Cariappa are the only two officers who have attained this rank. The Indian Army has seen military action in the Indo-Pakistani War of 1947, the Indo-Pakistani War of 1965,the Indo-Pakistani War of 1971, and others such as Operation Polo in 1948, the Sino-Indian War in 1962 over the McMahon Line, and the Kargil War against Kashmiri insurgents and the Pakistan military personnel

Currently, the Indian army has dedicated one brigade of troops to the UN's standby arrangements. Through its large, sustained troop commitments India has come in for much praise for taking part in difficult operations for prolonged periods.

The Indian Army has participated in several UN peace-keeping operations, including the ones in Cyprus, Lebanon, Congo, Angola, Cambodia, Vietnam, Namibia, El Salvador, Liberia, Mozambique and Somalia. The army also provided a paramedical unit to facilitate the withdrawal of the sick and wounded in Korea.

INDIAN NAVY

The Indian Navy is the naval branch of the armed forces of India. With 55,000 men and women, including 5,000 naval aviation personnel and 2,000 Marine Commandos (MARCOS), it is the world's fifth largest navy. The Indian Navy currently operates more than 155 vessels, including the aircraft carrier INS Viraat.

The navy is considered to have blue-water capabilities. It is fairly advanced in terms of technology and is in control of one of two Asian aircraft carriers. Two more aircraft carriers are on order and will be joining the Indian Navy. The ships of the Indian Navy are of Indian and foreign origin. In its maritime doctrine, the Indian Navy establishes its role in providing support to maritime neighbours during natural disasters. This was demonstrated during the Asian tsunami crisis during which the Indian Navy sent 35 ships to support relief efforts in neighbouring countries.

The Indian navy has taken part in UN missions in the coast of Somalia and has provided security to an African Union summit held in Mozambique. India uses its navy to enhance its international relations through joint exercises, port visits, and humanitarian missions, including disaster relief. The Indian Navy is increasing its capabilities as a true blue-water navy; the Indian Navy's doctrine states that this is for the collective good of nations.

INDIAN AIR FORCE

The Indian Air Force is the fourth largest air force in the world. In its history, it has generally relied on Soviet technology to support its growth. However, in recent times, India has begun building its own original aircraft, including the HAL Tejas, which is a 4.5 generation fighter.

Also India and Russia are currently building a 5th generation stealth aircraft jointly. India has also developed UAV called Nishant and HAL Dhruv, an advanced light helicopter. Recently it has completed a test of long range BVR air to air missile named Astra and also conducted a successful test of Anti ballistic missile defense system and hence became the 4th country after US,Russia and Israel to do so.

PARAMILITARY FORCES OF INDIA

Indian Nuclear Power

It is estimated that India possesses around 200-250 nuclear warheads which could be deployed at short notice.

Nuclear Doctrine

The Indian military possesses nuclear weapons and sufficient means — by means of missiles and aircraft — to deliver anything over long distances. However, India has a *nuclear no-first-use* and no use against non-nuclear weapons state policy. It also maintains a non-nuclear doctrine based on *credible minimum deterrence.*

India is not a signatory to the Nuclear Non-proliferation Treaty (NPT), arguing that it unfairly favours the established nuclear powers: While the treaty places restrictions on the non-nuclear weapons states, it does little to curb the modernization and expansion of the nuclear arsenals of the nuclear weapons states; it provides no provision for complete nuclear disarmament.

Gallantry Awards

The highest wartime gallantry award given by the Military of India is the Param Vir Chakra (PVC), followed by the Maha Vir Chakra (MVC) and the Vir Chakra (VrC). Its peacetime equivalent is the Ashoka Chakra. The highest decoration for meritorious service is the Param Vishisht Seva Medal.

Future

Several reports have mentioned that the Indian military will be an even greater force to reckon with in the future given the twin advantage of economic growth and an increasing population.

Analyses of the Central Intelligence Agency indicates that India is projected to possess the fourth most capable concentration of power by 2015. According to a report published by the US Congress, India is the developing world's leading arms purchaser.

ARMY

The army numbers about one million personnel and fields 34 divisions. Designed primarily to defend the country's frontiers, the army has become heavily committed to internal security duties in Kashmir and the Northeast.

In 2002 the Indian Army had 980,000 active troops, along with an Army Reserve consisting of: 300,000 first line troops (those within five years of full time service), and another 500,000 second line troops (subject to recall to service until 50 years of age). The Territorial Army numbered 40,000 first line troops (and 160,000 second line troops). In 1994 the army had approximately 940,000 men and women on active duty, and another 36,000 in the Territorial Army. As of 1998 the Army had a sanctioned troop strength of 1,045,000, but there was a shortage of about 59,000 troops.

At the beginning of World War II there were 170,000 soldiers in the Indian Army all regulars, but by June of 1948 there were 2,000,000. This was the reason British Officers were needed to help train and form new units. Each Battalion needed eight British Officers to take command, as all the lower ranks were manned by Indian Viceroy Commissioned Officers, and NCOs.

The army is headquartered in New Delhi and is under the direction of the chief of the army staff, always a full general. The chief of the army staff is assisted by a vice chief, two deputy chiefs, a military secretary, and the heads of four main staff divisions: the adjutant general, the quartermaster general, the master general of ordnance, and the engineer in chief.

The Army consists of a number of arms and services. These are: Armoured Corps, Regiment of Artillery, Corps of Engineers, Corps of Signals, Mechanised Infantry, Infantry, Army Service Corps, Military Nursing Service, Army Medical Corps, Army Dental Corps, Army Ordnance Corps, Corps of Electrical and Mechanical Engineers, Remount and Veterinary Corps, Military Farms Service, Army Education Corps, Intelligence Corps, Corps of Military Police, Judge Advocate General Department, Army Physical Training Corps, Pioneer Corps, Army Postal Service Corps and Defence Security Corps. In addition, the Army has its own Recruiting Organisation, Record Offices, Depots, Boys Establishments and Selection Centers and training institutions. These units are organized in twelve corps-level formations.

The army has five tactical area commands: the Northern Command headquartered at Udhampur in Jammu and Kashmir, the Western Command headquartered at Chandimandir in Chandigarh, the Central Command headquartered at Lucknow in Uttar Pradesh, the Eastern Command headquartered at Calcutta, and the Southern Command headquartered at Pune in Maharashtra. Each command is headed by a lieutenant general.

In the Indian context, Command Headquarter can be likened to a Field Army or even an Army Group Headquarter with a

General Officer Commanding-in-Chief presiding over matters in the rank of a (three-star) Lieutenant General. Next the line are the Corps Headquarters, which are Field Army Headquarters elsewhere. The Indian Army's combat formations are now grouped and tailored under many such Corps Headquarters (with some forces being retained under static Area Commands). As with the American Army, all Corps have numerical designations. They also have names, by which they are more commonly known. These names may derive from the city in which they are headquartered [XVI Corps / Nagrota Corps], or they may be evocative [IV Corps is Gajraj Corps, meaning "King Elephant."

The field force is grouped into Corps. Some of these are defensively oriented and have, over the years, acquired an unofficial-'Holding'. The others are called reserve or, unofficially again, 'Strike' Corps. The former is really a misnomer since these contain ample offensive potential. Corps Headquarters are designed to. handle an all-arms field army-of three to five divisions or their equivalents. Army Headquarters reserves could be mammoth-size or small, but powerful in either case. Heavy-tracked-Corps are an instance of the former, and the three parachute commandos (battalion-size units), which perform special forces duties, of the latter. Airborne, Air Assault or Parachute troops are usually held centralized. The mounts', in all cases, are provided by the Indian Air Force.

The Division and Independent Brigade Group are the lowest (or the highest, depending on the viewpoint) individual formations. They integrate in themselves all arms and services for sustained independent operations. There is great flexibility in their force mix, and in 'grouping for tasks'. Brigade (regiment in some armies) size combined-arms groups can be shed or added on at will. Standard Tables of Organization and Equipment do exist, but these are taken lightly for accounting purposes only. Divisions and independent brigade groups are designated by function, terrain of operation, or by their equipment mix.

The Army has in its Order of Battle, mountain divisions, infantry divisions, armoured divisions (in which tank units predominate) and mechanized divisions (in which mechanized infantry units predominate). An Infantry Division typically has about 15,500 combat troops, with 8,000 support elements (artillery, engineers, etc).

It consists of 3 to 5 Infantry Brigades, an Armoured Regiment and an Artillery Brigade. A Brigade is commanded by a Brigadier, and an Infantary Brigade consists of three Infantry Battalions. A regiment can be a type of battalion (eg. in the Artillery/Engineers) or a grouping of a number of battalions of the same type (eg. The Rajput Regiment). The approximate strength of an infantry battalion, commanded by a Colonel, may be taken as 900-1,000 personnel. A battalion may consist of three to four companies, and may be commanded by a Lieutenant Colonel or a Colonel. A company normally consists of 100-120 men and is commanded by a Major.

Independent brigade groups, as the name suggests, are vested with limited capability to carry out an independent mission. Independent brigade groups or independent brigade-sized formations may be armoured, mechanized, air defence (missile or gun), parachute, engineer, field artillery, electronic warfare or even standard infantry and mountain. These form 'Corps/Army troops', that is, they are held at Corps and Army levels for balancing out missions and task forces. At these levels, one would find heavy logistic support units in terms of supply, transport, field ordnance depots, and medical facilities.

An extensive body of schools and centers supports army operations. The officer corps is largely drawn from the National Defence Academy at Khadakvasla, Maharashtra, a joint services training institution that provides educational equivalents to the bachelor of arts or bachelor of science degrees to cadets for all three service arms.

Cadets spend their first three years at the National Defence Academy and then are sent to their respective service academies for further training before being commissioned in the armed forces. A preparatory school, the Rashtriya Indian Military College, at Dehra Dun, Uttar Pradesh, provides education to candidates for the National Defence Academy.

After completing their studies at the National Defence

Academy, army cadets are sent to the Indian Military Academy at Dehra Dun. Other Indian Military Academy cadets are graduates of the Army Cadet College or are direct-entry students who have qualified by passing the Union Public Service Commission Examination. They spend between twelve and twenty-four months at the Indian Military Academy before being commissioned in the army as second lieutenants. Still other officer training occurs at the Officers' Training Academy in Madras, Tamil Nadu, where a forty-four-week session is offered to university graduates seeking a short-service commission.

In addition to the Indian Military Academy, the army runs a number of military education establishments. The more prominent ones include the College of Combat at Mhow, Madhya Pradesh; the High Altitude Warfare School at Gulmarg, Jammu and Kashmir; and the Counter-Insurgency and Jungle Warfare School at Vairengte, Mizoram.

The army also operates the Defence Services Staff College at Wellington in the Nilgiri Hills in Tamil Nadu, which provides master of science-level joint-service training for mid-level staff appointments and promotes interservice cooperation.

In 1994 it was reported that there were 200 women in the armed forces. In the army, which employs women as physicians and nurses, the participation of women is small but growing. The Indian Military Nursing Service was formed in 1926 and has eight nursing schools (five army, two navy, and one air force) and one nursing college in Pune. Bachelor of science graduates are commissioned as lieutenants in the Medical Nursing Service and attached to the various components of the armed forces.

Ranks as high as colonel can be attained by career officers. In the mid-1990s, a small but increasing number of women officers were being assigned to nonmedical services. In 1994, there were fifty women nonmedical army officers and another twenty-five in training. They are university graduates who have been put through rigorous training and are reported to be eager for combat unit assignments.

3

India's Military Modernization

DEVELOPMENT AND MODERNISATION OF INDIAN ARMY

The Indian Army is the largest branch of the armed forces of India and bears responsibility for land-based military operations. Its primary objectives include defending India from external aggression, maintaining peace and security within the country, patrolling borders and conducting counter-terrorist operations. It also conducts rescue and humanitarian operations during calamities and other disturbances. The President of India is the Commander-in-Chief of the Indian Army. With more than 1,130,000 soldiers in active service and about 1,800,000 reserve troops, the Indian Army is the world's second largest. It is a completely voluntary service and although a provision for military draft exists in the Indian constitution, it has never been imposed.

The Indian Army was formed soon after India gained independence in 1947 and retained most of the regiments of the British Indian Army. The Army is deployed in many of the world's conflict zones as a part of the United Nations Peacekeeping forces. The force is currently headed by the Chief of Army Staff, General Deepak Kapoor. Field Marshal is the highest attainable rank in the Indian Army and is conferred by the President of India, on advice of the Union Government, only in exceptional circumstances. Two officers have attained this rank so far.

Objectives

The Indian Army doctrine defines the role of the Indian Army as - "The Indian Army is the land component of the Indian Armed Forces which exist to uphold the ideals of the Constitution of India." As a major component of national power, along with the Indian Navy and the Indian Air Force, the roles of the Indian Army are as follows :

- Primary: Preserve national interests and safeguard sovereignty, territorial integrity and unity of India against any external threats by deterrence or by waging war.
- Secondary: Assist Government agencies to cope with 'proxy war' and other internal threats and provide aid to civil authority when requisitioned for the purpose."

History

Upon India gaining independence in 1947, the British Indian Army was divided into two parts to serve the newly created nations of Union of India and Islamic Republic of Pakistan. Most units went to India; four Gurkha regiments were transferred to the British Army while the rest went to India.

FIRST KASHMIR WAR (1947)

Almost immediately after independence, tensions between India and Pakistan began to boil over, and the first of three full-scale wars between the two nations broke out over the then princely state of Kashmir. Upon the Maharaja of Kashmir's reluctance to accede to either India or Pakistan, an impatient Pakistan sponsored a 'tribal' invasion of parts of Kashmir. The men included Pakistan army regulars. Soon after, Pakistan sent in more of its troops to annex the State.

The Maharaja, Hari Singh, appealed to India, and to Lord Mountbatten, the Governor General, for help. He signed the Instrument of Accession and Kashmir acceded to India (a decision ratified by Britain). Immediately after, Indian troops were airlifted to Srinagar and repelled the invaders. This contingent included General Thimayya who distinguished himself in the operation and in years that followed, became a Chief of the Indian Army.

An intense war was waged across the state and former comrades found themselves fighting each other. Both sides made some territorial gains and also suffered significant losses.

An uneasy UN sponsored peace returned by the end of 1948 with Indian and Pakistani soldiers facing each other directly on the Line of Control, which has since divided Indian from Pakistani-held Kashmir. Tensions between India and Pakistan, largely over Kashmir, have never since been entirely eliminated.

Participation in UN peace-keeping operations

Presently, the Indian army has dedicated one brigade of troops to the UN's standby arrangements. The large number of sustained troop commitments made by India has been praised for taking part in long and difficult operations.

The Indian Army has participated in several UN peace-keeping operations, including the ones in Angola, Cambodia, Cyprus, Congo, El Salvador, Namibia, Lebanon, Liberia, Mozambique, Rwanda, Somalia, Srilanka & Vietnam. The army had also provided a paramedical unit to facilitate the withdrawal of the sick and wounded in Korea.

Inclusion of Hyderabad (1948)

After the partition of India, the State of Hyderabad, a princely-state under the rule of a Nizam, chose to remain independent. The Nizam, refused to accede his state to the Union of India. The following stand-off between the Government of India and the Nizam ended on 12 September 1948 when India's then deputy-Prime Minister Sardar Vallabhai Patel ordered Indian troops to secure the state. Within 5 days of intense fighting, the Indian Army, backed by the Indian Air Force, successfully defeated Hyderabad State forces. The following day, the State of Hyderabad was proclaimed as a part of the Union of India. Major General Joyanto Nath Chaudhuri, who led the Operation Polo was appointed the Military Governor of Hyderabad (1948-1949) to restore law and order.

Goa, Daman and Diu Operation (1961)

Even though the British and French vacated all their colonial possessions in the Indian subcontinent, Goa, Daman and Diu remained under Portuguese control. On 12 December, 1961, after repeated Portuguese refusals to negotiate their leaving, New Delhi launched Operation Vijay and ordered a small contingent of its troops to invade the Portuguese territories and secure them. Unable to withstand the assault that lasted twenty-six hours, Goa, along with Daman and Diu (enclaves lying to the north of Maharashtra) joined India.

Sino-Indian Conflict (1962)

Since 1959, India followed a "forward policy" under which Indian border patrol units continuously pushed their posts forward deep into territory claimed by the People's Republic of China (PRC). Small-scale clashes between the Indian and Chinese forces broke out as India insisted on the disputed McMahon Line being regarded as the international border between the two countries. Despite heavy casualties, Indian troops did not retaliate the cross-border firing by Chinese troops. China's misinterpretation of India's true intentions in Tibet created more rifts between the two countries.

Buoyed by the success of its military operations in Hyderabad and Goa, India took a more aggressive stance towards its border disputes with China. In 1962, the Indian Army was ordered to move to the Thag La ridge located near the border between Bhutan and Arunachal Pradesh and about three miles (5 km) north of the disputed McMahon Line. Meanwhile, Chinese troops too had made incursions into Indian-held territory and tensions between the two reached a new high when Indian forces discovered a road constructed by China in Aksai Chin. After a series of failed negotiations, People's Liberation Army attacked Indian Army positions at the Thag La ridge. This move by China caught India by surprise and by October 12, Nehru gave orders for the Chinese to be expelled from Aksai Chin. However, poor coordination among various divisions of the Indian Army and the late decision to mobilize the Indian Air Force in vast numbers gave China a crucial tactical and strategic advantage over India. On October 20, Chinese soldiers attacked India in both the North-West and North-Eastern parts of the border and captured vast portions of Aksai Chin and Arunachal Pradesh.

As the fighting moved beyond disputed territories, China called on the Indian government to negotiate, however India remained determined to regain lost territory. With no peaceful agreement in sight, China unilaterally withdrew its forces from Arunachal Pradesh. The reasons for the withdrawal are disputed with India claiming various logistical problems for China and diplomatic support to it from the United States, while China stated that it still held territory that it had staked diplomatic claim upon. The dividing line between the Indian and Chinese forces was christened the Line of Actual Control.

The poor decisions made by India's military commanders, and, indeed, its political leadership, raised several questions. The Henderson-Brooks committee was soon set up by the Government of India to determine the causes of the poor performance of the Indian Army. The report of committee apparently faulted much of the command of Indian Armed Forces and severely criticized the executive government for its failures on several fronts. The committee found that the major reason for the defeat was low deployment of troops on India's border with China even after hostilities began and also criticized the decision to not allow the Indian Air Force to target Chinese transport lines out of fear of Chinese aerial counter-attack on Indian civilian areas. Much of the blame was also targeted at the incompetence of then Defense Minister, Krishna Menon who resigned from his post soon after the war ended. Despite frequent calls for its release, the Henderson-Brooks report still remains classified.

Second Kashmir War (1965)

A second confrontation with Pakistan took place in 1965, largely over Kashmir. Pakistani President Ayub Khan launched *Operation Gibraltar* in August 1965 during which several Pakistani paramilitary troops infiltrated into Indian-administered Kashmir and tried to spark an anti-India rebellion. Pakistani leaders believed that India, which was still recovering from the disastrous Sino-Indian War, would be unable to deal with a military thrust and rebellion. However, the operation was a major failure since the Kashmiri people showed little support for such a rebellion and India quickly moved forces to drive the infiltrators out. Within a fortnight of the launch of the Indian counter-attack, most of the infiltrators had retreated back to Pakistan. Battered by the failure of Operation Gibraltar and expecting a major invasion by Indian forces across the border, Pakistan launched Operation Grand Slam on September 1, invading India's Chamb-Jaurian sector. In retaliation, the India's Army launched major offensive throughout its border with Pakistan, with Lahore as its prime target. Though the Indian Army's break through of the final phases of Pakistani defense was considerably delayed due to logistical issues, the conflict was largely seen as a debacle for the Pakistani Army.

Initially, the Indian Army met with considerable success in the northern sector. After launching prolonged artillery barrages against Pakistan, India was able to capture three important mountain positions in Kashmir. By September 9, the Indian Army had made considerable in-roads into Pakistan. India had its largest haul of Pakistani tanks when the offensive of Pakistan's 1 Armoured Division was blunted at the Battle of Asal Uttar which took place on September 10 near Khemkaran. Six Pakistani Armoured Regiments took part in the battle against three Indian Armoured Regiments with inferior tanks. By the time the battle had ended, the 4th Indian Division had captured about 97 Pakistani tanks in either destroyed, or damaged, or in intact condition. This included 72 Patton tanks and 25 Chafees and Shermans. 32 of the 97 tanks, including 28 Pattons, were in running condition. In comparison, the Indians lost only 32 tanks at Khemkaran-Bhikkiwind. About fifteen of them were captured by the Pakistan Army, mostly Sherman tanks. Pakistan's overwhelming defeat at the decisive battle of Assal Uttar hastened the end of the conflict.

At the time of ceasefire declaration, India reported casualties of about 2,000 were killed. On the other hand, it was estimated that about 3,800 Pakistani soldiers were killed in the battle, 9,000 were wounded and about 2,000 were taken as prisoners of war. About 300 Pakistani tanks were either destroyed or captured by India and an additional 150 were permanently put out of service. India lost a total of 190 tanks during the conflict and about 100 more had to undergo repair. In all, India lost about half as many tanks as Pakistan lost during the war. Given India's advantageous position at the end of the war, the decision to return back to pre-war positions, following the Tashkent Declaration, caused an outcry among the polity in New Delhi. It was widely believed that India's decision to accept the ceasefire was due to political factors, and not military, since it was facing considerable pressure from the United States and the UN to stop hostilities.

Bangladesh Liberation War (1971)

An independence movement broke out in East Pakistan which was brutally crushed by Pakistani forces. Due to large-scale atrocities against them, thousands of Bengalis took refuge in neighboring India causing a major refugee crisis there. In early 1971, India declared its full-support for the Bengali rebels, known as Mukti Bahini, and Indian agents were extensively involved in covert operations to aid them.

On November 20, 1971, Indian Army moved the 14 Punjab Battalion and 45 Cavalry into Garibpur, a strategically important town near India's border with East Pakistan, and successfully captured it. The following day, more clashes took place between Indian and Pakistani forces. Wary of India's growing involvement in the Bengali rebellion, the Pakistan Air Force (PAF) launched a pre-emptive strike on Indian military positions near its border with East Pakistan on December 3.

The aerial operation, however, failed to accomplish its stated objectives and caused India to declare a full-scale war against Pakistan the same day. By midnight, the Indian Army, accompanied by Indian Air Force, launched major military thrust into East Pakistan. The Indian Army won several battles on the eastern front including the decisive of battle of Hilli, which was the only front where the Pakistani Army was able to buildup considerable resistance. India's massive early gains was largely attributed to the speed and flexibility with which Indian armored divisions moved across East Pakistan.

Pakistan launched a counter-attack against India on the western front. On December 4, 1971, the A company of the 23rd Battalion of India's Punjab Regiment detected and intercepted the movement of the 51st Infantry Division of the Pakistani Army near Ramgarh, Rajasthan. The battle of Longewala ensued during which the A company, though being outnumbered, thwarted the Pakistani advance until the Indian Air Force directed its fighters to engage the Pakistani tanks. By the time the battle had ended, 34 Pakistani tanks and 50 armored vehicles were either destroyed or abandoned. About 200 Pakistani troops were killed in action during the battle while only 2 Indian soldiers lost their lives.

Pakistan suffered another major defeat on the western front during the battle of Basantar which was fought from December 4 to 16th. By the end of the battle, about 66 Pakistani tanks were destroyed and 40 more were captured. In return, Pakistani forces were able to destroy only 11 Indian tanks. None of the numerous Pakistani offensives on the Western front materialized. By December 16, Pakistan had lost sizable territory on both eastern and western fronts.

Under the command of Lt. General J.S Aurora, the three corps of the Indian Army, who had invaded East Pakistan, entered Dhaka and forced Pakistani forces to surrender on 16 December, 1971, one day after the conclusion of the battle of Basantar. After Pakistan's Lt. General A.A.K. Niazi signed the Instrument of Surrender, India took more than 90,000 Pakistani prisoners of war, which included about 38,000 armed forces personnel and 52,000 militia and bureaucrats of West Pakistani origin. At the time of the signing of the Instrument of Surrender, 9,000 Pakistani soldiers were killed-in-action while India suffered only 2,500 battle-related deaths. In addition, Pakistan lost 200 tanks during the battle compared to India's 80.

In 1972, the Simla Agreement was signed between the two countries and tensions simmered. However, there were occasional spurts in diplomatic tensions which culminated into increased military vigilance on both sides.

Siachen Conflict (1984)

The Siachen Glacier, though a part of the Kashmir region, is not officially demarcated. As a consequence, prior to the 1980s, neither India nor Pakistan maintained permanent military presence in the region. However, Pakistan started hosting a series of mountaineering expeditions to the glacier during the 1950s. By early 1980s, the government of Pakistan was granting special expedition permits to mountaineers and United States Army maps deliberately showed Siachen as a part of Pakistan. This practice gave rise to the contemporary meaning of the term *oropolitics*.

An irked India launched Operation Meghdoot in April 1984 during which the entire Kumaon Regiment of the Indian Army was airlifted to the glacier. Pakistani forces responded quickly and clashes between the two followed. Indian Army secured the strategic Sia La and Bilafond La mountain passes and by 1985, more than 1000 sq. miles of territory, claimed by Pakistan, was under Indian control.

The Indian Army continues to control more than 2/3rd of the glacier. Pakistan made several unsuccessful attempts to regain control over Siachen. In late 1987, Pakistan mobilized about 8,000 troops and garrisoned them near Khapalu, aiming to capture Bilafond La. However, they were thrown back after engaging the Indian Army personnel guarding Bilafond. During the battle, about 23 Indian soldiers lost their lives while more than 150 Pakistani troops perished. Further unsuccessful attempts to reclaim positions were launched by Pakistan in 1990, 1995, 1996 and 1999.

India continues to maintain a strong military presence in the region despite extremely inhospitable conditions and the conflict over Siachen is regularly cited as an example of mountain warfare. The highest peak in the Siachen glacier region, Siakangri, is strategically important for India because its immense altitude and proximity to the Karakoram Highway enables the Indian forces to keep check on any Pakistani or Chinese movement in the region. Maintaining control over Siachen poses several logistical challenges for the Indian Army. Several infrastructure projects were constructed in the region, including a helipad 21,000 feet (6,400 m) above the sea level. In 2004, Indian Army was spending an estimated US$2 million a day to support its personnel stationed in the region.

COUNTER-INSURGENCY ACTIVITIES

The Indian Army has played a crucial role in the past, fighting insurgents and terrorists within the nation. The army launched Operation Bluestar and Operation Woodrose in the 1980s to combat Sikh insurgents. The army, along with some paramilitary forces, has the prime responsibility of maintaining law and order in the troubled Jammu and Kashmir region. The Indian Army also sent a contingent to Sri Lanka in 1987 as a part of the Indian Peace Keeping Force.

Kargil Conflict (1999)

In 1998, India carried out nuclear tests and a few days later, Pakistan responded by more nuclear tests giving both countries nuclear deterrence capability. Diplomatic tensions eased after the Lahore Summit was held in 1999. The sense of optimism was short-lived, however, since in mid-1999 Pakistani paramilitary forces and Kashmiri insurgents captured deserted, but strategic, Himalayan heights in the Kargil district of India. These had been vacated by the Indian army during the onset of the inhospitable winter and were supposed to reoccupied in spring. The regular Pakistani troops who took control of these areas received important support, both in the form of arms and supplies, from Pakistan. Some of the heights under their control, which also included the *Tiger Hill,* overlooked the vital Srinagar-Leh Highway (NH 1A), Batalik and Dras.

Once the scale of the Pakistani incursion was realized, the Indian Army quickly mobilized about 200,000 troops and Operation Vijay was launched. However, since the heights were under Pakistani control, India was in a clear strategic disadvantage. From their observation posts, the Pakistani forces had a clear line-of-sight to lay down indirect artillery fire on NH 1A, inflicting heavy casualties on the Indians. This was a serious problem for the Indian Army as the highway was its main logistical and supply route. Thus, the Indian Army's first priority was to recapture peaks that were in the immediate vicinity of NH1a. This resulted in Indian troops first targeting the Tiger Hill and Tololing complex in Dras. This was soon followed by more attacks on the Batalik-Turtok sub-sector which provided access to Siachen Glacier. Point 4590, which had the nearest view of the NH1a, was successfully recaptured by Indian forces on June 14.

Though most of the posts in the vicinity of the highway were cleared by mid-June, some parts of the highway near Drass witnessed sporadic shelling until the end of the war. Once NH1a area was cleared, the Indian Army turned to driving the invading force back across the Line of Control. The Battle of Tololing, among other assaults, slowly tilted the combat in India's favor. Nevertheless, some of the posts put up a stiff resistance, including Tiger Hill (Point 5140) that fell only later in the war. As the operation was fully underway, about 250 artillery guns were brought in to clear the infiltrators in the posts that were in the line-of-sight. In many vital points, neither artillery nor air power could dislodge the outposts manned by the Pakistan soldiers, who were out of visible range. The Indian Army mounted some direct frontal ground assaults which were slow and took a heavy toll given the steep ascent that had to be made on peaks as high as 18,000 feet (5,500 m). Two months into the conflict, Indian troops had slowly retaken most of the ridges they had lost; according to official count, an estimated 75%–80% of the intruded area and nearly all high ground was back under Indian control.

Following the Washington accord on July 4, where Sharif agreed to withdraw Pakistani troops, most of the fighting came to a gradual halt, but some Pakistani forces remained in positions on the Indian side of the LOC. In addition, the United Jihad Council (an umbrella for all extremist groups) rejected Pakistan's plan for a climb-down, instead deciding to fight on. The Indian Army launched its final attacks in the last week of July; as soon as the Drass subsector had been cleared of Pakistani forces, the fighting ceased on July 26. The day has since been marked as *Kargil Vijay Diwas* (Kargil Victory Day) in India. By the end of the war, India had resumed control of all territory south and east of the Line of Control, as was established in July 1972 per the Shimla Accord. By the time all hostilities had ended, the number of Indian soldiers killed during the conflict stood at 527 while more than 700 regular members of the Pakistani army were killed. The number of Islamist fighters, also known as *Mujahideen*, killed by Indian Armed Forces during the conflict stood at about 3,000.

MAJOR EXERCISES

Operation Brasstacks

Operation Brasstacks was launched by the Indian Army in November 1986 to simulate a full-scale war on the western border.

The exercise was the largest ever conducted in India and comprised nine infantry, three mechanised, three armoured and one air assault division, and included three armoured brigades. Amphibious assault exercises were also conducted with the Indian Navy. Brasstacks also allegedly incorporated nuclear attack drills. It led to tensions with Pakistan and a subsequent rapprochement in mid-1987.

Operation Parakram

After the December 13, 2001 attack on the Indian Parliament, Operation Parakram was launched in which tens of thousands of Indian troops were deployed along the Indo-Pakistan border. India blamed Pakistan for backing the attack. The operation was the largest military exercise carried out by any Asian country. Its prime objective is still unclear but appears to have been to prepare the army for any future nuclear conflict with Pakistan, which seemed increasingly possible after the December attack on the Indian parliament.

Operation Sanghe Shakti

It has since been stated that the main goal of this exercise was to validate mobilisation strategies of the Ambala-based *II Strike* Corps. Air support was a part of this exercise, and an entire battalion of paratroops was paradropped during the conduct of the war games, with allied equipment. Some 20,000 soldiers took part in the exercise.

Exercise Ashwamedha

Indian Army tested its network centric warfare capabilities in the exercise Ashwamedha. The exercise was held in the Thar desert, in which over 300,000 troops participated. Asymmetric warfare capability was also tested by the Indian Army during the exercise.

Structure of the Indian Army

Initially, the army's main objective was to defend the nation's frontiers. However, over the years, the army has also taken up the responsibility of providing internal security, especially in insurgent-hit Kashmir and north-east. The army has a strength of about a million troops and fields 34 divisions. Its headquarters is located in the Indian capital New Delhi and it is under the overall command of the Chief of Army Staff (COAS), currently General Deepak Kapoor.

Commands

The army operates 6 tactical commands . Each command is headed by General Officer Commanding-in-Chief with the rank of Lieutenant General.

Each command is directly affiliated to the Army HQ in New Delhi. These commands are given below in their correct order of raising, location (city) and their commanders. There is also one training command known as ARTRAC.

Command	Command HQ	GOC-in-C
Southern Command	Pune	Lt Gen Pradeep Khanna, AVSM, VSM, ADC
Eastern Command	Kolkata	Lt. Gen. V K Singh,PVSM, AVSM, YSM
Central Command	Lucknow	Lt Gen. J K Mohanty, PVSM, UYSM, SM, VSM
Western Command	Chandimandir (Chandigarh)	Lt. Gen. TK Sapru, PVSM, YSM, ADC
Northern Command	Udhampur	Lt Gen P C Bhardwaj, PVSM, AVSM, VrC, SC, VSM
South Western Command	Jaipur	Lt Gen C K S Sabu, AVSM, VSM

CORPS

Field Formation

A Corps is an army field formation responsible for a sector within a Command. There are 3 types of Corps in the Indian Army: Strike, Holding & Mixed. A Command generally consists of 2 or more Corps. A corps has Army Divisions under its command. The Corps HQ is the highest field formation in the army.

Regimental Organisation

In addition to this (not to be confused with the Field Corps mentioned above) are the Regiments or Corps or departments of the Indian Army. The corps mentioned below are the functional divisions entrusted with specific pan-Army tasks.

Arms

1. Indian Infantry Regiments
2. Armoured Corps Regiments - The Armoured Corps School and Centre is at Ahmednagar.
3. Regiment of Artillery - The School of Artillery is at Devlali near Nasik.
4. Corps of Engineers - The College of Military Engineering is at Dapodi, Pune. The Centers are located as follows- Madras Engineer Group at Bangalore, Bengal Engineer Group at Roorkee and Bombay Engineer Group at Khadki, Pune.
5. Corps of Army Air Defence-Center at Gopalpur in Orissa State.
6. Mechanised Infantry - Regimental Center at Ahmednagar.
7. Corps of Signals
8. Army Aviation Corps(India)

Services

1. Army Dental Corps
2. Army Education Corps - Center at Pachmarhi.
3. Army Medical Corps - Center at Lucknow.
4. Army Ordnance Corps - Centers at Jabalpur and Secunderabad (HQ).
5. Army Postal Service Corps
6. Army Service Corps - Center at Bangalore
7. Corps of Electrical and Mechanical Engineers- Centers at Bhopal and Secunderabad .
8. Corps of Military Police [2] - Center at Bangalore
9. Intelligence Corps - Center at Pune.
10. Judge Advocate General's Deptt. - Institute of Military Law kamptee,Nagpur.
11. Military Farms Service
12. Military Nursing Service

13. Remount and Veterinary Corps
14. Pioneer Corps

Arms and services

Other Field Formations

- Division: An Army Division is an intermediate between a Corps and a Brigade. It is the largest striking force in the army. Each Division is headed by [General Officer Commanding] (GOC) in the rank of Major General. It usually consists of 15,000 combat troops and 8,000 support elements. Currently, the Indian Army has 34 Divisions including 4 RAPID (Re-organised Army Plains Infantry Divisions) Action Divisions, 18 Infantry Divisions, 10 Mountain Divisions, 3 Armoured Divisions and 2 Artillery Divisions. Each Division composes of several Brigades.
- Brigade: The Brigade is smaller than the Division and generally consists of 3 Infantry Battalions along with elements of various Combat & Support Arms & Services. It is headed by a Brigadier equivalent to a Brigadier General. The Indian Army also has 5 Independent Armoured Brigades, 15 Independent Artillery Brigades, 7 Independent Infantry Brigades, 1 Independent Parachute Brigade,3 Independent Air Defence Brigades, 2 Independent Air Defence Groups and 4 Independent Engineer Brigades. These Independent Brigades operate directly under the Corps Commander (GOC Corps).
- Battalion: A Battalion is commanded by a Colonel and is the Infantry's main fighting unit. It consists of more than 900 personnel.
- Company: Headed by the Major, a Company comprises 120 soldiers.
- Platoon: An intermediate between a Company and Section, a Platoon is headed by a Lieutenant or depending on the availability of Commissioned Officers, a Junior Commissioned Officer, with the rank of Subedar or Naib-Subedar. It has a total strength of about 32 troops.

- Section: Smallest military outfit with a strength of 10 personnel. Commanded by a Non-commissioned officer of the rank of Havildar Major or Sergeant Major.

ARMY MODERNIZATION: ENHANCING CAPABILITIES WITHOUT REDUCING MANPOWER

With personnel strength of 1.1 million soldiers (6 regional commands, a training command, 13 corps, and 38 divisions), the Indian Army has kept the nation together through various crises, including four wars since independence, Pakistan's "proxy war" in J&K since 1989–90, and insurgencies in many of the northeastern states. Given its large-scale operational commitments on border management and counterinsurgency, the army cannot afford to reduce its manpower numbers until these challenges are overcome. Many of its weapons and equipment are bordering on obsolescence and need to be replaced. The next step would be to move gradually toward acquiring network-centric capabilities for effects-based operations so as to optimize the army's full combat potential for defensive and offensive operations. The army is also preparing to join the navy and the air force in launching intervention operations in India's area of strategic interest when called on to do so in the future.

Lieutenant General J.P. Singh (retired), former deputy chief of the army staff (planning and systems), stated in an interview with the *CLAWS Journal* that "the critical capabilities that are being enhanced to meet challenges across the spectrum include battlefield transparency, battlefield management systems, night-fighting capability, enhanced firepower, including terminally guided munitions, integrated maneuver capability to include self-propelled artillery, quick reaction surface-to-air missiles, the latest assault engineer equipment, tactical control systems, integral combat aviation support and network centricity." The army's mechanized forces are still mostly "night blind." Its artillery lacks towed and self-propelled 155-mm howitzers for the plains and the mountains and has little capability by way of multi-barrel rocket launchers and surface-to-surface missiles. Infantry battalions urgently need to acquire modern weapons and equipment for counterinsurgency and counterterrorism operations to increase operational effectiveness and lower casualties.

Main battle tanks (MBT) and infantry combat vehicles (ICV) are the driving forces of India's conventional deterrence in the plains. This fleet is being modernized gradually by inducting two regiments of the indigenously developed Arjun MBT and importing 310 T-90S MBTs from Russia. A contract has also been signed for 347 additional T-90S tanks to be assembled in India. The BMP-1 and BMP-2 Russian ICVs, which have long been the mainstay of the mechanized infantry battalions, need to be replaced as well. The new ICVs must be capable of performing internal security duties and counterinsurgency operations in addition to their primary role in conventional conflicts.

Artillery modernization plans include the acquisition of towed, wheeled, and self-propelled 155-mm guns and howitzers for the plains and the mountains through import as well as indigenous development. The Corps of Army Air Defence is also faced with problems of obsolescence. The vintage L-70 40-mm air defence (AD) gun system, the four-barreled ZSU-23-4 Schilka (SP) AD gun system, the SAM-6 (Kvadrat), and the SAM-8 OSA-AK, among others, need to be replaced by more responsive modern AD systems that are capable of defeating current and future threats.

The modernization of India's infantry battalions is moving forward but at a similarly slow pace. This initiative is aimed at enhancing the battalions' capability for surveillance and target acquisition at night and boosting their firepower for precise retaliation against infiltrating columns and terrorists hiding in built-up areas. These plans include the acquisition of shoulder-fired missiles, hand-held battlefield surveillance radars, and hand-held thermal imaging devices for observation at night. A system called F-INSAS (future infantry soldier as a system) is also under development. One infantry division has been designated as a rapid reaction force for employment on land or in intervention operations and will have one amphibious brigade and two air assault brigades.

Similarly, the Indian Army proposes to substantially enhance the operational capabilities of army aviation, engineers, signal communications, reconnaissance, surveillance, and target acquisition branches in order to improve the army's overall combat potential by an order of magnitude. Modern strategic and tactical level command and control systems need to be acquired on priority for better synergies during conventional and sub-conventional conflict. Plans for the acquisition of a mobile corps-to-battalion tactical communications system and a battalion-level battlefield management system likewise need to be hastened. Despite being the largest user of space, the army does not yet have a dedicated military satellite for its space surveillance needs. Cyberwarfare capabilities are also at a nascent stage. The emphasis thus far has been on developing protective capabilities to safeguard Indian networks and C4I2SR (command, control, communications, computers, intelligence, information, surveillance, and reconnaissance) from cyberattack. Offensive capabilities have yet to be adequately developed. All these capabilities will make it easier for the army to undertake joint operations with multinational forces when the need arises and the government approves such a policy option.

NAVAL MODERNIZATION: MAJOR FLEET EXPANSION

The Indian Navy's ambitious Maritime Capabilities Perspective Plan seeks to dominate the Indian Ocean region by acquiring blue water operational capability while effectively countering current and emerging threats closer to the coastline. There is a perceptible shift in emphasis from an increase in the number of platforms to the enhancement of capabilities. According to a report tabled in the Indian Parliament in the last week of April 2012 by the Standing Committee on Defence, the navy's modernization plan seeks to achieve the following objectives:

- Augment airborne maritime surveillance, strike, anti-submarine warfare [ASW] and air defence capability through induction of shore-based aircraft, integral helos, carrier based aircraft, space based [assets] and UAVs [unmanned aerial vehicles], along with suitable weapons and sensors.

- Develop ASW capability through induction of suitable platforms, weapons and sensors.
- Build adequate stand off capability for sea lift and expeditionary operations to achieve desired power projection force levels, influence events ashore and undertake military operations other than war.
- Induct assets and develop suitable infrastructure to augment forces available for low intensity maritime operations (LIMO), protection of off-shore assets and [for] coastal security.
- Induct force multipliers like satellite based global communications, reconnaissance and network enabled platforms to achieve battle-space dominance capability and perform network centric operations.
- Induct state-of-the-art equipment and specialized platforms for special forces to enhance niche capabilities to conduct maritime intervention operations and other envisaged roles.
- Develop support infrastructure in island territories to support the planned force levels as well as support infrastructure for ships/submarines/aircrafts at ports and airbases.

According to Admiral Arun Prakash (retired), former chief of naval staff, India's naval modernization plans are designed to meet the following aims:

- Acquiring a capability for maritime domain awareness in the area of responsibility, including space-based surveillance, maritime reconnaissance, airborne early warning and control (AEW&C), and UAVs
- Developing the capability for expeditionary and joint warfare, supported by special operations
- Acquiring reach and sustainability through long endurance, tankers, turnaround facilities in friendly foreign ports, and longer intervals between maintenance cycles
- Acquiring modern capabilities in fields of tactical aviation, ASW, anti-air/anti-missile, land-attack, mine countermeasures, and electronic warfare

- Networking ships, submarines, and airborne platforms via satellite
- Committing to self-reliance and indigenization, with the objective of harnessing national strengths in shipbuilding, engineering, electronics, and IT

The Indian Navy has two operational fleets—the Eastern Naval Command and Western Naval Command—and has proposed to center both fleets around an aircraft carrier. Eventually the navy plans to graduate to three carrier battle groups. The INS *Chakra,* a nuclear-powered submarine leased from Russia, will join the fleet later in 2012, while the INS *Arihant,* the first of three to four indigenously designed and developed nuclear-armed submarines, is expected to become fully operational by late 2014. India has also begun to induct Russian Nerpa-class submarines, which will give the navy a much needed fillip to the submarine fleet and considerably enhance sea-denial capabilities. Three stealth frigates have only recently been added to the fleet.

The Indian Navy's modernization plans, though much delayed, have thus finally begun to pick up steam. Pointing out the navy's role as a key facilitator in promoting peace and stability in the Indian Ocean region, Defence Minister Antony observed while commissioning a stealth frigate in July 2012 that the present operating environment of the Indian Navy "dictates that we balance our resources with a strategy that is responsive across the full range of blue and brown water operations....The maintenance of a strong and credible navy and strengthening cooperation and friendship with other countries to promote regional and global stability is the need of the hour."

The navy plans to expand to a fleet of 150 ships in the next ten to fifteen years, with 50 warships now under construction and 100 new vessels in the acquisition pipeline. The navy is also engaged in setting up operational turnaround bases, forward-operating bases, and naval air enclaves with a view to enhancing India's surveillance efforts in the Indian Ocean region. Plans for accretions to the naval aviation fleet are likewise progressing smoothly: Boeing 737 P-8I maritime reconnaissance aircraft have begun to be inducted, and 5 additional Kamov Ka-31 AEW helicopters will be added to the existing fleet of 11 helicopters. Further, the navy's amphibious landing capability has been enhanced considerably by the acquisition of the INS *Jalashwa* (ex–USS Trenton) and other landing ships, and additional capabilities for amphibious warfare are being rapidly developed. As a result of these efforts, the Indian Navy is on the cusp of acquiring the capabilities necessary to join key strategic partners such as the U.S. Navy in safeguarding the sea lanes of communication in the northern Indian Ocean and ensuring unfettered freedom of the seas for trade and commerce.

AIR FORCE MODERNIZATION: AIR DOMINANCE AND FORCE PROJECTION

Until recently, India's traditional strategic sphere lay between the Gulf of Aden and the Strait of Malacca; but with India's global footprint expanding, the Indian Air Force should be ready to serve wherever the country's future strategic interests lie.

The air force is gearing up to provide the strategic outreach that India needs as a growing regional power and to project power where necessary in order to defend vital national interests. According to Kapil Kak, a retired air vice marshal and senior defence analyst, although there is a gap between vision and capability with regard to shaping India's strategic neighborhood, forward movement is now visible.

In his view, the modernization plans of the air force are aimed at achieving the following objectives:

- Air dominance and control of the air
- Deterrence, by both denial and punishment
- Long-range offensive reach—penetration, precision, persistence, and parallelity—in simultaneous operations at the tactical, operational, and strategic levels
- Strategic air-lift capability for power projection through both hard and soft power, such as humanitarian assistance and disaster relief operations and diaspora evacuation
- Build-up of capability for coercion
- Acquisition of force enablers and multipliers and related combat-support systems, including networking for tri-service command and control

- Capability of conducting cyberspace and information operations
- Indigenization of future capabilities for design and development

From a sanctioned strength of 39 squadrons, the Indian Air Force is down to 34 squadrons at present, due to decades of neglect, but hopes to enhance its strength to 42 squadrons by 2022. Yet plans to acquire 126 multi-mission, medium-range combat aircraft—in order to maintain an edge over the regional air forces—are stuck in the procurement quagmire. Tejas, the indigenously designed light combat aircraft, which is expected to replace the obsolescent Mig-21, is still a few years away from becoming fully operational. India is also developing a fifth-generation fighter jointly with Russia and aims to fly it in 2015. New fighter bombers include a fleet of 272 Sukhoi-30 MKIs, half of which have already been built. AEW aircraft are being acquired from Israel as well as being developed indigenously. India has also acquired 6 C-130J Super Hercules aircraft for its special forces and will likely order 6 more from the United States. C-17 Globemaster heavy-lift aircraft are also likely to be acquired shortly, which will take India's defence cooperation with the United States to a new level. Although a contract has been signed with a Swiss firm for 75 Pilatus PC-7 basic trainer aircraft, India's fleet of jet trainers continues to be deficient. In the rotary-wing category, the indigenously manufactured Dhruv utility helicopter has entered service. The air force is also in the process of acquiring medium-lift transport helicopters and attack helicopters.

In keeping with developments in the region, India's strategic forces are also modernizing at a steady pace. The Agni-I and Agni-II missiles are now fully operational. Immediate requirements include the Agni-V intermediate-range ballistic missile, which has a 5,000-km range, and nuclear-powered submarines with suitable ballistic missiles to provide genuine second-strike capability. As noted above, the INS *Arihant,* India's first indigenously built nuclear submarine, will likely become fully operational by late 2014. While India's emphasis is on mobile missile launchers, a small number of hardened silos are also being constructed. The armed forces do not currently have a truly integrated tri-service C4I2SR system suitable for network-centric warfare, which would allow them to optimize their individual capabilities; however, plans have been made to develop such a system in the next five to ten years. In fact, all new weapons and equipment acquisitions are now being planned on a tri-service basis to ensure interoperability.

India's Quest for Strategic Outreach

Given its growing power and responsibilities, India has been steadily enhancing its expeditionary and military intervention capabilities, which have been amply demonstrated in recent times. During the 1991 Gulf War, India airlifted 150,000 civilian workers, who had been forced to leave Iraq, from the airfield at Amman, Jordan, over a period of 30 days. This was the largest airlift since the Berlin airlift at the end of World War II. During the 2004 tsunami, the Indian armed forces were at the forefront of rescue and relief operations. Over 70 Indian Navy ships transported rescue teams and relief material to disaster zones in less than 72 hours, even though the country's eastern seaboard had itself suffered considerable casualties and damage. Likewise, Indian Navy ships on a goodwill visit to European countries during the Lebanon war in 2006 lifted and brought back 5,000 Indian civilian refugees.

From the ongoing modernization plans described above, it is evident that India is preparing to join the world's major powers in terms of the ability to undertake out-of-area contingency operations. Further, the acquisition of SU-30 MKI long-range fighter bombers with air-to-air refuelling capability, C-130J Hercules transport aircraft, and airborne-warning-and-control-system and maritime-surveillance capabilities over the next five to ten years will give India considerable strategic outreach. New Delhi has consistently favoured military interventions only under a UN umbrella. Though that position is unlikely to change in the near term, India is likely to join future coalitions of the willing even without UN approval when vital national interests are threatened and need to be defended. Shiv Shankar Menon, India's national security adviser, stated in a speech in August 2011: "As a nation state India has consistently shown tactical caution and strategic initiative, sometimes simultaneously. But equally, initiative and risk-taking must be strategic, not tactical, if we are to avoid the fate of becoming a rentier state." He went on to mention that India was cooperating extensively with other militaries to fight piracy off the Horn of Africa. Such cooperation will increase in the future as India adds to its intervention capabilities.

Given that India faces complex strategic scenarios and is located in an increasingly unstable neighborhood, it is in New Delhi's interest to encourage a cooperative model of regional security and work with all friendly countries toward that end. At the same time, New Delhi finds it pragmatic to hedge just in case worst-case scenarios—such as the collapse of China or China's use of military force for territorial gains—begin to unfold and threaten India's economic development or territorial integrity. The increasing emphasis on maritime cooperation, particularly with the United States, is part of India's continuing efforts to fulfil growing obligations and responsibilities as a regional power. New Delhi is now working to cooperate with all the major Asian powers in order to maintain peace and stability in the Indian Ocean and the Asia-Pacific more generally, though without aligning militarily with any one power. Toward this end, the armed forces are working together to achieve joint warfare capabilities for intervention operations in India's area of strategic interest. In sum, a rising India will soon become a net contributor to security in the Indian Ocean region, together with strategic partners such as the United States.

Nonetheless, India's modernization plans are moving ahead at a very slow pace. Policy paralysis in New Delhi due to the vagaries of coalition politics in a parliamentary democracy, along with the reduction in the defence budget as a share of India's GDP due to sluggish growth in the economy, has further exacerbated the difficulties in increasing the pace of modernization. However, the process is certainly underway, and there is hope that it will receive bipartisan support across the political spectrum because of the realization that no alternative exists for addressing emerging threats and challenges but for India to quickly modernize its armed forces.

India's military modernization, however slow it might be, will lead to a qualitative increase in defence cooperation with the United States and other strategic partners by enhancing the capabilities of the Indian armed forces for joint coalition operations, if they are in India's national interest. Overall, India will gradually acquire the capability to act as a net provider of security in South Asia and the Indian Ocean region. This positive development will allow strategic partners like the United States to reduce their military commitments to the region to a limited extent. Hence, India's modernization efforts will enhance and further cement U.S.-India relations.

4

Strength of Paramilitary Force in India

Paramilitary Forces was a term previously used without strict definitions and could include not only the current three forces, any of the Central Armed Police Forces and State Armed Police Forces and other organisations such as the Home Guard.

In March 2011, at the request of the Indian Army, the Indian government authorized the Indian Army to provide definitive terminology. A narrow definition of "paramilitary" was adopted which excluded services now known as the Central Armed Police Forces (CAPF) such as the Central Reserve Police Force, and services now known as the State Armed Police Forces. The Indian government's new terminology does not necessarily coincide with the existing terminology of the states of India. For example, the State of Bihar calls its state armed police force Military Police. It is not yet clear how (or whether) such discrepancies will be resolved. They are also compared to India's various State Armed Police Forces.

Assam Rifles

The Assam Rifles can trace their lineage back to a paramilitary police force that was formed under the British in 1835 called *Cachar Levy*. Since then the Assam Rifles have undergone a number of name changes before the name *Assam Rifles* was finally adopted in 1917. Over the course of its history, the Assam Rifles and its predecessor units have served in a number of roles, conflicts and theatres including World War I where they served in Europe and the Middle East, and World War II where they served mainly in Burma.

In the post World War II period the Assam Rifles has expanded greatly as has its role.

There are currently 46 battalions of Assam Rifles under the control of the IndianMinistry of Home Affairs (MHA) and they perform many roles including the provision of internal security under the control of the army through the conduct of counter insurgency and border security operations, provision of aid to the civil power in times of emergency, and the provision of communications, medical assistance and education in remote areas. In times of war they can also be used as a combat force to secure rear areas if needed.

HISTORY OF INDIAN PARAMILITARY FORCES

In addition to the regular armed forces, India also has paramilitary forces. These forces have grown dramatically since independence. There are twelve paramilitary organizations, which have an authorized strength of around 1.3 million personnel. In 1994, their reported actual strength was 692,500. These organizations include the Coast Guard Organisation and the Defence Security Force, which are subordinate to the Ministry of Defence. Paramilitary forces subordinate to the Ministry of Home Affairs include the Assam Rifles, the Border Security Force, the Central Industrial Security Force, the Central Reserve Police Force, the Indo-Tibetan Border Police, and the Rashtriya Rifles (National Rifles). The National Security Guards, a joint antiterrorist contingency force, are charged with protection of high-level persons (the so-called very very important persons—VVIPs) and are subordinate to the Office of the Prime Minister (also sometimes known as the Prime Minister's Secretariat.) The guards are composed of elements of the armed forces, the Central Reserve Police Force, and the Border Security Force. The Special Frontier Force also is subordinate to the Office of the Prime Minister. The Railway Protection Force is subordinate to the Ministry of Railways. At the local level, there is the Provincial Armed Constabulary, which is controlled by the governments of the states and territories. During the 1960s, 1970s, and 1980s, local police forces could not deal with the mounting array of sectarian, ethnic, and regional conflicts, and paramilitary forces were increasingly called on for assistance. In addition to security and guard duties, paramilitary organizations assist local and state-level police forces in maintaining public order and shield the army from excessive use in "aid-to-the-civil-power" operations. These operations essentially involve quelling public disorder when local police forces prove inadequate to the task.

The Coast Guard Organisation was constituted as an Armed Force of the Union in 1978 under the administrative control of the Ministry of Defence (although it is funded by the Ministry of Home Affairs), following its 1977 establishment as a temporary navy element. Its principal mission is to protect the country's maritime assets, particularly India's 200-nautical-mile exclusive economic zone and the marine resources contained in the area, which comprises nearly 2.8 million square kilometers.

The coast guard is also responsible for the prevention of poaching and smuggling, the control of marine pollution, and carrying out search-and-rescue missions. Under the command of a director general, the coast guard is organized into three national maritime zones: the Western Maritime Zone, headquartered at Bombay; the Eastern Maritime Zone, headquartered at Madras; and the Andaman and Nicobar Maritime Zone, headquartered at Port Blair. The zones are further subdivided into district headquarters, one each for the eight maritime states on the mainland and two in the Andaman and Nicobar Islands. In times of emergency, the coast guard is expected to work with the navy. In the late 1980s, coast guard units from the eastern zone supported Indian peacekeeping efforts in Sri Lanka. The coast guard's equipment includes about fifty ships, nine helicopters, and thirteen fixed-wing aircraft.

Another Ministry of Defence paramilitary organization has a security mission. The Defence Security Force guards Ministry of Defence facilities throughout India. The Border Security Force was established in the closing days of the 1965 Indo-Pakistani conflict. Its principal mission involves guarding the Indo-Pakistani line of actual control in Jammu and Kashmir as well as borders with Bangladesh and Burma. It works in internal security and counterinsurgency operations in Assam, Jammu and Kashmir, and Punjab. The border force has also been used to deal with communal rioting.

Another Ministry of Homes Affairs paramilitary force deployed in Jammu and Kashmir is the Rashtriya Rifles. In 1994 it had 5,000 troops, all of whom served in Jammu and Kashmir. Some observers expected the force to grow to thirty battalions, with around 25,000 personnel. In March 1995, Indian television referred to the Delta Force of the "fledgling" Rashtriya Rifles. It was reported that the force was operating against "terrorists" and "foreign mercenaries" in Doda District in south-central Jammu and Kashmir.

Founded in 1939, the Central Reserve Police Force is the country's oldest paramilitary organization. It maintains internal order when local and state-level forces prove inadequate to the task.

The Central Reserve Police Force in Assam, Jammu and Kashmir, and Punjab has worked in counterinsurgency operations. This force also was dispatched to Sri Lanka during India's 1987-90 involvement there. The Ministry of Defence's weekly armed forces magazine, *Sainik Samachar* , reported that the Mahila Battalion (Women's Battalion) of the Central Reserve Police Force had "proved its mettle in hot warlike conditions in Sri Lanka," and had established women as "a force to reckon with" in the paramilitary.

Another significant paramilitary organization is the Indo-Tibetan Border Police, established in 1962 in the aftermath of the war with China. It is primarily responsible for the security of the border with China.

The Special Frontier Force, established in 1962 in the aftermath of the war with China, is less well publicized by the government. Apparently it is an elite, parachute-qualified commando unit, nominally subordinate to the army and deployed along sensitive areas of the border with China, and recruited partially from among border-area hill tribes and Tibetan refugees. The Special Frontier

Force also appears to have a domestic security role; members of the force were involved in the Golden Temple siege in 1984. In 1994 its reported strength was 3,000, making it one of the smallest paramilitary forces.

PARAMILITARY FORCES: PERSONNEL INFORMATION

On 6 April 2010, killing of 76 CRPF personnel in an ambush by Maoists in Dantewada has stunned the nation and raised a question whether the Indian Police and Central Para- military Forces (CPMFs) are prepared to take on the highly motivated and very well trained cadres of Maoists or the government's policy is flawed. Attacks on the CPMFs, especially the CRPF deployed in the troubled Naxal-affected regions are getting frequent; the security forces have become a target for Naxal attacks in the 'Red Corridor.

Recurring attacks on security personnel and innocent civilians is indeed a challenge to our democratic set up. Security forces have suffered 226 casualties in counter-insurgency operations; so far this year (2010), in the Left Wing Extremism (LWE) affected States. In 2009, this number was 312 out of total 431 casualties. In 2008, more than 57% of total security forces casualties in insurgency-related violence were reported from the LWE states.

In a meeting of Politburo, CPI (Maoists) had decided to take on the Government head on and they have been able to bring about divisions in the Govt. Some UPA ministers and party members feel that Governments approach to tackle the issue is harsh and suggest dealing with them with 'Development Approach". These contradictions within the UPA have confused the public and diluted an effective and determined policy approach against the Maoists.

Due to structural and systematic deficiencies even after six decades of Counter Insurgency experience, we are still struggling in our efforts to contain Naxal violence. To deal with insurgencies and disorders, the Government has relied upon CPMFs, which are easily available and can be a rapidly deployed to tackle any crisis. But due to continuous expansion of the theatres of violence, CPMFs are under severe pressure and unable to co up with the situations. An analysis of the 'threat' dimension would define the role of the paramilitary forces; the 'capability' dimension defines the structures, manpower and resources needed to achieve the organisational objectives; and the time dimension defines the urgency of creating the required paramilitary capability. To deal effectively and proactively, to meet the existing and emerging challenges, tremendous efforts are required in building basic capability dimension of CPMFs. Are the troops in these areas, physically fit, well trained, mentally alert and logistically well-equipped to take on counter-insurgency operations in the tough terrains of LWE affected states?

The country's internal security situation demands a robust policing and paramilitary framework. Capabilities at Police Station level and in CPMFs at Platoon and Company level have to be adequate and go hand in hand to meet the challenges. In rapidly changing internal security scenario, the role assigned to CPMFs has undergone substantial changes. Para-military forces today, are multi task forces dealing with security, counter insurgency, law and order, border management, election duty, disaster management to list a few.

In sub-conventional operations requirements are different from conventional operations. Sub-conventional operations are the most difficult because concept of enemy cannot be applied to own people as a result the role of CPMFs has become more challenging. Having served both in the Army and BSF, I would not hesitate to say that life in Para- military forces is very tough as day in and out they are facing numerous challenges without any respite.

CPMFs have been expanding for the last 10-15 years, new battalions are being raised at break neck speed and at the same time proper training of the men; their equipment and logistics have not gone alongside. In spite of expansion at a large scale the Para-military Forces face grave challenges and have no respite. Mere increase in number of battalions will not enhance their efficiency when one views the weaknesses in command and control, organizational structure and state of training. Para-military Forces have not been able to innovate at the tactical level, lack of vigor at the junior levels of command, and not learning from the past mistakes are some of the reasons for their set backs. The Dantewada tragedy in which 75 CRPF personnel were brutally killed in an ambush is a serious operational failure and shows the inability of the Police and Para-military Forces to contain the Naxal violence.

Despite simmering resentment within the rank and file, life goes on. A middle ranking CRPF officer says, "Those who understand the ground realities do not have the power to decide and those who have the power to decide, do not understand the ground realities."

We must draw lessons from the actions of operationally deployed Platoons and Company's which are the source of rich ground experience, instead of strategy being worked out by inexperienced officers who have never served in the field, thus are unaware of the ground realities.

On the other hand the militarization and lethal capabilities of Naxals are on the rise. Naxalites have attacked Para-military camps and fought pitched battle for hours and they have well-coordinated, trained and ideologically brainwashed cadres and units. LWE tactics is to "Lure Forces into Trap." Armed Naxal cadres who have no fear of the presence of security forces can now gather in Bn / Brigade size groups at their time and place of choice. CPMFs have the obvious disadvantage of not knowing the local language, area, customs, traditions and it is here the role of well trained local Police comes to play. Police is a strong arm of the Govt., its strength and efficiency is essential for the Govts credibility. Civil police have roots in the society; they belong to that area, have deep knowledge of the terrain, know the local language and have bonds with the people, which are the key to success in any counter insurgency operation. Punjab and Andhra Pradesh provide an outstanding example of success achieved by the local police and Para-military forces in successful counterinsurgency campaigns.

No counterinsurgency campaign can succeed without the cooperation of the local police. Analyzing a series of Naxal incidents as case studies, grey areas in police training are:

a) Lack of physical and mental robustness.

b) Lack of soldierly and disciplinary traits

c) Lack of knowledge of field craft and tactics.

d) Poor firing skills.

A well trained, professionally committed and motivated local police with CPMFs can tackle any type of internal disorder. But at present there is a mismatch in training capabilities and infrastructure in most of the States. However STF personnel in most of the Naxalism- affected States are generally performing better as they are better trained; however they completely need to switch over to the combat role.

Paramilitary forces can achieve outstanding results against the insurgents only when they work in close coordination with the local police forces. But Para-military forces at times, feel hesitant in having close liaison with the Police and don't feel comfortable in taking orders or working under the directions of local Police.

Modernization of Police and Para-military forces should go hand in hand as their duties are complimentary to each other in counter insurgency operations. Modernize and strengthen the Police at the police station level instead of making it top heavy.

In order to enhance the capabilities of Police and Para-military Forces in Naxal affected States, the Centre and State Government's have initiated numerous steps. Combat capability of Special Police Forces, like raising of special anti-Naxal forces, specialized training to SPFs in counter insurgency and jungle warfare, providing better arms, ammunition, equipment and BP vehicles.

What are the challenges which are being faced by Para-military forces? We need to examine as to why different organizations with same weapons and manpower and from the same background perform differently in anti-terrorist and anti-insurgency operations. Difference in performance is due to lack of leadership, chain of command, neglect of training, higher age profile, professional ethos, manner of employment, regimentation, and logistics and its responsiveness.

BSF and CRPF are the main Para-military forces fighting Terrorism, Insurgency and Naxalism. BSF was raised in 1965 with 25 Bns has now 159 Bns. Each Bn has got 7 Companies with strength of 137 personnel in each company. But the effective strength of a company when it moves out to an operational area comes to only 75 to 80 personnel. Imagine if the Company is deployed in any operational area it will have fighting strength of only 60 -65 personnel after taking out personnel for administration and other duties.

Britishers raised Crown Representative Police in 1939 to quell "dacoity" in States. After Independence it became Central Reserve Police. It was deployed on Indo-China and Indo-Pak borders along with Army and did very well. In 1974 it became CRPF with the basic role of striking reserve to assist States/UTs in police operations to maintain law and order and to contain Insurgency. Besides the word Force, it still has the word Police and is treated as Police. It has various roles – crowd control, election duty, law and order problem, CI, personnel security, protection of flora and fauna etc. CRPF has got 208 Bns and is the biggest Para-military force in the world.

The question arises why our CPMFs are not being able to meet the challenges. The following factors can be attributed:-

a) Organizational structure at Functional level needs a change.
b) Inadequacy in training imparted to Police and CPMFs.
c) Lack of coordination between Police and CPMFs.
d) Non availability of reserves.
e) Lack of effective leadership
f) Lack of actionable Intelligence
g) Prolonged deployments
h) Lack of regimentation
j) Morale and Motivation
k) Political interference in working of Police and CPMFS.

Organizational Structure at Functional Level Needs a Change

Para-military forces should work on doctrines based on latest strategic perceptions and by structuring the organization accordingly. Internal Security duties demand a manpower intensive establishment at the activity level that is at the Platoon and Company level. In a Company effective strength available is 75 – 80 out of 137 personnel. Seven Companies with small functional strength affects the operational capability of a Battalion. So the number of Companies should be reduced to four, but at the same time increase the strength of the Company from 137 to 190, so that minimum 150 men are available in each Company for the operations. A weak Platoon or Company in terms of manpower does not instill confidence in a junior commander. So changes at the basic structural level are the need of the hour.

SPECIAL FORCES

The Special Forces of India are Indian military units with specialised training in the field of special operations such as Direct action, Hostage rescue, Counter-terrorism, Unconventional warfare, Special reconnaissance, Foreign Internal Defence, Personnel recovery, Asymmetric warfare, Counter-proliferation. The various branches include,

- Para (Special Forces): Formed in 1966, the Para (SF) are the largest and most important part of the Special Forces of India. They are a part of the highly trained Parachute Regiment of the Indian Army. They are the crack force and help the main army to get in the enemy lines without much damage. The main aim of having a Parachute Regiment is for quick deployment of soldiers behind the enemy lines to attack the enemy from behind and destroy their first line of defence. Para (SF) conduct series of joint exercises with US army special forces Called VJRA PRAHAR.
- Ghatak Force: Ghatak Platoon, or Ghatak Commandos, is a special operations capable infantry platoon. There is one platoon in every infantry battalion in the Indian Army. Ghatak is a Hindi word meaning "killer" or "lethal". They act as shock troops and spearhead assaults ahead of the battalion. Their operational role is similar to Scout Sniper Platoon, STA platoon of the USMC and the Patrols platoon of the British Army. A Ghatak Platoon is usually 20-men strong, consisting of a commanding Captain, 2 non-commissioned officers and some special teams like marksman and spotter pairs, light machine gunners, medic,

and radio operator. The remaining soldiers act as assault troopers. Most undergo training at the Commando Training Course in Belgaum, Karnataka. Often, other specialised training like heliborne assault, rock climbing, mountain warfare, demolitions, advanced weapons training, close quarter battle and infantry tactics are also given. Members of the platoon are also sent to the High Altitude Warfare School and Counterinsurgency and Jungle Warfare School.

- Marine Commandos (MARCOS): It is an elite special operations unit of the Indian Navy. It is specially organised, trained and equipped for the conduct of special operations in a maritime environment. The force has gradually acquired experience and a reputation for professionalism over the two decades it has been in existence. Now it is one of the finest Special Forces units in the world and among the few units qualified to jump in the water with a full combat load. The MARCOS are capable of undertaking operations in all types of terrain, but are specialised in maritime operations in Jammu and Kashmir through the Jhelum River and Wular Lake. To strengthen its capabilities to carry out special operations, the Navy is planning to procure advanced Integrated Combat System (ICS) for the MARCOS. The Navy wants the ICS for effective command, control and information sharing to maximise capabilities of individuals and groups of the MARCOS while engaging enemies. The individual equipment required by the Navy in the ICS includes light weight helmets, head-mounted displays, tactical and soft ballistic vests along with communication equipment. The group-level gear requirements include command and control and surveillance systems along with high speed communication equipment.
- Garud Commando Force: The Garud Commando Force is the Special Forces unit of the Indian Air Force. It was formed in September 2004 and has a strength of approximately 2000 personnel. The unit derives its name from Garuda, a divine bird-like creature of Hindu

Mythology. Garud is tasked with the protection of critical Air Force bases and installations; search and rescue during peace and hostilities and disaster relief during calamities. Garuds are deployed in Congo as part of the UN peace keeping operations.

INDIAN ARMED FORCES STAND ON ALLEGED HUMAN RIGHTS VIOLATIONS

The understanding of the "citizens in uniform" concept varies from country to country depending on history, military culture, transition from authoritarian rule to democracy, and experience with war and conflict. There is therefore no single model for protecting the human rights of armed forces personnel. A clear constitutional basis is recommended for the armed forces. However they do set the context for the functioning of the armed forces at home and abroad. Constitutional framework is especially important in countries where there has been a transition from civil war. Human rights education should be a core component of training, especially where armed forces have been involved in inter-communal conflict.

Indian Defence Minister A K Antony said at a seminar on 'Internal Security' though cases of human rights violations by security forces have been rare, even a single instance of human rights violation is totally unacceptable. Human rights are the lifeblood of a democracy and Terrorists have no regard for human life, or rights and attack the vary basis of a democratic set-up, but they underestimate, or overlook the resilience of a democratic country like ours. One of the major challenges in countering terror is that security forces, on the one hand, have to preserve the territorial integrity, sovereignty of the nation and give a sense of security to the people.

On the other hand, in the process of combating terrorism, they also run the risk of being dubbed as authoritarian and repressive. Through repeated terror attacks, the terrorists want the security forces to make mistakes which can be projected as a violation of human rights. Though cases of human rights violation by security forces have been rare, even a single instance of human rights violation is totally unacceptable. The Indian Armed Forces personnel are made aware of the respect for human rights and laws at every stage of their military training. This awareness must be translated into action on the ground. Our Armed Forces must consciously follow the twin ethics of 'minimum use of force' and 'good faith' during operations against an 'invisible and ruthless' enemy.

Though the constraints of the security forces are understandable, the security forces too must bear in mind that the process of 'winning the hearts and minds' of people is never an easy one task.

In India, the traditional application of humanitarian law to the armed forces is almost as old as the armed conflict themselves. The Indian Army took immediate cognizance of the protection of Human Rights Act, 1993. It established its Human Rights Cell in March 1993, six months prior to the establishment of the National Human Rights Commission in India. Its (COAS) Ten Commandments laying down the code of conduct for all ranks operating against armed insurgents and terrorists i.e. Do's or Don'ts, are recognized by the Indian Judicial System, and by the United Nations. The doubts about human rights conduct of the soldiers in India and abroad arise currently on account of lack of understanding about terrorism and insurgencies, the difficulties faced in dealing with them, and human rights aberration that take place in such operations.

The Armed Forces may be called upon to provide aid to civil authorities for maintenance of law and order, counter insurgencies, combat terrorism and help the public during natural calamities. While dealing in these types of situations, the Armed Forces come in contact with the public and unavoidably, uses some force, minimal though it may be. The Indian Armed Forces are faced with the dilemma of containing insurgency on one hand and to prevent violations of human rights on the other hand. The Indian Armed Forces especially Army frequently has been painted as 'monstrous institution of the state' perpetrating widespread human rights violations by those very countries that in the first place are responsible for funding separatism, insurgency and terrorism in

India. While the actions of the armed forces are closely monitored by human rights organizations, the same is not applicable to the acts by the militants. The media too, apparently is oblivious to the blatant human rights violations by the militants.

Sometimes the security forces tend to over react when some casualty occurs to their own comrade. The militants fire at the security forces and then merge with the local population. This Provo Cates the security forces to fire indiscriminately which in turn causes injuries to the local population resulting in violation of human right's. The Armed Forces are thus required to handle difficult situations during these situations with firmness and courtesy so that its reputation for being impartial, friendly and professionally component is maintained.

MODERNISATION ARMED FORCES

The Armed Forces of India are responsible for defending the country against external aggression and safeguarding the territorial integrity of the nation.

The Indian Army has to be extremely vigilant at all times to meet various challenges along the borders of the country encompassing different geographical and climatic conditions. Keeping in view the threat perceptions, advances in technology and geo-political environment, the Indian Army is suitably structured, equipped and trained to effectively perform its tasks.

Efforts are always continued to modernise and upgrade the weapons and weapon systems of the Army to prepare it to address the requirements of modern day warfare, and enhance its combat efficiency. Following are some of the notable efforts:-

Armoured Corps: As a part of the effort to equip the Armoured Corps with night fighting capabilities. Thermal Imager Based Stand Alone Sight and Thermal Imager Fire Control System for the T-72 Tanks are under process for procurement. Image Intensification Based Sights for the drivers of T-72 Tanks and Image Intensification Based Sights for the commanders, gunners and drivers of T-55 Tanks are undergoing trials and evaluation as part of the procurement process. Armoured Recovery Vehicle have also been contracted for procurement.

Mechanised Infantry: To enhance the combat efficiency, Konkurs-M Anti-Tank Guided Missiles have been acquired along with transfer of technology. Anti-tank Guided Missile Launchers of the Infantry Combat vehicle BMP-II are being equipped with the Thermal Imaging sights to enhance night-fighting capability. Image Intensification based Night Vision Devices for the drivers of BMPs are also in the process of procurement.

Artillery: To enhance the fire-power of the Army, efforts are being made of equip them with 155 mm Artillery Gun, for employment in various types of terrain. Besides, trials have been successfully completed for the Multi-barrel Rocket Launchers.

Trial Evaluation of the latest Artillery Ammunition System for induction viz Terminally Guided Munitions, Velocity Enhanced Long Range Artillery Projectiles and anti-radiation Ammunition is also in progress. Moreover, to enhance the Surveillance Capability of the Army, considerable progress has been made in the direction of acquisition of Long Range Reconnaissance and Observation System, Weapon Locating Radar and Unmanned Aerial Vehicle.

Air Defence Artillery: The negotiations for induction of improved version of Tunguska M1 Weapon system in Air Defence Artillery units of strike/ mechanised formations are going on. Air Target System 'Lakshya', developed by Aeronautical Development Establishment (ADE) of DRDO has also been recently evaluated by the Army and will be used for practice firing of Air Defence Weapon Systems.

In conjunction with the IAF, a revamp of the existing Control and Reporting System of Air Defence Artillery is being carried out. The thrust is towards automation of various warning and control systems and processes. A review of the requirement of modern Air Defence Weapon System has been carried out to replace the obsolescent equipment in a phased manner to enable it to meet emerging air threats.

Infantry: The combat potential, surveillance and counter-insurgency capability of the Infantry is being significantly improved by acquisition of following equipment and weapon systems:-

Fire Power: 20 mm Calibre and 14.5 mm Calibre Anti Material Rifles, Automatic Grenade Launcher-30, Multiple Grenade

Launcher, 84 mm MM Rocket Launcher MK II and Kornet –E Anti-Tank Guided Missile are under procurement.

Surveillance Devices: Battle field Surveillance Radars (BFRS), Hand-Held Thermal Imagers (HHTI) and various types of Unattended Ground Sensors (UGS) have been procured for surveillance in conventional and counter-insurgency roles and to monitor the intrusion across the Line of Control/ Actual Ground Position Line.

Mobility: A family of High-Mobility Vehicles, Bullet-Proof Vehicles and Anti-Tank Guided-Missile Vehicle are being procured to improve the mobility of the infantry.

Signals: Procurement of state-of-the-art communication equipment and system has brought about substantial qualitative improvements in the communications capability of the Army.

Some of the major procurements are: RS HX long-range frequncy-hopping high-frequency radio sets, Hand-Held Walkie-Talkie Radio Sets, Interception Receiver AR 5000, Radio Set 5 Watt/ 20 Watt VHF, and Radio Set 5 Watt/ 20 Watt VHF for Armoured Fighting Vehicles. A country wide – secured value-added backbone data network is also being established connecting the important Formation headquarters of the Army.

Engineers: After withdrawal of forces from the border, equipment to assist de-mining operations, have been procured to minimise the causalities. Trials and procurement of various equipment's is also underway which will improve capability for disaster-management during a nuclear, chemical and biological warfare scenario. Army's capability to fight against insurgency/ terrorism has been considerably bolstered by equipping them with more equipment.

In written reply to a clarification sought by the Committee in regard to the functioning and performance of recently inducted Arjun Tank, the Ministry have furnished the following details:-

The project on development of MBT Arjun was initially sanctioned in May 1974 at a cost of Rs. 15.50 Cr with a PDC of 10 years. Time and cost have undergone revision on 3 occasions (in 1980, 1987 and 2000).

The reason for revision in cost and time are-major changes in qualitative requirements, delay in import of sub-systems due to import embargoes, increase in number of prototypes, manufacture of pre-production series tanks, long and extended user trials, difficulties in organising for field evaluation, general inflation and devaluation of rupee etc.

MBT Arjun has been indigenously designed and developed as per the General Staff Qualitative Requirement (GSQR) given by the Army. It has been tested and evaluated exhaustively by the Army (user) in all types of terrains and weather conditions for more than a decade.

Various modifications suggested by the user, during pre-induction trials, have been systematically attended to and the performance of the tank improved as laid down in the GSQR.

The confidence of the Users in MBT Arjun is reflected very well, as they have already placed an order on DGOF for manufacture of 124 Nos. of ARJUN tanks.

During the presentation on the modernisation plans of the Indian Army, a representative of the Ministry of Defence provided detailed information as outlined below : "Modernisation is an ongoing process and sometimes mid-course corrections may become necessary to be undertaken because of the availability of various kinds of technologies or even changes in the overall geo-strategic perceptions and requirements of relevant force structures, the thrust we have given in the Tenth Plan is primarily to modernise the infantry battalions and the special forces. Our infantry battalions and special forces, for a long time since the 60's, had no major modernisation of their equipment and structures. So, this was given the highest priority by the Chief of the Army Staff.

Thereafter, we wanted our mechanised forces to be able to fight at night. Fighting by night has become a norm today in modern warfare and the removal of night blindness was given the next kind of priority.

Then there is the refurbishment of our medium artillery. As you would be aware, a bulk of our artillery comprises of very vintage 130 millimetre guns which were there from the 60's other than the Bofors of 155 millimetre calibre. So, a refurbishment of medium artillery will continue to mark our efforts right up to the end of Twelfth Plan and beyond.

Balanced modernisation of other arms and services and making up of deficiencies is what we call a hollowness in our structure". As regard the capability being looked for each arms, representative of the Ministry deposed as under: "I will take this up arm by arm and indicate to the Hon. Standing Committee as to what is the capability that we are looking for each of the arms. What are the kind of equipment we are providing to them?

The Committee note that modernisation of Armed Forces is a continuous process which requires long term planning and huge investments. The Ministry of Defence have undertaken a plan to modernise the Indian Army and to equip with the latest machine and equipment so that it can meet the security requirements of the country. The Committee note that during the three years of the Tenth Plan period, the stress primarily was on the modernisation of the infantry battalions and the special forces.

The Committee further note that as far as special forces are concerned, 40 items of various kinds have been identified for modernisation. Efforts are being made to modernise and upgrade the weapons and weapon systems of the Army to prepare it to address the requirements of modern day warfare.

These efforts cover the ability to exercise surveillance up to a distance of three kilometres of infantry battalion detection of infiltration by troops or vehicles in areas not physically held, destroying targets like vehicles, stores dumps and troop clusters, neutralise enemy commanders, various kinds of equipment, Battle Field Surveillance Radars, High Resolution Binoculars, Night Vision Devices, Thermal Imaging Sight for ATGM Launch, Mechanised Forces and their equipments, induction of T-90 and Arjun Tanks and T-72 Tanks.

From the presentation made by the Army before the Committee, it is observed that the number and type of weapons available with the Army are much less as compared to their requirements. The Committee, therefore, keeping in view the threat perceptions, advances in technology with special emphasis on Information Technology and geo-political environment, strongly recommend that there is an imperative need to prepare a long term policy to modernise the Indian Army and upgrade their weapon systems in areas identified by the Army and desire that a time bound programme should be drawn to acquire those weapons etc. and also ensure proper financial allocations for the purpose. The Committee desire that the quality of the equipment etc. should be the best available in the market which can enhance the combat efficiency of the soldiers in an effective manner. The Committee feel that our priority should be to equip the infantry man with superior light weight weapons and equipment & clothing.

The Committee are of the opinion that there needs to be a more focused thrust on development, production of indigenous equipment into the Army, with particular reference to the Arjun Main Battle Tank.

It is understood that though a limited order for 124 number of these tanks have been placed, the first production models are being further subjected to additional performance trials by the Army. This is primarily due to the unstated concern over quality control at the Ordnance Factory, Avadi at time of issue, which must be ensured by the Ordnance Factory Board to the satisfaction of the user. The Committee are surprised to note that instead of giving firm order for sufficient number of Arjun Tanks by indigenous production, only a very small order has been placed and the Government has decided to acquire tanks from a foreign country to meet its requirement.

Having incurred an expenditure of approximately Rs. 3,300 crores on the development and productionisation of the MBT Arjun, the Committee are of the firm opinion that the Arjun must be inducted into the Army in large numbers, for which an initial production order for 50 tanks must be placed on Heavy Vehicles Factory, Avadi. This does not absolve DRDO (AHSP for Arjun Tank) and the Ordnance Factory Board of their prime responsibility to ensure that the production model of the tank meets the user requirement in every respect. The procurement plan of the Army must be structured (or re-structured if necessary) to provide for induction of increased numbers of Ajrun Tanks by the 11th, 12th Army Plans, as a replacement for T-72 Tanks.

INDIAN NAVY: CHALLENGES BEYOND THE HORIZON

The Currency of Power

In the mid-1980s many commentators predicted the end of the role of military force as the "currency of power". Subsequent decades were however marked by global changes that significantly altered the distribution of international power. Radical shifts in the status of erstwhile subjugated states, the empowerment of newly developed and developing nations, and the displacement of totalitarian regimes across Europe, have altered the perception of the influence of military power in determining the course of global events. The freeing up of economies, which became the norm by the mid-1990s, resulted in a rise in expectations in many parts of the world. The spread of information made the disparities in living standards more glaring and national, political or ethnic groupings became assertive of their right to a share of the global wealth. As changing tectonic conditions result in periodic earthquakes which enable the earth's crust to adjust to the altered conditions, this instability created violent upheavals involving the use of military force to realign political or economic power. Predictions of the demise of military force as a currency of power were thus belied by the unilateral exercise of the military option in Central Europe and in West Asia. Far from the imagined era of stability (which is largely interpreted as the maintenance of the status quo) and the much vaunted "end of history" theory, the last two decades have been the most violent in history.

Apart from its being used as a means of forcibly redistributing political power within and between nations, military power is also being applied to further economic interests. The attack on Iraq by the US, and the current imbroglio in that unhappy country, had as much to do with the perceived energy requirements of the US as with any real or imaginary weapons of mass destruction. Similarly, it has been argued that Iraq's plans to trade its oil wealth in euros threatened the primacy of the dollar as the global currency, and the attack on Iraq was a measure to safeguard vital US economic interests. It is apparent therefore, that far from becoming irrelevant, or even waning in importance, military power is still considered a legitimate and viable option by countries that wish to impose their vision of the international order on recalcitrant lesser states. It is equally an unavoidable conclusion that states that wish to retain their freedom of manoevre in global affairs, must possess a sound economy, backed by a robust (even if defensive) military capability. Clearly the age has not yet arrived when nations can dispense with their armed forces. If anything, recent events would indicate the opposite-that failure to invest in national defence capability could cost a country dear.

The Nature of Future Wars

While it is fairly clear that nation states will continue to resort to military force, and we will need to maintain armed forces for the foreseeable future, it is much less clear, what size and shape and capabilities those forces will need to have. Warfare has begun to evolve away from the historical pattern, and massive wars on a global scale between evenly matched and industrialised opponents are generally accepted to be a phenomena of the past. Major influences on the nature of future warfare will be exerted by three main factors-economic interdependence and global-isation, redistribution and realignments of international power, and technology.

With the collapse of the USSR, socialist economic doctrines were rapidly discarded by all countries and they have embraced the free market philosophies of the West. The resultant free flow of capital, the increase in global movement of labour, and the offshoring of industrial production have bound countries together in a variety of ways-economic, social and cultural. It would be impossible under these conditions for a country to inflict severe or lasting damage to another with which it has close economic ties without itself suffering in the process. Globalisation has thus curtailed the freedom of the more powerful nations to act with impunity against weaker nations with well-developed economies, and with which they have economic relationships. The nature of conflict between such countries would necessarily be of brief durations and be focused on the achievement of narrow and specific (mainly economic) objectives.

The changed distribution and alignment of international power has various facets. The US, and under its leadership NATO, have resorted to military actions decisively against several countries in the last two decades. The object states of these actions are countries that are characterised by poor economic levels, political instability, and the absence of democratic forms of government. It is hard to see similar actions being taken against countries with a stable and democratic system in place, and which have well developed economic, social and cultural international linkages. Although the US has emerged as the sole superpower, it has been forced to become increasingly heedful to international opinion. Thus, while the end of the Cold War resulted in the emergence of a single super power, the economic globalisation that followed has swung the pendulum slightly back, resulting in a moderation of the superpower status.

The spread of satellite television brought distant wars to the homes of viewers, and the developed countries are finding it increasingly difficult to justify the loss of human life. The political cost of casualties in war has increased to the point where risk avoidance has become an important factor that impinges on war tactics in Western countries. These factors permit the following conclusions:

- Wars of the future are likely to brief and focused on economic objectives.
- They will be more in the nature of specific operations against unequal and weak states with poorly developed and insular economic and political systems.
- They will not be waged with equally industrialised or advanced countries.
- They will be increasingly subject to world opinion and approval.
- Risk avoidance will result in the use of long range weapons and aerial bombardment with precision weapons.

CIVIL DEFENCE

The Civil Defence Policy of the Government till the declaration of emergency in 1962 was confined to making the States and

Union Territories conscious of the need of Civil Defence measures and to ask them to keep ready Civil Defence Paper Plans for major cities & towns under the then Emergency Relief Organisation (ERO) Scheme. Two major incidents gave reason to the development of Civil Defence in India; the 1962 Indo-China and the 1965 Indo-Pak conflicts. This led to a considerable rethinking about the policy & scope of Civil Defence and as a result the Civil Defence Policy as it exists today, was evolved and Civil Defence legislation was enacted in the Parliament in 1968. In the 1971 Indo-Pak War, the Civil Defence acquitted itself commendably.

Civil Defence aims at saving lives, minimising damage to the property and maintaining continuity of industrial production in the event of an hostile attack. The Civil Defence Act of 1968, is though applicable throughout the country, but the organisation is only raised in such areas & zones which are tactically and strategically considered vulnerable from enemy attack points of view. At the moment Civil Defence activities are restricted to 135 categorised towns spread over 32 States/Union Territories. To meet the early warning communication requirement for an impending hostile attack, a reliable and flexible network, both on telephone lines and radio/wireless, have been established in most of the categorised Civil Defence Towns. Communication facilities, on telephone lines & radio, has also been planned and established in most of the Civil Defence towns for the purpose of command, control, coordination & liaison and also for mutual aid and cooperation.

Civil Defence is primarily organised on a voluntary basis except for a small nucleus of paid staff and establishment which is augmented during emergencies. The present target of Civil Defence volunteers is 394,000 personnel in 135 towns in 32 states. Apart from carrying out training and demonstration of Civil Defence measures during peacetime, Civil Defence volunteers are also deployed, on voluntary basis, in various constructive activities including assistance to the administration, relief & rescue work during natural calamities like floods, earthquakes, cyclones, droughts, etc. by the administration of the State Governments/ Union Territories of their own. Civil Defence Training is conducted in the country on a three-tier concept, i.e. Local/Town level, at

State level and National level. The National Civil Defence College at Nagpur, a subordinate training establishment of the Ministry, conducts various courses in civil defence and disaster relief management.

Civil Defence Capabilities of the Indian State

Few discussions of the implications of nuclear weapons in the India-Pakistan context make any mention of the civil defence capabilities of either state. It is generally assumed that the civil defence services in both countries will be rapidly overwhelmed by a nuclear attack and would be as good as useless. This may well be true – we have yet to find out - however, in India's case, the state has had enormous experience in dealing with some of the most catastrophic natural disasters known to man. While these may not approach the magnitude of a nuclear attack, they provide an interesting insight into the strengths and weaknesses of the Indian disaster management apparatus.

India maintains and trains a sizeable civil defence force and has laid down a reasonably comprehensive set of procedures and regulations governing civil defence operations in the event of war. While many of India's state governments do not implement these plans in peacetime, the fact that these plans exist and are periodically reviewed cannot be ignored. Moreover, as will be shown, the plans lay emphasis on rapid emergency measures rather than on a well-developed peacetime infrastructure.

In addition to the civil defence organization, India spends considerable money on a reserve body called the Home Guards and on the National Cadet Corps. These organizations do receive a modicum of civil defence training and are expected to reinforce and assist the regular emergency services in the event of war. India's huge police and paramilitary forces also have considerable experience in disaster management and would be a very valuable asset. The question as to how this set up will perform in the event of a nuclear war, however, remains unanswered.

The Development of Civil Defence in India

India's first steps in creating civil defence organization came at the start of the Second World War. Between the years 1939 and

1941, a cell in India's Home Department was established to deal with the subject of Civil Defence/Air Raid Precautions. A Lieutenant -Colonel of the Indian Army was placed in charge of this cell with effect from October 1939. This officer was given the status of a Deputy Secretary to the Government of India and his duties included extensive touring to advise and help Provincial Governments in preparing Civil Defence plans. Another officer was later appointed to act as a liaison between General Headquarters and the Home Department and to assist with technical advice on Air Raid Precautions matters.

It was not until June 1941, however, that an army Major was appointed as Deputy Assistant Director General - Indian Medical Service in order to deal with the medical aspects of civil defence. It can be seen from this that civil defence was not taken particularly seriously by the Indian government. Despite these developments, virtually no civil defence plans or organization existed on the ground. It took the start of the war in Europe for civil defence to receive more attention in India and in July 1941, a decision was taken to create a full-fledged Civil Defence Department. In September 1941, India's first Director General of Civil Defence was posted to the Home Department. The Civil Defence Department came into being on 24 October 1941 when Dr. E. Raghavendra Rao - the first Civil Defence Member of the Governor General 's Executive Council - arrived after training in England. The Air Raid Precautions cell in the Home Department was transferred to the new Civil Defence Department and was expanded.

Throughout 1942, the Indian Civil Defence Department expanded at a rapid pace as the threat of Japanese attack intensified. In close cooperation with the Provincial Governments - who were responsible for the implementation of the individual plans - a series of plans were drawn up to cope with the perceived threats. As the main Japanese threat came from the North-East, most of the civil defence efforts were concentrated in this area. The Civil Defence Department was responsible form planning, advice and provision of equipment while the provincial government was responsible for the distribution of civil defence instructions and on raising of fire-fighting and rescue units. The Civil Defence Department and the Provincial Governments did some remarkable work, but, civil defence activities in India were not particularly extensive or comprehensive. Compared to what existed before the war substantial progress had been made, but, compared to the massive civil defence efforts of, say, the United Kingdom, India's measures were woefully inadequate.

As the threat of Japanese attack faded, the Civil Defence Department was steadily wound down. In 1946 the Department was liquidated. A small cell - a mere shadow of the wartime organization continued to exist in the Home Department, but for all intents and purposes, India's civil defence organization ceased to exist. After independence, in 1948, the Emergency Relief Scheme existed as a cell in the Ministry of Home Affairs. This cell concerned itself with fire-fighting and fire-prevention and eventually led to the establishment of the National Fire Services College and the Central Emergency Relief Training Institute - now called the National Civil Defence College - at Nagpur in 1956-57. The formal initiation of civil defence in India started in 1953 when a civil defence plan was drafted. However, this failed to get accepted and was drastically revised. While the Civil Defence and Fire Service Colleges continued to run courses, for the first 15 years of Indian independence, there was no civil defence organization in existence on the ground. The Chinese invasion of 1962 changed all this.

As part of the massive rethinking and reorganization of India's national security policy, the British civil defence expert, General Irwin, was invited to draft the blueprint of a national civil defence plan and to give practical advice on how to meet both conventional and unconventional attacks. Two manuals were compiled and circulated to all state governments for the preparation of comprehensive civil defence plans in selected high priority towns which were categorized on the basis of their importance.

The Defence of India Act 1962 gave the State and Union Territory governments with all the powers necessary for the implementation of the measures outlined in General Irwin's manuals. These two manuals - ' The Master Plan for Civil Defence in India' and 'General Principles of Civil Defence' - form the structural basis for India's Civil Defence Organization to the present day. As regards the implementation of these plans, it was officially stated in the Indian Parliament in 1963, that while certain recommendations were implemented immediately, other measures regarding civil defence were to be kept on paper, to be implemented when needed. To this end, a comprehensive plan of operation was drawn up and directives issued to the State and Union Territory governments to make their own civil defence plans and to keep them, even if just on paper, in a state of readiness for their successful implementation in an emergency.

Over time, certain states have drafted a number of other emergency plans to cope with natural disasters such as cyclones and earthquakes as well as man-made calamities such as chemical and nuclear accidents. These plans tend to be kept in a higher state of readiness than the civil defence plans since the civil defence plan allows for the mobilization of resources in a phased manner to meet a threat for which there is considerable prior warning. In the case of natural disasters, this warning is not available.The 1965 and 1971 wars provided some experience for the Indian Civil Defence Organization. Despite this, no major changes have been recommended and the civil defence organization in India continues as envisaged in the Irwin Plan of 1962.

Strength, Organization and Structural Foundations

In 1995, the Indian Civil Defence Organization had a sanctioned strength of 676,000 volunteers in addition to a small (strength unknown) nucleus of professional staff which is to be augmented in an emergency. However, only 376,000 have actually been raised and of these, only 330,000 are fully trained. The civil defence staff and volunteers are a distinct and separately organized group from the other Indian emergency services - i.e. fire departments and paramedics. At present, civil defence units are raised and stationed in categorized civil defence towns. These towns are graded on both their vulnerability and on their strategic importance - a practice dating back to the Second World War. At present, there are 110 categorized towns spread over 24 states and union territories. This means that civil defence personnel and expenditure are concentrated in the areas where they are needed most. This is particularly important since the regular civil defence forces receive only Rs. 65 million from the central government. The Central

Government handles all matters regarding equipment and communications. All the central government ministries have civil defence cells which would be activated in wartime.

In addition to these volunteers, the Indian Civil Defence Organization relies heavily on the Home Guards and the National Cadet Corps. These two organizations are funded and, in the case of the NCC, trained separately from the civil defence volunteers. The Home Guards have a sanctioned strength of 573,793 and has a current raised strength of 418,493. Unlike the Civil Defence Organization, the Home Guards are spread across the country and extend into the rural as well as the urban areas. The Home Guards were created as an auxiliary to India's vast police and paramilitary forces and have an important role in the maintenance of law and order as well as internal security. In peacetime, the Home Guards assist communities in emergencies as epidemics, fires and floods, while their role in wartime extends to civil defence work as well as assisting the army in maintaining rear area security. The Home Guards have a budget of Rs.280 million - considerably higher than the Civil Defence Organization. The organization, since it is more geographically widespread, provides a veneer of civil defence cover to rural areas as well as reinforcing the civil defence units in the 110 categorized civil defence towns. Their training, as will be discussed later, prepares them for rescue and fire-fighting work. There is also provision for raising auxiliary Home Guards from the ex-soldiers population of India in case of extreme necessity - as in the case of the 1965 India-Pakistan war.

The National Cadet Corps are another important source of manpower for civil defence. But since the 1980s, 32 NCC officers and cadets are trained as civil defence instructors at the National Civil Defence College each year. The National Cadet Corps Act of 1948 states that NCC cadets have no military service liability. This means that they cannot be deployed on duties where they have to be armed - unless special legislation is passed. This, however, does not exempt them from civil defence work. On 9th. September 1965 - during the 1965 India-Pakistan war - the Indian Central Government drew up a list of duties which were to be performed by NCC personnel over the age of 17. These included the following:

(a) Passive Air Defence - including rescue work, first air, casualty evacuation fire fighting and removal of debris
(b) Manning of Civil Defence Posts - including civil defence patrols and look outs
(c) Maintenance of essential services - including motor transport, pioneer and engineering and water and power supply
(d) Traffic Control
(e) Manning Static Signal Installations
(f) Administration and running of evacuation camps

With these duties assigned to them, the NCC forms a very useful reinforcement for the Civil Defence Organization. This is even more obvious when it is realised that the NCC has 420,000 cadets in its Senior Division - made up of university students over the age of 17. The central and state governments contribute to the expenditure on the NCC in the ratio of 2:1. The budget for the NCC comes, in part from the Ministry of Defence - not the Home Ministry in the case of the Home Guards and Civil Defence Organization. It should be stated that the army regards the NCC as a waste of money. In addition to these organizations, the Indian government controls the Central Industrial Security Force and the Crisis Management Group of the Atomic Energy Regulatory Board. These two organizations, while not specifically created for the task of civil defence, could provide vital equipment, training and skilled personnel when operating in an environment of either radioactive or chemical contamination. As regards funding, the Indian central government maintains a sizeable calamity relief fund for use in the case of a natural disaster. This would provide a valuable source of reconstruction funds for post-war recovery. In fact, it can be said that the published expenditure on civil defence - Rs. 65 million - represents a relatively small fraction of the expenditure on a disaster relief/civil defence infrastructure. While little evidence of civil defence activities can be seen in peacetime, the extensive pool of manpower, combined with plans and an organizational set up, gives India to field a civil defence organization in wartime that is far better organized, larger and more capable than would first be apparent from the rather pathetic peacetime infrastructure.

5

Military Strength of India and Pakistan

MILITARY BUDGETS AND ECONOMIC IMPACT

Pakistan's defence budget for the year 2006-07 was $4.1 billion (~3% of GDP) in response to India's hike in defence budget of 2006-07 at $20.11 billion (~ 2.5% of GDP). Pakistan's hike in military budget would be partially funded by its government coffers and partially by borrowing whereas India's military spending would be entirely off its own funds. India's ambitious budget prompted Pakistan to up its own military budget, despite the country's widespread poverty and socio-political problems. Apart from its GDP, Pakistani military also gets a considerable funding from United States. Considering that India has a far larger economy overall, its military budget is also several times larger, despite being a smaller share of India's GDP.

Manpower and Ground Forces

As of 2005, India has the second largest military manpower in the world - at 3,773,300 personell, next only to China. Pakistan's manpower of 1,449,000 personell, although smaller in numbers, is proportionally higher than India in terms of their population ratios. Pakistan's ground forces are equipped with American or Chinese weapons like *FIM 92 Stinger* SAMs, *BGM-71 TOW* anti-tank missiles, *T-82* tanks and other equipments. Indian ground forces are equipped with mostly home-made and Soviet technologies like IR guided *9K35 Strela-10* SAMs, 3rd Gen IR guided *Nag* anti-tank missiles, UAVs and a large inventory of tanks and support vehicles. In terms of both numbers and equipments, Indian military dominates the Pakistani ground forces.

COMPARISON OF AIR FORCES

As of 2006, Indian Air Force (IAF) has over 170,000 personnel and 3,382 aircrafts, of which 1,330 are combat aircrafts operating off 61 airbases - making it the fourth largest air force in the world. India's strike fighters consist of Russian and French aircrafts like *Mikoyan MiG-29, Dassault Mirage 2000, Sukhoi Su-30* - the last one developed under dual licensing by HAL, India's aerospace industry in Bangalore.

In addition to these, Indian Air Force also owns ground attack aircrafts, reconnaissance aircrafts, UAVs and support helicopters - a majority of them either of Soviet or French origin. Pakistan Air Force (PAF) has about 530 combat aircrafts and 65,000 active personnel, operating out of 9 airbases. Its strike fighters consist of US, Chinese and ageing French fighters like *F-16 Fighting Falcon, JF-17 Thunder* and *Dassault Mirage ROSE-III*. It also has transport aircrafts like *Lockheed Martin C-130* and *Airbus A310*, however unlike India, there are no UAVs or reconnaissance aircrafts in the Pakistani Air Force.

Naval and Sea Based Forces

After the overwhelming losses in the 1971 war against India, Pakistan rapidly increased the size of its naval fleet which doubled in the 1980s after a massive 3.2 billion dollar military and economic aid by US President *Ronald Reagan*. At present, Pakistan's navy owns over 45 vessels , most of them of US or European origin which include submarines, destroyers, frigates, patrol and mine warfare boats. It operates from its sole naval port in Karachi and sometimes from naval facilities in UK, USA and France.

It had recently been involved in various humanitarian operations during the 2005 Tsunami in South East Asia. Indian Navy on the other hand, is a three dimensional naval force consisting of missile-capable warships, an aircraft carrier, mine sweepers and a host of marine aircrafts. Most of the warships in the Indian navy are indigenously built in its own dockyards. The navy operates from its major naval bases in Visakhapatnam, Mumbai, Goa and the Andaman Islands. Indian Navy has significant capabilities of being a true blue water Navy and is experienced both in war and peacekeeping operations in the Indian Ocean.

The Nuclear Club

India tested a nuclear bomb in 1974 using materials from Canada and technical help from Soviet Union. However, the embargo on heavy water export from Canada after the test stalled India's nuclear ambitions till 1998, when it shocked the world by conducting five nuclear detonations termed as *Shakti* tests. The highest yield was by a 48 kiloton staged fusion device, which India claimed was a thermonuclear bomb but seismic data on the tests proved otherwise. In the same year 1998, Pakistan conducted a series of six nuclear detonations in a test termed as *Chagai*. The highest yield was reported to be about 25 kiloton from a two stage boosted device. At present Pakistan's nuclear stockpile is slated to be around 30-40 warheads while India possesses 70-100 warheads. The nuclearisation of India and Pakistan became a turning point in the history of conflicts between these two countries with high tensions but no war, not very much unlike the US vs USSR Cold War.

Ballistic and Cruise Missile Proliferation

In the nuclear delivery front, both India and Pakistan have a series of ballistic and cruise missiles in addition to ground attack aircrafts. The maximum range among India's operational ballistic missiles is 2000 km achieved by Agni-2. India's Agni ballistic missiles are indigenously developed by its own missile defence industry known as *IGMDP*. The maximum range among Pakistan's missiles is by *Hatf V Gauri* which is reported to do over 2200 kms. Pakistan's Hatf missiles are based on North Korean *No-Dong* series of IRBMs. Both Pakistan's *Hatf* and India's *Agni* ballistic missiles are nuclear capable. India has also developed a supersonic cruise missile *BrahMos* which is by far the fastest cruise missile at Mach

2.6 and maximum range of 290 km. It is reported to be nuclear capable but it is not confirmed yet. On the Pakistan side, its *Babur* cruise missile has a reported range of 700 km and a maximum speed of 880 km/h (Mach 0.7). As with India *BrahMos, Babur* is also reported to be nuclear capable but there is no confirmation yet.

The Final Verdict

Both Pakistan and India are almost evenly matched head to head in nuclear and missile fronts, however India has strategic and technological superiority over the conventional forces of Pakistan. Indian Navy is larger in fleet and personnel size with a more varied range of ships including an aircraft carrier while Pakistan's Navy is smaller and has no aircraft carriers. Indian's IAF is equipped with highly capable fighters like 4.5th generation *Su-30*s and 4th gen *Mirage 2000*s which are technologically superior to Pakistan PAF's *F-16*s and *Mirage III*s. Additionally Indian pilots are better trained and more capable in air combat than Pakistani forces as was demonstrated by its various wars with Pakistan or joint exercises with US and UK. In the area of conventional ground forces both the Indian as well as Pakistani Army is well equipped and highly trained to survive in extremities of topography and climate in combat conditions, like wars in the high Himalayas.

If a purely conventional war were to take place between both these countries, India would most likely overpower Pakistan owing to its superior military technology and infrastructure, larger manpower, more territorial area and a strategic advantage in its sea and air forces. It must also be noted that a war between these two countries will matter more than India's conventional superiority as both these nations are nuclear powers on an equal deadlock. India has maintained a 'no first use' nuclear policy in the lines of a similar policy by China while Pakistan does not have any such policy, considering their only hope against India is in nuclear deterrance. It would be risky for India at the present scenario to go into any aggressive war against Pakistan as the repercussions would be serious a nuclear devastation for both countries.

Unfortunately India and Pakistan had adversarial relations since sixty years. After the Mumbai carnage Pakistan is under threat of pre-emptive strikes. Fourth Indo-Pakistan war could be triggered by another terrorist attack anywhere in India. This is a dangerous scenario. India and Pakistan have fought three wars, and war drums for the fourth war are getting louder.

It is in order therefore to comprehend Indian military capabilities, and Pakistan's ability to defend itself. Defense capability is an interplay of economic and military potential. Indian economy is booming, and its GDP growth is in double digits. The global recession has impacted Indian economy, but its defense capability remains intact.

Military power and capabilities are sustained by economic and industrial potential. Geography, demography, population, oil resources and reserves, industrial capability including defense production, dollar reserves, self reliance, education, quality of manpower and leadership have a bearing on military power. Seven lakh Indian troops are tied down in Jammu and Kashmir. India has over one hundred billion dollar reserves. The West, Israel and Russia are India's weapon suppliers.

Indian Army has eighteen Corps with 34 Divisions including four Rapid Action Divisions, which would spear head ground offensives. Pakistan Army has ten Corps and twenty five divisions. Indian Army has eighteen Infantry, ten Mountain, three Armored, and two Artillery Divisions. Besides it has five Infantry, one parachute, thirteen Air Defense, and four Engineering Brigades, designated as independent formations. In addition there are two Air Defense Groups, and fourteen Army Aviation Helicopter units. This is a sizeable force, capable of launching major offensives from several fronts.

The decentralized command structure will be an advantage, as compared to Pakistan's centralized Army command organization. Pakistan Army has an active force of 620,000 well trained personnel, with 528000 reservists, and 150000 para-military troops. Pakistan armed forces are seventh largest in the world. Pakistan Army's doctrine of "Offensive Defense", evolved by General Mirza Aslam Beg was put to test in 1989 in Exercise Zarb-e Momin.

The doctrine is to launch a sizeable offensive into enemy territory, rather than wait for enemy strikes or attacks. In case of Indian land offensive Pakistan Army and Air Force will respond with land and air offensives to gain and hold enemy territory. Before embarking on further offensive, gains shall be consolidated. In 1990 the Central Corps of Reserves was created to fight in the desert sectors , where enemy land offensives are expected. These dual capable formations trained for offensive and holding actions are fully mechanized.

Pakistan Army has ten Corps including the newly formed Strategic Corps. The Army has twenty six divisions (eight less than India). Two more divisions were raised as Corps reserves for V and XXXI Corps. Pakistan Army has two armored divisions, and ten independent armored brigades. Presently one hundred thousand troops are stationed on the Pak Afghan border to fight terror. Special Service Group-SSG comprises two airborne Brigades i.e. six battalions.

Pakistan Army has 360 helicopters, over two thousand heavy guns, and 3000 APC's. Its main anti-tank weapons are Tow, Tow Mk II, Bakter Shiken and FGM 148 ATGM. The Army Air Defence Command has S.A- 7 Grail, General Dynamics FIM-92 Stinger, GD FIM Red Eye, and ANZA Mk-I, Mk-II, Mk-III and HQ 2 B surface ti air missiles. Radar controlled Oerlikon is the standard Ack Ack weapon system.

The ballistic missile inventory of the Army is substantial. It comprises Ghauri III and Shaheen III IRB'S; medium range Ghauri I and II and Shaheen II, and short range Hatf I- B, Abdali, Ghaznavi, Shaheen I and M -11 missiles. All the ballistic missiles can carry nuclear war heads. Nuclear and conventional weapon capable Babur Cruise missile is the new addition to Pakistan's strategic weapon inventory. Number of ballistic missiles and war heads are almost the same as India has. So there is a parity in nuclear weapons, which is a deterrent.

Indian armor is of Russian origin. Out of 2295 Indian Army's Main Battle tanks, 2235 are of Russian origin. The main battle tanks are; 310 T-90-S Bishsma's (300 are on order), 1925 T-72M Ajeya's.. The T-90 and the T-72 have 125 mm smooth barrel guns. T-72 though old is the backbone of Indian Armor Corp's. 268 Ajeya's have been upgraded with Israeli Elbit thermal imaging systems. 1000 T-72 MBT's are awaiting up-gradation.

There have been several instances of T-72's gun barrel bursting. 124 Indian made Arjun (heavy 56 ton) MBT are on order. Sixty Arjun's are in operational service. Arjun's engine overheating problem has not been solved. Arjun has a 120 mm gun, but is unfit or desert operations. Pakistan Army is equally strong in armor, capable of giving a fitting response to any Indian military adventure.

Main Battle tanks Al-Khalid and Al-Zarrar are the backbone of Pakistan's armor Corp's. Both are Pakistan made. Pakistan's tank armory comprises :five hundred Al-Khalid MBT's; 320 Al-Zarrar type 85 II MBT's, 500 Al-Zarrar MBT's; 450 79II AP (Chinese type 81 upgrade, and 570 T-80 UD MBT of Ukranian make. In addition Pakistan has 880 Type 59, which were procured from China in 1970.This makes a total of three thousand six hundred and twenty tanks.

All Pakistani MBT's except T-59's have 125 mm smooth barrel guns. Indian armor offensives in Kashmir, Punjab, and Sind would be effectively challenged by Pakistani armor and mechanized formations, depending on PAF's ability to keep the skies over the battle areas clear of Indian Air Force. India's modern air defense system has Israeli Arrow anti-missile missiles, and 90,000 surface to air missiles-SAM's. India has one hundred nuclear armed ballistic missiles (Agni-1 and Agni II), and Brahmos the new supersonic cruise missile. Indian Army is well trained, equipped and highly professional, and so is Pakistan Army.

Air power is likely to play a key, if not a decisive role in any future major or minor India-Pakistan armed conflict. The aim of Indian pre-emptive strikes will be maximum destruction by surprise air attacks, combined with shock commando action. A possibe scenario is; intensive bombing of the target to be followed by attacks by armed helicopters and ground assault by heliborne Commandoes. An overview of Indian Air Force and Pakistan Air Force will help comprehension of IAF's offensive capabilities, and defensive capabilities of Pakistan Air Force.

Indian Air Force has 3000 aircraft including training, transport, helicopters and 800-1000 combat air craft, which operate from sixty air bases, including Farkhor airbase in Tajikistan.. Six hundred IAF's strike and air defense fighters are expected to be operational.

Pakistan Air Force has 630 aircraft, which include 530 combat aircraft, with 400 operational at any time. In 1996 India signed an agreement with Russia for the purchase of 90 Su 30 Mk-1 multi-role fighter-bombers. In 2004 a multi-billion licence was signed for building additional 140. 240 Su30-Mk-1's were ordered, 120 are already in service. With a maximum speed of Mach 2.3 and range of 8000 Km with refueling and ability to carry tons of conventional munitions and nuclear weapons, it is a lethal and menacing weapon system for the strike and interception role.

Other IAF's advanced strike and combat aircraft are: 51 Mirage-2000 (of Kargil fame), 60 Mig-29's (for air defense), 250 old Mig-21's (110 have been refurbished with Israeli help), 47 Jaguars and 70 Mig-27's for ground attack. 220 LCA Teja's under manufacture at HAL Bangalore will start entering service in 2010... IAF's fighter pilots are well trained and have out shone American pilots during joint exercises.

Pakistan Air Force has 200 rebuilt Mirage- 3's (for night air defense) and Mirage-5's for the strike role. They can carry nuclear weapons. They have been upgraded with new weapon systems, radars, and avionics. Additionally the PAF has 42 F-16's, 150 F-7's including 55 latest F-7 PG's. Manufacture of 150 JF 17 Thunder fighters (jointly designed) is underway at Pakistan Aeronautical Complex Kamra. The JF -17 Thunder is a 4th generation fly by wire multi-role fighter aircraft. Eight are already in PAF service. An order has been placed with China for the purchase of 36 JF-10, a Mach 2.3 -5th generation multi-role fighter, comparable in performance to the Su-30 Mk-1 with the Indian Air Force. PAF is on Red Alert, and is maintaining full vigil to intercept and destroy IAF intruders.

During the recent air space violation, the IAF intruders were in the sights of PAF's F-16's, but were allowed to escape unscathed to avoid a major diplomatic crisis. PAF pilots and technicians are well trained, high professionals, who will be able to prove their mettle in the future battle with India. A comparison of Indian Navy and Pakistan Navy reveals that Pakistan Navy could inflict substantial damage to the Indian Navy. Indian Navy has 16 submarines; Pakistan Navy has ten, some are brand new. Indian

Navy has 27 war ships, Pakistan Navy has ten. Indian Aircraft Carrier Veerat, will be a menace, and must be sunk by submarine or air attacks, if it attempts to block Pakistan's sea lanes or ports. It is hoped that better sense prevails and India desists from invading and attacking Pakistan. If it does, the consequences will be horrible for both the countries.

Manpower and Ground Forces

India has the second largest manpower in its military globally - at 3,773,300 personell (2005), next only to China. Pakistan has a much smaller manpower of 1,449,000 personell which is proportionally higher than India in terms of their population ratios. Pakistan's ground forces are equipped with American or Chinese weapons like FIM 92 Stinger SAMs, BGM-71 TOW anti-tank missiles, T-82 tanks and other equipments. Indian ground forces are equipped mostly by home-made or Soviet technologies like IR guided 9K35 Strela-10 SAMs, 3rd Gen IR guided Nag anti-tank missiles, UAVs and a large inventory of tanks and support vehicles. In terms of numbers and equipments, both Indian and Pakistani ground forces are on an closely equal footing.

Comparison of Air Forces

As of 2006, Indian Air Force (IAF) has over 170,000 personnel and 3,382 aircrafts of which 1,330 are combat aircrafts operating off 61 airbases - making it the fourth largest air force in the world. India's strike fighters consist of Russian and French aircrafts like Mikoyan MiG-29, Dassault Mirage 2000, Sukhoi Su-30 - the last one developed under dual licensing by HAL, India's aerospace industry in Bangalore. In addition to these, India's air force owns ground attack aircrafts, reconnaissance aircrafts, UAVs and support helicopters - a majority of them either of Soviet or French origin. Pakistan Air Force (PAF) has about 530 combat aircrafts and over 65,000 active personnel, operating out of 9 airbases. Its strike fighters consist of US, Chinese and French fighters like F-16 Fighting Falcon, JF-17 Thunder and Dassault Mirage ROSE-III. It also has transport aircrafts like Lockheed Martin C-130 and Airbus A310, however there are no UAVs or reconnaissance aircrafts in the Pakistani Air Force.

Naval and Sea Based Forces

After the overwhelming losses in the 1971 war against India, Pakistan rapidly increased the size of its naval fleet which doubled in the 1980s after a massive 3.2 billion dollar military and economic aid by US President Ronald Reagan. At present, Pakistan's navy owns over 45 vessels , most of them of US or European origin which include submarines, destroyers, frigates, patrol and mine warfare boats.

It operates from its sole naval port in Karachi and naval facilities in UK, USA and France. It had recently been involved in various humanitarian operations during the 2005 Tsunami in South East Asia. Indian Navy on the other hand, is a three dimensional naval force consisting of missile-capable warships, an aircraft carrier, mine sweepers and a host of marine aircrafts; most of its warships indigenously built in its own dockyards. The navy operates from its major naval bases in Visakhapatnam, Mumbai, Goa and the Andaman Islands. Indian Navy has significant capabilities of being a true blue water Navy and is experienced both in war and peacekeeping operations in the Indian Ocean.

The Nuclear Club

India tested a nuclear bomb in 1974 using materials from Canada and technical help from Soviet Union. However the embargo in heavy water export from Canada after the test stalled India's nuclear ambitions till 1998, when it shocked the world by conducting five nuclear detonations termed as Shakti tests. The highest yield was by a 48 kiloton staged fusion device, which India claimed was a thermonuclear bomb but seismic data on the tests proved otherwise. In the same year 1998, Pakistan conducted a series of six nuclear detonations in a test termed as Chagai. The highest yield was reported to be about 25 kiloton from a two stage boosted device. At present Pakistan's nuclear stockpile is slated to be around 30-40 warheads while India possesses 70-100 warheads. The nuclearisation of India and Pakistan became a turning point in the history of conflicts between these two countries with high tensions but no war, not very much unlike the US vs USSR Cold War.

Ballistic and Cruise Missile Proliferation

In the nuclear delivery front, both India and Pakistan have a series of ballistic and cruise missiles in addition to ground attack aircrafts. The maximum range among India's operational ballistic missiles is 2000 km achieved by Agni-2. India's Agni ballistic missiles are indigenously developed by its own missile defence industry known as IGMDP. The maximum range among Pakistan's missiles is by Hatf V Gauri which is reported to do over 2200 kms. Pakistan's Hatf missiles are based on North Korean No-Dong series of IRBMs. Both Pakistan's Hatf and India's Agni ballistic missiles are nuclear capable. India has also developed a supersonic cruise missile BrahMos which is by far the fastest cruise missile at Mach 2.6 and maximum range of 290 km. It is reported to be nuclear capable but it is not confirmed yet. On the Pakistan side, its Babur cruise missile has a reported range of 700 km and a maximum speed of 880 km/h (Mach 0.7). As with India BrahMos, Babur is also reported to be nuclear capable but there is no confirmation yet.

The Final Verdict

Both Pakistan and India are almost evenly matched head to head in nuclear and missile fronts, however India has strategic and technological superiority over the conventional forces of Pakistan. Indian Navy is larger in fleet and personnel size with a more varied range of ships including an aircraft carrier while Pakistan's Navy is smaller and has no aircraft carriers. Indian's IAF is equipped with highly capable fighters like 4.5th generation Su-30s and 4th gen Mirage 2000s which are technologically superior to Pakistan PAF's F-16s and Mirage IIIs. Additionally Indian pilots are better trained and more capable in air combat than Pakistani forces as was demonstrated by its various wars with Pakistan or joint exercises with US and UK. In the area of conventional ground forces both the Indian as well as Pakistani Army is well equipped and highly trained to survive in extremities of topography and climate in combat conditions, like wars in the high Himalayas.

If a purely conventional war were to take place between both these countries, India would most likely overpower Pakistan owing to its superior military technology and infrastructure, larger manpower, more territorial area and a strategic advantage in its sea and air forces. It must also be noted that a war between these two countries will matter more than India's conventional superiority as both these nations are nuclear powers on an equal deadlock. India has maintained a 'no first use' nuclear policy on the lines of a similar policy by China while Pakistan does not have any such policy, considering their only hope against India is in nuclear deterrence. It would be risky for India at the present scenario to go into any aggressive war against Pakistan as the repercussions would be serious a nuclear devastation for both countries.

India's numerical and technical superiority in a conventional war is beyond question - therefore Pakistan's low nuclear threshold and maintenance of the first-use option.

However, in a surgical kind of strike being talked about in Indian and Pakistani circles, over Muridke or Muzaffarabad , cruise missiles are likely to be used. The Pakistani and Indian capability is evenly matched in these except for India's supersonic cruise missile with a speed of Mach 2.6 which is an obvious advantage in this kind of a strike, but it only has a range of 290 kms - enough to reach Muridke if launched from East Punjab but not much more. Pakistan's answer is the Babur cruise missile with a range of 700 km and a speed of Mach 0.7 - sub-sonic but pretty fast.

UAV's was the other Indian advantage which has recently been matched by Pakistan.

With the evenly matched air, missile and nuclear capability, a surgical strike doesn't seem to be the best option. If India is to win, it will have to be a full-scale conventional war with both sides avoiding breaching the other's nuclear threshold.

MILITARY STRENGTH OF INDIAN AND PAKISTANI GROUND FORCES

Arjun

At the end of the 1971 war, the Indian army realized the limitations of their tank fleet in the harsh desert conditions of Rajasthan, a northwestern Indian state bordering Pakistan, so they initiated their own MBT design. The first "Arjun" (named after a mythical Hindu warrior prince) concept was laid out in 1974 by the Combat Vehicles Research and Development Establishment (CVRDE) of the Defence Research and Development Organization (DRDO). Based on 1971 battlefield experiences, the Arjun would have a locally-designed, rifled 120mm main gun, a German, MTU-based diesel powerplant (The Indians consider turbine engines fuel guzzlers), and a computerized fire control system with a laser rangefinder.

One of the early Arjun prototypes was unveiled in April 1985, with a number of prototypes undergoing technical testing while desert trials were scheduled for that summer.

At the time, it was reported to have a 120mm smooth-bore main gun and would use a 1400-hp MTU-based diesel until an indigenous one was ready. Weight would be about 50 tons, and the tank would cost about $1.6 million (U.S.). Development costs rose about 500 percent throughout the '80s, and through a development process plagued with delays, the end product visually resembles the German Leopard II, however, unlike the German vehicle, its future remains in doubt. As of mid-2000 India planned to acquire T-90 tanks, based on field trials which had already been completed. Although orders had been placed for the supply of 124 Arjun tanks through the Defence Research Development Organisation, it would be difficult to predict when these orders would be fufilled. Until such time, T-90 tanks would serve to counter Pakistan's T-85 tanks.

Pakistan's announcment in 1995 of a deal with Ukraine to purchase T-84s caused a flurry of activity in the Indian tank development community. And on 9 January 1996, the Arjun was formally unveiled and cleared for mass production. Considered comparable to the M1A2 Abrams, Leopard 2, and Leclerc, the 59-ton "15th Variant" can achieve a maximum speed of 70 kph (55 mph) and cross-country speed of 40 kph with its 1400-hp powerplant. The 1,610-liter fuel tank allows for a cruising range of 200 km (120 miles). To ensure crew survivability, production versions will have the indigenously-researched and developed 'Kanchan' composite armor, an automatic fire detection and suppression system, and an NBC protection system designed and built by the Bhabha Atomic Research Center.

The rifled 120mm gun, which includes a muzzle reference system, is made of ESR steel and is fitted with a thermal sleeve and fume extractor. All main gun rounds use a semicombustible cartridge case with increased energy propellant for higher muzzle velocity and greater penetration characteristics. In addition to the usual suite of rounds, an antihelicopter round is under development as well.

The Arjun's fire control system includes a laser rangefinder, ballistic computer, thermal imaging night sight, stabilized panoramic sight for the tank commander, and a secondary telescopic sight. The LRF (integral to the gunner's sight) has a range of nearly 10 km and a thermal imager (which can "see"' at around 5.5 km, recognize a target at 3.1 km and identify targets at 2.5 km). The Arjun fire control system's ability to fire on the move during the night is a major step forward for Indian armored forces.

The Chassis and Automative System of MBT Arjun comprises main chassis, power pack (1400 HP engine coupled to hydromech transmission), running gear with hydropneumatic suspension, integrated fuel system, advanced electrical system and other dedicated special systems like integrated fire detection and suppression system. The chassis is fabricated from rolled homogenous armour plate using advanced welding technique. Frontal armour is of Kanchan composite sandwitched between armour plates.

This fully integrated Arjun chassis and Automative System having smooth riding characteristics can be used as a mobile platform for any advanced weapon system. An extremely effective hydropneumatic suspension system has been developed for MBT Arjun. The suspension is externally mounted and provides vehicle springing and damping. It consists of one bogey wheel pair for each suspension station. Gaseous medium in the hydropneumatic suspension is for all terrain maneuverability for exploiting the power available. Casing and hub of the hydropneumatic suspension are sealed for preventing dust ingression and water seepage into the casing during operation in marshy area or shallow/medium fording. The MBT Arjun is fitted with double-pin steel track with detachable rubber pads. It is made out of steel casting having two bores for insertion of rubberised pins. It is an integral piece incorporating guide horns and has got a provision for insertion of detachable pads. The end connectors are induction-hardened in the area which comes in contact with the sprocket teeth to prevent wear.

The integrated fire and explosion suppression system developed for MBT Arjun is based on state-of-the-art technology. The indigenous development of this system is considered to be a breakthrough in the field of fire protection engineering. It is capable of suppressing hydrocarbon fuel fire/explosion resulting from an enemy hit on the tank or due to any malfunctioning of the engine, transmission or any electrical short circuiting. The system is based on infra-red detectors for the detection of fire/ explosion in the crew compartment of the battle tank and a continuous type of linear thermal detector popularly known as fire-wire for the engine compartment.

Halon-1301 has been employed as a fire extinguishing medium. The system is capable of detection and suppression of hydrocarbon fuel fire/explosion in the crew compartment within 200 milliseconds and in the engine compartment within 15 s thereby enhancing the chances of survivability of the crew and battle effectiveness of the tank. Further improvements were deemed necessary even after the Arjun design profile was accepted again in July 1996.

On 27 August 1996, the Defense Production and Supplies Secretary ordered 15 pre-production tanks from the Heavy Vehicles Factory, Avadi (at which point, estimates placed the project cost at $112 million). As of mid-1997 the list of faults after 20 years of development was not encouraging. In addition to numerous technical modifications to its fire and gun control systems, the fire control system in particular has been found unable to perform in temperatures above 42 degrees Celsius (108° F). The DRDO has been considering scrapping the current Arjun fire control system in favor of whatever is accepted for the T-72M1 upgrade program. Defects noticed during the user trials of the Arjun Mk.1 MBT, including over-heating of the engine in Rajasthan desert areas, had supposedly been "by and large overcome" while other complaints were being addressed.

The first 120 tanks to be built would cost $4.2 million each, while other cost estimates places the figure at $5.6 million each per tank by 2001, given a purchase of 124 tanks to equip two regiments. Production of the first batch of tanks might take more than the planned five years, given the capacity at the Avadi factory. Planned Arjun variants include mobile assault guns, an observation post vehicle, an air defense (gun or missile) version, a recovery vehicle, an engineer vehicle, and bridgelayers. New bridgelayers and recovery vehicles were necessary, given the Arjun's substantial weight increase over the T-72M1 series.

Specifications

ARJUN Mk 1 (15th Preproduction Model)

Weight 59 tons (58.5 tonnes)

Length (gun forwards) 10.19m

Width (over tracks) 3.5m (w/ skirts) 3.85m

Height (w/o 12.7mm AAMG) 2.32m

Engine 1400 HP MTU 838 Ka 501Diesel

Transmission Semi-automatic with 4 forward and 2 reverse gears.(also reported as ZF automatic)

Fuel 1610 ltrs

Performance

Max Speed 72-70 kph (55 mph)

Cross Country Speed 40 kph

Cruising Range 200 km (120 miles)

Ground Pressure . 84 kg/cm Square

Ground Clearance .45m

Slide Slope: 60%

Climbing Gradient 35°

Trench 2.43 m (also given as 3m)

Vertical Obstacle .9m

Ford 1.4 m

Armament

Main Gun 120mm, stabalized w/ MRS (APFSDS, HE, HEAT, HESH and smoke)

12.7mm AA Gun (probably NVST)

7.62mm Coax (probably PK-T)

2 X 9 Smoke Grenade Launchers

LRF Range 10 km

Sights Thermal (Max Rng 5.5 km)

Active and Passive

Defensive Systems 'Arena' a possibilty, probable Laser Warning System

105 mm Indian and Light Field Guns

(IFG/LFG)

The 105 mm Indian and Light Field Guns (IFG/LFG) are high performance guns meeting the conflicting requirements of mountain, plain and desert warfare. The Indian Field Gun is the mainstay of the Field Artillery Branch of the Indian Army covering a maximum range of 17 km. The LFG is a close in weapon, designed to provide the necessary range, mobility and fire power required in the present day battlefield scenario. A unique feature of LFG is its light weight which makes it capaple of being helilifted for quick deployment in mountain terrain. This has been achieved by using high strength alloy steel. The optimised design provides a compact, robust and small profile ideally suited for cross-country mobility.

The Government has recently announced that there would be no further need to import ammunition. This indeed is a great tribute to the constant efforts made by the armament group of laboratories. It is noteworthy that of the total production value from the Indian Ordnance Factories, 70 per cent is based on the design provided by the armament group of laboratories which amounts to more than Rs 5000 crore.

Effective illumination of an area for night operations in the battlefield enhances operational capability of the Army. DRDO has perfected the technology of illuminating ammunition and has developed a veriety of illuminating ammunition for the Indian

Army. These include 51 mm/81 mm/120 mm Mortar launched ammunition and 105 mm Indian Gun launched ammunition. The reliability and performance of indigenously developed illuminating ammunition is superior to the international standard.

PINAKA MULTIBARREL ROCKET LAUNCHER

The indigenously built Pinaka multi-barrel rocket launcher Weapon Area System can fire rockets with a range of 39-40 km, in a salvo of 12 rockets with 1.2 tons of high explosives within 40 seconds.

The complete system comprises a launch vehicle, a loader / replenishment vehicle, and a command post vehicle with a battery of six launchers. Pinaka can neutralise a target area of 350 square kilometres, and is meant as a supplement to the existing artillery system at a range beyond 30 km. It can be fitted with a variety of warheads ranging from blast-cum-pre-fragmented high explosives to anti-tank mines. This indigenously designed MLRS is far cheaper than the international competition, costing just Rs 23 million per system. By comparison the American M270 MLRS costs Rs 195 million, and the 9P140 URAGAN of Russia and the ASTROS-II of Brazil each cost Rs 38 million.

The Pune-based Armament Research and Development Establishment has successfully produced the 'Pinaka' Multi Barrel Rocket Launcher System for the Indian armed forces, to give it concentrated high volume firepower to destroy enemy targets as demanded by the top brass of the Indian army. The Pinaka system was tested at the interim test range (ITR) Chandipur-on-sea, and had undergone several tests since 1995. It has been subjected to user's trials by the Army, which was not entirely satisfied with the system, and additional tests were conducted in response to suggestions to improve its capability further.

In March 1999 the system was tested in the run-up to the country's largest ever air force exercise over the site of India's 1998 underground nuclear blasts, at the eastern Indian missile launch site of Balasore. Pinaka was finally put into field testing for assessing its capability during the Kargil conflict. Pinaka reportedly proved very successful during field testing in the high altitude conflict in

Kargil. In mid-1998 it was reported that production is on at various ordnance factories, and four public sector undertakings would meet the December 1998 delivery deadline.

But in May 1999 the Comptroller and Auditor General criticized the Defence Research and development Organisation (DRDO) for its failure to develop critical components of Pinaka, which led to a six-year delay in the induction of the system.

Far from reaching the production stage, the DRDO has yet to develop various critical components of the system despite an expenditure of Rs 42.45 crore. The Defence Ministry in 1981 had planned to induct "Pinaka" into Indian Army regiments by 1994, and the project was originally given a Rs 26.47 crore budget. The expected date of completion of development is late 2000 at a cost of around Rs 80 crore.

The Armament Research and Development Establishment (ARDE) has also developed a high performance artillery rocket system which can fire within a range between 70 km to 100 km. This is a highly sophisticated "shoot-and-scoot" high mobility system capable of firing a salvo of 12 rockets, each with a payload of 100 kg within a time span of 30 seconds. This new artillery rocket system comprises of an advanced family of warheads including terminally guided submunitions with autonomous target search and engagement capability besides remotely delivered intelligent bomblets and minelets with self-neutralising capability.

Specifications

Range 7 km - 40 km

Rocket Diameter 214 mm

Warheads

- fragmentation high explosive
- incendiary
- anti-tank and anti-personnel minelettes
- anti-tank bomlettes

Rate of Fire

- 40 seconds [typically reported]
- 24-44 seconds [variously reported]

ALL WEATHER AIR DEFENCE GUN SYSTEM

A high performance family of All Weather Towed and Self Propelled Air Defence Gun System is under development to complement the Defence Research and Development Organisation (DRDO) surface-to-air missile systems such as Trishul and Akash.

The new gun will feature twin-gun cyclic rate of fire of 2000 rounds per minute aimed to engage and neutralise high speed aircraft, helicopters, remote-piloted combat air vehicles and stand-off weapons. The integrated gun system is expected to have all weather day-night operations with on-mount passive suiteof electro-optic sensors like laser range finders, forward looking infra-red (FLIR), thermal imaging systems and low-light level TV, for tracking and engaging fast flying targets by means of a high precision computerised digital servo control system.

PAKISTAN – ARMY

Pakistan is a poor country riven with ethnic and religious tensions. Pakistan enjoys close ties with China and shares an antipathy and distrust of India. Half of Pakistan disappeared following its disastrous 1971 war with India.

The Pakistan Army is the largest branch of the Pakistan Armed Forces, and is mainly responsible for protection of the state borders, the security of administered territories and defending the national interests of Pakistan within the framework of its international obligations. The Pakistan Army a total strength of 520,000, about the size of the Army of the United States, with a reserve element of 500,000 who have a reserve obligation up to the age of 45 years. Reserve status lasted for eight years after leaving active service or until age forty-five for enlisted men and age fifty for officers.

The Pakistan Army structure in many ways has a close resemblance to the British Indian Army structure at the end of the nineteenth century. During that period, recruitment into individual, homogeneous regiments depended on class and caste, rather than on territory. Over time, these regiments became sources of immense pride to the men who served in them and to the ethnic group from which they were frequently recruited. Service in a specific regiment passed from father to son; the eventual shift from British to Pakistani rule went with hardly a ripple in the structure except for the change in nationality of the senior officer corps.

The British experimented with various forms of recruitment and of elevation to officer rank. During the period between the two world wars (1919-39), the British trained Indian officers to command at least Indian troops, and training establishments were set up to produce an indigenous officer corps. A small number of officer candidates were sent to Britain to the Royal Military Academy at Sandhurst; after 1932 the majority of candidates were trained at the Indian Military Academy at Dehra Dun.

A rank that predated that of the native officer was the viceroy's commissioned officer—an Indian who had risen from the ranks and performed officer functions (except for commanding officer), especially at the company level. The viceroy's commissioned officer came from the same social background as did the troops in his unit and performed a dual function: for the troops, he was a role model and figure of respect to whom they could turn for advice; he was also an invaluable intermediary between the troops and the British officer who commanded them.

The Pakistani military upon independence immediately became a central part of the national consciousness. Unlike their Indian counterparts, Pakistani soldiers did not bear the stigma of being antinational. The main base of army recruitment, Punjab, was at the heart of Pakistan, and the army was immediately called upon to defend the interests of the nation against a perceived security threat from "Hindu India."

The Pakistani army was fortunate in its political position, but less so in regard to the experience and technical expertise required to field an effective military force. Muslims had been significantly underrepresented in the Indian officer corps, and when partition occurred, there was a severe shortage of personnel. To lead the planned army of 150,000 men, 4,000 officers were needed, but there were only 2,500, and many of those, especially in the technical services, were underqualified. Only one major general, two brigadiers, and six colonels were available, and in the middle officer ranks the situation was equally bad. The first two commanders in chief of the army were British. The first Pakistani commander in chief—General Mohammad Ayub Khan—did not become commander in chief of the army until 1951.

Since the founding of Pakistan, the army has been key in holding the state together, promoting a feeling of nationhood among disparate peoples and providing a bastion of selfless service in the midst of a venal government system. All too frequently, the Pakistan Army has felt the need to take over the government, cleanse it of corruption and try to reform its bureaucracy before returning it to civilian control. Army control of the government has all too often led to a corrupt military regime that eventually collapsed.

The key holder of power in the armed forces and, along with the president and the prime minister, one of the triumvirate that runs the country is the chief of the army staff (COAS) — formerly called the commander in chief. The COAS operates from army headquarters in Rawalpindi, near Islamabad. From this position, Ayub Khan, Zia and Musharef all seized power.

Other senior staff positions, at the lieutenant general level, include a chief of general staff, who supervises army intelligence and operations; the master general of ordnance; the quartermaster general; the adjutant general; the inspector general for evaluation and training; and the military secretary. The headquarters function also includes the chief of the Corps of Engineers, the judge advocate general, and the comptroller of civilian personnel, all of whom report to the vice chief of the army staff.

The 20 Infantry & 2 Armored Divisions are grouped under 9 different Corps headquarters commanded by 3-star Lieutenant Generals. These are:

I Corps (Mangla)

II Corps (Multan)

IV Corps (Lahore)

V Corps (Karachi)

X Corps (Rawalpindi)

XI Corps (Peshawar)

XII Corps (Quetta)

XXX Corps (Gujranwala)

XXXI Corps (Bahawalpur)

There is also the Northern Area Command, headquartered at Gilgit, directly responsible to army general headquarters.

There is an army reserve of 500,000 whose members have a triennial attendance obligation to the age of 45. Refresher training is as adequate as can be expected of a three week period, but reserve service seems popular. Paramilitary organizations, which were mainly of symbolic importance, included the 185,000-member National Guard, comprising the Janbaz Force — locally recruited militia mainly charged with air defense — and two programs similar to the United States Reserve Officers Training Corps, the National Cadet Corps and the Women Guard.

The Women Guard, unlike the National Cadet Corps, included individuals trained in nursing, welfare, and clerical work. There were also some women in the Janbaz Force, and a very small number of women were recruited into the regular service in limited numbers to perform medical and educational work. The 180,000 strong National Guard would be useful in guarding vulnerable points. It consists of the Mujahid Force of 60,000, organized in battalions, some with light air defence capability, the Janbaz Force of 100,000, whose members are intended to serve close to their homes; and the National Cadet Corps in universities and colleges.

Pakistan has been faced with continuing dilemma of providing a credible defense in the face of large standing armed forces of the Indian adversary. Ideally, Pakistan would have a large, well trained and equipped standing army to provide effective deterrence. This Pakistan cannot afford. The only other way to fill the wide gap between the forces required and the force available is to have an effective organization of auxiliary forces which should be capable of supporting and supplementing the efforts of the regular standing army, during peace and war. In Pakistan, the requirement of such forces has been met to some extent by the Civil Armed Forces and the Organization of the National Guards with the passage of an Act of Parliament on 13 August 1973.

Every male citizen of Pakistan who is of such age as may be prescribed, may offer himself for enrolment in the Mujahid Force for service in any unit and any such person, who satisfies the conditions laid down in the Regulations may be enrolled for such period as laid down in the terms of service. Every Person enrolled shall, without unnecessary delay, be appointed in a unit to which he has applied for service. Every person offering himself for enrolment in the force shall be a male citizen of Pakistan between 18 to 30 years of age. Maximum age limit for ex servicemen is relaxable to 45 years. A large number of people of Azad Kashmir are serving in the Mujahid Force. After retirement they are denied the facilities of ex-Servicemen which is not justified.

Paramilitary internal security forces were organized on the provincial level but were subordinate to the Ministry of Interior and were commanded by seconded army generals. These forces were in effect an extension of the army for internal security duties. The Pakistan Rangers, headquartered in Lahore, dealt with unrest in Punjab, while the Mehran Force performed similar functions in Sindh.

In 1994 their strengths were 25,000 and 24,000, respectively, divided into "wings" of approximately 800 men each. The Frontier Corps, with a strength of 65,000, was based in Peshawar and Quetta with responsibility for the North-West Frontier Province and Balochistan. The corps was responsible to both the Ministry of States and Frontier Regions and to army headquarters. The corps was divided into twenty-seven local units—fourteen in the North-West Frontier Province and thirteen in Balochistan—and included the Chitral Scouts, the Khyber Rifles, the Kurram Militia, the Tochi Scouts, the South Waziristan Scouts, the Zhob Militia, and the Gilgit Scouts. There was also a Coast Guard, subordinate to the Ministry of Interior and staffed by army personnel.

In times of natural disaster army engineers, medical and logistics personnel, and the armed forces played a major role in bringing relief and supplies. The army also engaged in extensive economic activities. Most of these enterprises, such as stud and dairy farms, were for the army's own use, but others performed functions beneficial to the local civilian economy. Army factories produced such goods as sugar, fertilizer, and brass castings and sold them to civilian consumers.

The Pakistan military also assists in natural disasters in Pakistan such as the great floods of 1992, the floods in Balochistan in 2008 and the October 2005-devastating Kashmir earthquake; army engineers, medical and logistics personnel, and the armed forces played a major role in bringing relief and supplies.

In natural disasters there was no significant second wave of deaths from injury, cold, food shortages, or disease. And much credit for that probably goes to Pakistan Army.

Perhaps more than anything else, the quake relief effort demonstrated the growing importance of military forces in responding to disasters.

The entire fleet of Army Aviation flew innumerable sorties round the clock to take relief goods to the affected areas and brought back sick and injured back to base hospitals. Where helicopters could not reach, men carried relief goods on their back and reached the needy.

The undertaking of relief operation of this magnitude could only be taken by the men and machines of the Armed Forces of Pakistan. There are reports that the United Nations recommended the Pakistan military form a standby team to respond in disasters. Integrated military-civilian responses are most likely to be successful in natural disasters.

Several army organizations performed functions that were important to the civilian sector across the country. For example, the National Logistics Cell was responsible for trucking food and other goods across the country, the Frontier Works Organization built the Karakoram Highway to China, the Makran Coastal Highway, flood relief operations etcetera and the Special Communication Organization maintained communications networks in remote parts of Pakistan.

Pakistan Army is involved in relief activities not only in Pakistan but also in many other countries of the world, like they went for relief activities after Bangladesh was recently hit by floods. Pak Army also went to Indonesia, Bangladesh and Sri Lanka after they were hit by tsunami. Pakistan army and Navy sent ships and helicopters to the friendly nations for tsunami relief operation.

The army also engaged in extensive economic activities. Most of these enterprises, such as stud and dairy farms, were for the army's own use, but others performed functions beneficial to the local civilian economy. Army factories produced such goods as sugar, fertilizer, and brass castings and sold them to civilian consumers.

The Pakistani Army is a volunteer force and has been involved in many conflicts with India.

Combined with this rich combat experience, the Army is also actively involved in contributing to United Nations peacekeeping efforts. Other foreign deployments have consisted of Pakistani Army personnel as advisers in many African, South Asian and Arab countries.

Since the September 11th terrorist attacks, Pakistani military forces have been extensively engaged in the War on Terrorism against Taliban and Al Qaeda extremists.

Over 90,000 troops along with various paramilitary forces are involved in a protracted fight against extremists in the tribal areas of Pakistan. It is more important than ever for the army to build bridges with civilians, as success in fighting extremism and terrorism is dependent on this.

Army also provides opportunity to women to serve in the Pakistan Army. Currently, there are a sizable number of Women serving in the army.

The army sees itself as a national institution and thus many non-Muslim officers (including Qadiyanis) have achieved high ranks within the army. The army in Pakistan is most organized and powerful institution of a state, like all capitalist states, has the fundamental role of preserving and protecting the assets, social status, privileges and economic exploitation of the local ruling and imperialism.

The role of the military becomes more contentious as the immediate life-saving phase of an aid operation ends and the reconstruction phase takes over. It is therefore important for military actors to not only develop their capacity to respond to disasters, but also to develop their capacity to exit from disaster responses.

PARAMILITARY FORCES OF PAKISTAN

Pakistan's paramilitary forces - in the main subordinate to the Ministry of the Interior in peacetime (but to GHQ in war)- number some 100,000 and free the army and navy from most of the responsibilities of policing borders and economic zones.

Their officers are provided by the regular forces. the army's already severe shortage of junior officers is exacerbated by this requirement and consideration should be given to creating an officer corps solely for paramilitary elements such as the Pakistan Rangers (who police the border with India) and the Frontier Corps (responsible for the western border with Afghanistan and Iran).

In war, some of the higher calibre units would provide reinforcement for the army, as formed body of troops of company or even battalion size.

The Frontier Corps consists of 14 units based in the North West Frontier Province (NWFP) and 13 units based in Baluchistan, with HQ based in Peshawar and Quetta.

The Pakistan Rangers HQ is in Sialkot with subordinate HQ in Sialkot, Bahawalpur and Rahim Yar Khan. The Rangers are responsible for low level border security but can be deployed elsewhere as required by the internal security situation.

Reserves

There is an army reserve of 500,000 whose members have a triennial attendance obligation to the age of 45.

Refresher training is as adequate as can be expected of a three week period, but reserve service seems popular.

The 180,000 strong National Guard would be useful in guarding vulnerable points.

It consists of the Mujahid Force of 60,000, organized in battalions, some with light air defence capability.

The Janbaz Force of 100,000, whose members are intended to serve close to their homes; and the National Cadet Corps in universities and colleges. these elements have some value in providing poorly trained but enthusiastic reinforcements for rear area units.

Operational Art and Tactical Doctrine

From the time of the 65 war, through that of 71 and until the Indian Army excercise Brass Tacks in 1987, emphasis was on static defence of the LOC and the border. Penetration of Indian territory would be undertaken only on an opportunity basis. the doctrine was flawed, mainly because of lack of strategic depth in Pakistan, but no alternative was given serious consideration until it was realised that a "stand and fight" doctrine would probably result in deep penetration by Indian forces without Pakistani forces being able to manoeuver effectively. the Indian army would have gained and retained the initiative, enabling it to destroy Pakistani formations piecemeal as they reacted to Indian thrusts.

The "Riposte" is simple in concept: it is intended that the two strike corps conduct a limited advance along narrow fronts with the objective of occupying indian territory near the border, probably to a depth of 40 to 50 km. Pakistan considers that international pressure would result in a ceasefire after a maximum of three weeks of conflict, enough time to gain some territory to be used in subsequent bargaining. there would be acceptance of Indian penetration, which would be inevitable given the comparitive lack of mobility within the Infantry heavy divisions. Independent Armoured and Mechanized Brigades are intended for quick counter attack and exploitation and would add considerable weight to advances by the strike corps.

The "Riposte" is practiced at all levels. Major excercises involve the crossing of water obstacles and minefields at night with emphasis on subsequent break-out and rapid advance. So far as has been seen, the concept has been adequately translated into workable plans which are continuously being refined. However, complete mechanization of the strike corps and other formations was slowed by the effects of US sanctions and it will take some time for them to achieve desired mobility, although US army surplus equipment is now being rapidly delivered, and local manufacture and rebuilding of US supplied AFV/APC has received considerable impetus, thus improving the mechanization process.

The army took great interest in the Indian army/airforce excercise Vajra Shakti (Thunder Power, conducted in Punjab from

1-10 May 2005). in view of its emphasis on maintaining mobility while operating closed down against nuclear attack. Pakistan's own counter - nuclear preparedness is patchy, and it is doubtful that even the strike corps could fight through a nuclear battlefield.

India's doctrine of "Cold Start" involving swift penetration of Pakistan with the aim of isolating, destroying or capturing vital points (such as nuclear stores and other installations has resulted in some modification to the Riposte, in that acceptability of penetration could be fatal to counter-penetration plans. in the event of an indian advance reaching or crossing the line of the main Lahore-Karachi highway, it is likely there would be consideration of employment of tactical nuclear missiles.

6

Military Modernization in Strategic Asia

INTRODUCTION

On September 29, 2005, the Asia Program joined with the Seattle-based National Bureau of Asian Research (NBR) to host a conference exploring the ramifications of military modernization in Asia and the implications of defense transformation for the grand strategies of the region's principal powers, including the United States. Conference attendees sought to examine the drivers and gauge the progress of military modernization in Asia, and to assess the influence of these developments on the regional balance of power. This event was timed to mark the publication of the NBR report Strategic Asia 2005-06: Military Modernization in an Era of Uncertainty, edited by Ashley J. Tellis and Michael Wills.

China's rapid military modernization – in the context of a rising China more broadly – dominates the strategic thinking of the United States and the other major powers in Asia. George Washington University's **David Shambaugh** predicted that China's military power and regional reach will steadily increase in the years ahead, and will alter the balance of power in Asia. Nonetheless, Shambaugh cautioned against overestimating Chinese capabilities, or concluding that double-digit increases in China's military spending in each of the past 15 years mean that the Chinese military will be able to transform itself into a first-class fighting force with global reach in the near term. China's military possesses numerous deficiencies in both quantitative and qualitative terms, especially when compared to American capabilities. But when viewed in the context of a Taiwan Strait conflict, Shambaugh added, China has made steady and even surprising progress in increasing its strength. China's aspiration and plans regarding defense modernization, he judged, are much what one would expect for a nation of China's size, wealth, location, national interests, and global role.

The remainder of the first panel focused on the military modernization programs of Asia's other major powers, Japan, Russia, and India. **Christopher Hughes** argued that Japan is gradually forsaking its post-1945 pacifist tradition, and moving along a long-term trajectory toward assuming the military capabilities and security roles customarily expected of nations of Japan's size and wealth. Japan is acquiring enhanced power projection capabilities and will inevitably play a more active role in both regional and global security. While Japan has no realistic option other than to maintain its close security links with the United States, Washington can expect Tokyo to become a more assertive ally, one that demands greater reciprocity and more equal treatment from the United States.

Stephen Blank contended that despite rising defense outlays, the Russian military remains an archaic, dysfunctional, and inefficient force, and is unlikely to carry out a program of modernization that is capable of fulfilling Moscow's ambitious aims. Absent major systemic reforms reaching far beyond the defense sector, Blank asserted, Russian influence in Eurasia will continue to wane, to be replaced by a more visible Chinese presence in areas traditionally subject to Russian influence.

Volume co-editor **Ashley Tellis** characterized India's "very large and extremely proficient" military as capable of defending Indian territory and interests in a war with China, though not quite able to defeat Pakistan in a brief conventional war. The dramatic increases in India's defense spending over the past half dozen years, he explained, must be seen in the context of a decade of lean years for the Indian military in the 1990s. Tellis highlighted three facets of India's current modernization: 1) technological modernization, especially in air and sea power; 2) doctrinal innovation designed to enable India to field a sizable combat force 48 hours after mobilization; and 3) organizational innovations, such as an emphasis on smaller military units, that will facilitate the new emphasis on rapid response. India, Tellis added, has departed from its traditional posture of non-alignment and now has a new interest in coalition warfare, with the United States being a plausible coalition partner.

The morning's second panel explored how other Asian nations have responded to these developments in the major Asian powers. Looking at the Korean peninsula, **Jonathan Pollack** suggested that the ground force standoff that has long dominated peninsular security planning will decline in relevance in the years ahead. Pyongyang will increasingly focus on deterrence and longer-range strike capabilities, while Seoul will pursue deterrence without automatically assuming adversarial relations with the North. South Korea, Pollack added, will be increasingly unwilling to undertake major long-term defense investments based on a predominantly threat-based military strategy, a stance that may pose acute risks to the South Korean – U.S. alliance. In the discussion following this analysis, one participant noted that Seoul acts as if it believes that the United States needs South Korea more than Seoul needs Washington – which, if true, would mark a significant change in strategic thinking in South Korea.

Michael Swaine contended that modernization in Taiwan has been marked by inadequate funding, an absence of strategic clarity, misplaced priorities, and unaddressed vulnerabilities. Taiwan needs to be far more serious about its defense environment than it has been recently, Swaine asserted. Glaring shortcomings in Taiwan's military modernization efforts could lead to miscalculations in both China and on Taiwan, resulting in one side or the other undertaking dangerous or destabilizing actions. Nonetheless, both Taipei and Washington must continue to balance efforts to rectify Taiwan's defense deficiencies with the need to avoid an escalation of tensions with Beijing.

Turning toward the nations of Southeast Asia, **Sheldon Simon** of Arizona State University asserted that the region's security concerns are primarily internal, including separatism and ethnic and religious violence. Transnational threats such as piracy, terrorism, and the trafficking of contraband, people, and arms constitute the next tier of security threats in the region, while external threats from other nations are the least pressing of the security challenges Southeast Asia confronts. Simon reported that notable breakthroughs in multilateral security cooperation have taken place over the past several years, including coordinated naval patrols by Malaysia, Singapore, and Indonesia, and cooperation with the United States by several of the littoral states in anti-piracy patrols. Rising insurance rates for ocean-going commerce transiting Southeast Asian waters, Simon observed, have been an important factor pushing the region toward greater multilateral cooperation.

Kimberly Marten observed that military modernization in the five Central Asian republics has focused more on officer corps retraining and professionalization than on hardware acquisition. Regional leaders, she warned, often exaggerate the Islamist threat as a ploy to gain external support, including from the United States. Foreign defense assistance acquired in this fashion is then often used to suppress populist opposition movements and, as a consequence, to bolster authoritarian regimes while undercutting the human rights concerns of the donor nations. The opium trade originating in Afghanistan does constitute a major security concern for the region, but this threat cannot be successfully addressed by military modernization alone.

The day's final panel focused more directly on the implications for U.S. national security of these developments in the modernization of Asia's militaries. **Aaron Friedberg**, who spent the past two years as a senior advisor to Vice President Cheney, applauded Japan's retreat from its pacifist tradition of the past 60 years, as well as the improved tone in U.S. – India relations and India's greater ability to contribute to the maintenance of a regional balance of power. Among the troubling trends he highlighted were Russian sales of advanced weaponry to China, a problematic U.S. – Russia relationship, a growing divergence in strategic perceptions between the United States and South Korea, Taiwan's failure to spend "adequately" on its own self-defense, and skillful

Chinese diplomacy that is reaching out to traditional U.S. friends such as Australia, South Korea, and the Philippines.

The Brookings Institution's **Michael O'Hanlon** observed that for all the talk in the Pentagon of a "revolution" in thinking about American security needs, very little has actually been accomplished in this area. As one example of the continuity between the Bush administration and its predecessors, he noted that the Defense Department has still had no serious discussions with Tokyo about the U.S. Marine presence in Okinawa, notwithstanding the serious difficulties the Marine bases create for the Japanese government and for sustaining popular support for the U.S. alliance.

Robert M. Hathaway emphasized the need for American leaders tasked with managing the U.S. - China relationship to make choices among competing priorities, to realize that "we can't have it all." Even a step that is as widely supported among U.S. decision makers as Japan's movement in the direction of becoming a "normal" state is not cost-free – that is, such a Japan is going to become a less pliant partner for the United States, and could alarm not only China, but other Asian powers.

In the day's final presentation, **Ashley Tellis** offered three tests for American policy makers wondering if they ought to be concerned by Asia's military modernization: 1) what are the political aims of the country in question, and what is the character of the governing regime?; 2) is the modernization oriented toward denying U.S. capabilities (as much of China's is, Tellis added)?; and 3) how has the modernization impacted not only the technological base of the country's military, but its operational effectiveness?

Underlying the discussion throughout the day lay two fundamental questions: 1) do American interests in Asia require U.S. hegemony in the region?; and 2) is any enhancement of China's military capabilities, no matter how incremental, detrimental to the United States? The answers to these two queries supplied by American leaders in the years to come will go far in determining whether China's rise to power is accomplished without a repetition of the violence that accompanied the rise of Germany and Japan in the previous century.

INDIA'S MODERNISATION OF MILITARY POWER

China has taken serious note of India's growing military power over the last decade. India, which has traditionally talked of the power of argument began to talk of the argument of power. In fact, the 1998 nuclear tests themselves were indicative of the fact that India had begun to realize the role of hard power in securing its national interests and also in making her voice heard in international politics. India's growing military profile is especially evident in the maritime domain. The Indian navy has emerged as the net security provider in the Indian Ocean over the last decade. In 2004, it unveiled its first-ever naval doctrine that defined India's legitimate areas of interest stretching from the Persian Gulf to the Malacca Straits. It released its updated version in 2009, incorporating the rapid changes in the geo-strategic environment involving India. India's defense ties with the US have developed at a frenetic pace, which has played the central role in India's military modernization. For example, recent defense contracts signed with the US include US$ 1.1 billion for C-130J Super Hercules transport planes and US$2.4 billion for 10 Globemasters airlifters. In January 2009, the Indian Navy signed an agreement with the U. S. to buy eight P-8I planes worth nearly US$2.1 billion, so as to replace the aging long range aerial reconnaissance fleet of eight Russian-made Tu-142s and five IL-38 planes.

The tests of its China-centric Agni series missile systems and the development of a Ballistic Missile Defense system. India's future military plans are even more ambitious, which further complicates China's strategic calculations. For example, the Indian Ministry of Defense in late 2011 announced its biggest expansion package to date, a US$13 billion military modernization plan. Under this plan within next five years, the Indian army is set to deploy 90,000 more soldiers and raise four new divisions along India's border with China, the largest such mobilization since the Sino-Indian border clashes of 1962.

MODERNISATION PLANS OF THE INDIAN ARMY

Despite the army leadership's best efforts, the ongoing Revolution in Military Affairs (RMA) had, till recently, almost completely bypassed the Indian Army. For well over a decade the army's efforts to modernise had been thwarted due to political neglect and lack of adequate budgetary support. The funds made available for modernisation are extremely limited and a large portion of these funds is surrendered year after year. For Financial Year 2006-07, a sum of Rs 3,000 crore was surrendered as unspent. The fact that 155 mm ammunition for the Bofors howitzer had to be imported from South Africa during the Kargil conflict in 1999 tells its own tale of persistent shortages. Had the conflict not been confined to the 150 km frontage of the Kargil sector, T-72 and 130 mm medium gun ammunition too would have run short and it would have been politically embarrassing for the government as well as the army. In the plains the army would have had to fight with obsolete Vijayant tanks and several other vintage equipment that were unsuitable for combat. However, sustained efforts by Army HQ have now borne fruit and the army's modernisation drive is once again well underway.

In the prevailing era of strategic uncertainty, while terrorism has become the primary threat, the external and internal threats and challenges faced by India are such that a large army is still required to be maintained. Also, a high degree of preparation and operational readiness is still necessary as conventional war, though improbable, cannot be categorically ruled out. At the same time, heavy capital investments in modern defence equipment are undoubtedly a drain on a developing economy that is ill-equipped to handle the burgeoning defence expenditure. Several eminent analysts have recommended that qualitative upgradation should be accompanied by quantitative downsizing of personnel strength of the army. However, given its responsibilities for border management and the manpower-intensive low intensity conflict that the army is involved in, this is easier said than done.

Future conventional conflict on the Indian sub-continent will in all probability result from the ongoing low-intensity limited war on the Line of Control (LoC) with Pakistan or the unresolved territorial and boundary dispute with China and will be predominantly a land conflict. The Indian Army seriously lacks a potent firepower punch, especially in the mountain sector. Precision-guided munitions (PGMs) have still to enter service in numbers large enough to make a real difference. The reconnaissance, surveillance and target acquisition (RSTA) assets necessary for the optimum exploitation of even the existing firepower assets are grossly inadequate. Automated command and control and decision support systems have been on the drawing boards for several decades but are yet to mature.

In a future conventional war that will be fought under the nuclear shadow, manoeuvre will be extremely limited. This restriction will lead to much greater emphasis being placed on firepower to achieve the laid down military aim. Hence, it is imperative that artillery modernisation is undertaken with alacrity so as to generate firepower asymmetries on the future battlefield. After a long spell of keeping the powder dry, action on modernisation of the Indian artillery is livening up once again. Since January 2008, the Ministry of Defence (MoD) has issued three global tenders for 155mm guns and howitzers for the mountains, the plains and self-propelled guns for the deserts. Summer and winter trials are expected to be held over the next one year and, red tape permitting, contracts may be awarded as early as in the first half of 2010.

Artillery firepower had paved the way for victory during the Kargil conflict. Despite the lessons learnt in Kargil, modernisation of the artillery had continued to lag behind. The last major acquisition of towed gun-howitzers was that of about 400 pieces of 39-calibre 155mm FH-77B howitzers form Bofors of Sweden in the mid-1980s. This gun had proved its mettle in the Kargil conflict. Just when a contract for 120 tracked and 180 wheeled self-propelled (SP) 155mm guns was about to be concluded after years of protracted trials, South African arms manufacturer Denel, a leading contender for the contract, was alleged to have been involved in a corruption scam in an earlier deal for anti-material rifles (AMRs). The other two howitzers in contention, from Soltam of Israel and BAE (Bofors) of Sweden did not meet the laid down criteria according to the COAS and Army HQ recommended fresh trials, setting the programme back at least three to four years. Another key issue was that the howitzers that had been offered were technology demonstration models and not guns that were in actual service with the home country armies.

The probability of the next conventional war breaking out in the mountains is far higher than that of a war in the plains. With this in view, the artillery recently conceptualised a requirement for a light-weight towed howitzer of 155mm calibre for employment in the mountains. Neither the present Bofors howitzer nor its replacement will be capable of operations in the mountains. A light-weight 45-calibre 155mm howitzer weighing less than 5,000 kg, with a light but adequately powered prime mover, is ideal for the mountains. The gun-train should be capable of negotiating sharp road bends without the need to unhook the gun from the prime mover. The two British 45-calibre 155mm howitzers that competed for the US contract for a similar howitzer some years ago – the UFH (Ultra-lightweight Field Howitzer) and the LTH (Light-weight Towed Howitzer) – could be considered for licensed production with transfer of technology.

In January 2008, the MoD floated a Request for Proposal (RfP) for 140 pieces of ultra-light 39 calibre 155mm towed howitzers for use by the Indian Army's mountain formations and, presumably, by its rapid reaction divisions – as and when these are raised as it will be easy to transport by air. 140 howitzers will be adequate to equip seven medium artillery regiments and will cost approximately Rs 3,000 crore. The RfP has been reportedly issued to UK's BAE Systems (which now owns Bofors), for the M777 howitzer claimed to be the lightest in the world at under 4,220 kg, and to Singapore Technologies for the Pegasus SLWH.

India has floated a global tender for the purchase of 400 155mm towed artillery guns for the Army, to be followed by indigenous manufacture of another 1,100 howitzers, in a project worth a whopping Rs 8,000 crore. The RFP was issued to eight prospective bidders including BAE, General Dynamics, Nexter (France), Rhinemetall (Germany) and Samsung (South Korea). An RfP has also been issued for 180 wheeled self-propelled guns for around Rs 4,700 crore for employment by mechanised forces in the plains and semi-desert sectors.

Since the Bofors 155mm Howitzer was introduced into service, the indigenously designed and manufactured 105 mm Indian Field Gun (IFG) and its (not so) light version, the Light Field Gun (LFG), have joined the 75/24 Indian Mountain Gun, the 100mm Russian field gun and the 122mm Russian howitzer on the obsolescence list. Approximately 180 pieces of 130mm M46 Russian medium guns have been successfully "up-gunned" to 155mm calibre with ordnance supplied by Soltam of Israel. The new barrel length of 45 calibres has enhanced the range of the gun to about 40 km with extended range ammunition.

A contract for the acquisition of two regiments of the 12-tube, 300mm Smerch multi-barrel rocket launcher (MBRL) system with 90 km range was reported to have been signed with Russia's Rosoboronexport in early-2006. This will be a major boost for the long-range firepower capabilities of the army. If this weapon system had been available during the Kargil conflict, Pakistan's brigade HQ and forward airfield at Skardu and other targets deep inside POK could have been hit with impunity. Extended range (ER) rockets are being introduced for the 122 mm Grad MBRL that has been in service for over three decades. The ER rockets will enhance the weapon system's range from 22 to about 40 km. A Rs 5,000 crore contract has also been signed for the serial production of the Pinaka MBRL weapon system, another DRDO project plagued by time delays and completed with help from Larsen and Toubro and the Tatas.

The modernisation plan of tube artillery alone is likely to cost Rs 13,000 crore. The major acquisitions will be of initial lots of 400 towed howitzers of 155mm calibre, with a barrel length of 52 calibres, costing about Rs 4,000 crore, 140 ultra-light weight 155mm towed howitzers, with a barrel length of 45 calibres, costing Rs 3,000 crore and 180 SP 155mm howitzers costing Rs 5,000 crore. The "Shakti" project for a command and control systems for the artillery, called Artillery Combat Command and Control System (ACCCS), has reached the stage of maturity and is now being fielded up to the regimental level.

The BrahMos supersonic cruise missile (Mach 2.8 to 3.0), with a precision strike capability, very high kill energy and range of 290 km, was inducted into the army in July 2007. It is a versatile missile that can be launched from TATRA mobile launchers and silos on land, aircraft and ships and, perhaps in future, also from submarines. Fifty BrahMos missiles are expected to be produced every year. Efforts are underway to further increase its strike range. BrahMos Aerospace has orders worth Rs 3,500 crore from the army and the navy, which has opted for the anti-ship as well as the land attack cruise missile (LACM) versions. These terrain hugging missiles are virtually immune to counter measures due to their high speed and very low radar cross section and are far superior to sub-sonic cruise missiles like Pakistan's Babur. Chile, Kuwait, Malaysia and South Africa have shown interest in acquiring this missile.

The Indian army is extensively engaged in ongoing internal security (IS) and counter-insurgency operations (CI) and simultaneously needs to prepare itself for a future border conflict that may spill over to a larger conventional war in the plains. In keeping with these twin requirements, Army HQ have apparently decided to upgrade the IS and CI capabilities of infantry battalions as well as enhance their Infantry firepower-mobility-EW (electronic warfare) punch for a possible war in the plains against Pakistan or in the mountains against China. The Army Chief's modernisation vision is to "adapt to high-end technology, improve night-fighting capability... (and) information technology, information warfare and network centric warfare."

Despite its large-scale employment on border management and extensive commitments in Internal Security and Counter Insurgency operations, infantry modernisation had been languishing for several decades when the Ministry of Defence (MoD) finally cleared a visionary plan to modernise the army's infantry battalions by according "in principle" approval in the form of Modification 4B to the war establishment (WE) of a standard infantry battalion in 1998. However, no funds were specially sanctioned for this purpose till the BJP-led NDA government approved the expenditure of Rs 3,500 crore in September 2003. Thereafter, approval had to be sought on file for each new weapon system or piece of equipment on a "case-by-case" basis as has become the norm. It is by now well-known how each such case chronicles the saga of an uphill struggle to get approval first from the MoD, then MoD (Finance) and, finally, the Ministry of Finance (MoF). All this is only possible after the DRDO has first certified that the weapon system or equipment in question cannot be developed and manufactured indigenously and such a certificate is hard to come by.

While 250 Kornet-E anti-tank guided missiles (ATGMs) with thermal imaging sights have substantially increased the anti-tank capability of infantry battalions, most efforts to modernise the equipment held by infantry and Rashtriya Rifles (RR) units are aimed at enhancing their capability for surveillance and target acquisition at night and boosting their firepower for precise retaliation against infiltrating columns and terrorists holed up in built-up areas. About 200 hand-held BFSRs with practical ranges up to seven to eight km where clear line of sight is available, 2,000 hand-held thermal imaging devices (HHTIs) with ranges up to 2,000 metres for observation at night and stand-alone infra-red, seismic and acoustic sensors with varying capabilities have enabled infantrymen to dominate the Line of Control so completely that infiltration has come down to almost a trickle.

The newly acquired weapons, which complement these surveillance and observation devices, include: 1,500x84 mm rocket launchers, including some disposable ones; 1,000 AMRs (anti-material rifles); 8,000 UBGLs (under-barrel grenade launchers); 4,000 new generation carbines; 300 bullet proof vehicles; and, several hundred accurate sniper rifles. However, the numbers acquired and the ammunition stocks are still inadequate and need to be made up more rapidly. While the INSAS 5.56 mm assault rifles have now been in service for almost 10 years and proved to be effective, the light machine gun (LNG) version is still facing teething problems and the carbine version for close quarter battle has not found favour with the army. New 5.56 mm assault rifles of bull-pup design with an integrated laser range finder and grenade launcher are under development. Efforts are also being made to provide infantry platoons and sections with integrated GPS-based navigation system, secure light-weight walkie-talkie radio sets and better protective gear with a helmet that incorporates a built-in head-up display.

The mechanised infantry is now equipped with the BMP-2 ICV Sarath of which over 1,000 have been built since 1987. A new variant is the 81 mm Carrier Mortar Tracked Vehicle (CMTV) that is based on the chassis of the Sarath ICV and has been indigenously developed to enhance the integral firepower available to mechanised infantry battalions. Other variants include a command post, an ambulance, armoured dozer and engineer and reconnaissance vehicles. Mechanised reconnaissance and support battalions need better surveillance radars, fire-and-forget ATGMs and effective night fighting capability. However, their capabilities can be upgraded on a lower priority compared with infantry battalions that are engaged in border management and IS/CI operations.

The army's infantry battalions also need their own mini or micro UAVs like Elbit's Skylark or Rafael's Skylite, among others, to partly reduce the extent of patrolling necessary in internal security environment and to improve their surveillance capability in conventional conflict. These UAVs should have a range of about 10 to 15 km, should be light-weight (less than 10 kg), hand-launched, carry a single payload, e.g. a daylight video camera or infra-red camera for night operations, and should be inexpensive enough to be dispensable. A mini ground control station should be authorized at battalion HQ for planning and control. Ideally, these should be indigenously designed and developed and locally manufactured.

A new DRDO project, that is reported to be ongoing, aims to equip future soldiers with lightweight force multipliers. Soldiers of the future will have miniaturised communication and GPS systems, small power packs, weapon platforms and smart vests with fibre-optic sensors. The soldiers will also have better and lighter combat fatigues, boots, belts, ammunition pouches, rucksacks and rations in the form of meals-ready-to-eat. Though somewhat akin to the US Army's Land Warrior programme, the Indian Army programme for modernisation of infantry battalions will result in only incremental changes. However, these would be significant enough to make a difference on the battlefields of the Indian sub-continent. The infantryman's average combat load is approximately 27 kg, including the 3.06 kg 5.56 mm INSAS assault rifle and its "on weapon" ammunition. If this can be reduced by even a few kg, it will enable the soldier to improve his agility in battle and counter-insurgency operations. Ultimately an infantryman has to be prepared to engage in hand-to-hand combat and agility can make a difference between life and death.

For over 350 infantry battalions, plus about 150 Rashtriya Rifles, Assam Rifles and Territorial Army battalions, these major changes will be extremely costly to implement and will spill over at least 10 to 12 years – that is, if the funds can be found. What is certain is that there is no alternative to making the financial commitment that is necessary to enhance the operational capabilities of the army's infantry battalions. Without modernising this cutting edge of its sword, the army will soon begin to resemble the armies of India's lesser neighbours.

The indigenously designed Arjun main battle tank (MBT) has been in the pipeline for over two decades. Though the tank has many good features, it has consistently failed to meet the army's GSQR for an MBT and orders have been placed for only 124 tanks to be manufactured. The lack of progress on the Arjun MBT had slowed down the pace of armour modernisation. India then signed a deal with Russia to acquire 310 T-90S tanks in the year 2000. Subsequently, India began to assemble these tanks at Avadi. It has recently been reported that in addition to these, India has decided to acquire another 347 T-90S tanks and assemble them within the country.

The first Indian assembled T-90S (Bhishma) rolled off the production line on January 8, 2004. While T-90S Russian tanks have provided new teeth to India's strike formations in the plains and corrected the imbalance that had resulted from Pakistan's acquisition of T-80 UD from Ukraine and the Al Khalid tanks jointly designed with China, a large number of T-72 (Ajeya) tanks are still awaiting modernisation. The lack of a suitable fire control system and night fighting capability are major handicaps. As soon as the obsolescent Vijayanta tanks are phased out of service, it will be time to also discard the old T-55s as well as they can no longer be either upgraded or modernised. Armour modernisation is now proceeding apace and can be classified as a success story.

The air defence (AD) of mechanised forces is another area that is crying for attention. The Kvadrat missile system that has been the backbone of AD for strike formations since the early 1970s are now ageing and need urgent replacement. With the DRDO's indigenous Akash medium-range and Trishul short-range missile projects not making major headway, it is time to start looking at import substitutes. In fact, the assets of Army Air Defence corps of the army are grossly inadequate to provide effective protection against enemy aircraft during war. This young corps requires substantial capital infusion to really come into its own.

Another DRDO project that is way behind schedule is the Nag anti-tank missile system. The antiquated Jonga-mounted SS-11 B1 anti-tank guided missile (ATGM) system has been replaced in missile battalions by MILAN shoulder-fired ATGMs. However, a vehicle-mounted missile system like the Nag is definitely necessary for reconnaissance and attrition tasks. The experimental Plan AREN tactical communications system for strike formations needs early replacement. The ability to carry broadband data needs to be enhanced in particular. Even the more recent static communications network called ASCON lacks ISDN capability for the real-time transmission of maps and streaming video.

While some Stentor long-range BFSRs have been in service for over a decade, medium-range radars are still to be acquired. At least about 30 to 40 weapon locating radars (WLRs) are required for effective counter-bombardment, especially in the plains, and only a few have been procured so far. Israeli Searcher-I unmanned aerial vehicles (UAVs) have been introduced into service but these are few in number and it will be a long time before these will really make a difference by providing a real-time surveillance capability so that ground forces can initiate action even as a fresh input is received. Only a small number of Searcher – II UAVs, with an upper ceiling that makes them suitable for the mountains, have been acquired.

An automated command and control and decision support system for use by the General Staff is still a far cry and so are supporting systems like the battlefield surveillance system and air space management system. The urgent requirement of real-time satellite reconnaissance systems has still not been accepted despite the nuclear overhang under which the armed forces now operate.

Even though the cameras on India's remote sensing and cartographic satellites now have sharply enhanced resolutions, less than one metre, military-grade photographs of still better resolution are needed to be purchased from the open market. These sources may dry up quickly during war.

A "system of systems" approach must be followed so that scarce RSTA and communications resources can be synergistically configured and optimally exploited. The war in Iraq fought in March-April 2003 was based on the concept of "network-centric warfare" in which surveillance sensors, targeting systems and "shooters" are fused together in a seamless "system of systems" that reduced response time between the acquisition of a target and its destruction to 15 to 20 minutes. While such a system may take over a decade to establish, a beginning must be made right away.

PGMs are increasingly gaining currency as weapons of choice in conflict on land, both to accurately destroy critical hard targets quickly as well as to avoid or at least minimise collateral damage. During the Gulf War I in 1991, despite all the CNN-generated hype of smart bombs flying unerringly through ventilators, PGMs formed less than 10 percent of the total high explosive dropped over Iraq and were rather inaccurate. The "collateral" destruction of an air raid shelter harbouring women and children has been too well documented to bear recounting. The coalition forces did not destroy a single Iraqi Scud missile launcher. In Kosovo, PGMs accounted for about 30 per cent of the ordnance dropped and accuracies had improved considerably by 1999. In the post-September 11, 2001 retribution inflicted on the Taliban militia and its al Qaeda supporters in Afghanistan, the share of PGMs had risen to nearly 60 percent. In Gulf War II in Iraq, the ratio of PGMs went up to nearly 70 per cent. The Indian artillery does not have any PGMs worth the name. Only limited quantities of the Russian Krasnopol PGM have been imported for the Bofors 155 mm howitzer. Among others, the Bofors Bonus PGM is a suitable candidate, subject to successful trials in the deserts and the mountains.

Finally, the approach to army modernisation must be more focused; the priorities must be clearly established and then adhered to. The government must give a firm commitment in terms of funds and the Ministry of Defence must streamline its procedures and processes for speedy procurement of high priority weapons and equipment. It is time to institute a rolling, non-lapsable defence modernisation fund of Rs. 25,000 crores as a viable method of ensuring that defence procurement is not subjected to the vagaries of annual budgets. The present situation is disturbing and, if allowed to go on indefinitely, will seriously compromise the army's preparedness to fight the next border war that inimical neighbours like Pakistan can be expected to thrust on India.

MODERNISING THE INDIAN INFANTRY

Why has it taken the Army so long to conceive an upgrade package for the oldest, most potent and intensely employed fighting arm, the Infantry, even after the so-called revolution in military affairs? The foot soldier, the original and most versatile weapon system that is always taken for granted, has emerged from the dubious shock and awe strategy of recent campaigns as its ultimate arbiter. India has paid dearly for the neglect of its infantry in terms of cost, casualties and over-stretch of battle. But the Infantry has never let us down. Kargil was its finest hour. Gen VP Malik, the Army Chief of the time, wryly noted: "We will fight with what we have."

So when for the first time an international conference of Army and defence industry was launched last week to put the forgotten soldier centre-stage, some misgivings were natural. While Army Chief Gen JJ Singh outlined his vision for the soldier system of the future, the conspicuous and total absence of Government - MoD - robbed the conference of any sanctity. In sharp contrast, for a MoD-sponsored defence finance seminar earlier in the month, Government officials and ministers were stepping over each other at Vigyan Bhavan.

Free India's Army came into being in 1947 and within weeks, the Infantry soldiers landed in Srinagar to save J&K from being gobbled up by Pakistani tribal raiders. Since then, the Infantry has not ceased fighting proxy wars there and later, elsewhere too. A former Army Chief, Gen SR Choudhury, who was not from the Infantry, described the Infantry as the Army and vice versa. Field

Marshal Montgomery said: An army is considered only as good as its Infantry.

The experience of four wars, several border skirmishes, two out-of-area missions, the ceaseless campaign to counter cross-border terrorism in Kashmir, numerous other insurgencies in the North-East, internal stability operations elsewhere in the country and UN peace keeping operations make the Indian Infantry the most battle-hardened and combat rich force in the world. The simple and uncomplaining infantryman has given so much to so many for so little. The modernisation of the infantry was first attempted - halfheartedly - in the mid-1980s by the Perspective Planning branch of the Army Headquarters. The bias for mechanised warfare, zealously pursued by Gen Sundarji, was so pronounced that the Infantry modernisation plan was skipped altogether. Guns, tanks, APCs were the weapons in demand. The Infantry was ignored. Had a modest upgrade package been undertaken at that time, infantry would have been more combat contemporary and effective.

Instead, till recently, some soldiers were still using World War II equipment and clothing. Shameful as it was, soldiers had to buy rucksacks and other accoutrements from the market. DRDO is still to come out with a light bulletproof vest. The Army failed to accurately visualize the nature of combat it would fight in the future. Pakistan-sponsored insurgency in Punjab did not alert the nation and the Army to the proxy war brewing in J&K. We defaulted on both counts - anticipating low intensity conflict and cross border terrorism and preparing the Infantry for it.

Despite the sustained counter-insurgency and counter-terrorism campaign in J&K and the North-East since the 1990s, the Army was sluggish in investing in the infantry. The first Gulf War reintroduced the fiction that wars could be won from the air. The air campaigns in Bosnia and Kosovo temporarily turned fiction into reality. But 9/11 broke the myth of supremacy of air power. Operation Enduring Freedom in Afghanistan lasted 76 days; 65 of these were air operations.

The 11-day land offensive secured a temporary and incomplete victory against the Taliban. Operation Iraqi Freedom on the other hand, fought for 20 days was bereft of any preparatory air campaign though a secret air war preceded it. Unhappily for the US/NATO-led coalition forces, despite their pyrrhic military victories, low intensity wars in Afghanistan and Iraq are continuing in full blaze.

The recent 34-day war in Lebanon and the ongoing campaign in Gaza demonstrate the limits of Israel's military power. Used to decisive victories in less than 10 days, Israeli Defence Forces (IDF) were badgered by Hassan Nasrallah's jihadi militia. Reliance on air power, tanks and guns in Lebanon as substitute for ground troops - infantry - was motivated by casualty aversion. We too have to be sensitive to casualties.

The wars in Lebanon, Iraq and Afghanistan spurred by the growing cult of Osama bin Laden and Hassan Nasrallah require a redefinition of the concept of power and military success. Success would necessarily be an inclusive military victory encompassing post-conflict stability and reconstruction. For this we need Infantry.

The Indian Army should not get overly seduced by high-sounding warfare like 'netcentric' that the West is being diverted into. This is not to suggest we ignore the strides in high-tech warfare. But as a former US NATO Commander noted recently: "This netcentric stuff is great but our men in Baghdad are being blown up with their Humvees by IEDs." He suggested that we address the battle we are fighting before switching to the one we will fight in the future.

India's supreme operational challenge is and will be the maintenance of internal security. Just last month, Prime Minister Manmohan Singh stated this ground reality. The Infantry is at the heart of counterinsurgency and counter-terrorism operations and may well get sucked into anti-Naxal operations as well. Keeping the Army operationally ready for both conventional and unconventional missions is imperative but the emphasis has to be on the business of the day: CI and CT.

The Indian Infantry is belatedly embarking on a modernisation programme to enhance its combat skills through increased lethality, communications, surveillance, mobility and suvivability. These force multipliers will enable the soldier to fight all-weather, 24x7 and on any terrain in the right battle-configuration albeit with the accent on LIC. The GSQR for the Future-Infantry-Soldier-As a System (F-INSAS) must empower not encumber the soldier. DRDO must compete with domestic and international industry. DRDO has one more chance to make amends for its omissions and commissions. F-INSAS must strike the right balance between the surge of technology and sensibility of the soldier keeping the battle of the future in mind. Defence Minister AK Antony should accord F-INSAS the highest strategic priority.

ROLE OF FOREIGN MILITARY TECHNOLOGY

Following the withdrawal of Soviet aid and advisers in 1960, which crippled the defense industry and weapons production for several years, China stressed self-reliance in developing its own weaponry. The acquisition of foreign military technology became a contentious issue at times, particularly in the 1970s, when Maoists stressed complete self-reliance and more moderate leaders wished to import some foreign technology.

The signing of an agreement to coproduce Rolls Royce Spey engines in 1975 signaled the resolution of that debate in favor of selective importation. Beginning in 1977, Chinese military delegations traveled abroad, particularly to Western Europe and, in the 1980s, to the United States, to visit Western defense manufacturers and to inspect the state of the art in military equipment. Chinese representatives showed great interest in a wide variety of weapons systems, but they made few purchases of complete weapons systems, concentrating instead on acquisition of selective components, equipment, or technologies and on concluding coproduction agreements.

China's selective approach to acquiring foreign military technology stemmed from the limited funds available for military modernization and the desire of Chinese leaders to avoid dependence on any one supplier. The selective approach also reflected the knowledge that assimilation of foreign technology could present problems because of the low level of Chinese military technology and lack of qualified personnel. Finally, the leadership realized that China's past emphasis on modifying foreign weapons and on reverse engineering had greatly limited China's weapons development capacity. To overcome weapons deficiency in the short run and achieve indigenous military research, development, and production in the long run, China's leaders combined the selective import of weapons and technology with improved technical training of defense personnel and development of the civilian economy.

China primarily was interested in obtaining defensive weapons from abroad to correct the PLA's most critical weaknesses. These weapons and equipment included antitank and antiaircraft missiles, armor-piercing ammunition, helicopters, trucks, jeeps, automobiles, and tank fire-control systems, engines, and turrets for the ground forces; antiship missiles, air defense systems, antisubmarine warfare systems, and electronic countermeasures systems for the Navy; and avionics, including fire control and navigation systems, for the Air Force. Observers opined that the entire military needed improved command, control, communications, and intelligence equipment and computers for command and logistics.

Arms Sales

China's entrance into the international arms market in the 1980s was closely related to reforms in the defense industry and the leadership's desire to acquire the foreign technology needed to modernize PLA weaponry. Before 1980 China provided arms to friendly Third World countries at concessionary prices (see Foreign relations of the People's Republic of China). Because China transferred arms based on ideological and foreign policy considerations, terms were generous. Around 1980 China decided to sell weapons for profit to absorb excess capacity in the defense industry, make defense enterprises more economically viable, and earn the foreign currency required to purchase foreign military technology. China continued to sell military hardware at generous terms to some of its traditional friends and weapons customers, such as Pakistan, North Korea, Egypt, Sudan, and Somalia.

Hard-currency sales to Middle Eastern countries, however, particularly Iran and Iraq, accounted for the rapid increase in Chinese weapons sales in the 1980s. United States Arms Control and Disarmament Agency studies indicated that from 1979 to 1983 Chinese arms sales ranked eighth in the world, for a total of about

US$3.5 billion, of which an estimated US$2.1 billion went to Middle Eastern countries. In 1979 arms sales accounted for 0.9 percent of total exports; in 1983 arms sales rose to 6.3 percent of total exports. By 1987 China had jumped to fifth place, ranking behind the United States, the Soviet Union, United Kingdom, and France.

In the 1980s the defense industry and the PLA established a number of trading corporations to sell Chinese military hardware and to acquire foreign technology. The most prominent of these corporations were the China Xinshidai Corporation, affiliated with the NDSTIC; China Northern Industrial Corporation (commonly known as NORINCO), affiliated with the State Machine-Building Industry Commission; China National Aero-Technology Import and Export Corporation (CATIC), affiliated with the Ministry of Aeronautics; Great Wall Industrial Corporation and China Precision Machinery Import and Export Corporation, both affiliated with the Ministry of Astronautics; China Electronics Import and Export Corporation, affiliated with the Ministry of Electronics Industry; China Shipbuilding Trading Corporation, affiliated with the China State Shipbuilding Corporation; and China Xinxing Corporation, affiliated with the PLA General Logistics Department. In 1984 these corporations began promoting Chinese weapons, actively seeking technology transfer and coproduction agreements with foreign defense companies at international defense exhibitions in 1984.

Civilian Production

In late 1978 China initiated a policy of integrating civilian and military industry more closely in order to promote overall civilian economic development. This policy entailed civilianizing the machine-building ministries to make the defense industry more responsive to civilian control and needs; increasing defense industry production of civilian goods, particularly consumer goods; and transferring technology from the more advanced defense sector to the civilian sector of the economy. Production of civilian goods totaled 6.9 percent of total defense industry output in 1975. In 1980 it rose to 18 percent, and by 1985 it had jumped to 41.8 percent of total output. Chinese officials predicted that by 1990 about 80 percent of defense industry output would be civilian goods. The large excess capacity of the defense industry, resulting from declining orders from the PLA, made possible the rapid growth in civilian output. The defense industry manufactured a wide variety of goods for civilian use, including motor vehicles, optical equipment, television sets, electrical appliances, pharmaceuticals, and medical instruments and prostheses. Many of these products were consumer goods in high demand. For example, in 1985 the Ministry of Ordnance Industry manufactured 500,000 motorcycles, representing two-thirds of total motorcycle output, as well as 250,000 cameras, 450,000 bicycles, and 100,000 refrigerators.

Following the formulation of regulations and mechanisms for such transfers, defense industries began transferring technology to civilian industries on a large scale in the mid-1980s. Technology transfers provided defense enterprises with additional, lucrative sources of income and furnished civilian enterprises with a wide range of useful, advanced technology to modernize production. For example, the Ministry of Astronautics disseminated aerospace technology to light industry and to the petroleum, chemical engineering, machine-building, textile, communications, medical, and electronics industries.

Economic Roles of the PLA

The PLA played a role in economic development practically from its inception. Beginning in the late 1930s and early 1940s, when the party was headquartered in Yan'an, the Red Army raised its own food. After 1949 the PLA became involved in economic reconstruction tasks—building railroads and factories, reclaiming wasteland, digging irrigation canals, establishing state farms, and participating in disaster relief operations. The PLA accepted its role as a force in economic construction and devoted segments of its structure, such as the Engineering Corps, Railway Engineering Corps, Capital Construction Engineering Corps, Signal Corps, and Production and Construction Corps, to building up the national infrastructure. However, PLA regional- and main-force units played a much smaller role in aiding the civilian economy.

This pattern continued into the 1980s. The PLA remained self-sufficient in food, participated in selective infrastructure development projects, and aided in disaster relief. From 1981 to

1985, the PLA contributed 110 million workdays to 44,500 construction projects, including the diversion of river water from the Luan He to Tianjin, construction of the Shengli oilfield in Shandong and the Huolinhe open-cut coal mine in Shaanxi, expansion of Zhanjiang port in Guangdong, and afforestation work involving the planting of 290 million trees.

The PLA contributed to economic development in two additional ways. First, in November 1984 the government decided to transfer some military facilities to civilian control or joint military-civilian use. These facilities included airfields, ports, docks, railroads, depots and warehouses, and recreational areas. The devolution of these facilities to civilian control helped to alleviate problems that plagued the civilian economy. Second, beginning in the late 1970s, the PLA operated a large-scale program of dual-use training, whereby PLA personnel learned skills useful to the growing economy. Under this program, officers and soldiers received military training and training in specialized skills, such as livestock breeding, cultivation, processing, construction, machine maintenance, repair of domestic appliances, motor vehicle repair, and driving. In 1986 the PLA trained more than 650,000 soldiers in 25,000 training courses at over 6,000 training centers. In early 1987 surveys indicated that over 70 percent of demobilized PLA personnel left the armed forces with skills they could use as civilians.

CHINA'S MILITARY MODERNIZATION

China has been steadily building up its strategic and conventional capabilities since the 1990s. Eighteen years ago, experts say, China had a "bare-bones" military: basic capabilities, but nothing sophisticated or top-of-the-line.

But two decades of double-digit spending increases have changed that picture. China says its 2008 defense budget is $61 billion, though the Pentagon has historically challenged Beijing's reported figures.

In its annual report to Congress, the U.S. Defense Department estimated China's total military-related spending for 2007 to be between $97 billion and $139 billion, as compared to $52 billion reported by China. All that spending has gone to building a sophisticated, modern military: a large, increasingly capable submarine fleet, an air force stocked with Russian warplanes, and technical strides which have improved China's ballistic missile arsenal, as well as satellite surveillance, radar, and interception capabilities.

China continues to stress that its military modernization is in line with its peaceful rise in the world. Its latest White Paper on national defense emphasizes it will never seek hegemony or engage in military expansionism.

However, this has not alleviated concerns among its neighbors and regional rivals, say experts. A CFR Independent Task Force report (PDF) in 2007 on U.S.-China relations noted that many of China's neighbors and potential adversaries were making adjustments to their own defense plans and expenditures to balance China's growing military capabilities.

Japan: Japan and China compete over a host of issues, from regional security to international trade to access to energy. The two countries have a centuries-old history of conflict, including two Sino-Japanese wars that began in 1894 and 1931, and a bloody Japanese occupation of China during World War II. As this Backgrounder points out these animosities surface in recurring cycles, often involving Chinese anger over Japan's perceived lack of contrition for wartime crimes.

But concrete territorial and economic issues also aggravate the relationship, including Japan's close alliance with the United States, trade frictions, and ongoing disputes over ownership of various islands in the East China Sea. In 2007, China and Japan ranked third and fifth respectively in national defense expenditures (PBS), both spending only a small fraction of the U.S. budget even after adjusting for gross underreporting by Beijing.

China's military modernization fuels Japanese fears that China will use its growing economic leverage and military prowess to throw its weight around and dominate the region. Tanaka Akihiko of the University of Tokyo, speaking at a December 2008 CFR symposium on U.S.-Japan relations said China's growing military forces might change the balance of power in East Asia, which "would necessitate for Japan and the United States to readjust its force structure and other military management."

Japan has significantly upgraded capabilities over the past 15 years, deploying the Aegis radar and accompanying missile systems for its navy and warplanes armed with advanced air-to-air missiles for its air force.

Since 1998, when a North Korean missile test violated Japanese airspace, Toyko has been working in partnership with the United States to develop theater missile defenses which have obvious application in the event of any conflict with China.

Over the past decade the U.S.-Japanese security alliance has been strengthened through revised defense guidelines, which expand Japan's noncombatant role in a regional contingency, allows for the deployment of an X-Band radar system in Japan as part of a missile defense system, expands bilateral cooperation in training and intelligence sharing, and allows a nuclear-powered U.S. aircraft carrier in the Yokosuka Naval Base. In September 2007 Japan joined a multinational naval exercise with the United States, Australia, Singapore, and India in the area west of the Malacca Straits.

The exercise reinforced the U.S.-led campaign of strengthening security ties among its democratic allies and "the strategic countering (PDF) of Chinese military power," argues a December 2008 U.S. Congressional Research Service report.

In 2005, a joint statement by U.S.-Japan Security Consultative Committee 2005 for the first time included Taiwan as a common strategic objective where the parties would "encourage the peaceful resolution of issues" through dialogue. Though Japan's foreign affairs ministry said this did not change the country's position on Taiwan, many experts believe the shift indicates that Japan is increasingly concerned with China's growing military capabilities.

Taiwan: It is the main driver for China's militarization drive and biggest concern for the United States as this Backgrounder points out. Taiwan is also pursuing modernization goals which include procurement of army attack helicopters, army utility helicopters, PAC-3 missile defense systems, fighter jets, and diesel-electric submarines, as well as transformation of the military.

Relations between China and Taiwan have improved dramatically under the administration of President Ma Ying-jeou, although U.S. arms sales to Taiwan remains contentious.

In its white paper on national defense, China says the United States continues to sell arms to Taiwan "causing serious harm to Sino-US relations as well as peace and stability across the Taiwan Strait." In October 2008, Beijing suspended military contacts with the United States in protest of the U.S. decision to sell $6.4 billion in defense equipment and services to Taiwan.

South Korea: It has undertaken a major modernization drive, replacing antiquated fighter aircraft, frigates, tanks, and artillery pieces with advanced systems, many of them purchased from the United States or developed in partnership with U.S. defense industries, notes the 2007 CFR report (PDF). However, most experts say South Korea's military initiatives are more in response to a possible conflict with a nuclear North Korea.A thorough look at the status of South Korea's military is contained in CFR's Crisis Guide: The Korean Peninsula.

Russia: The country is China's largest supplier of advanced military hardware as well as a potential great power rival.

Moscow experienced a significant decline in its overall military capabilities during the 1990s, but buoyed by strong oil revenues in the past decade, it has been increasing its defense expenditure, in what most experts see as a sign to counter U.S. influence in the region.

The 2009 defense budget is expected to be $50 billion, a 25.7 percent increase from previous year. Fedor Lukyanov, chief editor of *Russia in Global Affairs,* told a January 2009 CFR meeting that there are limits to Russian military cooperation and arms sales to China. "We sold everything we could without making damage to Russian security," he said. CFR's Senior Fellow on Russian and Eurasian Studies, Stephen Sestanovich says Russia's relationship with China is based on the interests of some elites—those in the energy sector, the nuclear power sector, and the arms exports, that see China as an important market.

China and Russia also formed a security alliance to solve border disputes, which has grown into an important regional organization, the Shanghai Cooperation Organization (SCO), and includes Central Asian countries Kazakhstan, Kyrgyzstan, Tajikistan, and Uzbekistan. China and Russia have held a number of joint military exercises under the SCO. In October 2007, the SCO also signed a memorandum of understanding with the Collective Security Treaty Organization, a military alliance of several former Soviet states.

Some analysts see the SCO as a vehicle for Russia and China to curb U.S. access to the region's vast energy supplies. But others say Russia and China have very different objectives in Central Asia. Russia wants to reassert its regional leadership there, while China seeks energy ties, note some analysts. In 2008, China and Russia resolved (BBC) their last remaining border dispute involving islands in the eastern part of the border which had seen armed clashes between the two sides during the Cold War.

Southeast Asia: Experts say Southeast Asian countries, including Indonesia, the Philippines, and Thailand, are currently calculating whether the political and economic benefits of closer ties with a strong China outweigh the military risks. Bilateral trade between China and all ten countries within the Association of Southeast Asian Nations (ASEAN) is expected to exceed $200 billion in 2008 up from $ 190 billion in 2007.

The region is now China's fourth-largest trading partner. Despite the economic windfall, ASEAN countries want the United States to pay more attention to the new security trends in the region, experts say. While these countries are not very vocal about their fears, experts say they are nervously looking over their shoulders at China's military buildup and wondering where it's headed.

Border disputes with some countries also complicate China's relations with its Southeast Asian neighbors. Vietnam and China each assert claims to the Spratly and Paracel Islands, archipelagos in a potentially oil-rich area of the South China Sea. Malaysia, the Philippines, and Taiwan also claim all or part of the South China Sea.

China's assertion of "indisputable sovereignty" over the Spratly Islands and the entire South China Sea has elicited concern from

Vietnam and its Southeast Asia neighbors, according to the U.S. State Department. Vietnam has been pursuing closer military relations with the United States through joint military exercises, and sharing intelligence on terrorism, drugs, and other transnational threats. Vietnam has also hosted U.S. warships at its ports.

India: It has long-time rivalry with China over disputed borders and these two Asian giants also fought a war in 1962. New Delhi watches Beijing's military buildup closely and has undertaken military reforms of its own. It is currently building a nuclear submarine and is trying to acquire two more aircraft carriers in addition to the one it possesses.

It also launched its first unmanned moon mission in October 2008, another step in what many analysts see as a race with China in space. It has also been expanding its military cooperation with the United States. In June 2005, New Delhi and Washington agreed on a new framework for their defense relationship, including increases in defense trade, technology transfers, and joint exercises for the next ten years.

China's close military cooperation with Pakistan also concerns New Delhi. Each country helps the other to check India's power, say experts. China remains a key supplier of arms to Pakistan and in 2008, agreed to help Pakistan build two nuclear power plants. China also supplies Pakistan with nuclear technology and assistance, including what many experts suspect was the blueprint for Pakistan's nuclear bomb.

Pakistan's army has both short- and medium-range ballistic missiles that experts say came from China. According to Thomas C. Reed, a former U.S. Air Force secretary, China probably helped Pakistan test a nuclear weapon inside China in 1990. Reed adds that this weapon was most likely based on a Chinese design.

Central Asia: Several Central Asian countries— Kazakhstan, Kyrgyzstan, Tajikistan, and Uzbekistan —have forged closer relations with China as part of the Shanghai Cooperation Organization. Experts say tensions in China's western province of Xinjiang is one of the major reasons behind Beijing's eagerness to improve relations with the Central Asian states.

Xinjiang is largely made up of Uighurs, predominantly a Muslim community with ties to Central Asia, and China has been concerned that Central Asian states may back a separatist movement in Xinjiang. Beijing also seeks energy ties in the region. Under the SCO, the countries conduct joint military exercises. Problems with their own Muslim fundamentalist groups have led these countries to assist China in its struggle against separatists from Xinjiang, say experts. However, some experts say the Central Asian states still view China and Russia as possible hegemonic powers.

7

Military Strength of Pakistan Army

HISTORY OF THE PAKISTAN ARMY

1947 - 1958

The Pakistani Army was created on 30 June 1947 with the division of the British Indian Army and Pakistan received six armoured, eight artillery and eight infantry regiments compared to the forty armoured, forty artillery and twenty one infantry regiments that went to India. Fearing that India would take over the disputed region of Kashmir, the newly created Pakistani Army sent in irregulars and tribal groups in 1947 which lead to the Indo-Pakistani War of 1947.

Regular army units joined the invasion later on but were stopped on UK pressure but not before occupying the northwestern part of Kashmir. During the 1950s, the Pakistani Army received large amounts of economic and military aid from United States and Great Britain after signing two Mutual Defense Treaties, Central Treaty Organization, (Cento) also known as the Baghdad Pact and SEATO, (South East Asian Treaty Organization) in 1954. This aid greatly expanded the Army from its modest beginnings.

The sole division HQ that went to Pakistan was the 7th. 8th and 9th Divisions were raised in 1947; 10, 12 and 14 Division were raised in 1948. 15 Div was raised in 1950. At some point before 1954, 6 Div was raised and 9 Div disbanded. 6 Div was disbanded at some point after 1954 as US assistance was available only for 1 armed and 6 infantry division. 1st Armoured Div was raised in 1956.

1958 - 1969

The Army seized control of Pakistan for the first time when General Ayub Khan came to power through a bloodless coup in 1958. Tensions with India continued in the 1960s and a brief border skirmish was fought near the Rann of Kutch area during April 1965, in which the Indian Army was repulsed with moderate casualties. Emboldened, the Pakistan Army leaders carried out Operation Gibraltar, an attempt to take Kashmir, that was launched later in the year, resulting in the Indo-Pakistani War of 1965, after the Pakistani infiltrators were discovered, India counter-attacked.

The 3-week war ended in a U.N. mandated ceasefire culminating in the Tashkent Declaration. However, the military generally considers the 1965 war as a victory over a rival that outnumbered it by almost 3 to 1 in all military aspects. In that regard, the valour of Major Raja Aziz Bhatti of thwarting an entire Indian Brigade planning to break into Lahore and the Battle Of Chawinda are considered to be one of the most courageous feats in the army.

At Chawinda the Pakistan Army was vastly outnumbered in terms of personnel and equipment but it is said that victory was achieved when Pakistani East Bengal Regiment soldiers tied bombs to their bellies in order to stop the advancing Indian tanks. An uprising against General Ayub Khan, during 1968 and 1969 resulted in Ayub Khan relinquishing his office as President and Chief of Pakistan Army in favor of General Yahya Khan who assumed power in 1969.6 Armoured and 11 Infantry Divisions were raised in adhoc form 1964-65. 16, 18 and 23 Divisions were raised at some point between 1966-69; and 9 Division was re-raised in this period.

1969 - 1977

During the rule of General Yahya Khan, the Bengalis protested their poor conditions and civil unrest broke out in East Pakistan amidst incidents of massive human rights abuses carried out and genocide by the Pakistani Army and military.

India joined the war on the side of Bangladesh following seven months of civil war in November 1971, and on the 16th of December, 1971, over 50,000 Pakistani Armed forces personnel (army, air force and navy) around 40,000 government and civil employees surrendered to the Indian forces and Bangladesh became a republic. Consequently, the Pakistan army was modernized at a faster pace than ever before. After the war, General Yahya Khan resigned and Zulfikar Ali Bhutto took over the reins.

1977 - 1999

In 1977 the Pakistan Army took over the government of Pakistan after a coup by General Zia ul-Haq, which saw the end of another democratically elected government leading to the hanging of Zulfikar Ali Bhutto, after he was tried and found guilty of conspiracy of murdering a politician named Kasuri. General Zia ul-Haq ruled as a military dictator until his mysterious explosion aircraft death in 1988.

Pakistani army also helped the Saudi Arabian Government in regaining the control of the Kaaba with the help of French Commandos. Pakistani and French security forces retook the Kaaba in a battle which left approximately 250 dead, and 600 wounded. The Pakistanis and French were called in after poor results from assaults by the Saudi Arabian National Guard (SANG). 127 were reported to have been killed.

In the mid-1970s the Pakistani Army was involved in fighting an uprising in Balochistan. Various Balochi factions, some with the oblique support of the USSR, wanted independence or at least greater provincial rights. The rebellion was put down but the Army suffered heavy casualties.

With the Soviet invasion of Afghanistan, the United States began to provide large scale military and economic aid to Pakistan to modernize its conventional military capability and, ostensibly at least, prevent any Soviet attacks on it. This aid was also intended as an incentive for Pakistan to aid guerrilla forces (called "Army of GOD") in Afghanistan. The SSG created a unit called the Black Storks in which SSG commandos were dressed up as Afghan Mujahideen during the Soviet-Afghan war. They were then flown into Afghanistan and provided the Mujahideen with support. The

United States allocated about 40% of its assistance package to non-reimbursable credits for military purchases, the fourth largest program after Israel, Egypt and Turkey. The remainder of the aid program was devoted to economic assistance.

After the Soviets withdrew by 1989 and the Pakistani Nuclear weapons program nearing maturity, Pakistan was placed under sanctions by USA in 1990. Various weapon systems ordered by Pakistan such as F-16 Jets were not delivered but various amendments have authorized return of spare parts and end items already paid for by Pakistan. There was a period of international sanctions due to Pakistan's nuclear tests. During 1999 the Pakistan Army for the fourth time overthrew a democratically elected government which resulted in additional sanctions being placed against Pakistan

The Army fought a brief border skirmish with India in Kargil 1999 after the Pakistan Army sent in their para-military NLI troops dressed as mujahiddin into Indian territory. There was a danger of the war spiraling out of control when Nawaz Sharif, under immense pressure from Washington, eventually ordered a withdrawal. This decision and the resulting Pakistani casualties created great resentment in the Army against the Prime Minister and is rumored to have contributed to his eventual over throwing by the COAS.

40 and 41 Divs were raised in the 1980s; Two more divs have been raised under the rubric "Corps Reserves" for V and XXXI corps.

1999 - Present

In October 1999 the Pakistan Army for the fourth time, with popular support, overthrew a democratically elected government which resulted in additional sanctions being placed against Pakistan, resulting in General Pervez Musharraf coming to power in a bloodless coup. Musharraf stepped down as President in August 2008.

Since the 9/11 incident, Pakistan unrecognized the Taliban and has become a key ally of the United States in the fight against terrorism. As part of the U.S.'s War on Terrorism, the army has moved over 100,000 troops to the Pakistan-Afghan border to patrol against extreme elements cross border infiltration.

The Pakistan Army commenced operations in Balochistan during 2006, resulting in the killing of the leader of the Balochis, Nawab Akbar Bugti and has resulted in the crushing of a rebellion by the Balochistan Liberation Army.

POLITICAL POWER OF THE ARMY

The Pakistani army has always played an integral part of the Pakistan government since its inception. It has virtually acted as a third party that has repeatedly seized power in the name of stabilizing Pakistan.

General Ayub Khan came to power in 1956 due to political turmoil within the ruling party. The situation was so dire that the speaker of the National Assembly was beaten to death right in front of the assembly hall.

Ayub Khan reluctantly agreed to take power as a favour to the nation. Later on, General Yahya Khan would assume power in 1969. After the 1971 war, democracy was restored only to be cut short in 1977 after a coup which saw the hanging of Zulfikar Ali Bhutto, the Pakistani Premier. General Zia ul-Haq ruled as a dictator virtually unopposed until his death in 1988. Despite the exit of the army from mainstream politics, the political muscle of the military is everpresent. The former President, General (ret) Pervez Musharraf, came to power in a bloodless coup in October 1999 overthrowing the last democratically elected government led by Nawaz Sharif.

Fauji Foundation

Fauji Foundation (established in 1954) is a charitable trust, operating on a completely self sustaining basis, channeling approximately 80% of the profits from commercial ventures into social protection programmes that serve a beneficiary population representing approximately 7% of the country's population.

Spending more than Rs. 21 billion since inception on welfare, the Foundation provides services in the areas of healthcare, education, educational stipends, technical and vocational training.

Over 2.1 million patients treated per year through the FF Healthcare System

- Approximately 38,000 students enrolled in the FF Education System
- Approximately 70,000 educational stipends dispersed each year
- Over 6,000 individuals trained annually through the Vocational & Technical Training Centres

Considered the most sustainable social protection mechanism in the country, Fauji Foundation provides welfare services to approximately 10 million individuals on a completely sustainable basis. Running autonomously for over 50 years, the foundation has been providing healthcare, education, vocational and technical training to over 7% of the country's population through 294 welfare projects.

PERSONNEL TRAINING

Enlisted Ranks

Most enlisted personnel used to come from rural families, and many have only rudimentary literacy skills, but with the increase in the litracy level the requirements have been raised to Matriculate level (10th Grade). Recruits are processed gradually through a paternalistically run regimental training center, taught the official language, Urdu, if necessary, and given a period of elementary education before their military training actually starts.

In the thirty-six-week training period, they develop an attachment to the regiment they will remain with through much of their careers and begin to develop a sense of being a Pakistani rather than primarily a member of a tribe or a village. Enlisted men usually serve for eighteen years, during which they participate in regular training cycles and have the opportunity to take academic courses to help them advance.

Officer Ranks

About 320 men enter the army bi-annually through the Pakistan Military Academy at Kakul in Abbottabad in the North West

Frontier Province; a small number—especially physicians and technical specialists—are directly recruited, and these persons are part of the heart of the officer corps. The product of a highly competitive selection process, members of the officer corps have completed twelve years of education and spend two years at the Pakistan Military Academy, with their time divided about equally between military training and academic work to bring them up to a baccalaureate education level, which includes English-language skills.

The army has twelve other training establishments, including schools concentrating on specific skills such as infantry, artillery, intelligence, or mountain warfare. A National University of Science and Technology (NUST) has been established which has absorbed the existing colleges of engineering, signals, electrical engineering and medicine. At the apex of the army training system is the Command and Staff College at Quetta, one of the few institutions inherited from the colonial period. The college offers a ten-month course in tactics, staff duties, administration, and command functions through the division level. Students from foreign countries, including the United States, have attended the school but reportedly have been critical of its narrow focus and failure to encourage speculative thinking or to give adequate attention to less glamorous subjects, such as logistics.

The senior training institution for all service branches is the National Defence University. Originally established in 1971 at Rawalpindi, to provide training in higher military strategy for senior officers, the school house was relocated to Islamabad in 1995. It also offers courses that allow civilians to explore the broader aspects of national security. In a program begun in the 1980s to upgrade the intellectual standards of the officer corps and increase awareness of the wider world, a small group of officers, has been detailed to academic training, achieving master's degrees and even doctorates at universities in Pakistan and abroad.

Pakistani officers were sent abroad during the 1950s and into the 1960s for training in Britain and other Commonwealth countries, and especially to the United States, where trainees numbering well in the hundreds attended a full range of institutions ranging from armored and infantry schools to the higher staff and command institutions. After 1961 this training was coordinated under the International Military Education and Training (IMET) program, but numbers varied along with vicissitudes in the United States-Pakistan military relationship.

Of some 200 officers being sent abroad annually in the 1980s, over two-thirds went to the United States, but the cessation of United States aid in 1990 entailed suspension of the IMET program. In 1994 virtually all foreign training was in Commonwealth countries. However, after the 9/11 attacks, Pakistan again has begun sending officers to US Army schools. Today there are more than 400 officers serving in foreign countries. Officers retire between the ages of fifty-two and sixty, depending on their rank.

RELIEF OPERATIONS AND ECONOMIC DEVELOPMENT

In times of natural disaster, such as the great floods of 1992 or the October 2005 devastating earthquake, army engineers, medical and logistics personnel, and the armed forces played a major role in bringing relief and supplies. The army also engaged in extensive economic activities. Most of these enterprises, such as stud and dairy farms, were for the army's own use, but others performed functions beneficial to the local civilian economy. Army factories produced such goods as sugar, fertilizer, and brass castings and sold them to civilian consumers.

Several army organizations performed functions that were important to the civilian sector across the country. For example, the National Logistics Cell was responsible for trucking food and other goods across the country; the Frontier Works Organization built the Karakoram Highway to China; and the Special Communication Organization maintained communications networks in remote parts of Pakistan. Pakistan Army is involved in relief activities not only in Pakistan but also in many other countries of the world, like they went for relief activities after Bangladesh was recently hit by floods. Pak Army also went to Indonesia, Bangladesh and Sri Lanka after they were hit by tsunami. Pakistan army and Navy sent ships and helicopters to the friendly nations for tsunami relief operation.

Women and Minorities in the Army

Women have served in the Pakistani Army since its foundation. Currently, there is a sizable number of Women serving in the army. Most women are recruited in the regular Army to perform medical and educational work. There is also a Women's Guard section of Pakistan's National Guard where women are trained in nursing, welfare and clerical work and there are also women recruited in very limited numbers for the Janbaz Force. Only recently has Pakistan began to recruit women for combat positions and the Elite Anti-Terrorist Force In 2007, several female graduates were nominated to be Sky Marshalls for Pakistan based airlines. In addition recently eight of the 41 cadets from the Pakistan Military Academy at Kakul became the first women guards of honour. Pakistan is the only country in the Islamic world to have women Major *Generals* in the Army.

Recruitment is nationwide and the army attempts to maintain an ethnic balance but most enlisted recruits, as in British times, come from a few districts in northern Punjab Province and the adjacent Azad Kashmir and the North West Frontier Province. Pakistan's Officer Corps are also mostly from Punjab and the North West Frontier Province and of middle-class, rural backgrounds.

Minorities in Pakistan are allowed to sit in all examinations, including the one conducted by Inter Services Selection Board however the proportion of religious minorities in the Pakistan army is still considerably very less. The army sees itself as a national institution although not many minorities have seen high ranks.

MILITARY STRENGTH OF PAKISTAN

The military history of Pakistan encompasses an immense panorama of conflicts and struggles extending for more than 3,000 years across areas constituting modern Pakistan, and the greater Indian subcontinent. The history of the modern-day military of Pakistan begins from post-1947, after Pakistan achieved its independence as a modernnation-state. The military holds a significant place in the history of Pakistan, as the Pakistani Armed

Forces have played, and still continue to play, a vital role in the Pakistani establishment and shaping of the country since its inception. Although Pakistan was founded as a democracy after its independence from the British Raj, the military has remained one of the country's most powerful institutions and has on occasion overthrown democratically elected civilian governments on the basis of mismanagement and corruption.

Successive governments have made sure that the military was consulted before they took key decisions, especially when those decisions related to the Kashmir conflict and foreign policy. Political leaders of Pakistan's developing democracy know that the military has stepped into the political arena before at times of crisis through Coup d'état to establish military dictatorships, and could do so again.

The military was created in 1947 by division of the British Indian Army and was given units who had a long and cherished history during the British India such as the Khyber Rifles, and had seen intensive service in World War I and World War II. Many of the early leaders of the military had fought in both world wars.

The military draws on inspiration from the rich combat history that has occurred within the area of modern day Pakistani soil and uses example of sacrifice and perseverance to embolden troops, and has named medals of valor, nickname for combat divisions, and indigenous weapons; Such as the short-range ballistic missiles Ghaznavi, which is named in honour of Mahmud of Ghazna who founded the Ghaznavid Empire, and ruled from 997 to 1030.

Since the time of independence, the military has fought three major wars with India. It has also fought a limited conflict at Kargil with India after acquiring nuclear capabilities. In addition, there have been several minor border skirmishes with neighbouring Afghanistan. After the September 11 attacks, the military is engaged in a protracted low intensity conflict along Pakistan's western border with Afghanistan, with the Taliban and Al-Qaeda militants, as well as those who support or provide shelter to them.

In addition, Pakistani troops have also participated in various foreign conflicts usually acting as United Nations peacekeepers. At present, Pakistan has the largest number of its personnel acting under the United Nations with the number standing at 10,173 as of 31 March 2007.

550 BCE–1857

Ancient Empires

The region of modern day Pakistan (part of India before 1947) formed the most populous and richest satrapy of the Persian Achaemenid Empire for almost two centuries, starting from the reign of Darius the Great (522-485 BCE). The first major conflict erupted when Alexander the Great overthrew the Achaemenid empire in 334 BCE, and marched eastwards. Eventually, after defeating King Porus in the fierce Battle of the Hydaspes (near modern Jhelum), he conquered much of the Punjab region. But, his battle weary troops refused to advance further into India to engage the formidable army of Nanda Dynasty and its vanguard of trampling elephants, new monstorities to the invaders. Therefore, Alexander proceeded southwest along the Indus valley. Along the way, he engaged in several battles with smaller kingdoms before marching his army westward across the Makran desert towards modern Iran. Alexander founded several new Macedonian/Greek settlements in Gandhara andPunjab.

As Alexander the Great's Greek and Persian armies withdrew westwards, the satraps left behind by Alexander were defeated and conquered by Chandragupta Maurya who founded the Maurya Empire, which ruled the region from 321 to 185 BC. The Mauryas Empire was itself conquered by the Sunga Empire, which ruled the region from 185 to 73 BCE. Other regions such as the Khyber Pass was left unguarded, and a wave of foreign invasion followed. TheGreco-Bactrian king, Demetrius, capitalized and he conquered southern Afghanistan and Pakistan around 180 BC, forming the Indo-Greek Kingdom. The Indo-Greek Kingdom ultimately disappeared as a political entity around 10 AD following the invasions of the Central Asian Indo-Scythians. Their empire morphed into the Kushan Empire who ruled until 375 AD. The region was then conquered by the Persian Indo-Sassanid empire who ruled until 565 AD before the entire Sassanid Empire was conquered by the Arabs including the region of modern Pakistan.

Muslim Conquests

In 712 CE, a Syrian Muslim chieftain called Muhammad bin Qasim conquered most of the Indus region (stretching from Sindh to Multan) for the Umayyad empire. In 997 CE, Mahmud of Ghazni conquered the bulk of Khorasan, marched on Peshawar in 1005, and followed it by the conquests of Punjab (1007), Balochistan (1011), Kashmir (1015) and Qanoch (1017). By the end of his reign in 1030, Mahmud's empire extended from Kurdistan in the west to the Yamuna river in the east, and the Ghaznavid dynasty lasted until 1187. In 1160, Muhammad Ghori conquered Ghazni from the Ghaznavids and became its governor in 1173. He marched eastwards into the remaining Ghaznavid territory and Gujarat in the 1180s, but was rebuffed by Gujarat's Solanki rulers. In 1186-7, he conquered Lahore, bringing the last of Ghaznevid territory under his control and ending the Ghaznavid empire. Muhammad Ghori returned to Lahore after 1200 to deal with a revolt of the Rajput Ghakkar tribe in the Punjab. He suppressed the revolt, but was killed during a Ghakkar raid on his camp on the Jhelum River in 1206. Muhammad Ghori's successors established the first Indo-Islamic dynasty, the Delhi Sultanate. The MamlukDynasty, (*mamluk means "slave" and referred to the Turkic slave soldiers who became rulers throughout the Islamic world*), seized the throne of the Sultanate in 1211. Several Turko-Afghan dynasties ruled their empires from Delhi: the Mamluk (1211–90), the Khalji(1290–1320), the Tughlaq (1320–1413), the Sayyid (1414–51) and the Lodhi (1451–1526). Although some kingdoms remained independent of Delhi - in Gujarat, Malwa (central India), Bengal and Deccan - almost all of the Indus plain came under the rule of these large Indo-Islamic sultanates. Perhaps the greatest contribution of the sultanate was its temporary success in insulating South Asia from the Mongol invasion from Central Asia in the 13th century; nonetheless the sultans eventually lost Afghanistan and western Pakistan to the Mongols.

Mughal Empire

From the 16th to the 19th century, the formidable Mughal empire covered much of India. In 1739, the Persian emperor Nader Shah invaded India, defeated the Mughal Emperor

Muhammed Shah, and occupied most of Balochistan and the Indus plain. After Nadir Shah's death, the kingdom of Afghanistan was established in 1747, by one of his generals, Ahmad Shah Abdali and included Kashmir, Peshawar, Daman, Multan, Sind and Punjab. In the south, a succession of autonomous dynasties (the Daudpotas, Kalhoras andTalpurs) had asserted the independence of Sind, from the end of Aurangzeb's reign. Most of Balochistan came under the influence of the Khan of Kalat, apart from some coastal areas such as Gwadar, which were ruled by the Sultan of Oman. The Sikh Confederacy (1748–1799) was a group of small states in the Punjab that emerged in a political vacuum created by rivalry between the Mughals, Afghans and Persians. The Confederacy drove out the Mughals, repelled several Afghan invasions and in 1764 captured Lahore. However after the retreat of Ahmed Shah Abdali, the Confederacy suffered instability as disputes and rivalries emerged. The Sikh empire (1799–1849) was formed on the foundations of the Confederacy by Ranjit Singh who proclaimed himself "*Sarkar-i-Wala*", and was referred to as the Maharaja of Lahore. His empire eventually extended as far west as the Khyber Pass and as far south as Multan. Amongst his conquests were Kashmir in 1819 and Peshawar in 1834, although the Afghans made two attempts to recover Peshawar. After the Maharaja's death the empire was weakened by internal divisions and political mismanagement. The British annexed the Sikh empire in 1849 after two Anglo-Sikh wars.

1857–1947

British Raj

The British Raj lasted from 1858 to 1947, the period when India was part of the British Empire. After the mutiny, the British took steps to avoid further rebellions taking place including changing the structure of the Army. They banned Indians from the officer corp and artillery corp to ensure that future rebellions would not be as organized and disciplined and that the ratio of British Soldiers to Indians would be drastically increased. Recruiting percentages changed with an emphasis on Sikhs and Gurkhas whose loyalties and fighting prowess had been proven in the conflict and new caste and religious based regiments were formed.

The World Wars

During World War I the British Indian Army fought in Egypt, Palestine, Mesopotamia, Gallipoli, and France and suffered very heavy casualties.

The British Indian Army's strength was about 189,000 in 1939. There were about 3,000 British officers and 1,115 Indian officers. The army was expanded greatly to fight in World War II. By 1945, the strength of the Army had risen to about two and a half million. There were about 34,500 British officers and 15,740 Indian officers. The Army took part in campaigns in France, East Africa, North Africa, Syria, Tunisia, Malaya, Burma, Greece, Sicily and Italy. It suffered 179,935 casualties in the war (including killed (24,338), wounded (64,354), missing (11,762) and POW (79,481) soldiers). Many future military officers and leaders of Pakistan fought in these wars.

Birth of the Modern Military

On June 3, 1947, the British Government announced its plan to divide British India between India and Pakistan and the subsequent transfer of power to the two countries resulted in independence of Pakistan. The division of the British Indian Army occurred on June 30, 1947 in which Pakistan received six armoured, eight artillery and eight infantry regiments compared to the forty armoured, forty artillery and twenty one infantry regiments that went to India. At the Division Council, which was chaired by Rear Admiral Lord Mountbatten of Burma, the Viceroy of India, and was composed of the leaders of the Muslim League and the Indian National Congress, they had agreed that the British Indian Army of 11,800 officers and 500,000 enlisted personnel was to be divided to the ratio of 64% for India and 36% for Pakistan.

Pakistan was forced to accept a smaller share of the armed forces as most of the military assets, such as weapons depots, military bases, etc., were located inside the new Union of India, while those that were in the new Dominion of Pakistan were mostly obsolete. Pakistan also had a dangerously low ammunition reserve of only one week. By August 15, 1947, both India and Pakistan had operational control over their armed forces. General Sir Frank Messervy was appointed as the first Army Commander-in-Chief of the new Pakistan Army. General Messervy was succeeded in this post in February 1948, by General Sir Douglas Gracey, who served until January 1951.

The Pakistani Armed Forces initially numbered around 150,000 men, many scattered around various bases in India and needing to be transferred to Pakistan by train. The independence created large scale communal violence in the India. In total, around 7 million Muslims migrated to Pakistan and 5 million Sikhs and Hindus to India with over a million people dying in the process.

Of the estimated requirement of 4,000 officers for Pakistani Armed Forces, only 2,300 were actually available. The neutral British officers were asked to fill in the gap and nearly 500 volunteered as well as many Polish and Hungarian officers to run the medical corps.

By October 1947, Pakistan had raised four divisions in West Pakistan and one division in East Pakistan with an overall strength of ten infantry brigades and one armoured brigade with thirteen tanks. Many brigades and battalions within these divisions were below half strength, but Pakistani personnel continued to arrive from all over India, the Middle East and North Africa and from South East Asia. Mountbatten and Field Marshal Sir Claude Auchinleck, the last Commander-in-Chief, India, had made it clear to Pakistan that in case of war with India, no other member of the Commonwealth would come to Pakistan's help.

1947–1965

The War of 1947

Pakistan had its first taste of war almost immediately in the First Kashmir War where it sent its forces into Kashmir. Kashmir, had a Muslim majority population, but the choice of which country to join was given to the Maharaja Hari Singh of Kashmir he was not able to decided whether to join India or Pakistan. By late October, the overthrow of the maharaja seemed imminent. He sought military assistance from India, for which he sign an instrument of accession with India. The Army was pushed back by the Indians but not before occupying the northwestern part of Kashmir (roughly 40% of Kashmir), which Pakistan still controls, the rest remaining under Indian control except for the portion ceded by Pakistan to China

U.S. Aid

With the failure of the United States to persuade India to join an anti-communist pact, it turned towards Pakistan, which in contrast with India was prepared to join such an alliance in return of military and economic aid and also to find a potential ally against India. By 1954, the Americans had decided that Pakistan along with Turkey and Iran would be ideal countries to counter Soviet influence. Therefore Pakistan and USA signed the Mutual Defense Assistance Agreement and American aid began to flow in Pakistan. This was followed by two more agreements. In 1955, Pakistan joined the South East Asian Treaty Organization (SEATO) and the Baghdad Pact later to be renamed as Central Asian Treaty Organization (CENTO) after Iraq left in 1959. Pakistan received over a billion dollars in military aid from United States between 1954 and 1965. This aid greatly enhanced Pakistan's defense capability as new equipment and weapons were brought into the armed forces, new military bases were created and existing ones were expanded and upgraded and two new Corps commands were formed. Shahid M Amin, who has previously served in the Pakistani foreign service, writes in his book *Pakistan's foreign policy: A reappraisal*, "It is also a fact, that these pacts did undoubtedly secure very substantial US military and economic assistance for Pakistan in its nascent years and significantly strengthened it in facing India, as seen in the 1965 war."

American and British advisers trained Pakistani personnel and the USA was allowed to set up bases within Pakistan's borders to spy on the Soviet Union. In this period, many future Pakistani presidents and generals went to American and British military academies that lead to the development of the Pakistani army on Western models, especially the British one.

After Dominion status ended in 1956 with the formation of a Constitution and a declaration of Pakistan as an Islamic Republic, the military took control in 1958 and held power for more than 10 years. During this time, Pakistan had developed close military relations with many Middle Eastern countries to whom Pakistan sent military advisers and this relationship continues to the present day.

First Military Rule

Since its independence, the democratic system has been disturbed by the Pakistan Army's generals. In 1951, the Military Intelligence foiled a conspiracy against the government of first Prime minister Liaqat Ali Khan. The M.I. under Major-General Syed Shahid Hamid arrested Major-General Akbar Khan, along with other senior officers. Akbar was subsequently court-martialed was relieved from his service. On October 16, 1951, Liaqat Ali Khan was assassinated by Afghan national Said Akbar, hired by the United States and Pakistan Army. After his death, the political turmoil further destabilized the country. In 1958, retired Major-General and President Iskander Mirza took over the country and deposed the government of Prime minister Feroz Khan Noon, and declared first martial law on October 7, 1958. President Mirza personally appointed his close associate General Ayub Khan as the Commander-in-Chief of Pakistan Army.

However, Khan ousted Mirza shortly when he became highly dissatisfied by Mirza's policies. It was said that, at that time when Khan took over the control, Ayub Khan had slapped Mirza and disrespected him and night to pack Mirza off to exile in England. Now as President and Commander-in-Chief Ayub Khan himself appointed him as 5-star Field Marshal and built up the relationship with the United States and the West. A formal alliance including Pakistan, Iran, Iraq, and Turkey was formed and was called the Baghdad Pact (later known as CENTO), which was to defend the Middle East and Persian Gulf from Soviet communists designs.

Border Clashes with Afghanistan

Armed tribal incursions from Afghanistan into Pakistan's border areas began with the transfer of power in 1947 and became a continual irritant. Many Pashtun Afghans regarded the 19th century Anglo-Afghan border (historically called the Durand Line) treaties as void and were trying to re-draw the borders with Pakistan or trying to help create an independent state (Pashtunistan) for the ethnic Pashtun people. The Pakistan Army had to be continually sent to secure the country's western borders. Afghan-Pakistan relations were to reach their nadir in 1955 when diplomatic relations were severed with the ransacking of Pakistan's embassy in Kabul and again in 1961 when the Pakistan Army had to repel a major Afghan incursion in Bajaur region.

Pakistan used American weaponry to fight the Afghan incursions but the weaponry had been sold under the pretext of fighting Communism and the USA was not pleased with this development, as the Soviets at that time became the chief benefactor to Afghanistan. Some sections of the American press blamed Pakistan for driving Afghanistan into the Soviet camp.

In retaliation to continuous Pashtun Afghan claims on Northwestern Pakistan, Pakistan's military provided support for the non-Pashtun populations of Afghanistan to re-unite with their ethnic groups who constitute a majority in neighbouring countries of Afghanistan, which gained independence after the fall of the USSR.

All this changed after the rise of the Taliban movement, which mainly consisted of Pakhtuns. Seeing the Taliban as a tool to maintain stability, Pakistan's military then shifted its support to the Pashtun-dominated Taliban; losing the trust of the non-Pashtun majority it traditionally supported right until the Soviet-Afghan war era.

Alliance with China

After India's defeat in the Sino-Indian War of 1962, India began a rapid program of reforming and expanding its military. A series of conferences on Kashmir was held from December 1962 to February 1963 between India and Pakistan. Both nations offered important concessions and a solution to the long-standing dispute seemed imminent. However, after the Sino-Indian war, Pakistan had gained an important new ally in China and Pakistan then signed a bilateral border agreement with China that involved the boundaries of the disputed state, and relations with India again became strained.

Fearing a communist expansion into India, the USA for the first time gave large quantities of weapons to India. The expansion of the Indian armed forces was viewed by most Pakistanis as being directed towards Pakistan rather than China. The US also pumped in large sums of money and military supplies to Pakistan as it saw Pakistan as being a check against Soviet expansionist plans.

1965–1979

The War of 1965

In Pakistan, after the Sino-Indian War in 1962, the military of India was seen as being weakened. This analysis was proven true when a small border skirmish occurred between India and Pakistan in the Rann of Kutch on April 1965 where the Indian Army was caught unprepared. The skirmish occurred between the border police of both countries due to poorly defined borders and later the Armies of both countries responded. The result was a decisive one for the Pakistan Army that was praised back home. Emboldened by this success, Operation Gibraltar, a covert infiltration attempt in Kashmir was launched later in the year. The plan was to start a rebellion among local Kashmiris and attack the rebuilding Indian Army thus capturing Kashmir by force, as the Pakistan Army Command believed that it had a qualitative superiority over their neighbours. However this proved over-ambitious as Indian Kashmiris did not support the intruding Pakistan Army and a full-fledged war across the international border (the Indo-Pakistani War of 1965) broke out between India and Pakistan. Pakistan Air Force and Indian Air Force were indulged massive air warfare in this war. Pakistani Army could not achieve the goal of taking over Indian controlled Kashmir while Indian Army failed to fulfill its aspiration of capturing Lahore and Sialkot, while on the offensive both the armies were occupying some of each other's territory resulting in a stalemate.

US had imposed an arms embargo on both India and Pakistan during the war and Pakistan was affected more by the arms embargo as it had no spare parts for its Air Force,tanks, and other equipment while India's quantitative edge making up for theirs. The war was finally ended in a ceasefire.

Rebuilding the Armed Forces

The United States was disillusioned by a war in which both countries fought each other with equipment, which had been sold for defensive purposes and to stop the spread of communism. Pakistan's claims that an Indian attempt to fully integrate Indian Controlled Kashmir into the union of India had compelled it to act fell on deaf ears in the Johnson Administration and by July 1967, the United States withdrew its military assistance advisory group. In response to these events, Pakistan declined to renew the lease on the Peshawar military facility, which ended in 1969. Eventually, United States-Pakistan relations grew measurably weaker as the United States became more deeply involved in Vietnam and as its broader interest in the security of South Asia waned.

The Soviet Union continued the massive build-up of the Indian military and a US arms embargo forced Pakistan to look at other options. It turned to China, North Korea, Germany, Italy and France for military aid. China in particular gave Pakistan over 900 tanks, Mig-19 Fighters and enough equipment to fully equip 3 Infantry divisions. France supplied some Mirage aircraft, submarines and even the Soviet Union gave Pakistan around 100 T-55 tanks, Mi-8 helicopters but that aid was abruptly stopped under intense Indian pressure. Pakistan in this period was partially able to enhance its military capability.

Involvement in Arab Conflicts

Pakistan had sent numerous military advisers to Jordan and Syria to help in their training and military preparations for any potential war with Israel. When the Six Day war started, Pakistan assisted by sending a contingent of its pilots and airmen to Egypt, Jordan and Syria. PAF pilots performed excellently and downed about 10 Israeli planes including Mirages, Mysteres, Vautours without losing a single plane of their own.

Jordan and Iraq decorated Pakistani Flight Lieutenant Saif-ul-Azam. Israelis praised the performance of PAF pilots too. Eizer Weizman, then Chief Of Israeli Air Force wrote in his autobiography about Air Marshal Noor Khan (Commander PAF at that time):

"...He is a formidable person and I am glad that he is Pakistani..." No Pakistani ground forces participated in the war.

After the end of the Six-Day War, Pakistani advisors had remained in Jordan and were training the Jordanian Forces. In 1970, King Hussein of Jordan decided to remove the PLO and its forces from Jordan by force after a series of terrorist acts attributed to the PLO, which undermined Jordanian sovereignty. On September 16, King Hussein declared martial law. The next day, Jordanian tanks attacked the headquarters of Palestinian organizations in Amman. The head of Pakistan's training mission to Jordan, Brigadier-General Zia-ul-Haq (later President of Pakistan), took command of the Jordanian Army's 2nd division and helped Jordan during this crisis.

Pakistan again assisted during the Yom Kippur War, sixteen PAF pilots volunteered for service in the Air Forces of Egypt and Syria. The PAF contingent deployed to Inchas Air Base (Egypt) led by Wing Commander Masood Hatif and five other pilots plus two air defence controllers. During this war, the Syrian government decorated Flight Lieutenant Sattar Alvi when he shot down an Israeli Mirage over the Golan Heights. The PAF pilots then became instructors in the Syrian Air Force at Dumayr Air Base and after the war Pakistan continued to send military advisers to Syria and Jordan. Apart from military advisers, no Pakistani ground forces participated in this war.

In 1969, South Yemen, which was under a communist regime and a strong ally of the USSR, attacked and captured Mount Vadiya inside the province of Sharoora in Saudi Arabia. Many PAF officers as well Army personnel who were serving in Khamis Mushayt training the Saudi Air Force (the closest airbase to the battlefield), took active part in this battle in which the enemy was ultimately driven back.

During the Gulf War in 1990, the Pakistani government joined the international community in condemning the Iraqi invasion of Kuwait. Pakistan also joined the Coalition forces to expel Saadam Hussein's forces from Kuwait. However that was not an easy decision as the CoAS of the Pakistani Army was against sending Pakistani soldiers to fight the fellow Muslim nation of Iraq. This caused a rare strain in the relationship between Saudi Arabia and Pakistan. Later on, Pakistan agreed to send forces to assist the coalition forces and most of these forces were deployed along the Saudi border with Yemen, which sided with Iraq during the conflict, and Pakistani forces were also stationed around various religious sites throughout Saudi Arabia. Pakistan suffered no casualties in the conflict and later joined the UN in rebuilding Kuwait's destroyed infrastructure.

The War of 1971

The first democratic elections in Pakistan were held in 1970 with the Awami League winning with a substantial majority. However Yahya Khan banned the Awami League and declared martial law after talks on sharing power failed. Bhutto was famously heard saying "break the legs" if any member of [People's Party] attend the inaugural session at the National Assembly. Fearing on capitalization on West Pakistan, West-Pakistanis fears of East Pakistani separatist, and Bhutto demanded to form a coalition with Mujib. Both Mujib and Bhutto were agreed upon the coalition government, with Bhutto as President and Mujib as Prime minister. The Military government and General Yahya Khan was kept unaware of such of these developments. Both Bhutto and Mujib continued a political pressure on Khan's military government. Pressured by his own military government, General Yahya Khan postponed the inaugural session, and ordered to arrest Mujib and put Bhutto on house arrest. Military Police subsequently arrested Bhutto and put him on house arrest, and Mujib was sent to military court where his case was headed by Judge Advocate General Branch's Brigadier-General Rahimuddin Khan.

Faced with popular unrest and revolt in East-Pakistan, the Army and Navy clamped down through violence. The Military government of General Yahya Khan ordered Rear-Admiral Mohammad Shariff, Commander of Eastern Naval Command of the Pakistan Navy, and Lieutenant-General Amir Abdullah Khan Nazi, Commander of the Eastern Military Command of Pakistan Army, to curb and liberate East Pakistan from the resistance. The navy and army crackdown and brutalities during the Operation Searchlight and Operation Barisal and the continued killings throughout the later months resulted in further resentment among the East Pakistanis of East Pakistan. With India assisting and funding the Mukti Bahini, war broke out between the separatist supporters in Bangladesh and Pakistan (Indo-Pakistani War of 1971). During the conflict, the coordination between the armed forces of Pakistan were ineffective and unsupported.

On major decision, the army, navy, marines and air force were not taken on confidence. Each forces had led their own independent operations without notifying or taking on confidence the higher command. To release the pressure from East Pakistan the Pakistan Army opened new front at western sector when 2000 strong Pakistan army attacked Indian outpost at Longewala. where merely 120 Indian army of 23 Punjab regiment was protecting the post. The attack was backed by tank regiment but without any air support. The battle was decisively own by the Indian army with the help of Indian Air Force & resulted sutting down of western front. It was a shere example of poor coordination of Army & Airforce.

The result was the Pakistan Armed Forces's surrender to the Indian forces upon which 93,000 Pakistan Armed Forces officials and 93,000 soldiers and officers became POWs, the largest since World War II. The official war between India and Pakistan ended in just a fortnight on December 16, 1971, with Pakistan losing East Pakistan, which became Bangladesh. The official Bangladesh Government claim puts the number of Bengali civilian fatalities at 3 million.

Recovery from the 1971 War

The Military government was collapsed as a result of the war, and the control of the country was handed over to the Zulfikar Ali Bhutto. Bhutto became country's first Chief Martial Law Administrator as well as first Commander-in-Chief of Pakistan Armed Forces. As becoming the leader of his country in January 1972, Bhutto made his move and started the nuclear deterrence programme under Munir Ahmad Khan and his adviser Abdus Salam. In July 1972, Bhutto proceeded the *Shimla Agreement* with Indira Gandhi of India, and brought back 93,000 Pakistan Armed Forces personnel and recognized East-Pakistan as Bangladesh.

As part of re-organizing the country, Bhutto first disbanded the "Commander-in-Chief" title in the Pakistan Armed Forces. He also decommissioned the Pakistan Marines as a unit of Pakistan Navy. Instead, Chiefs of Staff were appointed in the three branches and Bhutto appointed all 4 star officers as the Chief of Staff in the Pakistan Armed Forces.

General Tikka Khan, infamous for his role in Bangladesh Liberation War, become the first Chief of Army Staff of Pakistan Army; Admiral Mohammad Shariff, as first 4-star admiral in the navy and as the first Chief of Naval Staff of Pakistan Navy; and, Air Chief Marshal (General) Zulfiqar Ali Khan, as first 4-star air force general, and the first Chief of Air Staffof Pakistan Air Force. Because the coordination between the armed forces were unsupported and ineffective, in 1976, Bhutto also created the office of Joint Chiefs of Staff Committee for maintaining the coordination between the armed forces.

General Muhammad Shariff, a 4-star general, was made its first Chairman of the Joint Chiefs of Staff Committee.

Pakistan's defense spending rose by 200% during the Bhutto's democratic era but the military balance between India-Pakistan, which was at a rough parity during the 1960s was growing decisively in India's favour.

Under Bhutto, the education system, foreign policy, and science policy was rapidly changed. Under Bhutto's government, the funding of science was exponentially increased; Pakistan Atomic Energy Commission's and Kahuta Research Laboratories's classified projects were launched under Bhutto. Bhutto also funded the classified military science and engineering projects, entrusted and led by Lieutenant-General Zahid Ali Akbar of the Pakistan Army Corps of Engineers.

The United States once again became a major source for military hardware following the lifting of the arms embargo in 1975 but by then Pakistan had become heavily dependent on China as an arms supplier. Heavy spending on defense re-energized the Army, which had sunk to its lowest morale following the debacle of the 1971 war. The high defense expenditure took money from other development projects such as education, health care and housing.

Baloch Nationalist Uprisings

The Baloch rebellion of the 1970s, was the most threatening civil disorder to a United Pakistan since Bangladesh's secession. The Pakistan Armed Forces wanted to establish military garrisons in Balochistan Province, which at that time was quite lawless and run by tribal justice. The ethnic Balochis saw this as a violation of their territorial rights. Emboldened by the stand taken by Sheikh Mujibur Rahman in 1971, the Baloch and Pashtun nationalists had also demanded their "provincial rights" from then Prime minister Zulfikar Ali Bhutto in exchange for a consensual approval of the Pakistan Constitution of 1973. But while Bhutto admitted the NWFP and Balochistan to a NAP-JUI coalition, he refused to negotiate with the provincial governments led by chief minister Ataullah Mengal in Quetta and Mufti Mahmud in Peshawar. Tensions erupted and an armed resistance began to take place.

Surveying the political instability, Bhutto's central government sacked two provincial governments within six months, arrested the two chief ministers, two governors and forty-four MNAs and MPAs, obtained an order from the Supreme Court banning the NAP and charged them all with high treason, to be tried by a specially constituted Hyderabad Tribunal of handpicked judges.

In time, the Baloch nationalist insurgency erupted and sucked the armed forces into the province, pitting the Baloch tribal middle classes against Islamabad. The sporadic fighting between the insurgency and the army started in 1973 with the largest confrontation taking place in September 1974 when around 15,000 Balochs fought the Pakistani Army, Navy and the Air Force. Following the successful recovery of the ammunition in the Iraqi embassy, shipped by both Iraq and Soviet Union for the Baluchistan resistance. The Naval Intelligence launched the investigation, and cited that arms were smuggled from the coastal areas of Balochistan. The Navy acted immediately, and jumped in the conflict. Vice-Admiral Patrick Simpson, commander of Southern Naval Command, began to launched the series of operation with also applying the naval blockage.

The Iranian military fearing a spread of the greater Baloch resistance in Iran also aided the Bhutto-sent Pakistan military in brutally putting down the insurrection. After three days of fighting the Baloch tribals were running out of ammunition and so withdrew by 1976. The army had suffered 25 fatalities and around 300 casualties in the fight while the rebels lost 5,000 people as of 1977.

Although major fighting had broken down, ideological schisms caused splinter groups to form and steadily gain momentum. Despite the overthrow of the Bhutto government in 1977 by General Zia-ul-Haque, Chief of Army Staff of Pakistan Army, calls for secession and widespread civil disobedience remained. The military government then appointed General Rahimuddin Khan as Martial Law Administrator over the Balochistan Province. The provincial military government under the famously authoritarian General Rahimuddin began to act as a separate entity and military regime independent of the central government.

This allowed General Rahimuddin Khan to act as an absolute Martial Law Administrator, unanswerable to the central government. Both General Zia-ul-Haq and General Rahimuddin Khan supported the declaration of a general amnesty in Balochistan to those willing to give up arms. General Rahimuddin then purposefully isolated feudal leaders such as Nawab Akbar Khan Bugti and Ataullah Mengal from provincial policy. He also militarily put down all civil disobedience movements, effectively leading to unprecedentedsocial stability within the province. Due to Martial Law, his reign was the longest in the history of Balochistan (1977–1984).

Tensions have resurfaced recently in the province with the Pakistan Army being involved in attacks against an insurgency known as the Balochistan Liberation Army. Attempted uprisings have taken place as recently as 2005.

Second Military Rule

During the 1977 elections, there were rumours of wide spread voter fraud and as such the civilian government under Zulfikar Ali Bhutto was overthrown in a bloodless coup of July 1977 and the new ruler and Bhutto's own appointed Chief of Army Staff General Zia-ul-Haq became Chief Martial Law Administrator in 1978. General Zia-ul-Haq was appointed by this position by Bhutto after Bhutto forced seventeen senior general officers to retire from the army. General Zia appointed Mushtaq Hussain, chief jurist for Bhutto's case. Mushtaq Hussain was famously known in the public as extreme hater of Bhutto, and played a controversial role in Bhutto's removal as Foreign minister in 1965. Mushtaq Hussain, now judge, disrespected Bhutto and his hometown, and further denied any appeals. Under Zia's direction and Mushtaq's order, Bhutto was controversially executed in 1979 after the Supreme Court upheld the High Court's death sentence on charges of authorizing the murder of a political opponent. Under Zia's Martial Law military dictatorship (which was declared legal under the *Doctrine of Necessity* by the Supreme Court in 1978) the following initiatives were taken:

- Strict Islamic law was introduced into the country's legal system by 1978, contributing to current-day sectarianism and religious fundamentalism, as well as instilling a sense of religious purpose within the youth.
- Pakistan fought a war by proxy against the Communists in Afghanistan in the Soviet-Afghan War, greatly contributing to the eventual withdrawal of Soviet forces from Afghanistan.
- Secessionist uprisings in Balochistan were put down by the province's authoritarian Martial Law ruler, General Rahimuddin Khan, who ruled for an unprecedented seven years under Martial Law.
- The socialist economic policies of the previous civilian government, which also included aggressive nationalisation, were gradually reversed; and Pakistan's Gross National Product rose greatly.

General Zia lifted Martial Law in 1985, holding party-less elections and handpicking Muhammad Khan Junejo to be the Prime Minister of Pakistan, who in turn rubber-stamped Zia remaining Chief of Army Staff until 1990. Junejo however gradually fell out with Zia as his political and administrative independence grew. Junejo also signed the Geneva Accord, which Zia greatly disliked. After a large-scale explosion at a munitions store in Ojhri, Junejo vowed to bring those responsible for the significant damage caused to justice, implicating several times the Inter-

Services Intelligence (ISI) Director-General Akhtar Abdur Rahman. President Zia, infuriated, dismissed the Junejo government on several charges in May 1988. He then called for the holding of fresh elections in November. General Zia-ul-Haq never saw the elections materialize however, as he died in a plane crash on August 17, 1988, which was later proven to be highly sophisticated sabotage by unknown perpetrators.

Under Zia, real defence spending increased on average by 9 percent per annum during 1977–88 while development spending rose 3 percent per annum; by 1987–88 defence spending had overtaken development spending. For 1980s as a whole, defence spending averaged 6.5 percent of GDP. This contributed strongly to large fiscal deficits and a rapid buildup of public debt.

1979–1999

Development of Atomic Bomb Projects

Soon after Bhutto came to assumed the control of Pakistan, Bhutto made his move to established the nuclear weapons development. In January 20, 1972, Abdus Salam, after being request by Zulfikar Ali Bhutto, arranged and managed secret meeting of academic scientists and engineers, in Multan city, to meet with Zulfikar Ali Bhutto who assumed the control of his country shortly after the Indo-Pakistani war of 1971 and the Bangladesh Liberation War. It was here that Bhutto orchestrated, administrated, and led the scientific research on nuclear weapons as he announced the official nuclear weapons development programme. In 1972, Pakistan's core intelligence service, the ISI, secretly learned that India was close to developing an atomic bomb, under its nuclear programme. Partially in response, defence expenditure and funding of scienceunder then-Prime minister Zulfikar Ali Bhutto increased by 200%. In the initial years and starting years, Dr. Abdus Salam, a Nobel laureate, headed the nuclear weapons program as he was the Science adviser to the Prime minister. He is also credited in bringing hundreds of Pakistani scientists, engineers, and mathematicians who would later go on to develop the nuclear weapons program and later on formed and headed *"Theoretical Physics Group"* (TPG), the special weapons division of

Pakistan Atomic Energy Commission (PAEC) that developed the designs and completed the crucial mathematical and physics calculations of the nuclear weapons.

Throughout the time, the foundations were laid down to develop a military nuclear capability. This includes the nuclear fuel cycle and nuclear weapons design, development and testing programme. The fuel cycle program included the uranium exploration, mining, refining, conversion and Uranium Hexafluoride (UF_6) production, enrichment and fuel fabrication and reprocessing facilities. These facilities were established in the Pakistan Atomic Energy Commission or PAEC by its Chairman Munir Ahmad Khan. He was appointed as Chairman of Pakistan Atomic Energy Commission (PAEC) on January 20, 1972 at the Multan Conference of senior scientists and engineers. Earlier, Munir Ahmad Khan was serving as Director of Nuclear Power and Reactors Division, IAEA. He was credited to be the "*technical father*" of Pakistan's atom project by a recent International Institute of Strategic Studies, London, (IISS) Dossier on history of the Pakistan's nuclear development, with Zulfikar Ali Bhutto as the father of Pakistan's nuclear developmental programme. Munir Ahmad Khan, an expert in Plutonium technology, had also laid the foundation and groundbreaking work for the Plutonium reprocessing technology. Khan, built the *New Laboratories*, a plutonium reprocessing plant located in Islamabad.

After Chief Martial Law Administrator (later President) and Chief of Army Staff General Zia-ul-Haq came to power, further advancements were made to enrich uranium and consolidate the nuclear development programme. On March 11, 1983, PAEC under Munir Ahmad Khan carried out the first successful cold test of a working nuclear device near at the Kirana Hills under codename *Kirana-I*. The test was led by CERN-physicist Dr. Ishfaq Ahmad, and was witnessed by other senior scientists belonging to Pakistan Armed Forces and the PAEC. To compound further matters, the Soviet Union had withdrawn from Afghanistan and the strategic importance of Pakistan to the United States was gone. Once the full extent of Pakistan's nuclear weapons development was revealed, economic sanctions were imposed on the country by several other countries, particularly United States. Having been developed under both Bhutto and Zia, the nuclear development programme had fully matured by the late 1980s. Dr. Abdul Qadeer Khan, a metallurgical engineer, greatly contributed to the uranium enrichment programme under both governments. Dr. A.Q. Khan established an administrative proliferation network through Dubai to smuggle URENCO nuclear technology to Khan Research Laboratories. He then established Pakistan's gas-centrifuge program based on the URENCO's Zippe-type centrifuge. Dr. Abdul Qadeer Khan is considered to be the founder of Pakistan's HEU based gas-centrifuge uranium enrichment programme, which was originally launched by PAEC in 1974.

The PAEC also played its part in the success and development of the uranium enrichment programme by producing the uranium hexafluoride gas feedstock for enrichment.PAEC was also responsible for all the pre and post enrichment phases of the nuclear fuel cycle. By 1986 PAEC Chairman Munir Ahmad Khan had begun work on the 50MW plutonium and tritium production reactor at Khushab, known as Khushab Reactor Complex, which became operational by 1998. After India, by the order of the Indian Premier Atal Vajpayee, successfully tested five underground nuclear tests (codename *Pokharan-II*) in Pokhran region in 1998. Pakistan, under Prime Minister Nawaz Sharif, to the distaste of the international community, successfully carried out six underground in Ras Koh region of the Chagai Hills on nuclear tests on May 28 (codename *Chagai-I*) and on Kharan region (codename *Chagai-II*) on May 30, proving Pakistan's nuclear capability. These tests were carried out by the supervision of the PAEC. These tests were supervised and observed by physicist Dr. Samar Mubarakmand and other senior academic scientists from PAEC and the KRL.

U.S. Sanctions

U.S. Senator Pressler introduced the Pressler Amendment, which imposed an embargo on all economic and military aid to Pakistan for developing nuclear weapons. This whole episode caused very negative publicity in Pakistan towards the USA as many people in Pakistan as well as the Pakistani Armed Forces believed they had risked a great deal in helping the USA give the

Soviet Union its own Vietnam in Afghanistan and when the task was done, Pakistan was promptly abandoned. Pakistan was hosting a very large Afghan refugee population and drugs from Afghanistan had infiltrated Pakistan and the use of heroin was growing to be a very widespread problem that further compounded the situation.

The embargo continued for five years and in 1995, the Brown Amendment authorised a one-time delivery of US military equipment, contracted for prior to October 1990, worth US$368 million. However, the additional 28 F-16 aircraft costing US$658 million and already paid for by Pakistan were not delivered. Unable to purchase American or NATOweaponry, Pakistan tried to develop an indigenous weapons industry, which has yielded some successes such as the development of the Al-Khalid Tank and JF-17 Strike Fighter.

Soviet-Afghan War

During the Soviet occupation of neighbouring Afghanistan, the alliance between USA and Pakistan was greatly strengthened as the USA needed Pakistan as a staging area from which to send weapons to the Mujahideens who were fighting the Soviets. Apprehensive of the threats on two front to Pakistan from India and from Soviet occupied Afghanistan, the U.S. in 1981 offered a military aid package of over $1.5 billion, which included 40 F-16 fighters, 100 M-48 tanks, nearly 200 artillery guns and over 1,000 TOW anti-tank missiles, which considerably enhanced Pakistan's defence capability. During the course of the war, Pakistan experienced several air intrusions by Afghan/Soviet pilots and claims to shooting down about 8 Afghan/Soviet aircraft over the years as well as losing one F-16 from its own fleet.

The Pakistani Military, aided by the United States and financed by Saudi Arabia, began helping the Mujahideen in setting up training camps and arming them. United States President Jimmy Carter had accepted the view that Soviet aggression could not be viewed as an isolated event of limited geographical importance but had to be contested as a potential threat to the Persian Gulf region. The uncertain scope of the final objective of Moscow in its sudden southward plunge made the American stake in an independent Pakistan all the more important.

Pakistan's Inter-Services Intelligence and Special Service Group now became actively involved in the conflict against the Soviets. Pakistan's SSG created a unit called the Black Storks who were SSG men dressed as Afghan Mujahideen during the Soviet-Afghan war. They were then flown into Afghanistan and provided the Mujahideen with support. AfterRonald Reagan became the new United States President in 1980, aid for the Mujahideen through Zia's Pakistan significantly increased. In retaliation, the KHAD, under Afghan leader Mohammad Najibullah, carried out (according to the Mitrokhin archives and other sources) a large number of terrorist operations against Pakistan, which also suffered from an influx of weaponry and drugs from Afghanistan. Pakistan also took in 3 million Afghan refugees (mostly Pashtun) who were forced to leave their country due to heavy fighting including genocide by the communist forces of Soviet Union. Although the refugees were controlled within Pakistan's largest province, Balochistan, then under martial lawruler General Rahimuddin Khan, the influx of so many refugees - believed to be the largest refugee population in the world - into several other regions had a heavy impact on Pakistan and its effects continue to this day.

PLO and Lebanese weapons captured by the Israelis in their invasion of Lebanon in June 1982 were of Soviet origin and were then covertly transferred into Afghanistan through Pakistan. Later, when American support for the Mujahideen became obvious, Stinger Missiles and other high-technology American weaponry were transferred through Pakistan into Afghanistan. However some of these weapons may have been siphoned off by the ISI for reverse engineering purposes. The arrival of the new high-technology weaponry proved to be quite helpful in organizing stiff resistance against the Soviet Union. Many Army regulars fought in Afghanistan along with the resistance and were partly instrumental in the withdrawal of Soviet forces from Afghanistan in 1989.

1st Gulf War

When Iraq occupied Kuwait The Saudi government reached agreement with Pakistan to have several brigades brought into the country to help in its defense. These brigades were placed under the orders of the Ministry of Defense and deployed in Tabuk and Khamis Mushayt.

Taliban Takeover of Afghanistan

After the Soviet withdrawal, Pakistan for the first time since 1947, was not concerned about a threat on two fronts. Further, the emergence of five independent Muslim republics in Central Asia raised hopes that they might become allies and offer Pakistan both the political support and the strategic depth it lacked. As long as Afghanistan was in chaos, Pakistan would lack direct access to the new republics.

Fighting between the Communist government in Kabul and the Mujahideen forces continued until 1992 when the Mujahideen forces, led by Ahmed Shah Massoud, removed the Soviet-backed government of Mohammad Najibullah. By 1993, the rival factions who were vying for power agreed on the formation of a government with Burhanuddin Rabbani as president, but infighting continued. Lawlessness was rampant and became a major hindrance to trade between Pakistan and the newly independent Central Asian states. Pakistan appointed the Taliban to protect its trade convoys because most of the Taliban were Pashtun and were trained by the ISI and CIA in the 1980s and could be trusted by Pakistan. With Pakistan's backing, the Taliban emerged as one of the strongest factions in Afghanistan. Pakistan then decided to the end the infighting in Afghanistan and backed the Taliban in their takeover of Afghanistan to bring stability to its western border and establish a pro-Pakistan regime in Kabul.

Pakistan solicited funds for the Taliban, bankrolled Taliban operations, providing diplomatic support as the Taliban's virtual emissaries abroad, arranged training for Taliban fighters, recruited skilled and unskilled manpower to serve in Taliban armies, planned and directed offensives, providing and facilitating shipments of ammunition and fuel, and on several occasions senior Pakistani military and intelligence officers help planned and execute major military operations. By September 1996, the Taliban under the leadership of Mullah Muhammad Omar seized control of Kabul. However, the stability in Afghanistan led to Osama bin Laden and Zawahiri to come to Afghanistan, which caused the Taliban to implement a very strict interpretation of Islamic law. The Taliban continued to capture more Afghan territory until by 2001 they controlled 90% of the country.

Siachen Glacier

After the 1971 war, another border flare-up occurred between India and Pakistan in 1984. The area of the dispute was the Siachen Glacier - the world's highest battlefield. The Glacier was under territorial dispute, but in the late 1970s and early 1980s, Pakistan began organizing several tourist expeditions to the Glacier.

India, irked by this development, mounted Operation Meghdoot, and captured the top of the Glacier by establishing a military base that it still maintains to this day at a cost of more than US$1 million per day. Pakistan on the other hand spends just under US$1 million per day, though as a percentage of GDP Pakistan spends 5 times as the Indian Military does to maintain its share of the glacier. Pakistan tried in 1987 and in 1989 to retake the whole Glacier but was unsuccessful.

The Pakistanis control the glacial valley just five kilometers southwest of Gyong La. The Pakistani Army has been unable get up to the crest of the Saltoro Ridge, while the Indians cannot come down and abandon their strategic high posts.

The line between where Indian and Pakistani troops are presently holding onto their respective posts is being increasingly referred to as the Actual Ground Position Line(AGPL).

Kargil War

After the failure of the 1989 attempt to re-take the glacier, a new and much more daring plan was developed by the Pakistan Army to re-take the glacier by blocking the Indian supplies reaching the Indian base at the top of the glacier. The plan was ready in the late 1980s but was put on hold due to the fear that this operation could lead to an all out war with India. Pakistan had recently been placed under US military sanctions for developing Nuclear weapons and the Pakistani military hierarchy believed that they did not have the proper military deterrent if the situation escalated into an all out war with India.

In the winter of 1998, a modified version of the plan was approved due to the fact that months earlier both India and Pakistan had conducted nuclear tests. Pakistan believed that it now had a deterrent to prevent all out war with India and believed that once it had taken the Kargil hills, the international community, fearing a nuclear war, would urge a secession of hostilities. Pakistan would emerge with an improved tactical advantage along the LOC and bring the Siachen Glacier conflict to the forefront of international resolution.

Some elements of the Pakistani SSG Commandos, Northern Light Infantry Forces as well as Indian Kashmiri militants planned to take over the abandoned Indian bunkers on various hills that overlooked the vital Srinagar-Leh highway that serviced the logistics base from which supplies were ferried through helicopter to the Indian Army at the top of the Siachen Glacier. The Indian Army routinely abandoned the bunkers in the winter due to the cold and snow and re-occupied them in the spring.

The Pakistani backed forces took over the bunker complex around April and May 1999, but the winter snows had melted earlier than usual and an Indian reconnaissance team sent to inspect the bunkers was wiped out by them. The Indian Army, alerted to the presence of these militants, responded quickly, forcefully and massed a huge force of around 30,000 men to re-take the Kargil hills. The Pakistani backed forces were detected very early in the operation and were not adequately prepared as they still needed another month or so before they properly established themselves on the Kargil hills, as they were short on heavy weaponry, ammunition, food, shelter, and medicine. However Pakistani troops initially managed to retain most of the heights in spite of continuous Indian attacks. Two months into the conflict, Indian troops had slowly retaken most of the ridges that were encroached by the infiltrators; according to official count, an estimated 75%–80% of the intruded area and nearly all high ground was back under Indian control.

Faced with the possibility of international isolation, the already fragile Pakistani economy was weakened further. The morale of Pakistani forces after the withdrawal declined as many units of the Northern Light Infantry suffered heavy casualties. The government refused to accept the dead bodies of many officers, an issue that provoked outrage and protests in the Northern Areas. Pakistan initially did not acknowledge many of its casualties, but Sharif later said that over 4,000 Pakistani troops were killed in the operation and that Pakistan had lost the conflict.

1999-Present

Third Military Rule

Many people in Pakistan blamed Sharif for retreating from Kargil under American pressure. Growing fiscal deficits and debt-service payments mainly due to American sanctions after Pakistan tested its Nuclear Weapons in May 1998 as a response to India had led to a financial crisis. When asked about his reason for backing down from Kargil, Sharif said that Pakistan had only enough fuel and ammunition for 3 days and the nuclear missiles were not ready at that time. This comment made many Pakistanis brand Nawaz Sharif a traitor as Army doctrine called for having at least 45 days of fuel and ammunition and to have stand by nuclear missiles ready.

Fearing that the Army might take over, Sharif attempted to dismiss his own appointed Chief of Army Staff and Chairman of Joint Chiefs of Staff Committee General Pervez Musharraf and install an ISI director-general Lieutenant-General Ziauddin Butt as Chief of Army Staff. General Musharraf, who was out of the country, boarded a commercial flight to return to Pakistan. Senior Army generals refused to accept Musharraf's dismissal. Sharif ordered the Karachi airport to prevent the landing of the airline, which then circled the skies over Karachi. In a coup d'état, the generals ousted Sharif's administration and took over the airport. The plane landed with only a few minutes of fuel to spare, and Musharraf assumed control of the government. Prime Minister Nawaz Sharif was put under house arrest and later exiled.

The coup d'état in Pakistan was condemned by most world leaders but was mostly supported by Pakistani populace. The new military government of Pervez Musharraf was heavily criticized in the United States, Saudi Arabia, United Kingdom and when

President Bill Clinton went on his landmark trip to South Asia, he only made a last minute stop in Pakistan for a few hours but spent more than five days touring and visiting India. Pakistan was also suspended from the Commonwealth Nations while Musharraf pledged to clean corruption out of politics and stabilize the economy.

On 18 August 2008, General Pervez Musharraf resigned from the post of President under impeachment pressure from the coalition government. Consequently, his website was removed since he was no longer President. He was succeeded on 6 September 2008 by Asif Ali Zardari, duly elected as Pakistan's 11th President since 1956.

Standoff with India

In response to a militant attack on the Indian Parliament on December 13, 2001 during which fourteen people, including the five men who attacked the building, were killed. India claimed that the attacks were carried out by two Pakistan based militant groups fighting Indian rule in Kashmir, Lashkar-e-Taiba (LeT) and Jaish-e-Mohammad (JeM), both of whom, were backed by Pakistan's Inter Services Intelligence (ISI) agency, a charge Pakistan denied. This led to a military standoff between India and Pakistan that resulted in the amassing of troops on either side of the International Border (IB) and along the Line of Control (LoC) in the region of Kashmir. In the Western media, coverage of the standoff focused on the possibility of a nuclear war between the two countries and the implications of the potential conflict on the United States-led War on Terrorism. Tensions de-escalated following international diplomatic mediation, which resulted in the October 2002 withdrawal of Indian and Pakistani troops from the International Border.

Military Assistance to Sri Lanka

Pakistan and Sri Lanka enjoy a strong relationship and Pakistan International Airlines planes ferrying Pakistan Army reinforcements to East Pakistan, now Bangladesh, refueled in Colombo after India denied Pakistan overflight permissions before the actual outbreak of the Indo-Pakistan war of 1971. Pakistan has sent military advisers, ammunition and other equipment to Sri Lanka during previous offensives against the LTTE. Many Sri Lankan officers are trained in Pakistan. Pakistan, by supplying high-tech military equipment such as 22 Al-Khalid main battle tanks, 250,000 rounds of 60 mm, 81 mm, 120 mm and 130 mm mortar ammunition worth and 150,000 hand grenades and along with positioning of some of its highly trained army officers in Sri Lanka, played a key role in the ultimate defeat of Tamil Tigers in May 2009. Back in 2000, when a LTTE offensive code-named Operation Ceaseless Waves overran Sri Lankan military positions in the north and captured the Elephant Pass Base and entered Jaffna, and it was being feared that the LTTE would run down thousands of Sri Lankan troops stationed in Jaffna, Pakistan supplied Multi-Barrel Rocket Launcher System and other high-tech weaponry, which halted the offensive.

War in the North-West Region

After the September 11 attacks in the United States, Pakistan joined the US-led War on Terror and helped the U.S. Military by severing ties with the Taliban and immediately deploying more than 72,000 troops along Pakistan's western border to capture or kill Taliban and al-Qaida militants fleeing from Afghanistan.

Pakistan initially garrisoned its troops in military bases and forts in the tribal areas. After several high profile terrorist attacks inside Pakistan and assassination attempts on Pervez Musharraf that Pakistan in May 2004. As Chief of Army Staff, General Pervez Musharraf ordered XII Corps and XI Corps to be stationed in FATA region and take forceful action against al-Qaedamembers in Pakistan's mountainous Waziristan area (in the Federally Administered Tribal Areas), which escalated into armed resistance by local tribesmen. On March 2004, a battle began to take place in Wana, South Waziristan. It was reported that Al-Qaeda's second-in-command dr. Ayman al-Zawahiri was among with these fighters. Pakistan responded to deploy its 10th Mountaineering Division under Major-General Noel Israel. After a week of fighting, the army suffered a major casualties with hundreds of fighters being captured. However, army was unable to Ayman al-Zawahiri as he either escaped or was never among these fighters.

Clashes erupted between the Pakistani troops and al-Qaeda's and other militants joined by local rebels and pro-Taliban forces. The Pakistani actions were presented as a part of the War on Terrorism, and had connections to the war and Taliban insurgency in Afghanistan. However, the offensive was poorly coordinated and the Pakistani Army suffered heavy casualties as well public support for the attack quickly evaporated.

After a 2-year conflict from 2004 until 2006, the Pakistani military negotiated a ceasefire with the Tribesmen from the region in which they pledged to hunt down al-Qaedamembers, stop the Talibanization of the region and stop attacks in Afghanistan and Pakistan. However, the militants did not hold up their end of the bargain and began to regroup and rebuild their strength from the previous 2 years of conflict.

The militants emboldened by their success in FATA moved into Islamabad where they sought to impose an extremist Sharia government on Pakistan. Their base of operations was the Lal Masjid in Islamabad. After a 6-month standoff fighting erupted again in July 2007 when the Pakistani Military decided to use force to end the Lal Masjid threat. Once the operation ended, the newly formed Pakistani Taliban, an umbrella group of all militants based out of FATA vowed revenge and launched a wave of attacks and suicide bombings erupted all over North-West Pakistan and major Pakistani cities throughout 2007.

The militants then expanded their base of operations and moved into the neighbouring Swat Valley and imposed a very harsh Sharia law on the scenic valley. The Army launched an offensive to re-take the Swat Valley in 2007 but was unable to clear it of the militants who had fled into the mountains and waited for the Army to leave to take over the valley again. The militants then launched another wave of terrorist attacks inside Pakistan.

The Pakistani government and military tried another peace deal with the militants in Swat Valley in 2008. This was roundly criticized in the West as abdicating to the militants. Initially pledging to lay down their arms if Sharia Law was implemented, the Pakistani Taliban used Swat Valley as a springboard to launch further attacks into neighbouring regions and reached to within

60 km of Islamabad. The public opinion turned decisively against the Pakistani Taliban when a video showing a flogging of a girl by the Pakistani Taliban in Swat Valley finally forced the army to launch a deceive attack against the Taliban occupying Swat Valley in April 2009. After heavy fighting the Swat Valley was largely pacified by July 2009 although there are isolated pockets of Taliban activity continues.

The next phase of Pakistani Army's offensive was the formidable Waziristan region. A US drone attack killed the leader of the Pakistani Taliban, Baitullah Mehsud in August in atargeted killing. A power struggle engulfed the Pakistani Taliban for the whole of September but by October a new leader had emerged, Hakimullah Mehsud. Under his leadership, the Pakistani Taliban launched another wave of terrorist attacks throughout Pakistan killing hundreds of people.

The Pakistani Army had been massing over 30,000 troops and 500 Commandos to launch a decisive offensive against the Pakistani Taliban's sanctuaries. After a few weeks of softening up the targets with air strikes and artillery and mortar attacks, the Army moved in a three pronged attack on South Waziristan. The fighting is currently continuing.

Since the conflict began, Pakistan has lost more than three times the number of its soldiers compared to the number of US troops killed in Afghanistan. However, as of 2009, the confirmed bodycount of militants killed by the Pakistan Army reached the 7,000 mark.

8

Evaluating China's Military Strength

The Department of Defence recently released its long-overdue annual report on China's military power. The document tells us much about how the Democratic Congress and the Obama administration would like to approach relations with China, and not nearly enough about China's military modernization. It suggests we have a Congress that does not take the China challenge seriously and a White House that is uncertain how to tackle it.

The problems started with the 2010 National Defence Authorization Act (NDAA), which revised the 2000 NDAA—the law that requires an annual DOD report to Congress on China's military power—in a number of ways. Most noticeably, the 2010 NDAA changed the report's title from "Military Power of the People's Republic of China" to "Military and Security Developments Involving the People's Republic of China," which obscures the report's purpose by framing China as a passive actor. China's development of an anti-satellite (ASAT) capability, for example, is not a military development involving China; it is a decision by China to enhance its military power.

Also, before the 2010 NDAA, the report's scope included "the tenets and probable development of Chinese grand strategy"; now, Congress has stripped away every mention of "grand strategy." DOD had in the past been instructed to provide analysis of "trends in Chinese strategy that would be designed to establish [China] as the leading political power in the Asia-Pacific region and as a political and military presence in other regions of the world." Now, DOD must report on "trends in Chinese security and military behavior that would be designed to achieve, or that are inconsistent with," "the goals... shaping Chinese security strategy and military strategy."

Further, since its inception, the report's purpose has been to inform the Senate and House about Chinese military power so that Congress can adequately fund U.S. defence needs; this is why the law requires that the report be submitted by March 1 of each year, long before the NDAA debates take place. But this year, not wanting to anger the Chinese—who have complained about the report year after year—the White House delayed its release, presumably excising declassified information that it deemed too provocative. (The Chinese complained anyway.) By the time the administration released the report to the public, Congress was in recess and the rest of Washington on vacation. Published too late to have the impact that it should on the congressional debate over the 2011 NDAA, and at a time when few members of Congress are likely to comment, the report has failed in its purpose: to inform Congress as it prepares the coming year's defence-spending bill.

It seems that the White House wishes to avoid an open, honest, and public debate about China's military modernization and intentions in Asia. Such a debate might make it more difficult for the administration to pursue a cooperative approach to relations with Beijing. While the recent decisions to wade into the South China Sea territorial disputes and to send the USS George Washington to exercise in the Yellow Sea—both of which elicited strident Chinese objections—suggest that the White House might be abandoning that approach, the report's handling should make outside observers think twice. At best, it suggests a confused China policy; at worst, that the president prefers "business as usual"—or rather, business as in 2009. This president seems most comfortable when he is extending an open hand; he is unlikely to quickly set aside the "strategic reassurance" policy articulated last year. If that means manipulating the public's perceptions of a rising China, then so be it.

The irony of this state of affairs, unfortunately, seems to be lost on this administration. It is Beijing—not any report produced by the Defence Department—that is primarily responsible for how China is perceived. As the new report notes, "the limited transparency in China's military and security affairs enhances uncertainty and increases the potential for misunderstanding and miscalculation." Beijing fails to satisfactorily explain the reasoning behind its aggressive military modernization, thus generating concern and suspicion amongst its neighbours and in the United States.

Unfortunately, the DOD report also fails to adequately explain Chinese military modernization. A close reading reveals that the modernization is robust, and is occurring across all of the service branches. But the report (like its predecessors) does not explain how these developments are related to each other or to Beijing's strategic goals. What role will they play in China's security strategy? In China's military strategy?

For example, this year's report, like last year's, notes that China is developing an aircraft carrier and that its navy has already started training pilots for carrier-borne aviation. But it does not explain that aircraft carriers are the quintessential instrument of military power projection. A nation does not build them if it does not see a need to project air power to distant shores. With Chinese carriers patrolling the seas, Guam, Australia, all of Southeast Asia, and the entirety of India will for the first time be in range of People's Liberation Army tactical aircraft. The 2010 report similarly lacks analysis of the developments in China's missile force. While it mentions the 2nd Artillery Corps's development of an anti-ship ballistic missile (ASBM), few details are provided, and no attempt is made to explain the impact it will have on the U.S. Navy's ability to operate in the Western Pacific.

The report is vague about the PLA's overall missile buildup as well. It notes that "China is fielding an array of conventionally armed ballistic missiles [and] ground-and air-launched land-attack cruise missiles... to hold targets at risk throughout the region." But again, there is no explanation of what this might mean for U.S. forces in the region. Can those missiles hit American bases and those of our allies? What kind of damage can they inflict?

Though you wouldn't know it from reading the report, China likely envisions using ASBMs, other ballistic and cruise missiles, future carriers, and other capabilities—including nuclear and quiet conventional attack submarines, cyber-and space-warfare assets, and an integrated air-defence system—in pursuit of its regional goals. Those goals are, in short, to unify Taiwan with the mainland, to settle East and South China Sea disputes in China's favour, and, more broadly, to assert its primacy in the region.

In a Taiwan Strait crisis, for example, the PLA could use its missile force to strike American aircraft carriers in the Western Pacific, and airbases in Japan and potentially on Guam. Strike-group ships that survived could be stalked by multiple, increasingly stealthy submarines. Meanwhile, the now-limited number of tactical aircraft that the U.S. could send to the fight would face a highly sophisticated air-defence system on the Chinese mainland, but only if they could bypass or punch through combat air patrols launched from Chinese carriers in the East China and Philippine Seas. Chinese cyber and space operations would further complicate American efforts to bring force to bear. This would leave China's air force, ground forces, and smaller surface warships to focus their efforts on Taiwan.

This is a relatively straightforward story, and one that the DOD reports have failed to tell over the years. China, thankfully, has a long way to go before it will be able to successfully pull off such an operation. But American forces in Asia are vulnerable, and increasingly so as Chinese military modernization continues. The administration should provide the American people and the U.S. Congress with a full accounting of PLA modernization and Chinese strategic goals, and of how they are linked; armed with such an accounting, Congress would be in a position to fund the military America needs for the Asia-Pacific region. Congress, of course, also has a responsibility to ensure that it is getting the information it requires. Last year's changes to the DOD China report were ill considered and should be revisited. When it comes to China, this administration seems to be pulled in two directions. It spent much of 2009 trying to reassure China that the U.S. welcomes its rise; the White House's handling of the report was one effort in that broader campaign. At the same time, there has been the occasional glimpse of a more confrontational approach to Beijing: Secretary Clinton's Internet-freedom speech, arms sales to Taiwan, Secretary

Gates's remarks at the International Institute for Strategic Studies' Asia Security Summit, and the recent diplomatic contretemps over the South China Sea.

Hopefully, the president is learning that these two approaches need not be mutually exclusive. With an honest recognition that the United States and China share some interests but not others, the president should, sooner or later, settle on the proper course: to cooperate with China on issues where goals intersect, and to vigorously defend those U.S. interests that China threatens. If the two countries can find a way to cooperate on climate change or in international economic forums, they should do so. But Washington should be less concerned with "reassuring" Beijing and more concerned with deterring it from upsetting the American-led international order.

This requires both an unwavering commitment to the security of U.S. allies and partners in Asia—including Taiwan—and the maintenance of an American preponderance of military power in the region. The role of U.S. forces in the Asia-Pacific region should be, first and foremost, to deter Chinese aggression. Absent a robust, resilient force in the region, Beijing will be tempted to resort to force to achieve its goals. And absent an honest public debate in this country about China's rise—a debate the report fails to foster—that robust, resilient force may one day be a thing of the past.

CHINESE ARMY MODERNIZATION

The Chinese People's Liberation Army (PLA) is in the third decade of a comprehensive program of modernization and transformation that began in 1979 after the PLA's last major campaign against a foreign enemy, its "self-defensive counterattack" against Vietnam. The program continues with renewed vigore into the new century.

Chinese military modernization encompasses all four services with priority of effort directed toward the PLA Navy (PLAN), the PLA Air Force (PLAAF), and the strategic missile force (known as the Second Artillery). The ground army, which previously had been the centre of gravity of the Chinese Armed Forces, remains the largest service and still provides the bulk of senior leadership for the military, but it has felt the brunt of force reductions as the PLA's mission emphasis has shifted. U.S. Army personnel who served in the post-Vietnam and post-Gulf War military should be able to appreciate the scope of what the Chinese are attempting and understand the time period required to achieve their goals.

The strategic underpinning for a long-term military modernization process was set in 1985 when China's supreme military command, the Central Military Commission (CMC), headed by paramount leader Deng Xiaoping, declared the most likely military contingency China faced to be "local, limited war" (replacing the threat of the "early, major, and nuclear war" foreseen by Mao Tse-tung).

Because the threat of major war was deemed low, senior Chinese leaders made the critical strategic decision to subordinate military modernization to other aspects of national economic development, such as agriculture, industry, and science and technology. Thus, in the 1980s and early 1990s, the Chinese Government did not spend vast sums of money and national resources to rapidly modernize the PLA. The "bloated" PLA could take its time to reform, focusing first on downsizing its 4-million-plus force.

For the first 10 years of modernization, China perceived its major potential foe to be the Soviet Union. Using force to reunify Taiwan with the mainland was low on the list of China's military priorities. By the mid-1990s, the situation between the mainland and Taiwan had changed considerably. A multiparty democratic form of government was taking hold on the island, and voices for independence had risen. After the 1995-1996 crisis in the Taiwan Strait, China's leaders decided they needed to develop military capabilities more rapidly to prevent what Beijing perceived as further steps toward Taiwanese independence.

Although Chinese leaders preferred peaceful reunification of the island with the mainland, they knew Taiwan and its supporters in the United States had to see China's military power as credible. As a result, after 1999 the intensity of the PLA's modernization process increased, focusing principally on the goal of deterring Taiwan's independence and, if necessary, on imposing the will of

Chinese leaders by force. Although the Taiwanese scenario became the top planning priority, training for a variety of military missions continued throughout the country and in all PLA units.

The acceleration of PLA modernization after 1999 became possible to a large extent because of the confluence of a more specifically defined mission, the availability of increased resources, a smaller force, and 20 years of previous effort that had laid the groundwork for what was to follow.

In particular, many advances in the PLA since 1999 have taken advantage of the Nation's impressive economic growth during the 1990s, especially developments in the Chinese electronics industry. The end of the Soviet threat, along with the availability of advanced military weapons from a cash-strapped Russian Government, also contributed to changes in China's strategic posture in the late 1990s. Still, despite some marked improvements in China's military capabilities, the effectiveness of PLA modernization has yet to be proven in battle against a hostile force.

Elements of Modernization

By the turn of the 21st century, several distinct but interrelated elements have been seen in the PLA's modernization program. The following components of modernization were directly linked to developments of the previous two decades and enhanced by increased resources available since 1995:

* Reduction in force size.
* Changes in force structure.
* Reform of the structure and missions of the reserves and militia.
* Changes in the personnel system.
* An influx of new equipment.
* Doctrinal revision to prepare the PLA to fight and win Local Wars Under Modern High-Technology Conditions or Local Wars Under Informationalization Conditions.
* Improvements in the frequency, content, and methods of military training, with emphasis on joint operations.
* Transformation of the PLA logistics system.

* Enhancement of all soldiers' standard of living, pay, and lifestyle.
* Modification of the professional military education system.

Members of the U.S. Army will appreciate the complexity of the PLA's transformation, its long-term nature, and the difficulty of the tasks Chinese military leaders face. The PLA is also pursuing modernization with a much smaller resource and combat experience base than did the U.S. Army in the 1970s and 1990s. On the positive side, the PLA's modernization goals are more manageable because, unlike the U.S. Army, the PLA does not seek to project force across oceans, and it limits its scope of operations to what it considers protection of Chinese sovereignty (which, by definition, includes Taiwan and much of the South China Sea). The PLA does not have to man foreign bases and respond to a web of defence commitments throughout the world. Moreover, unlike the U.S. Army, the PLA remains a party-army bonded by loyalty to the Chinese Communist Party.

Security apparatus. The PLA is one of three elements of the Chinese Armed Forces, each of which is a separate, distinct organization, although all are closely related. According to China's National Defence Law of March 1997, Chinese Armed Forces are composed of the—

* PLA, both active and reserve units.
* People's Armed Police (PAP) Force.
* People's militia (ordinary and primary units).

The PLA is primarily responsible for defending China from external threats, with the secondary mission of domestic security in accordance with the law; that is, when requested by local authorities and approved by the central leadership. The ultimate command authority for the PLA is the CMC, with command running through four general headquarters departments in Beijing to the forces deployed in seven military regions throughout the country. The PLA, PAP, and militia wear similar but distinct uniforms, have similar organizational and rank structures, and undergo similar basic training, but they have separate systems for command and control, funding, promotion, education, and training. All three support national economic development with labour and service projects and can be mobilized to provide rescue and relief support in the event of floods, earthquakes, and other natural disasters. The PAP and militia are paramilitary organizations. By law and in practice, the PAP is not part of the PLA, although it is sometimes mistakenly called military police by Chinese and foreign sources alike. The PAP's primary mission, worked in conjunction with the Ministry of Public Security police force, is internal security. The PAP has a dual command structure that includes the CMC and the State Council through the Ministry of Public Security. Its secondary mission is to help the PLA in local defence against external enemies.

The militia supports the PLA in time of war and also helps maintain public order when necessary. The PLA chain of command and local civilian governments are in the militia's command structure. They cooperate through established joint civilian-military organizational mechanisms. The 1.7-million-person civilian Ministry of Public Security police force is primarily responsible for law enforcement and domestic security. It and the Ministry of State Security, with the missions of counterespionage and domestic and foreign intelligence, respond to the State Council and are not part of the Chinese Armed Forces. However, in its annual human fights reports, the U.S. Department of State (DOS) includes the Ministry of Public Safety with the PLA, the PAP, the Ministry of State Security, and "the state judicial, procuratorial, and penal systems" as part of the Chinese Government's security apparatus.

According to a recent DOS report, "[c]ivilian authorities generally maintained effective control of the security forces." What kind of control they exercised is not altogether clear because "[s]ecurity policy and personnel were responsible for numerous human rights abuses.... At times, police used excessive force against demonstrators." There is no recent confirmed evidence of the PLA being used routinely to control domestic demonstrations or dots, although that could change if the civilian police force and PAP fail in their missions.

The PLA is also distinct from the civilian-run (but mostly government-owned) defence industrial sector composed of some 2 million workers and thousands of enterprises that produce and sell military equipment and civilian goods and services.

Reductions in force. The PLA has undergone two large reductions in force in the past decade, starting with about 3 million people in 1995 and losing 500,000 people from 1997 to 2000 and another 200,000 from 2003 to 2005. By the end of 2005 the PLA have about 2.3 million people on its active duty roster. As the largest component of the PLA with the lowest priority in modernization, army ground forces suffered the largest proportion of cuts. Current estimates put the number at 1.6 million—town about 500,000 from 1995. Reserve personnel, most of whom are in reserve army units, number about 800,000. The PAP might have up to 1.5 million in its ranks. The primary militia, according to a 2004 defence white paper, has 10 million members, but the number of ordinary militia, presumably a larger force, was not announced.

While PLA active duty forces have been cut by approximately 23 percent over the past 10 years, the officially announced defence budget has nearly quadrupled from about 64 billion yuan in 1995 to 248 billion yuan in 2005. Yet these figures do not account for the total funds available to the PLA from extra-budgetary sources, such as support from local governments and special budgets for the purchase of foreign weapons. The PLA-watching community has debated exactly what should be included in estimates of actual Chinese defence expenditures and what factor should be applied to announced budget numbers to arrive at true defence spending. Estimates range from about 1.5 to 3 times (or greater) the announced figure. Whatever the true amount of funds available, such a large force is still relatively resource-constrained; thus, PLA leaders constantly look for ways to save money as new equipment enters the force and training opportunities increase. Future personnel reductions with increased defence budgets would not be surprising.

ARMY OF THE FUTURE

In the past, some defence specialists insisted a Chinese attack on Taiwan would be a "million-man swim" across the Taiwan Strait because of the country's lack of troop-carrying ships. "We left the million-man swim behind in about 1998, 1999," the senior Pentagon official said. "And in fact, what people are saying now, whether or not that was ever useful, is that it's a moot point, because in just amphibious lift alone, the Chinese are doubling or even quadrupling their capability on an annual basis."

Asked about a possible Chinese attack on Taiwan, the official put it bluntly: "In a time frame, a capability was there that a year ago we would have said was very, very unlikely. We now assess that as being very likely to be there." Air Force Gen. Paul V. Hester, head of the Pacific Air Forces, said the U.S. military has been watching China's military buildup but has found it difficult to penetrate Beijing's "veil" of secrecy over it. While military modernization itself is not a major worry, "what does provide you a pause for interest and concern is the amount of modernization, the kind of modernization and the size of the modernization," he said during a recent breakfast meeting with reporters. China is building capabilities such as aerial refueling and airborne warning and control aircraft that can be used for regional defence and long-range power projection, Gen. Hester said.

It also is developing a maneuverable re-entry vehicle, or MARV, for its nuclear warheads. The weapon is designed to counter U.S. strategic-missile defences, according to officials who spoke on the condition of anonymity. The warhead would be used on China's new DF-31 long-range missiles and its new submarine missile, the JL-2. Work being done on China's weapons and reconnaissance systems will give its military the capability to reach 1,000 miles into the sea, "which gives them the visibility on the movement of not only our airplanes in the air, but also our forces at sea," Gen. Hester said.

Beijing also has built a new tank for its large armed forces. It is known as the Type 99 and appears similar in design to Germany's Leopard 2 main battle tank. The tank is outfitted with new artillery, anti-aircraft and machine guns, advanced fire-control systems and improved engines. The country's air power is growing through the purchase of new fighters from Russia, such as Su-30 fighter-bombers, as well as the development of its own fighter jets, such as the J-10.

Gen. Hester compared Chinese warplanes with those of the former Soviet Union, which were less capable than their U.S.

counterparts, but still very deadly. "They have great equipment. The fighters are very technologically advanced, and what we know about them gives us pause for concern against ours," he said. Missiles also are a worry.

"It is their surface-to-air missiles, their [advanced] SAMs and their surface-to-surface missiles, and the precision, more importantly, of those surface-to-surface missiles that provide, obviously, the ability to pinpoint targets that we might have out in the region, or our friends and allies might have," Gen. Hester said. The advances give the Chinese military "the ability... to reach out and touch parts of the United States — Guam, Hawaii and the mainland of the United States," he said. To better deal with possible future conflicts in Asia, the Pentagon is modernizing U.S. military facilities on the Western Pacific island of Guam and planning to move more forces there. The Air Force will regularly rotate Air Expeditionary Force units to Guam and also will station the new long-range unmanned aerial vehicle known as Global Hawk on the island, he said.

It also has stationed B-2 stealth bombers on Guam temporarily and is expected to deploy B-1 bombers there, in addition to the B-52s now deployed there, Gen. Hester said.

Projecting power

China's rulers have adopted what is known as the "two-island chain" strategy of extending control over large areas of the Pacific, covering inner and outer chains of islands stretching from Japan to Indonesia. "Clearly, they are still influenced by this first and second island chain," the intelligence official said. The official said China's buildup goes beyond what would be needed to fight a war against Taiwan. The conclusion of this official is that China wants a "blue-water" navy capable of projecting power far beyond the two island chains. "If you look at the technical capabilities of the weapons platforms that they're fielding, the sea-keeping capabilities, the size, sensors and weapons fit, this capability transcends the baseline that is required to deal with a Taiwan situation militarily," the intelligence official said. "So they are positioned then, if [Taiwan is] resolved one way or the other, to really become a regional military power as well."

The dispatch of a Han-class submarine to waters near Guam, Taiwan and Japan was an indication of the Chinese military's drive to expand its oceangoing capabilities, the officials said. The submarine surfaced in Japanese waters, triggering an emergency deployment of Japan's naval forces. Beijing later issued an apology for the incursion, but the political damage was done. Within months, Japan began adopting a tougher political posture toward China in its defence policies and public statements. A recent Japanese government defence report called China a strategic national security concern. It was the first time China was named specifically in a Japanese defence report.

Energy supply a factor

For China, Taiwan is not the only issue behind the buildup of military forces. Beijing also is facing a major energy shortage that, according to one Pentagon study, could lead it to use military force to seize territory with oil and gas resources. The report produced for the Office of Net Assessment, which conducts assessments of future threats, was made public in January and warned that China's need for oil, gas and other energy resources is driving the country toward becoming an expansionist power. China "is looking not only to build a blue-water navy to control the sea lanes [from the Middle East], but also to develop undersea mines and missile capabilities to deter the potential disruption of its energy supplies from potential threats, especially in the case of a conflict with Taiwan," the report said. The report said China believes the United States of America already controls the sea routes from the oil-rich Persian Gulf through the Malacca Strait. Chinese President Hu Jintao has called this strategic vulnerability to disrupted energy supplies Beijing's "Malacca Dilemma."

To prevent any disruption, China has adopted a "string of pearls" strategy that calls for both offensive and defensive measures stretching along the oil-shipment sea lanes from China's coast to the Middle East. The "pearls" include the Chinese-financed seaport being built at Gwadar, on the coast of western Pakistan, and commercial and military efforts to establish bases or diplomatic ties in Bangladesh, Burma, Cambodia, Thailand and disputed islands in the South China Sea. The report stated that China's ability to use these pearls for a "credible" military action is not certain.

The rapid Chinese naval buildup includes the capability to project power to these sea lanes in the future. "They are not doing a lot of surface patrols or any other kind of security evolutions that far afield," the intelligence official said. "There's no evidence of [Chinese military basing there] yet, but we do need to keep an eye toward that expansion." The report also highlighted the vulnerability of China's oil and gas infrastructure to a crippling U.S. attack.

"The U.S. military could severely cripple Chinese resistance [during a conflict over Taiwan] by blocking its energy supply, whereas the [People's Liberation Army navy] poses little threat to United States' energy security," it said. China views the United States as "a potential threat because of its military superiority, its willingness to disrupt China's energy imports, its perceived encirclement of China and its disposition toward manipulating international politics," the report said.

'Mercantilist measures'

The report stated that China will resort "to extreme, offensive and mercantilist measures when other strategies fail, to mitigate its vulnerabilities, such as seizing control of energy resources in neighbouring states." U.S. officials have said two likely targets for China are the Russian Far East, which has vast oil and gas deposits, and Southeast Asia, which also has oil and gas resources. Michael Pillsbury, a former Pentagon official and specialist on China's military, said the internal U.S. government debate on the issue and excessive Chinese secrecy about its military buildup "has cost us 10 years to figure out what to do" "Everybody is starting to acknowledge the hard facts," Mr. Pillsbury said. "The China military buildup has been accelerating since 1999. As the buildup has gotten worse, China is trying hard to mask it."

Richard Fisher, vice president of the International Assessment and Strategy Centre, said that in 10 years, the Chinese army has shifted from a defensive force to an advanced military soon capable of operations ranging from space warfare to global non-nuclear cruise-missile strikes. "Let's all wake up. The post-Cold War peace is over," Mr. Fisher said. "We are now in an arms race with a new superpower whose goal is to contain and overtake the United States."

CHINA'S GROWING MILITARY

China's defence budget rose 10.7% this year to USD114.3 billion. The White Paper claims, "Over the years, the PLA has been proactively and steadily pushing forward its reforms in line with the requirements of performing its missions and tasks,and building an informationised military."

The PLA is becoming more mobile with smaller modular units, yet it has also shrunk dramatically after undergoing progressive downsizing in 1985, 1997 and 2003. These programmes reduced the armed forces by one million, 500,000 and 200,000 personnel respectively. In other words, the PLA cut its size by 40+% over a ten-year period! Today the army service of the PLA has total manpower of 850,000. The PLA Navy (PLAN) is a major beneficiary of new equipment under China's offshore defence strategy; a blue-water capability is necessary to conduct mobile operations, cooperate internationally and counter non-traditional security threats. The PLAN has 235,000 personnel and the PLA Air Force (PLAAF) 398,000 people.

Modernisation of the armed forces cannot be separated from the transformation of Chinese society in general. The PLA was a very late starter in terms of modernisation. In the 1980s, expenditure was static so the defence budget started from a very low baseline. Since then the budget has grown in parallel with the economy as a whole. Rather than raw figures, the percentage of GDP is a better indicator of defence spending levels. In the past decade it has varied from 1.22% to 1.42%, which is not outlandish. In contrast, the USA averaged 4.7% in 2010-11. Furthermore, unlike Europe and the USA, China does not have a network of alliances and international technological partners with which it can jointly develop weaponry. China is not pursuing a sudden arms race, but it is gradually upgrading a hopelessly obsolete force. Much spending goes to improving pay and living conditions – for example, in 2011 salaries and benefits for non-commissioned officers (NCO) increased 40%.Despite new equipment reaching the PLA, older weapon systems predominate. For instance, only a third of in-service ground systems can be considered modern. Similarly, just 25% of naval surface vessels and aircraft are modern. Comparing raw numbers of weapons on paper does not reflect just how outdated PLA equipment in China's inventory actually is. China recognises its equipment cannot compete directly with that of the USA, for instance. Additionally, the aircraft and amphibious vessels necessary to project power from Chinese shores are also lacking. Most analysts agree that the PLAN's capability still falls behind that of Japan's navy.

China has no recent combat experience either. Our recently commissioned Liaoning aircraft carrier is an all-new capability and it will take years to master its use. In comparison, the US Navy has a wealth of accumulated wisdom after operating carriers for 91 years. It is inevitable a nation will develop its military as its economic power rises. During the Cold War, the Soviet Union was launching a new submarine every month. In comparison, China's build-up has been measured and unhurried.

Defence Minister Liang Guanglie told US Defence Secretary Robert Gates in January 2011, "I also firmly believe that in terms of the level of modernisation of the PLA, we can by no means call ourselves an advanced military force. The gap between us and that of advanced countries is at least two to three decades."

It is true there are maritime territorial disputes in the East China and South China Seas. However, the PLA has been careful not to get involved. These are the domain of the China Marine Surveillance (CMS) agency. It is hoped these disputes can be solved diplomatically, as China has strong historical claims on these territories. Another half-baked idea thrown around, particularly by Indian media, is the 'string of pearls' notion of Chinese naval ports stretching across the Indian Ocean. This theory has no truth, something confirmed by Jane's Intelligence Review in an article entitled 'Harbouring Ambitions' published in November 2009. China contributed financially to build commercial ports in Myanmar (Sittwe), Bangladesh (Chittagong), Sri Lanka (Hambantota) and Pakistan (Gwadar), but these are not used for naval purposes. Conversely, the USA maintains bases or has access to facilities in Japan, South Korea, the Philippines, Guam, Australia and Singapore. This is the equivalent of China possessing naval bases in Canada, Mexico, Cuba and Greenland to surround the North American continent. Such an action would doubtlessly make Americans feel uncomfortable. The Chinese people feel the same way about this robust US presence. To date, China has made no effort to establish overseas bases, and it even declined an offer from the Seychelles Islands.

Painful History

The USA complains the PLA is "not transparent". It must be remembered that China is emerging from a very turbulent past. While the military may not yet have attained the standards of US or European openness, it is making progress. A series of White Papers has given progressively more information as the country moves towards greater transparency. Since 2002, the PLA has held 28 joint exercises and 34 joint training sessions with 31 different countries as it opens up. Indeed, on 6 September three PLAN warships sailed into Hawaii to begin a three-day search-and-rescue exercise with the US Navy. The last such visit to US territory was seven years ago.

Remember, too, that history has scarred the Chinese psyche. European nations invaded and imposed unfair treaties on China (e.g. the opium wars). Japan's invasion from 1937-45 caused terrible suffering and resulted in numerous atrocities. That conflict left 20 million dead and 100 million internal refugees. Japan has not fully admitted to many atrocities (e.g. the Nanjing Massacre), and this is a deep-seated irritant in Sino-Japanese relations. An increasingly nationalistic Japan is thus a great source of concern. Prime Minister Shinzo Abe's promise to restore his country's "greatness" is like a red rag to our nation. China has already suffered from Japanese nationalism, and we remain mistrustful of European, US and Japanese intentions based on past injustices.

Multiple Tasks

In fact, the PLA has little time for 'regional or global domination'! Common threats frequently highlighted by the

Chinese government are terrorism, separatism and extremism. Uygur separatists in Xinjiang Province, for example, are constantly fomenting trouble. The country has 22,000km of land borders with 14 neighbours, plus an 18,000km coastline. Safeguarding these borders is difficult and arduous, and it occupies a good proportion of the country's manpower.

The PLA is also responsible for providing support in cases of natural disaster and public-health outbreaks (e.g. SARS). For example, in 2008, the armed forces/ militia contributed 1.26 million members to combat snowstorms in southern China. Another 221,000 mobilised after the deadly Sichuan earthquake that year. In 2011-12, the PLA contributed 370,000 servicemen, 197,000 vehicles/pieces of equipment, obilised 870,000 militiamen/reservists and flew 225 sorties to support rescue operations.

The PLA is constitutionally required to support national and local plans for economic and social development too. It commits personnel and assets to key infrastructure projects, environmental protection and poverty alleviation measures. The PLA does much more than defend the country, for it is an integral component of societal development and improving people's livelihood.

Greater Reach

Fuelled by a booming economy, the PRC needs to import a continuous stream of raw materials. It must then send its commodities to export markets, primarily by sea. Last year, China's imports and exports were worth USD3.87 trillion, surpassing the USA for the first time and making China the globe's largest trader. The country thus needs to protect its sea lines of communication (SLOC), and non-traditional security threats such as piracy in the Gulf of Aden have demonstrated the need for countries to protect domestic shipping. China, as a responsible global player, has worked closely with other nations to successfully thwart would-be pirates. Since the first naval task force was despatched to the Gulf of Aden on 26 December 2008, the PLAN had escorted 4,984 ships till the end of last year.

Some say China does not contribute enough to international alliances, but the facts reveal otherwise. The PLA has despatched 22,000 personnel to 23 United Nations (UN) peacekeeping missions to date. As at July 2013, 1,703 officers and soldiers were deployed on UN missions. Of the five permanent members of the UN Security Council, China supplies more personnel than any other. The USA, for instance, had a mere 24 servicemen on UN missions, and the UK just 278. Furthermore, since 2002, the PLA has conducted 36 international humanitarian-aid missions to 27 disaster-struck countries.

The PLAN conducted a landmark evacuation of nationals from Libya in 2011. In the PRC's largest ever overseas evacuation, the rescue of 35,860 nationals was assisted by a frigate (on a Gulf of Aden escort mission at the time) and four aircraft. Such crises demonstrate the need for a capable navy, as China does not wish to rely on external powers like the USA to protect its people and interests.

CHINA'S MILITARY PREPARING FOR 'PEOPLE'S WAR' IN CYBERSPACE, SPACE

China's military is preparing for war in cyberspace involving space attacks on satellites and the use of both military and civilian personnel for a digital "people's war," according to an internal Chinese defence report.

"As cyber technology continues to develop, cyber warfare has quietly begun," the report concludes, noting that the ability to wage cyber war in space is vital for China's military modernization.

According to the report, strategic warfare in the past was built on nuclear weapons. "But strategic warfare in the information age is cyber warfare," the report said.

"With the reliance of information warfare on space, cyberspace will surely become a hot spot in the struggle for cyberspace control," the report said.

The new details of Chinese plans for cyber and space warfare were revealed in a report "Study on Space Cyber Warfare" by four engineers working at a Chinese defence research centre in Shanghai.

The report presents a rare inside look of one of Beijing's most secret military programs: Cyber warfare plans against the United States in a future conflict. "Cyber warfare is not limited to military personnel. All personnel with special knowledge and skills on information system may participate in the execution of cyber warfare. Cyber warfare may truly be called a people's warfare," the report says.

People's War was first developed by China's Communist founder Mao Zedong as a Marxist-Leninist insurgency and guerrilla warfare concept. Chinese military theorists are adapting Mao's peasant uprising stratagem for a future conflict with the United States.A defence official said the report was recently circulated in military and intelligence circles. Its publication came as a surprise to many in the Pentagon because in the past, U.S. translations of Chinese military documents on similar warfighting capabilities were not translated under a directive from policy officials seeking to prevent disclosure of Chinese military writings the officials feared could upset U.S.-China relations.

A Chinese government spokesman could not be reached for comment. However, Chinese spokesmen in the past have denied reports that China engages in cyber attacks.

The study links China's space warfare development programs with its extensive cyber warfare capabilities. Both programs are considered "trump card" weapons that would allow a weaker China to defeat a militarily stronger United States in a conflict.

"Cyber warfare is an act of war that utilizes space technology; it combines space technology and cyber technology and maintains and seizes the control of cyberspace," the study says.

Because cyberspace relies on satellites, "space will surely be the main battlefield of cyber warfare," the report said.

Satellites and space vehicles are considered the "outer nodes" of cyber space and "are clear targets for attack and may be approached directly," the report said, adding that ground-based cyberspace nodes are more concealed and thus more difficult to attack.

Additionally, satellites have limited defences and anti-jamming capabilities, leaving them very vulnerable to attack.

The report reveals that China's military, which controls the country's rapidly growing space program, is preparing to conduct space-based cyber warfare—"cyber reconnaissance, jamming, and attack"—from space vehicles. Space-based cyber warfare will include three categories: space cyber attack, space cyber defence, and space cyber support. The space cyber support involves reconnaissance, targeting, and intelligence gathering.

"A space cyber-attack is carried out using space technology and methods of hard kill and soft kill," the report said. "It ensures its own control at will while at the same time uses cyberspace to disable, weaken, disrupt, and destroy the enemy's cyber actions or cyber installations."

Soft-kill methods are designed to disrupt or damage cyberspace links using jamming, network cyber attacks, and "deceit" in the electromagnetic domain.

The cyber attacks include launching computer viruses, theft and tampering of data, denial of service attacks, and "detonation of [a] network bomb that can instantaneously paralyze or destroy enemy's information network."

"Soft kill measures are well concealed, fast in action, and the attack can be accomplished before the enemy even has time to discover it," the report said. "Soft kill measures are deceptive and well hidden; they are difficult to detect and monitor."

Hard-kill cyber attack weapons include missiles and other "kinetic" weapons along with directed energy, including lasers, radio frequency weapons, and particle beam weapons.

Chinese cyber warfare capabilities are one of the People's Liberation Army's (PLA) most closely guarded secrets, along with its anti-satellite missile and jamming program.

The topic of military cyber warfare was recently discussed by U.S. and Chinese military and defence officials at a meeting earlier this month of the U.S.-China Strategic and Economic Dialogue in Washington.

The *Washington Free Beacon* obtained a copy of the recently translated report, dated December 2012 and published in the journal Aerospace Electronic Warfare. The journal is a bimonthly publication of the Institute 8511, part of the China Aerospace Science and Industry Corp. (CASIC), a state-run missile manufacturer and high-technology aerospace research centre.

Institute 8511 develops electronic warfare offense and defence weapons, countermeasure technologies, and command and control systems for aircraft and missiles. The institute in the past also developed China's DF-21D anti-ship ballistic missile, a unique weapon that uses precision guidance to attack U.S. aircraft carriers at sea.

The defence official said Institute 8511 is located close to the PLA's premier cyber warfare headquarters in Shanghai, known as Unit 61398. That unit was identified in a report last February by the security firm Mandiant as the main origin of widespread military cyber attacks on the West.

According to the report, China's goal for cyber war calls for using high-technology weapons in cyberspace to achieve military objectives.

"Since cyberspace is boundless and transcends land, sea, air, and space, cyber warfare is not constrained by territorial land or territorial sea, and there is no difference between the front and the rear of the battlefield," the report said. "The advantage of cyber warfare is its global nature; it has global alert, global resources, and global access."

Additionally, war in cyberspace is not constrained by nighttime, weather, or geography and can be conducted at any time, key factors that have limited conventional warfighting in the past.

In line with Chinese military doctrine that calls for sudden attacks and the element of surprise, the report said cyberwarfare is ideal for rapid attacks that are difficult for an enemy to identify.

"This suddenness can often leave cyber warfare without a trace and without damaging the physical installation or personnel, and yet it can change the trend and outcome of war by affecting the operational effectiveness in an instance."

A second recently translated military report by two PLA colonels calls for China to adopt a new military doctrine called "trump card and data link-centric warfare" that is based on the U.S. war fighting doctrine called "network-centric warfare."

The two colonels, Sr. Col. Du Wenlong and Sr. Col. Xie Zhaohui, call for a new strategic concept designed to attack and defeat the United States using advanced command, control, communications, computers, intelligence, surveillance, and reconnaissance, what the military calls C4ISR and the key to conducting combined arms warfare. The colonels call for new weapons and other military capabilities "to penetrate and to strike as quickly as possible ... and ensure that our military will win the warfare under the informatized conditions."

"Should the United States military's transformation model of 'network-centric warfare' become a success, it will undoubtedly and completely change the mode and means of warfare, making warfare even more sudden and its outcome even quicker to come, generating unmatched asymmetrical advantages," the colonels said. "This will inevitably greatly strengthen its arrogance, enabling it to have its own way to an even bigger extent and to promote its politics of hegemony."

Publication of the new cyber warfare report provides a more recent example of the contradiction between internal Chinese military writings and public statements. A 1999 book produced for the Pentagon's Office of Net Assessment and edited by China specialist Michael Pillsbury first reveals the contradiction.

The book, "Chinese Views of Future Warfare," influenced many senior Pentagon and military leaders' views of China by showing that internal Chinese military writings discussed plans for war with the United States, considered China's main enemy. The writings contrasted sharply with frequent public statements by China that its arms buildup is purely defensive and not directed at any country.

Richard Fisher, a Chinese military affairs expert, said the Chinese report reveals China's merger of cyber warfare and space warfare efforts. Fisher said the Chinese military understands that U.S. satellites are critical to relaying computer data traffic and are vulnerable to direct attack.

"China has already demonstrated two anti-satellite weapons: ground based lasers in 2006 and then the SC-19 [anti-satellite] missile in 2007. A higher Medium Earth Orbit (MEO) capable ASAT called DN02 may have been tested recently," Fisher said.

China also is pressing for a space arms agreement at the same time it is building up its space forces, Fisher said.

"The bottom line today is that China's first priority is building the means to win wars in space while using space diplomacy to disarm its potential enemies," he said. U.S. cyber warfare strategy was recently disclosed in a top-secret Presidential Policy Directive-20 that was made public by former National Security Agency contractor Edward Snowden.

The directive outlines the use of military cyber attacks that "can offer unique and unconventional capabilities to advance U.S. national objectives around the world with little or no warning to the adversary or target and with potential effects ranging from subtle to severely damaging."

A third Chinese document from 2005 that was translated recently by the U.S. government reveals that Chinese military planners are preparing to destroy or disable up to eight Global Positioning System satellites. The satellites are critical for U.S. military precision guided missiles and bombs.

"Eliminating two groups of GPS satellites can prevent GPS satellites from providing navigation service around the clock," the study stated. "The effect of dropping these GPS satellites on the navigation accuracy of GPS satellites is quite obvious," the study, "Research on Voidness of GPS," said.

A STRATEGIC CROSSROADS FOR CHINESE MILITARY POWER

The 2005 Department of Defence Annual Report to Congress on "The Military Power of the People's Republic of China" is to be commended for providing context, up-to-date information, and some new details about the complex subject of the People's Liberation Army's (PLA) modernization program. The Report raises the question of choices China's leaders must make as the country faces "a strategic crossroads," grows economically, and expands its international influence. It highlights many capabilities the PLA is developing, but also casts doubt on the intentions of the Chinese leadership with statements such as:

"China does not now face a direct threat from another nation. Yet, it continues to invest heavily in its military, particularly in programs designed to improve power projection. The pace and scope of China's military build-up are, already, such as to put regional military balances at risk. Current trends in China's military modernization could provide China with a force capable of prosecuting a range of military options in Asia – well beyond Taiwan – potentially posing a credible threat to modern militaries operating in the region."

Shortly after the release of the Report, Joint Chiefs Vice Chairman General Peter Pace reminded that military threats include both capabilities and intent. Hopefully, the Report can become a vehicle to spur informed discussion about Chinese military capabilities and intentions, and perhaps result in a better understanding of the often confusing and contradictory signals and implications of PLA modernization.

However, the full content of the Report must be carefully examined before conclusions can be drawn. For example, in the Executive Summary, there are at least five qualifiers in the forecast "Over the long term, if current trends persist, PLA capabilities could pose a credible threat to other modern militaries operating in the region." Change any qualifier and the meaning of the sentence changes. Simplify the sentence by omitting a phrase (as headlines often do) and the meaning is changed. In the next paragraph, the Report makes this current assessment: "The PLA is working toward these goals…We assess that China's ability to project conventional military power beyond its periphery remains limited." While frustrating for those who want certain, unambiguous judgments, such craftsmanship reflects the Report's acknowledgement that, "the findings and conclusions are based on incomplete data." Unfortunately, to some extent, the Report itself is not as complete as it could be.

The Report is correct to mention "the PLA's routine publication of a biannual Defence White Paper demonstrates some improvement in transparency," but also notes that "China's leaders continue to guard closely basic information on the quantity and quality of the Chinese armed forces." What the Report didn't say was that in 2004 foreign observers (including U.S. allies) were invited to watch 1) a marine brigade conduct amphibious operations at Shanwei, Guangdong, 2) the 127th Light Mechanized Division execute joint training at a regional combined arms training centre, and 3) a hostage-rescue demonstration conducted by the Beijing

Military Region's Special Operations unit at its garrison. While not an "all access pass" to these exercises, these are notable steps in allowing outsiders to observe conditions in PLA combat forces. Marines and Special Operations units are identified in the Report as among the small number of PLA "expeditionary forces," and the 127th is the first division of its type to be transformed. However, in each case, U.S. observers were not invited (unlike in 2003 when they viewed an exercise in Inner Mongolia).

Though the Report contains much information, some elements could have been presented more clearly and in more detail. While it should be credited with the first-time enumeration of both numbers of missiles and launchers in the short-range ballistic missile force and listing specific naval vessel acquisitions, the Report did not give any indication of either the number of third and fourth generation aircraft, such as Su-27/30, F-10, F-11, FC-1, and FB-7, or their percentage in the force. Moreover, no assessment was included about pilot proficiency, tactics, and maintenance for these new aircraft. Later, an important judgment about the training of expeditionary forces is made: "Combined training for all these units [airborne, special operations, amphibious, and marine units] is seldom conducted in a major amphibious assault exercise." This conclusion is a significant change from the 2002 Report which stated, "In 2001, PLA training emphasized maritime and amphibious operations, integrating conventional ground units with marines, airborne, and special operations forces."

In describing the Chinese military as the largest in the world, the Report noted, "China's military comprises four services...A fifth element consists of the paramilitary People's Armed Police (PAP) and reserves. The combined total...exceeds 3.2 million." Instead of trying to formulate its own explanation of the composition of the Chinese military, in this case the authors would be better advised to use the description in China's National Defence Law of 1997, which defines the armed forces of the People's Republic of China to be composed of 1) the active and reserve units of the PLA, 2) the PAP, and 3) the people's militia. (Unlike most other countries, the PLA also includes uniformed civilians on its active rolls.) The Law also defines the PLA's primary mission to be defence from external threats with the secondary mission of domestic security in accordance with the law, i.e., when requested by local authorities and approved by the central leadership, and the PAP's mission to be internal security with a secondary mission of external defence. The Report is correct to call the PAP a paramilitary organization; it is sometimes incorrectly called "military police" by both Chinese and foreign sources. Though the PLA and PAP have similar organizational and rank structures, they have separate systems for command and control, funding, promotion, education, and training. In short, the PAP is not part of the PLA, but reserve units are.

The Report notes that official Chinese sources only give the personnel strength of the active PLA as 2.3 million (at the end of 2005) and 10 million in the primary militia. The Chinese do not reveal the size of each service, the reserves, or the PAP. Nonetheless, The Military Balance estimates reserve personnel to number about 800,000 and the PAP up to 1.5 million. If these forces are added to active PLA numbers (like the Report suggests) the total is closer to 4.6 million personnel, not the 3.2 million the Report inexplicably cites.

Like previous reports, the Report mentions "Assassin's Mace" weapons: "We assess that this conclusion [by China's leaders that the PLA is unable to compete directly with other modern military powers] might have given rise to a priority emphasis on asymmetric programs and systems to leverage China's advantages while exploiting the perceived vulnerabilities of potential opponents – so called Assassin's Mace (sha shou jian) programs...Reflecting the emphasis China appears to be placing on anti-access strategies, most of the capabilities believed to fall under the Assassin's Mace program are designed to blunt adversaries' military advantages or deny entry into the theatre of operations."

Leveraging one's advantages while exploiting enemy weakness is not a unique insight into the conduct of war. While "Assassin's Mace" weapons are often perceived to be exotic technologies, such as high powered microwave weapons, electromagnetic pulse, or maneuverable warheads, the Chinese consider a much broader range of weapons to be "Assassin's Mace," including fighter bombers, submarines, anti-ship missiles, torpedoes, mines, nuclear weapons, and even rapid runway repair equipment. One American observer quoted a PLA officer that sha shou jian can be "whatever the PLA needs to win future local wars...[including] weapons systems and equipment and every type of combat method." Chinese doctrinal writings, such as Zhanyi Xue (The Study of Campaigns) quoted in the Report, go to great lengths to stress that modern joint operations must combine all elements of military power, such as firepower, manoeuvre, information operations, and special operations, to achieve victory. PLA doctrine and practice on the training field increasingly include all combat elements as well as the use of deception, surprise, and stratagem and incorporate "Assassin's Mace" weapons and techniques into operational methods for a weaker force to defeat a stronger enemy. In this regard, the Chinese concept of "Assassin's Mace" is not that remarkable.

In a similar manner, "People's War" is often identified as China's magic weapon, relying upon mobilization of the Chinese population and economy. The Report mentions continued emphasis on mobilization of the civilian economy to support the PLA in war and peace. Much more could have been said about the system of National Defence Mobilization Committees, which extends from national to county level, integrating military, government, and communist party leaders at all echelons. These committees are involved in the coordinated development of the national economy and military modernization and in all aspects of civilian mobilization (personnel, material, transportation, air defence, national defence education). Many committees are prepared to set up joint military-civilian command posts in times of crisis. Tremendous effort has been expended over the past decade to build this system. It is likely to be a key element in any extended future military operation.

This year's DOD report is an excellent starting point for additional examination of Chinese military modernization and transformation. It should be read along with the Chinese Defence White Papers by anyone interested in the developments of this rising power. These documents do not provide answers to every question, but form a basis for further investigation into an extremely complicated and important issue.

DEVELOPMENTS IN CHINESE MILITARY DOCTRINE

China's military doctrine—commonly referred to as "local war under high tech conditions" while still defined by the precepts of People's War and active defence is focused on preparing Chinese military forces to fight small-scale, regional conflicts along China's periphery. Execution of this doctrine requires smaller, more specialized quick-reaction forces capable of rapidly dealing with border incursions or striking outside China's borders. By implication, this doctrine, although defensive in nature, requires that the PLA possess a limited offensive and force projection capability; it also includes the option of pre-emptive military action. Chinese military planners are working to incorporate the concepts of modern warfare attributed to the *Revolution in Military Affairs* to Chinese military doctrine, particularly as they relate to information operations and strike warfare. Beijing is engaged concurrently in a weapons modernization program intended to fill short-term gaps in it defence and to improve, over the longer term, the military's capability to counter more powerful forces. For example, Beijing is developing or seeking to acquire such force multipliers as mobile ballistic missile systems, land-attack cruise missiles, and advanced surface-to-air missiles. China also is working to ameliorate weaknesses in C4I, training, and logistics so as to improve gradually the PLA's overall warfighting capability.

AREA OF NUCLEAR WEAPONS DEVELOPMENT

China has embarked on a ballistic missile modernization program, and a warhead modernization program probably exists to complement the missile program. The evaluation of new warhead technologies likely was completed by July 1996, when China announced its nuclear test moratorium. However, China's experience with the presumed newer warhead technologies is limited.

DEVELOP LONG-RANGE AIR-TO-AIR OR AIR DEFENCE MISSILES

There is little evidence to suggest China has or is developing an air-to-air missile (AAM) specifically designed to counter special mission aircraft such as the Airborne Warning and Control System and the Joint Tactical Surveillance Targeting and Reconnaissance System. However, there are AAMs in China's inventory which could be used against these aircraft and Beijing is acquiring more modern missiles which could threaten them, to include indigenous versions of an advanced medium-range air-to-air missile (AMRAAM).

Surface-to-Air Missiles

The capabilities demonstrated by coalition forces against Iraq during the early stages of Operation Desert Storm provided a vivid demonstration to Beijing that its vision of an adequate air defence fell woefully short in the face of precision weapons, cruise missiles and stealth aircraft. In the aftermath of the Persian Gulf War, Beijing embarked on a measured effort to procure a modern, integrated air defence system. To date, China has purchased from Russia two variants of the SA-10/GRUMBLE long-range surface-to-air missile (SAM) system, as well as the SA-15/GAUNTLET short-range tactical air defence missile system.

China also is developing a number of indigenous air defence systems including the HQ-9 advanced long-range SAM and the HQ-7 short-range tactical SAM. The HQ-9 is intended to counter high-performance aircraft, cruise missiles, and tactical ballistic missiles. The HQ-7—also known as the FM-80—includes both land-based and naval variants. China's air defence capability is expected to improve over time as it develops its own indigenous SAM systems and procures additional missiles and technology from foreign sources with the ultimate goal of integrating these systems into a cohesive infrastructure. While it may take several decades to realize this goal, Beijing already has demonstrated a rudimentary local integrated air defence capability with its mobile Tactical Air Defence System.

STRATEGIC, OPERATIONAL, AND TACTICAL LEVELS OF WAR

In recent years, the PLA has shown an exceptional interest in information warfare (IW) and has begun programs to develop IW capabilities at the strategic, operational and tactical levels as part of its overall military modernization effort. The PLA's interest in IW is reflected particularly in the number of articles which appear frequently in military publications and in the use of IW-related scenarios in exercises and wargames. The PLA's desire to develop a capability to conduct IW at the strategic level is best mirrored in the numerous articles and papers on military strategic and doctrinal issues as they relate to IW. These articles suggest that the PLA, at a minimum, understands the requirements involved in integrating the technical and operational elements of IW in order to attack the enemy's decision-making systems, apply military deception, and conduct operational security, psychological operations, and electronic warfare. There also are recurring references to innovative training and education programs designed to prepare China's military forces for "local war under high tech condition," which includes an IW dimension.

At the operational level, Chinese military writers often have noted that information gathered by the U.S. prior to and during the 1991 Gulf War provided coalition forces with a critical advantage over the forces of Saddam Hussein. In an effort to counter this advantage, the PLA is improving its indigenous capabilities to collect, process and disseminate information. The PLA also is said to be incorporating IW—including concepts learned from exploiting U.S. military doctrine—in studies and exercises aimed at improving its staff planning process and moving the PLA toward "jointness." Recently, a series of articles in the official *Liberation Army Daily* described military exercises which incorporated such IW concepts as computer network attack and computer network defend exercises at both the operational level and tactical levels. These exercises also included elements of electronic warfare, psychological operations, military deception, operations security, and physical destruction, representing the full spectrum of IW at the operational level.

At the tactical level, the Chinese military appears to be focused largely on information warfare as it relates specifically to electronic warfare (EW). China recognizes that the army which is capable of achieving "information superiority" on the battlefield in future high-tech wars will seize the initiative and attain victory. As such, the PLA views EW as an integral part of its IW planning and is currently emphasizing improvements in EW training and acquisitions of more modern EW equipment.

CAPABILITIES IN THE AREA OF ELECTRONIC WARFARE

China views electronic warfare (EW) as a fourth dimension of ground, naval, and air combat. It currently is engaged in an extensive program to upgrade its EW technology equipment and training. China's current inventory of EW equipment includes; combination of 1950s to 1980s vintage technology. This equipment appears to be fielded haphazardly, with a few "select" units receiving the most modern equipment. China is seeking to procure state-of-the-art intercept, direction finding, and jamming equipment, upgrade poorly equipped ground-based, shipborne and airborne forces, and to serve as a template for a robust reverse-engineering effort. In so doing, China has establish close commercial ties with electronic companies in numerous foreign countries.

Ground Forces

The PLA ground forces consider EW a critical area for modernization efforts, as it can act as a combat multiplier, whether on offense or defence. The PLA will employ assets to support all echelons through the use of electronic countermeasures (ECM) consisting of active and passive jamming of communications and non-communications targets, and electronic support measures (ESM) consisting of intercept and direction-finding systems. Physical destruction of the enemy's communications and non-communications systems also is considered a component of EW. EW is employed to disrupt the enemy's use of the electromagnetic spectrum during time frames critical to enemy operations to render the enemy ineffective in achieving his objectives. EW also serves to protect critical friendly point targets, such as command posts, key weapons sites, troop formations, and logistics nodes.

The PLA will attempt to establish EW dominance on the battlefield during the early, critical stages of battle. The PLA would use EW to support military operations by denying or degrading enemy use of radar and communications systems, as well as protecting friendly use of the electromagnetic spectrum. PLA ground force EW capabilities likely will increase qualitatively and quantitatively over the next 20 years. Although the Chinese have written about applications of radio frequency (RF) weapons and a Navy official has been quoted as stating that RF weapons are among those weapons that the Chinese military will need in present century, the Chinese do not have an RF weapon capability at this time. They are, however, developing high-power microwave (HPM) sources that could form the basis for some types of RF weapons. They are also are conducting studies of electronics susceptibility to HPM pulses and of HPM propagation through the atmosphere.

An analysis of publications in technical journals suggests that one RF weapon concept the Chinese are investigating is the HPM missile warhead. This is an explosively powered RF system that would be delivered to the vicinity of a target and, upon detonation, would emit a single intense pulse of HPM energy to upset or damage electronics in enemy equipment. If this type RF weapon is feasible—and it is at present unclear whether it is possible to produce enough RF energy to negate electronics at a greater range than a high-explosive warhead of the same size would cause blast—then the Chinese should be able to deploy such weapons by 2015.

Another possibility is a directed-energy RF weapon in which a RF beam is propagated over kilometre ranges against targets such as manned aircraft and guided missiles. Chinese deployment of such RF weapons by 2015 is assessed to be technically feasible, although as with the HPM warhead the critical unresolved issue is whether these RF weapons would be more effective at accomplishing the desired military mission than would more conventional weapon systems. A less stressing RF weapon concept for which the requisite technology is now mature and that therefore could be deployed in the near term is a countermine system on a ground vehicle to dud or predetonate mines with electronic fuzes.

Naval Forces

The PLA Navy's (PLAN's) major combatants (frigates, destroyers, and eventually aircraft carriers) are expected to have an extensive electronic warfare (EW) suite. The suite will have intercept systems designed to detect and locate enemy radar and communications signals, along with the capability to employ various types of countermeasures against radar, communications, and electro-optical/infrared threats. Minor combatants (missile patrol boats) will have at least radar intercept systems and capabilities for countering radar and electro-optical/infrared threats. Shipboard EW equipment will be integrated together via automated data exchange interfaces between the intercept and jamming systems. Intercept systems against radar signals cover from 500 MHz to 40 GHz. Some combatants could have intercept capabilities against communications and data signals. Jamming capabilities will consist of both active and passive methods for targeting airborne surveillance and fire control radars and missile seekers. Some ships may have jamming capabilities against communications and data transmissions. Submarines (attack and ballistic missile) are expected to carry passive intercept systems for detecting and locating enemy radar emissions. These systems will cover from around 500 MHz to 40 GHz. PLAN combat aircraft could have self-protection jamming systems for use against enemy fire control radars and missile seekers. Some aircraft will be modified to conduct offensive EW missions in support of anti-surface warfare. Unmanned aerial vehicles may be used for surveillance and jamming support missions. The Chinese are expected to produce the majority of the naval EW systems; however, some foreign systems or components will be imported from various sources, mostly likely in Europe and Russia. However, the performance of Chinese naval EW systems probably will continue to lag behind state-of-the-art Western EW systems.

The PLAN will emphasize multiple methods and techniques for protecting its own radar and communications from enemy electronic attack operations. For radars, electronic protection (EP) features will include frequency agility (RF hopping), antennas designed to significantly reduce signal sidelobe levels, digital processing for sidelobe cancelling, trackers operating in the millimeter wave region, and electro-optical/infrared trackers. Communication EP features will emphasize the use of frequency hopping signals and extensive use of fiber-optic cabling for shore-based communications networking. Strict communications security (COMSEC) and emission control (EMCON) procedures will be emphasized.

Air Forces

The PLA Air Force (PLAAF) is in the process of upgrading its EW capability through technology acquisition, reverse engineering, and indigenous research and development. At present, the capabilities of most airborne EW equipment in the PLAAF inventory are extremely limited by Western standards. China's new designs, offered for sale at air shows, while displaying significant improvements over older systems, remain simple by modern standards.

Moreover, China's current inventory of deployed EW assets is inadequate both in size and capability to significantly influence the outcome of combat against a more modern adversary. China is developing a number of new standoff EW aircraft which are likely to enter the inventory over the next 20 years. These assets may be augmented by escort jamming aircraft. Additionally, China is expected to increase the capabilities of self-protection jammers on all of its new tactical aircraft. The PLAAF can be expected to pursue new airborne SIGINT collection platforms in various EW configurations.

DEVELOPMENT OF ADVANCED INTELLIGENCE, SURVEILLANCE, AND RECONNAISSANCE CAPABILITIES

China has the capability to launch military photoreconnaissance satellites, the technology employed is outdated by Western standards. The Chinese do not possess a real-time photoreconnaissance capability. China eventually may deploy advanced imagery reconnaissance and earth resource systems with military applications.

The Chinese also may attempt to deploy a near-real-time electro-optical imaging satellite within the next decade, as well as a high-resolution film-based photoreconnaissance satellite. In the interim, the Chinese can be expected to exploit commercial SPOT and LANDSAT imagery. Use of other commercial satellite imagery also can be anticipated as it becomes available. China already has launched two low-orbit meteorological satellites and a geosynchronous weather satellite. Although China has received some degree of foreign technological assistance in the areas of reconnaissance, surveillance and targeting capabilities, its system development efforts appear to have a substantial indigenous component. In the future, however, Beijing could be expected to acquire and incorporate greater amounts of foreign technology and hardware to expedite program development.

Over the past decade. China has invested heavily in its infrastructure to develop and produce new ballistic and cruise missiles. Beijing currently is upgrading and expanding the size of its ballistic missile force, as well as developing new types of ballistic and cruise missiles.

SRBMs/MRBMs

China's CSS-6 (DF-15) or M-9 road-mobile short-range ballistic missile (SRBM) has been operational since 1994. This missile can deliver a 500-kilogram payload to a maximum range of 600 kilometres, enabling Chinese forces to attack with conventional firepower area which previously were unreachable, even by air platforms. The 300-kilometer range CSS-X-7 SRBM—better known by its export designator, the M-11—has not yet been deployed by Chinese forces. However, an improved, longer-range version of this missile may be under development. Application of satellite-assisted navigation technology would improve the accuracy of both missiles. China's first road-mobile, solid-propellant ballistic missile is the CSS-5 (DF-21) medium-range ballistic missile (MRBM). Is has been operationally deployed since around 1991. Development of a longer-range version may be underway.

ICBMs/SLBMs

In the first decade of the twenty-first century, China is expected to begin deployment of two new road-mobile, solid-propellant intercontinental ballistic missiles (ICBMs) currently in development: the DF-31 will have an estimated range of about 8,000 kilometres; the other ICBM will have an estimated range of some 12,000 kilometres. China's first generation submarine-launched ballistic missile (SLBM), has not yet reached initial operational capability (IOC), even though a follow-on SLBM already may be under development.

Cruise Missiles

China is seeking foreign cruise missile and production-related technologies; it already may have acquired engine, guidance and control, and low-observable technologies. This high level of investment could allow China to increase the pace of cruise missile development; however, Beijing could encounter problems with propulsion systems and mass production capabilities.

China is attempting to purchase from Russia two SOVREMENNYY-class destroyers, together with SS-N-22/ SUNBURN antiship cruise missiles (ASCMs). The acquisition of. two SUNBURN-equipped SOVREMENNYYs would have marginal impact on the balance of power in the region; however, were China to obtain a significant number of additional missiles, it could retrofit them on other major combatants and improve the PLA Navy's offensive punch against surface naval targets.

Any attempt to reverse-engineer the SUNBURN missile probably would take ten years. In the interim, technological improvements that the Chinese are said to be making to the C-801/SARDINE and the C-802/SACCADE could provide a modest upgrade to China's antiquated ASCM force. In addition, the Chinese are said to be working on a submerged-launch version of the C-802.

China is developing land-attack cruise missiles (LACMs) for theatre warfighting and strategic attack. These missiles appear to have a relatively high development priority. Chinese research and development of LACMs is aided by an aggressive effort to acquire foreign cruise missile technology and subsystems, particularly from Russia. The first LACM to enter production probably would be air-launched from bombers and could be operational early in the next century. A second generation, longer-range LACM probably would be fielded several years later.

9

Military Power and Strategy of the China

MILITARY MODERNIZATION

Establishment of a professional military force equipped with modern weapons and doctrine was the last of the Four Modernizations announced by Zhou Enlai and supported by Deng Xiaoping. In keeping with Deng's mandate to reform, the PLA has demobilized millions of men and women since 1978 and has introduced modern methods in such areas as recruitment and manpower, strategy, and education and training. In 1979, the PLA fought Vietnam in the Sino-Vietnamese War. In the 1980s, the PLA shrunk its military considerably on the theory that freeing up resources for economic development was in its interest.

In June 1989, party hardliners called on PLA to enforce martial law in Beijing and suppress the student-led demonstrations in Tiananmen Square. Over 200,000 troops from a dozen group armies were sent to Beijing in one of the largest mobilizations since the Korean War. Ideological correctness was temporarily revived as the dominant theme in Chinese military affairs. Reform and modernization appear to have since resumed their position as the PLA's priority objectives, although the armed forces' political loyalty to the Communist Party of Chinaremains a leading concern. One other area of concern to the political leadership was the PLA's involvement in civilian economic activities. Concern that these activities were adversely impacting PLA readiness has led the political leadership to attempt to remove the PLA's economic enterprises.

During the 1980s and 1990s, the PLA became extensively involved in creating a business empire including companies in areas not normally associated with the military (i.e., travel and real estate). Much of the motivation for this was to supplement the PLA's normal budget, whose growth was restricted. Mao's belief that people and groups should be self-sufficient also played a role in the PLA's varied business interests.

In the early 1990s, the leadership of the Communist Party and the high command of the PLA became alarmed that these business transactions were in conflict with the PLA's military mission. The business interests of the PLA were eroding military discipline, and there were reports of corruption resulting from the PLA businesses.

As a result, the PLA was ordered to spin off its companies. Typically, the actual management of the companies did not change, but the officers involved were retired from active duty within the PLA and the companies were given private boards of retired PLA officers. Military units were compensated for the loss of profitable businesses with increased state funding.

Beginning in the 1980s, the PLA tried to transform itself from a land-based power, centered on a vast ground force, to a smaller, mobile, high-tech military capable of mounting defensive operations beyond its coastal borders.

In the mid-1980s, Deng Xiaoping began to redefine PLA orientation radically, beginning with a reassessment in 1985 of the overall international security environment that lowered the probability of a major or nuclear war. Instead, Deng asserted that China would be confronted with limited, local wars on its periphery.

The natural consequence of this sweeping reassessment was an equally comprehensive reorientation of the Chinese military. The number of military regions was reduced from 11 to 7, and the 37 field armies were restructured to bring "tank, artillery, anti-aircraft artillery, engineer, and NBC defence units under a combined arms, corps-level headquarters called the Group Army." Between 1985 and 1988, the 37 field armies were reduced to 24 group armies, and thousands of units at the regimental level and above were disbanded. —James C. Mulvernon, 'The PLA Army's Struggle for Identity,' in The PLA and China in Transition, INSS/NDU, 2003, 111. The motivation for these large-scale changes was that a massive land invasion by Russia is no longer seen as a major threat, and the new threats to China are seen to be a declaration of independence by Taiwan, possibly with assistance from the United States, or a confrontation over the Spratly Islands. In addition, the economic centre of gravity of China has shifted from the interior to the coastal regions and China is now more dependent on trade than it has been in the past. Furthermore, the possibility of a militarily resurgent Japan remains a worry to the Chinese military leadership.

The PLA's power projection capability is limited; one Chinese general has characterized China's military as having "short arms and weak legs". There has however been an effort to redress these deficiencies in recent years. The PLA has acquired some advanced weapons systems, including Sovremenny class destroyers, Sukhoi Su-27 and Sukhoi Su-30 aircraft, and Kilo-class diesel submarines from Russia. It is also currently building 4 new destroyers including 2 AAW Type 052C class guided missile destroyers.

However, the mainstay of the air force continues to be the 1960s-vintage J-7 fighter. In addition, the PLA has attempted to build an indigenous aerospace and military industry with its production of the J-10, which currently is in production. It reportedly contains technology supplied by Israel from its Lavifighter program as well as technology reverse-engineered from an F-16 reportedly given to China by Pakistan. The PLA launched a new class of nuclear submarine on December 3, 2004 capable of launching nuclear warheads that could strike targets across the Pacific Ocean.

China's military leadership has also been reacting to the display of American military might during the Gulf War and the 2003 invasion of Iraq.

PERCEPTION OF THREAT

In the late 1980s, China viewed the Soviet Union as its principal military opponent. Simmering border disputes with Vietnam and

India were perceived as lesser threats to security. China's burgeoning opening up policy, its claims to the Paracel and Spratly Islands, and the presence of offshore oil deposits made the South China Sea an area in which Beijing saw potential threats to its interests. Finally, although it did not regard Taiwan as a military threat, China nevertheless refused to rule out the use of force as a means of achieving reunification with Taiwan.

Soviet Union

Despite common ideological roots, considerable Soviet assistance in the past, and warming relations since 1982, China in 1987 regarded the Soviet Union's military strength and foreign policy as the major threat to its security. Tensions in relations between the two countries had begun to escalate in the mid-1950s. The 1968 Soviet invasion of Czechoslovakia and the buildup of Soviet forces in the Soviet Far East raised Chinese suspicions of Soviet intentions. Sharp border clashes between Soviet and Chinese troopsoccurred in 1969, roughly a decade after relations between the two countries had begun to deteriorate and some four years after a buildup of Soviet forces along China's northern border had begun. Particularly heated border clashes occurred in the northeast along the Sino-Soviet border formed by the Amur River and the Ussuri River, on which China claimed the right to navigate. Border provocations occasionally recurred in later years—for example, in May 1978 when Soviet troops in boats and a helicopter intruded into Chinese territory—but major armed clashes were averted.

In the late 1970s, China decried what it perceived as a Soviet attempt to encircle it as the military buildup continued in the Soviet Far East and the Soviet Union signed friendship treaties with Vietnam and Afghanistan. In April 1979, Beijing notified Moscow that the thirty-yearTreaty of Friendship, Alliance, and Mutual Assistance—under which the Soviets aided the PLA in its 1950s modernization—would not be renewed. Negotiations on improving Sino-Soviet relations were begun in 1979, but China ended them when the Soviet Union invaded Afghanistan late that year. In 1982, China and the Soviet Union resumed negotiations on normalizing relations. Although agreements on trade, science and technology, and culture were signed, political ties remained frozen because of Chinese insistence that the Soviet Union remove the three obstacles to improved Sino-Soviet relations. Although Chinese leaders publicly professed not to be concerned, the Soviet base at Cam Ranh Bay in Vietnam, Soviet provision of MiG-23 fighters to North Korea, and Soviet acquisition of overflight and port calling rights from North Korea intensified Chinese apprehension about the Soviet threat.

Soviet Communist Party General Secretary Mikhail Gorbachev's 1986 offer to withdraw some troops from Afghanistan and the Mongolian People's Republic were seen by Beijing as a cosmetic gesture that did not lessen the threat to China.

In the mid-1980s, the Soviet Union deployed about one-quarter to one-third of its military forces in its Far Eastern theater.

In 1987, Soviet nuclear forces included approximately 171 SS-20 intermediate-range ballistic missiles, which China found particularly threatening, and 85 nuclear-capable long-range Backfire bombers. Approximately 470,000 Soviet ground force troops in 53 divisions were stationed in the Sino-Soviet border region, including Mongolia.

Although 65 percent of these ground force divisions were only at 20 percent of full combat strength, they were provided with improved equipment, including T-72 tanks, and were reinforced by 2,200 aircraft, including new generation aircraft such as the MiG-23/27 Flogger fighter.

Chinese forces on the Sino-Soviet border were numerically superior—1.5 million troops in 68 divisions—but technologically inferior. Although the PLA units in the Shenyang and Beijing military regions were equipped with some of the PLA's most advanced weaponry, few Chinese divisions were mechanized. The Soviet Union held tactical and strategic nuclear superiority and exceeded China in terms of mobility, firepower, air power, and antiaircraft capability.

Chinese leaders reportedly did not consider a Soviet attack to be imminent or even likely in the short term. They believed that if the Soviets did attack, it would be a limited strike against Chinese territory in north or northeast China, rather than a full-scale invasion.

Vietnam

China's relations with Vietnam began to deteriorate seriously in the mid-1970s. After Vietnam joined the Soviet-dominated Council for Mutual Economic Cooperation (Comecon) and signed the Treaty of Friendship and Cooperation with the Soviet Union in 1978, China branded Vietnam the "Cuba of the East" and called the treaty a military alliance. Incidents along the Sino-Vietnamese border increased in frequency and violence. In December 1978, Vietnam invaded Cambodia, quickly ousted the pro-Beijing Pol Pot regime, and overran the country. In February 1979, China attacked along virtually the entire Sino-Vietnamese border in a brief, limited campaign that involved ground forces only. In March, Beijing declared its "lesson" finished and withdrew all its troops.

After the war, both China and Vietnam reorganized their border defences. The border war strengthened Soviet-Vietnamese relations. The Soviet military role in Vietnam increased during the 1980s as the Soviets provided arms to Vietnam; moreover, Soviet ships enjoyed access to the harbors at Da Nang and Cam Ranh Bay, and Soviet reconnaissance aircraft operated out of Vietnamese airfields. Low-level conflict continued along the Sino-Vietnamese border as each side conducted artillery shelling and probed to gain high spots in the mountainous border terrain. Border incidents increased in intensity during the rainy season, when Beijing attempted to ease Vietnamese pressure against Cambodian resistance fighters. In 1986 China deployed twenty-five to twenty-eight divisions and Vietnam thirty-two divisions along their common border.

India

Beijing considered recurring Sino-Indian border clashes a potential threat to its security. Negotiations since the 1962 Sino-Indian border war failed to resolve the conflicting border claims, and each side improved its military and logistics capabilities in the disputed regions. Since the war, China has continued its occupation of the Aksai Chin area, through which it built a strategic highway linking Xizang and Xinjiangautonomous regions. China had a vital military interest in maintaining control over this region, whereas India's primary interest lay in Arunachal Pradesh, its state in the northeast bordering Xizang Autonomous Region. In 1987, although India enjoyed air superiority, rough parity on the ground existed between the two military forces, which had a combined total of nearly 400,000 troops near the border. The Indian Army deployed eleven divisions in the region, backed up by paramilitary forces, whereas the PLA had fifteen divisions available for operations on the border. After a 1986 border clash and India's conversion of Arunachal Pradesh from union territory to state, tensions between China and India escalated. Both sides moved to reinforce their capabilities in the area, but neither ruled out further negotiations of their dispute. Most observers believe that the mountainous terrain, high-altitude climate, and concomitant logistic difficulties and economic trade make it unlikely that a protracted or large-scale conflict would erupt on the Sino-Indian border.

South China Sea

The South China Sea area was strategically important to Beijing because of the discovery of offshore oil in China's 200-nautical-mile (370 km) exclusive economic zone, increased foreign trade in the South China Sea, and China's territorial claims there. The Xisha and Nansha islands also were claimed, and some occupied, by Vietnam, Taiwan, the Philippines, and Malaysia. Beijing's claims to these island groups predated all others except those by the Guomindang authorities. In 1974 the PLA Navy ousted South Vietnamese forces from the Xisha and occupied some of the islands, which were valuable as Chinese fishing bases and guano sites. Although Chinese occupation of the Xisha effectively expanded its exclusive economic zone, the discovery of offshore oil deposits near Hainan Island intensified China's interest in both island groups. With the expansion of Chinese foreign trade, Beijing's interest grew in maintaining a naval presence in theXisha Islands, which sit astride the strategic Hong Kong–Singapore shipping route. Chinese fishermen also used the Nansha Islands, but most of these were occupied by Vietnam, Taiwan, and the Philippines. In the 1980s, the PLA Navy built up the South Sea Fleet, strengthened its naval facilities and deployments in the Xisha

Islands, and conducted naval exercises in the South China Sea. To strengthen its military position in the Xisha Islands and protect itself against the Soviet base at Cam Ranh Bay, Beijing also reinforced its claim to the Nansha Islands.

Taiwan

Taiwan does not pose a military threat to China, despite Taipei's previous vow to "recover the mainland." Tensions in the Taiwan Straitdecreased beginning in the late 1970s, when China called for peaceful reunification with Taiwan and reduction of PLA forces in Fujian Province opposite Taiwan. Nevertheless, Beijing refused to rule out the use of force against Taiwan in the event that Taiwan had serious internal disturbances or declared independence. In the late 1980s, a Chinese attack against Taiwan was considered unlikely by most observers. The Navy lacked the amphibious forces necessary to mount a full-scale invasion. The Navy had the capability to mount a blockade of Taiwan, but this measure also was considered unlikely.

DEFENCE TECHNOLOGY

China is accelerating reform and innovation in its defence-related science, technology and industry, promoting strategic and specialization-oriented restructuring of defence industry enterprises, enhancing the capabilities of independent innovation in the R&D of weaponry and equipment, and striving to establish a new system of defence-related science, technology and industry which caters to both military and civilian needs, and channels military potential to civilian use.

Promoting Innovation in Structures and Mechanisms

To meet the needs of weaponry and equipment development, as well as development of the socialist market economy, China is constantly reforming its management system of defence-related science, technology and industry. According to the Plan for Restructuring the State Council passed by the First Session of the Eleventh National People's Congress in 2008, the Science, Technology and Industry Commission for National Defence of the People's Republic of China has been superseded by the State

Administration of Science, Technology and Industry for National Defence.

In 2007, the State Council approved Some Opinions on Deepening the Reform of the Investment System of Science, Technology and Industry for National Defence, which explicitly proposes a new investment system featuring effective government regulation and control, participation of social capital, standardized intermediary services, vigorous supervision and management, and positive military-civilian interaction. As a result, an open development pattern for defence-related science, technology and industry is taking shape. The investment field has been further broadened, and investment structure further optimized. Ways of investment have been diversified to include not only direct investment, but also injection of capital and investment subsidies.

China is speeding up the transformation of the structures and mechanisms of the defence industry enterprises, and is in the initial stage of establishing a new system of defence-related science, technology and industry that features a small core, extensive cooperation and a large military potential reserve among civilians. Structural contradictions in defence-related science, technology and industry have been gradually and fundamentally solved through strategic restructuring and the streamlining of the main body of the defence industry. China is steadily promoting the transformation of defence industry enterprises into joint-stock enterprises, actively exploring approaches to diversifying the structure of property rights, giving priority on helping qualified competitive enterprises to be reorganized and listed on the stock market, and encouraging specialization-oriented restructuring and the integration of the efforts of enterprises, universities and research institutes. Relevant laws and regulations have been improved to standardize and supervise the process of reorganizing the defence industry enterprises and getting them listed on the stock market.

Improving the Weaponry and Equipment Research and Production System

Establishing a sound licensing system for weaponry and equipment research and production. In accordance with the Implementation Measures for Weaponry and Equipment Research and Production Licensing promulgated in May 2005, the defence-related science, technology and industry has adopted a licensing system for weaponry and equipment research and production featuring management of categorization. While maintaining state control over weaponry and equipment research and production, the document allows the non-public sector to enter this field and compete for research and production projects. In March 2008 the State Council and the CMC issued the Regulations on the Licensing Administration of Weaponry and Equipment Research and Production, further improving the system.

Enhancing the basic capabilities of weaponry and equipment research and production. Defence-related science, technology and industry are striving to enhance the informationization of weaponry and equipment design and development, and to render product design more digitalized, modularized, standardized and reliable. It has built digital simulation and hardware-in-the-loop(HIL) simulation facilities and a number of important advanced experimentation and demonstration facilities, which has resulted in a higher design capability and R&D success rate.

This sector has also increased final assembly and integration capabilities, and a number of key enterprises have realized systems integration of assembly, experimentation and testing. This has substantially raised core manufacturing capabilities by giving priority to resolving processing and technical issues in complex parts processing, precision manufacturing and special welding.

In addition, a number of large-scale basic experimentation facilities serving the entire industry have been constructed, as well as specialized testing and experimentation centres for reliability testing and burn-in screening of components and parts, and improved measures, standards and other basic support conditions for defence industries have been put in place. With the improvement of basic capabilities, a leapfrogging development in the ability to provide weaponry and equipment has been achieved.

Building a dynamic innovation system for defence-related science, technology and industry. The government has taken the lead to create a favourable environment for innovation and guide innovation activities through policies and investments.

With the research institutes and enterprises of the defence industry as the backbone and with institutes for basic research and institutions of higher learning as a vital new force, China is giving full play to the advantages of integrating enterprises, universities and research institutes, and making efforts to increase its capability for independent innovation in defence-related science, technology and industry.

To consolidate the foundation of human resources for the innovative development of defence-related science, technology and industry, both the national major projects of science and technology and important projects for defence scientific research and weaponry and equipment R&D have been taken as platforms to identify, cultivate, employ and attract talented people.

Enhancing Cooperation with Other Countries

Following the principles of mutual benefit and common development, China is conducting cooperation with foreign countries in defence-related science, technology and industry. It emphasizes exchanges and cooperation with developed countries in defence industry technology to draw on their experience in technological development and management.

It enhances mutually beneficial cooperation with developing countries, and engages in joint R&D and production in major cooperative projects, in accordance with the national conditions and specific requirements of the partners. On the export of military items, it adheres to the following principles: It should only serve the purpose of helping the recipient state enhance its capability for legitimate self-defence; it must not impair peace, security and stability of the relevant region or the world as a whole; and it must not be used to interfere in the recipient state's internal affairs.

China's defence-related science, technology and industry actively conduct cooperation with other countries in the field of hi-tech industries, combining military and civilian needs, and makes great efforts to develop hi-tech civilian products with high added value. Major breakthroughs have been made in developing the international market for space products.

China has exported its first satellite; and the earth resources satellite project with Brazil has played an important role in both countries' economic development. China has significantly enhanced its cooperation with other countries in aviation products and technologies, and made new headway in developing the international market for civil aircraft.

China's shipbuilding industry has exported products for civil use in series and batches, further increasing its share in the international market for such products.

MISSILE TECHNOLOGY CONTROL REGIME (MTCR)

The Missile Technology Control Regime (MTCR) is a set of guidelines regulating the export of missiles, unmanned air vehicles (UAVs), and related technology for those systems capable of carrying a 500 kilogram payload at least 300 kilometres, as well as systems intended for the delivery of weapons of mass destruction (WMD). The MTCR was formed in 1987 by the G-7 partners, and is an informal voluntary arrangement, not a treaty or an international agreement. The MTCR consists of common export policy applied to a common list of controlled items. Each member implements its commitments in the context of its own national export laws. In addition to the MTCR's members, a number of countries unilaterally observe — or "adhere to" — the Guidelines.

The MTCR considers "missiles" to include: ballistic missiles, space launch vehicles (SLVs) and sounding rockets. UAVs include: cruise missiles, drones, and remotely piloted vehicles (RPVs). The MTCR Guidelines specifically state that the Regime is "not designed to impede national space programs or international cooperation in such programs as long as such programs could not contribute to delivery systems for weapons of mass destruction." The MTCR was originally concerned only with nuclear capable delivery systems. In January 1993, the Partners extended the guidelines to cover delivery systems capable of delivering all WMD (nuclear, chemical, and biological).

The MTCR's annex of controlled equipment and technology is divided into "Category I" and "Category II" items. It includes equipment and technology, both military and dual-use, that are relevant to missile development, production, and operation. According to the Guidelines, export of Category I items is subject to a presumption of export denial. Category I includes complete rocket systems, unmanned air-vehicle systems such as cruise missiles, target and reconnaissance drones, specially-designed production facilities for these systems; and certain complete subsystems. Category II covers a wide range of parts, components and subsystems such as propellants, structural materials, test equipment and facilities, and flight instruments. These items may be exported at the discretion of the MTCR Partner government, on a case by case basis, for acceptable end-uses. They may also be exported under government-to-government assurances, which provide that they not be used on a missile system capable of delivering a 500 kilogram payload to a range of at least 300 kilometres.

November 2000 Pledge

On 21 November 2000, the Chinese Foreign Ministry issued its most stringent and specific policy statement on missile nonproliferation to date. The Chinese government promised, for the first time, to issue export control laws covering missile technologies. In the past, Chinese officials have stated that its controls on missile exports were governed by internal documents and not public laws. The Chinese pledged that the new laws would include such regulations as license application and review, end-user certifications, and a "catch-all" clause. The Chinese statement did not, however, specifically reference the MTCR or its control list and the statement did not mention when China would issue the new export control law. Some experts argued that the latter elements represented a loop-hole in the accord. The Chinese government also denied that it engaged in illegitimate trade with either Iran or Pakistan. The *China Daily* reports Chinese Foreign Ministry spokesman, Sun Yuxi refuting US allegations that China supplied Iran and Pakistan with missiles. Sun denounced the allegations as "rumors with ulterior motives." Sun said the PRC had exercised strict control on the export of missile technologies.

On the same day, the State Department announced that it was waiving sanctions on Chinese entities for the past sales of missile technologies to entities in Iran and Pakistan. These exports, which date back to 1992, violated the 1990 Missile Control Act which calls for sanctions on entities engaged in export of MTCR-controlled items. The sanctions were for the export of both MTCR category I and category II items. The US also pledged to resume discussions with China as soon as possible on extending the 1995 US-China Agreement on International Trade in Commercial Launch Services. Under this accord, US companies can export satellites to China for launch on Chinese rocket boosters.

Old Problems Arise

The November 2000 deal did not hold for very long. On 1 September 2001 the US government imposed economic sanctions on a Chinese company for shipping missile technology to Pakistan in violation of a bilateral agreement in November 2000 and US law. The US government said that the China Metallurgical Equipment Corporation in late 2000 and early 2001 shipped missile technology to Pakistan that would assist its Shaheen 1 and Shaheen 2 programs. The sanctions, under the 1990 Missile Control Act, ban US companies from doing business with the Chinese entity for two years. The Bush administration has also invoked a ban on new licenses for U.S. companies to put their satellites on Chinese rockets or transfer satellite technology. These transfers were subsequently confirmed in September CIA report on global proliferation developments.

The Chinese government vociferously denied a Chinese company had shipped proscribed missile technology to Pakistan. The Foreign Ministry spokesman said: Over a period of time, the US has repeatedly alleged that MECC was engaged in missile proliferation activities according to its so-called "intelligence information". In-depth investigations by the Chinese side indicate that MECC has never engaged in any activities as alleged by the United States and the US allegation is groundless. However, the US side is bent on making the erroneous decision based on its wrong intelligence information, in disregard of the constructive position and the investigation results of the Chinese side. Such a

US move is totally groundless and irresponsible, which the Chinese side can never accept.

The Foreign Ministry called for the US to immediately lift the sanctions. China threatened repercussions of the sanctions were not lifted. "China strongly urges the US side to immediately withdraw its wrong decision, so as to avoid any damage to Sino-US cooperation in non-proliferation. Otherwise, the US side should bear all the responsibilities for the consequences arising therefrom."

2002 Regulations

In the aftermath of the September 11th terrorist attacks, US-China relations showed signs of improvement. Beijing extended its support to the US-led campaign against global terrorism. However, the Bush administration continued to stress that the issue of nonproliferation and export control was essential to further improvements in bilateral relations. In an effort to resolve bilateral tension, in August 2002 Beijing announced new export control regulations and an expanded control list, fulfilling its November 2000 pledge to issue export control laws covering missile technologies. The announcement coincided with a visit by Deputy Secretary of State Richard Armitage to Beijing, and was seen as an aspect of preparations for President Jiang Zemin's upcoming visit to the US in October 2002.

The new regulations included both the MTCR's "presumption of denial" approach, end-user certifications, and a "catch-all" clause. The new regulations appeared to mark a realization in China's leadership of the dangers of the proliferation of WMD and their delivery systems to its own security, as well as an attempt to remove this issue as a barrier to bilateral cooperation. The 2002 regulations and control list are comprehensive and closely follow the MTCR. The discrepancies with the MTCR were explained by senior Chinese diplomat Liu Jieyi as: "If you compare the List with MTCR, you will find that the categorization is a bit different for the sake of easy administration.

There are items not contained in MTCR in the List. So in this respect, this List covers a wider area than MTCR. Of course there is also a very limited number of MTCR items that are not in the list because they are not really that relevant, either because we don't have them, or they have never come into the picture, or because our experts do not know exactly what they are. Some discrepancies, however, may still allow for license-free export of some technologies that would be useful for countries to establish indigenous missile programs.

The US response to the regulations was cautious, with many in the Bush administration taking a "wait-and-see" approach before making a final judgment as to whether Beijing had fully committed itself to comprehensive implementation of these regulations. In an example of this cautious attitude, State Department spokesman Richard Boucher stated that: "It is an important part to have the regulations in place, it is an equally important part to see that they are enforced." On 9 May 2003, the U.S. expressed its dissatisfaction with China's implementation of its new export control regulations and control list by imposing sanctions on North China Industries Corporation (Norinco) for allegedly supplying missile technology to Iran. The sanctions barred all exports to the US by Norinco and its subsidiaries, and forbade any contracts between the company and US government agencies. The measure was expected to have more of an impact than previous sanctions; in 2002, Norinco exported an estimated $100 million worth of products to the US.

STRATEGIC PLANNING OF DEFENCE EXPENDITURE OF CHINA

China's declaration (March 5) raising its military budget for 2014 by 12.2% to almost $132 billion should not be surprising. In fact, it would have been surprising if China had cut its defence budget or made a small increase.

Instead, what should be catching the eye would be Premier Li Keqiang's assertion in his report to the National People's Congress' (NPC) annual session on March 5 "We will safeguard the victory of Second World War and the post-war international order, and will not allow anyone to reverse the course of history". According to some senior experts of Chinese institutions this was, perhaps the first time that such words were mentioned in the government's work report and they were a strong warning to Japan.

Premier Li's report went on to make the following three points (i) China will work for peace but would resolutely safeguard its sovereignty and the post war international order, (ii) The country will resolutely safeguard its sovereignty, security and development interests, and fully protect the legitimate rights and interests of Chinese citizens and business overseas, and (iii) China will play a constructive role in resolving global and hotspot issues and work to make the international order more just and equitable.

This is a new, assertive and daring official position taken by the People's Republic of China, and it is obvious that this position is quite openly backed by its growing military power. Enough signals have been received from China that late senior leader Deng Xiaoping's theory of "building strength while keeping a low profile" is no longer in vogue among China's leadership. But it is very difficult to say with certainty whether Deng's advice has been cast overboard or kept aside.

The NPC report makes it clear that the Chinese government is no longer satisfied playing a regional role, but demands a global role commensurate with its clout as the second largest economy in the world after the United States.

Li Keqiang's government report was accompanied by a barrage of articles from the official media, especially the *Xinhua*, justifying the continuous rise of defence expenditure. It was argued that every country needs a military budget that meets its defence needs; the size of the country and its roles as a key cornerstone of regional and global peace, as well as the largest contributor to UN peace keeping missions demand that its defence outlays increase relatively. In the same breath it was said that the expenditure is both in proportion to GDP and per capita terms. Worries of China's neighbours including Japan were dismissed as "unfounded and misplaced".

The *Xinhua* propaganda barrage reiterated that military power (of China) ensured peace, China faced several challenges, and the real threats to regional security were mainly the "mounting assertiveness" of some of the South China Sea claimants, the US re-balancing to the Asia Pacific region and resurgence of Japanese radical nationalism.

Part of President Xi Jinping's repeated emphasis on the People's Liberation Army (PLA) for combat readiness and to win a war and his "China dream" vision to return the country to its "central kingdom" status could be felt in this new discourse on defence in the government report. But there appears to be some difference on the speed and ambit of the process. It is understood that the process should begin from its neighbourhood. Pledging to safeguard the post war international order is a clear reference to Japan over the Senkaku (Diaoyu in Chinese) chain of islands. China claims the Diaoyu as both historical and post-war settlement, while Japan controls them. The US-Japan security treaty covers the Diaoyu, but the US is also against Japan provoking a situation. The matter was precipitated when the Japanese government purchased the islands from a private Japanese owner, with Beijing fearing Tokyo was closing any scope for negotiations. One of Tokyo's apprehensions was that a rising powerful China may in a sudden sweep take over these uninhabited islands, as it did with the Paracels from Vietnam in the South China Sea.

Beijing's sudden declaration of Air Defence Identification Zone (ADIZ) in the East China Sea raised concerns, though both Japan and South Korea had denoted theirs much earlier. But the claimed air space clash, with those of Japan and South Korea through rhetorics over the issue appears to have subsided.

Equally volatile is the situation in South China Sea over the sovereignty of the Spratly group of islands. China, Taiwan and Vietnam claim the entire group of islands, while the Philippines, Malaysia and Brunei claim small parts. China's nine-dashed lines claim 80 percent of the South China Sea. The nine-dashed lines do not have any legal or historical basis, but Beijing continues to emphasize that its claims are non-negotiable. The only discussion it is willing to enter is on the basis that the other party acknowledges Beijing's sovereignty. China has categorically rejected international laws in South China Sea because its claims do not stand.

The South China Sea issue is a major question of security and stability in this part of the world. Not is only the water around the Spratly Islands are estimated to have huge hydrocarbon deposits and is rich in marine life, the South China Sea is the waterway for almost 50% of the world trade.

For some years now China has been trying to persuade the US to agree that South China Sea is China's "core interest", that is, China can use its military to establish control over these waters. The US (read Secretary of State Hillary Clinton) refused. The US has too many interests in the region to hand over the Asia-Pacific region to China even under a G-2 (US-China supreme) condition to manage the world. Nevertheless, US President Barack Obama had offered China a G-2 position during his first visit to China in his first term as president, but the Chinese leadership declined.

The main Chinese leadership still remains cautious and prefers a step by step approach even in their 'China dream' pursuit. First to deal with it is what can be called its main adversary, the Japanese led by Prime Minister Shinzo Abe. Japan must be contained first, but how is the question.

Simultaneous is the question of the South China Sea. China's main conflict at the moment is now with the Philippines over maritime territory. Declaration of the controversial fishing zone in the Sea under China's Hainan province followed by more aggressive naval patrols have added to the tension. Manila taking the case to the UN Commission of the Law of the Seas (UNCLOS) has also irritated Beijing. Compounding the issue is the fact that the US has a defence security agreement with the Philippines.

Vietnam is working with China for better relations and economic development, but has a keen eye on its own interests. It is building its navy, especially the submarine arm with Russian transfers, and has virtually offered berthing facility to the US Navy. US- Vietnam military contacts have ensued.

China also intends to secure its overseas interests including its businesses and people. It demonstrated its ability, evacuating Chinese workers in Libya during the Libyan civil war. The Chinese navy has done some commendable job in anti-piracy work off Somalia.

As China's interests spread across the globe, so does its scouting for energy resources, raw material, and business opportunities. Beijing expects not to rely on others but to do the job of protection themselves. At the moment the area envisioned by Beijing is the first island chain in the Pacific Ocean, the Indian Ocean region,

Africa, Gulf and West Asia. This envisages not only a huge naval force of competing modernization, but also bases in friendly foreign countries.

Similarly, to resolve global issues and hotspots, as stated by Li Keqiang, China has to acquire the status and military strength of a super power. To that end, China's military expenditure has to increase and rapidly. Experts assess the current $ 132 billion budget announced for 2014 does not show the real expenditure in critical military area. At least another 50 to 60 billion dollars would have to be added. In fact, the 12.2% increase in the budget appears to have been a little cautious to address international reactions especially from its maritime neighbours. During the Jiang Zemin and Hu Jintao leaderships the budget grew at an average of 15% to 16%.

There have been harsh and threatening rhetorics from a section of Chinese strategic experts mainly connected to the military-statements like China is entitled to use all means at its disposal to settle disputes to its satisfaction in the South China Sea, including "employing its full capacities to assert sovereignty".

The ever predictable Maj. Gen (Rtd) Luo Gan's recipe for Japan is to teach Tokyo a lesson. Maj Gen (Rtd) Qian Lihua, a member of the National Committee of the Chinese People's Political Consultative Conference (CPPCC) was of the opinion that China was not what it was in 1894-5 or 1930s and 1940s and can contain the development of Japan's militarism.

Yet, the official Chinese line on Japan though strong, does not cross the red line. The aggressiveness is reserved for Shinzo Abe and his supporters, calling them right wing militarists. Abe's quest to alter the post-war peace constitution and pledge to build an independently strong military has disturbed China. His resumption of talks with India in the peaceful nuclear field is read by China with strong apprehension. A militarily strong Japan capable of independently defending itself against China could get out of US control under a proud Japanese leader wanting to erase the shame of World War II.

Therefore, the official Chinese line encourages peace and stability and a win-win economic cooperation. If Japan starts moving its investment away from China, it can find other destinations including India, and Beijing can be a net loser. But no such signs are visible. Whether China is ready for a quick strike local war is the question. The countries of the region are tied in a cobweb of alliances and agreements mainly with the US. Russia has returned its focus of interest in the region and is unlikely to encourage Chinese military adventurism.

China's modern war record is not encouraging. Except for winning the 1962 border conflict with India, it has lost twice to Japan (1894-5, and 1930s and 40s). In trying to teach Vietnam a lesson in 1979, it got a bloody nose.

China is currently trying to bolster its access denial armament like DF-26C and DF-21D missiles, stealth fighters and information warfare capabilities.

China's internal situation is under considerable stress and challenges. Minority issues are rising. Global attention is returning to the Tibet issue and the Dalai Lama. Pro-independence Uighur militants have taken to a more desperate path which is nearing suicide attacks. Last year 13 Uighur related incidents took place. This year, already two have happened.

On the other hand, the Chinese leaders have to control ultra-nationalism which they have fomented. Within the tight system freedom of speech has gained a new momentum, and the authorities do not appear to be winning. The budget for internal security has reached the level of the defence budget.

Hence, there are balances and counter-balances ensuring stability unless something goes wrong drastically.

Nevertheless, China will continue with its defence modernization and accumulation. The old Ukranian aircraft carrier the "Varyag" has been refurbished and inducted in the navy as the "Liaoning". A second carrier is under construction. After that, another three are expected. The stress on the navy is followed by the air force.

In the next five to ten years, Chinese task forces can be expected firmly placed in both ends of the Indian Ocean. The coming scenario makes for an interesting study for Indian defence planners and managers.

FUTURE LOGISTICS MODERNIZATION AND STRENGTH

Deng Xiaoping attaches great importance to the logistics modernization of our armed forces, considering the question of logistics construction in the context of the overall strategic situation. He has made many important statements on logistics in accordance with the new requirements of modern warfare and the new situation that our logistics construction faces in the new era. He has emphasized the importance of the modern logistics to the modern army and modern war. He asks us be subordinate to the overall situation of national economic construction, making full use of the limited defence budget. We should race against time and prepare for anti-aggression war. We should pay special attention to the study of the new situation and the new problems facing our logistics. We should improve the standard of management in our logistics, and learn to do more work with less spending. Things should be straightened out in our logistics, and the good tradition of hard and honest work should be carried on. His instructions have become important parts of the theories on defence building in the new era, and have given guidance to the revolutionizing modernization, and regularization of our logistics.

A Clear Understanding of Logistics

As the modernization of the armed forces progresses, the role and function of logistics become more important. The fourth Middle East war in the 1970s, the war over Malvinas in the 1980s, and the Gulf War in the early 1990s have all attested to this. In the early days of our Republic, Mao Zedong pointed out, "To the modern army, it is of extreme great importance to organize good logistics in the rear area." Deng Xiaoping said in 1978, "As military science and technology develops, and our military equipment gradually improves, we have to come up with new situations in our logistics. In the past, ours was an army of millet and rifles, and our dependence on logistics was not great. Now that the situation has changed, our military supplies, arms and ammunition, and military equipment are all dependent on the supply from a strong rear." President Jiang Zemin also pointed out, "There would be no high combat effectiveness without a strong logistics supply. Fighting under the condition of modern technology, there is the problem of a big consumption of materials, the complexity of the technical aspect, and the demands of time requirements. The dependance on logistics and technology is much greater. We should fully recognize the role and function of logistics supply, and continuously strengthen our logistics construction."

Faced with this new situation, we should not only make sure that the army is well prepared for military struggle, but also make sure that the army maintains a good standard of living, that army cohesiveness is strengthened, and that combat effectiveness is improved. Our logistics department staff should clearly understand the responsibilities they bear and be firmly committed to servicing the army. Catering to the needs of the grass-roots units and servicing the army wholeheartedly should be the point of departure for our logistics. We should strive to ensure good service and efficient supply; our motto should be "we serve." We should make sure that our logistics serve the army, our department offices serve the grass-roots units, and higher levels of authority serve the lower levels. Warehouses, hospitals, recreation centres, supply stations, and army service stations are windows on the spirit of logistics. We should improve the quality of our service through promoting good service activities, and create good images. Good service for the armed forces in the remote and hardship areas should be our priority. The investment of expenditures and materials should favour the grass-roots units and the remote and hardship areas. We should continuously improve the level of logistics service to facilitate overall army modernization.

Modernize Logistics Within National Economic Construction

Military modernization being subordinated to the overall situation of economic construction is a scientific policy that will ensure a prosperous country and a strong army. Military power in the final analysis is based on economic power. The scale, speed, and quality of army building are all conditioned by the country's economy. On a weak economic foundation, military maintenance is constrained by economic conditions; thus it is difficult to develop and strengthen the military. Only when the economy is developed and the economic power strengthened will it be possible to build a strong and solid national defence. Deng Xiaoping has therefore emphasized, "The four modernizations can be summed up as economic construction. There would not be the modernization of national defence without the necessary economic foundation.... The modernization of national defence can only be based on the development of the whole sector of industry as well as agriculture." Therefore, we must exercise restraint and adhere to the central task of economic construction.

We should strive to develop our national economy, because without the development of our national economy there will be no military modernization. Stressing military reconstruction but ignoring the national economic construction will certainly affect the speed of economic development and fundamentally constrain the speed of military modernization. To gain the initiative in the next century, many countries in the world now choose the road of giving priority to the development of the economy, science, and technology. Deng Xiaoping's idea that military modernization be subordinated to the overall goal of national economic construction is suitable for the conditions of our country and of our military and is absolutely correct.

An important principle of logistics in the new period is to serve and be subordinated to the overall situation of national economic construction. We should attach importance to the overall situation, starting out from the overall interests of the nation and the military. We should give up individual or local interests for the sake of the whole, and immediate interests for the sake of long-term interests. We should firmly establish the concept of the overall situation, and overcome and prevent selfish departmentalism and decentralism. We should conscientiously put the interests of our unit or department under the interests of our nation and the military. Just as military modernization is subordinated to the overall situation of economic construction, logistics construction should be subordinated to overall military modernization. The fact that we show consideration for the overall situation does not mean that we are passively exercising restraint, attempting nothing and accomplishing nothing. We should be eager to make progress in the context of "subordination and restraint." We should liberate our minds, renew ideas, and use our brains to find our way toward reform. New ideas and new ways should be tried in our efforts to strive for the continuous development of logistics modernization.

Improve Logistics Supply Capability

In the field of logistics, doing an excellent job for combat readiness is an important aspect of being prepared for an anti-aggression war. Modern wars, especially high-tech local wars, have raised new and higher requirements for combat readiness in the field of logistics. We should carefully study and seek new ways to deal with the question of combat readiness in the field of logistics. We should closely follow military strategic policy in this new era, to ensure that the entire armed forces are well prepared for military struggle, and at the same time greatly improve the combat readiness of the logistics itself. We should pay close attention to the building of emergency support forces for logistics, and make serious adjustments in the structure of combat material stockpiling. The portion of high-technology materials should be increased. Materials stockpiling should be combined with that of production capability, and stockpiling by the military should be combined with that of civilians. The logistics mobilization structure should be improved and we should study and formulate rules and regulations concerning mobilization during wartime. The building of a logistics reserve force should be strengthened, and preparation work for logistics mobilization should be carried out. In light of the characteristics of a high-tech war, we should stress the study of theories, principles, and methods of wartime supply.

Equipment for logistics is an important component part of military equipment and an important factor in fighting capability. Acceleration of the modernization of logistics is a key way to improve the capabilities of logistics supply. In future wars, without an advanced logistics supply, costs will increase and the time it takes to win a war will be prolonged. We should have a sense of urgency about updating our logistics. There should be a unified plan for overall logistics and for combat equipment, as well as a coordinated development between the two. Priority goals should be set with an obvious focal point. Currently, we should first of all increase the mobility of logistics supply and improve the capability of emergency supply. Human beings are the decisive factor in war, including the area of logistics supply. It would be impossible to improve wartime capability of logistics supply without high-quality personnel suited to high-technology war.

Therefore, the training and education in the field of logistics should be strengthened and be seen as a basic project in the improvement of logistics supply capability. In order to strengthen training and education in the field of logistics, training and education reforms should be implemented. We are in a time of rapid development in science and technology. High-technology arms have come into the combat field, with many features of modern warfare. Training in and education of logistics should incorporate the realities of modern war, quickly changing from coping with general warfare to dealing with the problems of logistics supply on a high-technology battlefield. We should pay attention to the needs of supply under high-technology conditions.

The intensity and degree of difficulty of training should be raised, and the contents and methods be reformed. We should try to find different ways to train various logistics forces. Training on new equipment, with new technology, to gain new knowledge, should be increased. Training in the areas of mobility, supply, rescue operation, repair work, and protection under different conditions should be stressed. Real combat situation training should be increased. Methods of training in the field for night warfare and for expedient materiel supply should be studied. Training and real combat situations should be closely related. Modern science and technology are the most important factors of logistics capability. Research in logistics will generate great cost effectiveness not only for the military but for the economy as well. Therefore, strengthening research in logistics will be of great significance to logistics modernization and improvement of logistics supply capability. In order to do this, our leaders at various levels should strengthen their awareness of science and technology. The idea of building a strong army by relying on science and technology and improving logistics through science and technology should be genuinely fostered. Scientific research work should be put on the agenda, and an atmosphere should be created so that the entire logistics forces attach importance to science and technology. Scientific research should focus on logistics modernization and on logistics supply under high-technology conditions. President Jiang Zemin stated, "In the field of defence science and technology, we should focus on researching and developing some key technologies," and we should concentrate our manpower, material, and budget on a number of high-technology items that influence overall logistics work. We should give full play to our scientific research department's skills and knowledge and tap their potential. On the basis of high-quality research and achievements, we should promote popularizing and utilizing the results of scientific research by organizing the transfer of research results, offering technical service and consultation, and signing technical contracts. Our logistics department has a lot of intellectuals and technical professionals and is a department with a high concentration of skills and knowledge. We should uphold Deng Xiaoping's policy of "respect knowledge, respect talents," and create an environment in which people's talents will emerge and be fully utilized. We should give full play to our scientific research workers' talents and creativity.

Reform the Logistics Field

As the country has set up its socialist market economy system, the environment of military logistics reconstruction has seen great changes. For a long time, logistics reconstruction was been carried out under the planned economy system. The various aspects of the logistics construction are all suited to the planned economy system. As the economic system changes, logistics construction faces new situations. We should keep in mind Deng Xiaoping's instruction: "Pay attention to the study of the new situations and new problems of logistics work under new historical conditions." We should raise our reform consciousness, follow the development of the situation, and make sure that the guiding ideology, our goals, supply system and logistics methods in this new era are in step with the establishment of the socialist market economy system. Logistics reconstruction should be pushed to a new phase.

In the defence industry we should adhere to the method of "linking peacetime and wartime production, and having compatible utility for both the military and civilians." In the last few years, we have made some progress and had some pleasing results. The defence industry has been connected with the civilian industry. After ensuring that the military has all of its needed supplies, the defence industry has entered the market place, and reform has been carried out in all production areas. We have organized the transfer of defence industry technology to commercial use.

The portion of commercial products made by the defence industry has increased year by year, thus creating wealth for the country and greatly invigorating the industry itself. Furthermore, logistics department units have made improvements in the long-time problem of single-product and low-efficiency manufacturing, by tapping potential markets and expanding plant functions. On the basis of accomplishing various logistics tasks, they have provided services to society, which both facilitated their own development and also brought about greater economic and social cost effectiveness. Social forces to improve logistics supply have also greatly promoted military logistics reconstruction. We have trained a great many people, providing them with skills suitable for defence and commercial sectors, thus providing a source of talents for both military reconstruction and civilian economic development. Practice has shown that, under the conditions of a socialist market economy, it is correct and practical that the logistics industry adhere to the principle of linking peacetime and wartime production that has both defence and commercial applications.

According to the principle of linking unified supply with separate supply, it will be a long-term task to carry out adjustmenta and reform in the logistics supply system. Currently, the materials and services that various military forces use should be procured according to the principle of proximity and convenience, and we shall further improve the supply system by allocating supplies, medical services, and repair work according to region. This will meet the needs of the army to strengthen combined forces and raise efficiency and will also be in accord with the market economy trend of to strengthening cross sectorial ties and raising efficiency.

The essential criterion is to improve the capability of logistics supply and to improve the combat effectiveness of the armed forces. We should deepen the reform of the logistics supply system and gradually establish a centralized, unified, flexible and highly efficient logistics supply system suited both to the military strategic policy of the new period as well as to the development of the socialist market economy.

We should actively carry out reform in a way that will allow us to raise money, stockpile and provide supplies. At present, the logistics department should work with the main channels of government. We should take the initiative in reporting to the relevant government departments our military supply needs and gaining support of the country. We should work through legislation to ensure there is a large stockpile of necessary military materials for the armed forces. In addition, we should study new channels, methods, and measures for increasing military materials and stockpiles, by actively exploring the market. With regard to stockpiling military materials, Deng Xiaoping pointed out that the army "should not store too much, otherwise there will be waste.... What is the use of storing too much. We should not store too much because the service life of materials is limited, and things become useless after storing them for too long."

In the future, apart from storing combat-use materials according to regulations, materials and equipment that have both defence and commercial applications should be ordered by contract according to market conditions. We should use specially designated civilian enterprises to supply the set amount of materials at agreed upon times, and let society shoulder more responsibility. We should have various and useful ties with the large and medium-size commercial enterprises and establish stable channels of supply. Army supply stations should be connected, exchange and redistribution of supplies should be strengthened, and unified supply should be organized. When logistics has really adapted to the new track of the market economy, when it can better use the market mechanisms and work according to market prices, we will be able to closely follow the steps of the national economic reform, and the reform of logistics will continuously progress.

Strengthen Logistics Management

The shortage of defence funds has always been a bottleneck constraining the modernization of our military, and the tension between supply and demand is not likely to ease. Under the conditions of scarce funds and big demands of reforms, we should strengthen logistics management and use the limited amount of funds efficiently. We shall use less money, accomplish more, and do a better job, for this is the only option for us in the strengthening of our army's logistics construction in the new era.

To strengthen logistics management, we should above all manage according to rules and regulations. Deng Xiaoping pointed out, "In the past, we did not have much property. But we have more things now. It is a new problem for us to manage the logistics work well. We need to have a whole series of rules and regulations that are suited to the new situation and can solve the problems. We should fight against those who have no regard for the financial rules and regulations, and oppose extravagance and waste." Rules and regulations governing logistics work should be perfected and be strictly followed in order to regulate the various activities of logistics work. We should prevent wilful use of funds, materials, and equipment, and conduct technical operations. Logistics work should gradually become systematized, standardized, and regularized. All those actions that violate financial regulations should be seriously dealt with, and the maintenance of a system of standards and financial disciplines should be taken seriously.

Financial administration is the key to strengthening of logistics management. Military logistics is, in a certain sense, financial administration. On the premise that the defence budget cannot increase much, the rate of defence modernization is, to a large degree, determined by the management of logistics and especially the management of the defence budget. Deng Xiaoping said, "Those who do the logistics work should learn how to manage things well, and should learn to use less money and do more chores....The defence budget as a portion of the government budget can not be increased now, and it is the job of the army to use the money effectively. It takes a lot of knowledge to know how best to spend money, and we need to study carefully... strict budgeting.

The policy should be correct, and the method right." We should examine the annual budget and its implementation, to make sure the money is correctly spent and the amount is appropriate. Because the defence budget is tight, we should concentrate our financial resources and focus on key projects. Taking into consideration the need to continually improve the living standard of the troops, the military expenditure should be tilted toward equipment, key forces, and key direction. That is to say, to ensure stability of the armed forces, we must modernize the armed forces. At the same time, we should closely follow and assess the results of the actual spending after the funds have been distributed. Auditing and supervision by the broad masses should be perfected, in order to meet the requirement put forward by Deng Xiaoping that "the money should be put to better, rational use, and should be used genuinely to improve combat effectiveness."

The foundation of logistics management lies at the grass-roots level, and when the performance of logistics management at the grass-roots unit is good, the whole logistics management system will be excellent. Therefore, leaders at different levels should attach importance to logistics management at the grass-roots level. "Regulations on Logistics Management at the Grass-roots Level," issued by the Central Military Committee, lists important regulations for grass-roots level reconstruction of the whole military. These are regulations for the standardized management of logistics at the grass-roots level.

Each level should work according to headquarters requirements and consider the implementation of the regulations to be part of its day-to-day management. Emphasis should be laid on improving the quality of the managers and raising the standard of management. The self-managing capability at the grass-roots level should also be strengthened. We should rely on the masses to do a good job in logistics management at the grass-roots level in order to ensure that everyone cares about management, everyone takes part in it, and everyone encourages its development.

Logistics management is a scientific matter, and the strength of the members of the logistics department determines the results of the management. Deng Xiaoping has repeatedly emphasized the importance of training logistics personnel. We must use various ways and means to strengthen the training of logistics personnel to increase the number of good managers. Better software for logistics management is the essential solution to the improvement of the logistics management.

Strengthen Improvement of the Logistics Department

Logistics personnel, especially the leaders, should set good examples, and not take advantage of being in a favored position. They should be honest in performing official duties and be good managers.

According to the plan of the Party and Central Military Commission, we should further carry out our anticorruption policy and advocate honesty. Army logistics is in charge of money and materials and is vulnerable to the corrupting influences of pleasure seeking, money worshipping, and extreme individualism that exist in a developing socialist market economy. To carry on the excellent tradition of hard work and thrift in the new era, anticorruption and pro-honesty activities should be seriously carried out and not conducted perfunctorily or superficially. We should reform our production and management, and maintain the distinctive character of the people's army. The army is basically dependent on public revenue, but it is necessary to undertake some production in order to make up for the deficiency of public funds.

But the army should not attempt to completely support itself. It would be extremely dangerous to put all its energy into business and making money. The level of corps must not engage in business activities, but instead engage in agricultural and side-line production. Production and business activities should be grouped together and be under the unified management of a larger unit. The financial affairs of production and business activities should be strictly managed and earnings from production should be distributed in a unified way. It should be stressed that illegal acts will not be tolerated in production and business activities. This is an important policy for the military in the new era, and should be resolutely, earnestly, and fully implemented. We should fully understand the significance of rectification and reform in our production and management. Through rectification and reform, we can carry on the fine tradition of hard work and thrift, strengthen the development of honest administration and Communist Party style in the army, and better perform the essential duties and functions of our army.

STRATEGY FOR WEAPONS AND EQUIPMENT DEVELOPMENT

Weapons are tools used to carry out armed conflicts. It is an important component of the military's combat power. It is the major element that determines the success and failure of a war. The development of modern weaponry, contained and controlled by national defence science and technology and national defence economic realities, have affected a succession of military scientific theories.

The Development of Modern Weaponry and National Defence Science and Technology

On June 7, 1981, the Israeli Air Force sent out 14 aircraft and bombed a nuclear reactor 20 km southeast of the Iraqi capital of Baghdad. "The bombs landed precisely on the main building where the nuclear reactor was located." On May 2, 1982, during the Falklands War between England and Argentina, England's SSN Conqueror fired two wire-guided TIGERFISH torpedoes and sank the only 13,000-ton large cruiser, General Belgrano, in the Argentina Navy. Two days later, the Argentina air force flying the French manufactured SUPER ETENDARD fighters needed only one EXOCET AM39 air-to-ship missile to sink the large, superbly equipped and costly ($200 million) SHEPHERD class destroyer from a distance more than 45 km away. On May 25, Argentina sank the British Navy's 18,000-ton troop transport, an ATLANTIC SEA TRANSPORT [Daxiyang Yunsongze] class ship. In June 1982, in the air battle above Syria's Bekka Valley, the Israeli Air Force won an important battle by using all types of jamming methods and precision-guided weapons like air-to-surface missiles and television and in 2 days completely destroyed all the surface-to-air missile sites in the Bekka Valley. In the surprise attack on Grenada on October 25, 1983, the United States used many surveillance methods and sent out an E-2C high-altitude, early-warning aircraft with antijamming capability, and hi-tech F-15s and F-16s, which had been remodeled and equipped with infrared sighting equipment, laser-guided bombs, and radar-guided self-seeking air-to-surface missiles, to achieve its predetermined military objectives with very little cost. During the military conflict over the Gulf of Sidra between the United States and Libya between March 24-25, 1986, and in the air attack on Libya by the United States on April 15, the United States used hi-tech weapons such as laser-guided bombs, "Rockeye" cluster bombs, TRIDENT radar-guided, self-seeking air-to-surface missiles and for the first time, used its high speed antiradiation missile "HARM" as well as other hi-tech equipment such as new infrared sighting equipment. The United States lost only one F-111 fighter-bomber and in turn sank and seriously damaged two Libyan cruisers, destroyed one missile launching site, destroyed about 5 to 12 Soviet made MIG-23s and 3 to 5 IL-76 transports, and achieved combat successes on 5 predetermined targets. Since the 1980s, several local area conflicts have vividly shown, and people have clearly understood even before the smoke cleared, that modern weapons have assumed some new characteristics under the impetus given them by the advances made in national defence science and technology.

One is electronics. With the development of microelectronics, computers, satellite communications, lasers, and other technologies and greater improvements seen in communications, navigation, radar, telemetering, remote control, remote sensing, and modern electronic command, control, and communications systems because of electronics and the radio, various kinds of weapons systems are extensively using electronic equipment and technology. From the perspective of the cost accounting of weapons systems, the percentage of the costs of the electronic equipment within each of these weapons systems is relatively sizable. In aircraft, it is 33 percent; in missiles, 45 percent; in space vehicles, 66 percent; in military vessels, 22 percent; and in combat vehicles, 24 percent. Electronic equipment has already become an indispensable component of modern weapons systems. It has also become the nerve center of modern weapons systems. With the development of the fifth generation of computers, artificial intelligence, and robotic technology, it is possible that troops could be equipped with simple artificial intelligence weapons systems in the future.

Second is the change in guidance systems. Since the 1950s, along with the development and discovery of new technologies like wireless, television, infrared, laser, microwave, inertia guidance, photoelectricity, acousto-electronics, sensors, and precision measuring and automation, precision-guided weapons systems (cruise missile, surface-to-air missile, air-to-surface missiles, air-to-air missiles, surface-to-surface missiles, ship-borne missiles and antitank missiles) have appeared along with terminal precision-guided weapons warheads for guided artillery shells, guided bombs, and guided torpedoes. The guidance system changes in these weapon systems have greatly increased their capabilities for automatic searches and identification and attack, and have increased tenfold the precision of these weapons systems, to the point of near perfect accuracy.

Third is covertness. Weapons are tools for the destruction of the enemy but at the same time, they are also the major target of offensives by the enemy. The new technological revolution has searched for and provided advanced equipment, ways, and methods for the modern battlefield, and together with troops, weapons have now become a serious threat. In the history of combat, to increase battlefield survivability of weapons, man has thought of many kinds of decoys and camouflage. With the development of invisible light technology (like infrared, ultraviolet, laser, microwave, and others), surveillance technology and various anticamouflage technology, original camouflage mechanisms have lost a great deal of their effectiveness. To increase their battlefield survivability, weapons systems have begun moving toward the direction of concealment. "Concealment" is the use of various types of scientific technology to decrease detection by radar, infrared, photoelectricity, and weapons sighting systems. It is the adoption of a specialized technology through systems research and design. Major "concealment" methods include:

- Having the weapons system's structural distribution and design be scientifically rational and still be able to decrease the effective reflecting surfaces of radar, electromagnetic spectrum, and laser.

- Decreasing infrared radiation and the noise level of engines within the propulsion system in the weaponry.
- Selecting coatings that will absorb and shield radar waves and infrared radiation as well as effectively reduce radar reflecting surfaces. For coating on surfaces of the weaponry, new wave-absorbing structured materials made of composite materials and electromagnetic spectrum "absorbing material" are now being selected. There is also the use of different kinds of concealment technology and use of different methods for different weapons systems, such as missiles, aircraft, ships, tanks, vehicles, and artillery. The U.S.'s B-1B bomber is a weapons system that uses rather advanced stealth technology. Structurally, it uses swing-wing. The outer shape of the body and wings are designed for radar reflecting surfaces. It uses a turbofan engine and a bypass culvert that dispenses the mixed hot and cold air to decrease the heat radiation strength of the jet. It uses the radioactive isotope polonium 210 and curium 242 as well as ferrite as its surface coating. Cover coating the aircraft surface with these substances decreases the radar reflecting surfaces and will furthermore absorb and shield radar, electromagnetic spectrum, and laser radiation. From what we have seen in localized wars during recent years, covert technology has raised the survivability of weapons systems in close concealed contact with the enemy and in surprise attacks. It has also played a role in decreasing wastefulness in terms of consumption.

Fourth, focused energy, is different from radiation mass destruction weapons like chemical, atomic, and nuclear weapons. A focused- energy weapon directs energy into beam power that kills the enemy or destroys a target directly. (It is also called a directed energy or directed beam energy weapon.) The rapid rise of laser technology, particle beam technology, microwave technology, and plasma technology has provided the foundation for the creation of focused-energy technology. In recent years, there has been rapid development in focused-energy weapons, and at present, the phase of theoretical experimentation has largely been completed and has entered the prototype stage of research.

According to reports, the Soviet Union is in the process of researching three kinds of high energy laser weapons for its anti-air defence. It could complete the research work for a practical model against a star wars weapon in the 1990s and deploy a small quantity of them. There is intense research going on for various kinds of tactical laser artillery and guns and the coming of directed-energy weapons in theaters of war are not far away. The combined use of these and conventional weapons systems will result in greater casualties and destruction.

War and the need for the development of weapons power are the motivations for weapons development. As long as war, an abnormal development of mankind, persists, the military will strive to find more sophisticated weaponry and suggest the need for development of weapons. With this "demand as an incentive," opposing sides, all wanting victory, will initiate national defence construction "monitors" for "military expenditures" for large investments in national defence science and technology and support for research work in the leading edge of technology and advanced weapons systems. The greatest "investment returns" in weapons development for national security and arms superiority would be a pioneering spirit in new ideas, exploitation, and creation of new technologies. In other words, national defence science and technology could apply all kinds of new technologies to both the research of weapons and their production, thus acting as "technology boosters." In this way, the research disciplines within national defence science and technology could become the "breeding grounds" for high technology development; furthermore, the new achievements of science and technology would most appropriately find their first applications within the military.

Weapons Development and the National Defence Economy

It is common knowledge that modern warfare is not only the competition of weapons on the battlefield but is also, at the same time, an all-out competition of the total strength of the opposing side's politics, economics, military, and science and technology. During the development of weaponry, the four aspects of politics, economics, military and science and technology are completely brought into play. In today's climate of rapid development of national defence science and technology and the daily emergence of new weapons, the material base of the actual national defence economy should be not only strong but also exceptional.

- With the upgrade in the tactical and technical performances of weapons, manufacturing costs would correspondingly be also more expensive. Since the end of WWII, science and technology development has flourished. There has been a multitude of achievements in science and technology that have continuously increased weapon precision, its powers to cause casualties, and its military effectiveness. The explosive power of a small atomic bomb has the same effectiveness as 100 bombers from WWII. The fire power of today's tank is tenfold greater than that of WWII. A mission to destroy 60 percent of the equipment of a tank division would today require only 1 percent of the aircraft used 40 years ago. During the Falklands War between England and Argentina, the EXOCET missile, which cost only $200,000, fired by the Argentinean Air Force was able to sink a British SHEPHARD missile destroyer that costs $200 million. The ratio of the two costs effectiveness is 1:1,000. The precision of precision-guided bombs and artillery shells is 2 to 3 times better than that of non-guided bombs and artillery shells. However, the upgrading of weapons performance has also brought with it the consequence ofmore expensive manufacturing costs. The cost of scientific research and technical components compared to the cost of a system with microcomputer technology, new materials, and new techniques imported in great quantities would appear to be prominently greater. Each of the U.S.'s HELLFIRE antitank missile costs about $28,100 to buy, but the scientific research to produce it costs $310 million. Each of the LEOPARD-II tanks of the Federal Republic of Germany costs $3.58 million to buy, yet the scientific research cost was $360 million. The research cost of Japan's MODEL 61 tanks cost •500 million to research and develop in the 1950s, its MODEL 74 tanks cost •2.5 billion to develop in the 1960s, and the MODEL 88 tanks that currently are under research and development have a budgeted cost that could reach •25 billion. The research and development expenditures of three generations of tanks seem to have increased geometrically. According to statistics, the costs of fighters and tanks increase about tenfold every 20 years and the costs of aircraft carriers increase by tenfold every 30 years. Weapons development has come to rely more and more on the national defence economy, causing great burdens for many countries.

- The increase in weapon power has also created battlefield situations where the consumption of battlefield material and economic losses are immense. It requires a huge quantity of material reserves. The 4th Middle East War lasted only 18 days and both sides, Egypt and Israel, suffered economic losses of over $5 billion. The loss of aircraft by both sides was comparable to the combined loss in aircraft in a year by all of the participant countries during WWII. In the first 3 days after the war started, the total number of tactical missiles launched by both sides was equivalent to the combined total of all the reserves of the countries in NATO. The loss of tanks was equal to one-third the number of those in the possession of NATO countries at that time. Both sides strategic reserves and materials were exhausted a week into the war. We can infer the amount of economic loss that could be created by modern warfare from this. In the Falklands War, the English spent a total of $2.16 billion, about $1.2 million every hour. This kind of consumption, to fight one mid-size modern war, is difficult for even an economically great power to support.

In addition to the above, research and production of weapons, ammunition, technical facilities and engineering equipment all consume large amounts of metal and various kinds of nonferrous metals. They also need the support of the chemical industry and energy resources, as well as military industrial products. According to the statistics from affiliated departments at the United Nations,

15 to 16 percent of the world's copper output and 10 percent of it tin, nickel, lead, and zinc outputs are used for weapons production and toward the building of other national defence installations. The consumption of energy resources is even greater. During WWI, the consumption of fuel by each soldier for each day averaged about 6 kg. During WWII, it was increased to 20 kg for each person each day. In the several local area wars fought in recent years, the fuel consumption of each man each day increased to 90 kg. The consumption level is shocking! This not only raises problems for logistics support, it also increases the economic and energy resources burden.

- The rapid increase and shorter intervals in the updating and replacement of weaponry have sharply increased military expenditures and expenses. The advancements of science and technology have caused new weapons to emerge in an endless stream and greatly accelerated replacement and updating of weaponry. Before and after WWI, the time period for a weapons system to go from research and design, through trial tests and production to its deployment within the service required about 20 to 30 years. At present, this procedure requires only 10 to 15 years or an even shorter period. According to the analysis of a Soviet economist, Maj. Gen. Guluofu, a new weapons system for the Soviet military from research to its deployment in the services requires 10 - 15 years. Since the 1960s, Soviet missiles have already been updated three generations. The majority of its aircraft, submarines, and surface ships underwent updating long ago. Its anti-air defence missiles, radar, command equipment, communications equipment, and other equipment have also been through several generations of updating. The research of new weapons and the updating of existing weapons have greatly increased the military expenditures and expenses of every country. According to an analysis by western observers, "The world economy is already shouldering a burden of massive destructive weapons, poverty, and debt. Militarization will further sap its strength." Since the 1960s, the global expenditure for weapons has been about $14 trillion. In 1985 it was about $800 billion, in 1986 about $900 billion. Every second of every year about $1.7 million are spent. Immense military expenditures have become serious economic problems for each of the world's countries.

- The research and production of modern weapons have made even greater demands on the national defence economy and national defence industries. Since WWII, especially during the 1960s and 1970s, the unceasing discovery of new technology has led to a great revolution in weapons and military-use equipment.

In 1945, the atomic bomb appeared. The research of computers for weapons use came in 1946. In 1952, the first transistorized computer was developed. In 1953, the world's first hydrogen bomb was exploded. In 1955, the first nuclear-powered submarine was launched. In August 1957, the first intercontinental ballistic missile was fired, and in October of that same year, the first manmade satellite was orbited.

In 1960, mankind recovered its first satellite. In 1961, the world's first manned satellite did an orbit around the earth and returned to the surface. In 1967, the first integrated circuit was successfully developed. In 1969, man had his first landing on the moon. In 1977, the neutron bomb was researched and developed. In April 1981, the world's first spacecraft flew. The research and production of all these new weapons and equipment and a large portion of the new technology that entered into the sphere of the national defence economy not only greatly changed the production and industrial structure of the national defence economy, it also added a series of new production and industrial sectors. These changes helped to restructure the traditional national defence industries, moving them in the direction of technological improvement, and development of a technological reserve. The diffusion of a large quantity of high technology made it possible to turn a consuming national defence economy into a propagating field of national defence economy.

Weapons development is reliant on the development of the national economy. It also encourages the growth of national defence science and technology. Military high-technology also gave impetus to the development of the economy. Looking at this from two-dimensional space, this big "O" cycle could possibly expand further. Analyzing it from a three-dimensional space, this kind of spiraling trend is perfectly suited to the objective laws of material development.

Weapons and Equipment Development and Military Scientific Theory

"Technology determines the tactics." The appearance of large quantities of technical equipment inevitably brings about great transformations in military theory and tactics; this in turn leads to great changes in strategic thinking, patterns of combat, combat style, and military structures:

- Weapons development enhances man's strategic consciousness, deepens his strategic reflections, and increases the emphasis on strategic projections. In today's world, strategic research is extremely dynamic. With the development of strategic rockets and various spacecrafts, as well as the gradual development of energy beam weapons, kinetic energy weapons, and other space weapons systems, war has extended from the surface, air, and sea toward outer space. The areas of man's activities have already extended beyond the earth and moved into space. This has opened up man's field of vision and expanded his modes of thinking. In the wideness of space, the earth is no longer "boundless and limitless," but has become one of the "global villages" in the universe. In the eyes of the strategist, the earth has become small and man's strategic reflection is becoming more profound and his strategic consciousness has been greatly enhanced. Man's heart embraces the whole of the universe. The development of strategic research is even more important than at any time in history and has become an especially important issue for all countries globally. What is coming will be conflicts in space. One of the conflicts will be the military struggle for "control of the high ground in space." The other will be exploitation and use of space, the struggle for the resources of space. For this reason, every country in the world is busily formulating and developing strategic plans. In March 1983, the United States became the first to formulate a "Star Wars Plan." This caused global commotion in strategy research. The Soviet Union responded with "defensive measures" to the "Star Wars Plan." Western Europe came up with the "Eureka Plan." Each of the COMECON countries announced a "Plan for the integrated advancement of science and technology by the year 2000." Japan had its "Policy outline for science and technology;" China had a "Policy for a new technological revolution;" India came out with "Policy statements for new technology;" South Korea had its "Conceptions for long range national growth;" and Yugoslavia had its "National science and technology development strategy." To rank within the world's family of nations, to live and survive in the "global village" in this universe, each nation must come up with ideas for a "grand strategy." "To stand shoulder to shoulder with the giants" one must intensely fix one's eye on the growth of national defence construction and weapons in the next century.

- Modern weapons are not only direct combat strengths between opposing combat opponents, they are also strategic deterrents and tools for international political struggles. The appearance of offensive strategic weapons like missiles, atomic bombs, nuclear-powered submarines, and long-range bombers has caused great changes in military strategy. The research, production, and large stockpiles of strategic weapons are already more than needed to seek out and kill an enemy. It has turned into a tool for political and diplomatic struggle. The large-scale arms race have caused the United States to stockpile over 9,400 nuclear warheads with a total nuclear weight equivalent of over 4 billion tons. The Soviet Union's stockpile of over 8,000 nuclear warheads has a total nuclear weight equivalent of over 5 billion tons. The quantity of nuclear warheads possessed by these two nuclear powers comprises above 97 percent of the global total. Both have the capacity to destroy the other several times over. Living under these conditions, the military strategy of both sides has gone through many changes; strategic ideologies have been revised about every 10 years. However, pressure from the threat that "destroying the enemy doesn't necessarily mean one's own survival" has kept them from crossing the "nuclear threshold" and taking the next step of pressing the button to launch those nuclear missiles. England, France, and China have independently and on their own developed into national nuclear powers. The limited power of these countries is not enough to compete with the capabilities of the United States and the Soviet Union, but they do play a role in the even development of political, economical, and military affairs within the world. This power is entirely a symbol of a country's independence and its existence within the world of politics, economics, military affairs, and science and technology.

In addition to nuclear weapons, the emergence of strategic weapons has definitely caused reforms within the military, changing past combat theories that we must go through war and campaigns to achieve strategic objectives to the possibility that strategic weapons could directly attack the opponent's strategic targets and achieve the strategic objectives. The development of various space weapons has not only intensified military struggles in space, it has also increased ways in which strategic objectives could be directly achieved.

- Today's weapons systems are very mobile. They also have long range, high accuracy, and great power, causing the time and spatial aspects as well as the intensity of war to change greatly. The development of these weapons and the great number of these weapons being deployed within the services have caused the arenas of war to be extended into deep sea and space, the length of war to shorten, and the suddenness, destructiveness, savageness, and mutation to increase unprecedentedly. In the "blitzkrieg" of the German armoured troops during WWII, they could advance only about 30 km daily. Today, under normal circumstances, the Soviets could do 50 km and under nuclear conditions it could reach above 100 km. When the Soviet Union invaded Afghanistan, its push towards Kabul, a distance of 900 km took only 6 days. The time it takes for an intercontinental ballistic missile to travel its whole distance is only slightly more than 30 minutes and there is no more than 20 minutes of early warning for its defence.

During the Falklands War, England's SHEFFIELD class missile destroyer did not even have the opportunity to react before it was hit by Argentina's EXOCET missile. With this short span of time, it is very difficult to react. This has made even greater demands on command and control. The largeness of the battlefield and the number of troops involved have given rise to immense increases in technical weaponry and specialized technology and have caused even greater problems in the coordination of operations and commands. According to reports, there were only 20 different military specialties during Word War I. It grew to 160 during World War II, and at present, the number of military technologies and specializations exceed 2,000. During combat, the army, navy, air force, and the other different service branches are all involved at the same time. The types of weapons used are never less than a dozen and usually are in the hundreds. This alone would demand that the commander prepare detailed plans and coordinate his commands well. There must be no mistakes in differentiating missions, allotting time, and coordinating activities. Any small error could lead to major mistakes and even greater disasters.

First strike has always been the combat phase that militarists attach greatest importance to. The success or failure of the first strike impacts the whole battle. In modern combat, because of the short time needed for combat, the phases of combat are no longer clearly delineated. The long range surprise attack or the counterattack during the preliminary period of the combat has become the main combat model for first strike. Thus, every nation has given special attention to studying the first strike phase of a war. The United States emphasizes that "every preparation must be made to win with the first strike." The Soviet Union also believes that "surprise attacks are the most effective combat opening moves to implement in future wars.... Victory can basically be determined in the first phase of a war." This will demand that commanders make complete preparations for first strikes. Intelligence, reconnaissance, personal observations with automatic and rapid analysis, processing and judgment, decisionmaking, formulating careful plans, and even reactions must be quick and accurate because only then could the "first strike win" objective be achieved.

- The extensive use of modern weapons has caused great changes in military structures. Before WWI, the military was basically composed of land forces that included the infantry, artillery, calvary, and navy. Before WWII, there was a great deal of aircraft and tanks in the military, thus the air force, armoured troops and motorized troops came into existence. The air force itself was divided into bomber, fighter, and attack aircraft forces. There were surface vessels, submarines, naval aviation forces and marines in the navy. After WWII, strategic rocket forces, army airborne forces and other service branches were formed. With the development of space technology and the successful development of various spaceflight vehicles as well as the development of various space weapons, the militarization of space will possibly strengthen the military deployment of a new independent military service branch "Space Forces." In 1982, the United States established the Air Force Spaceflight Command (a command comparable to the Strategic Air Force and Tactical Air Force Commands combined), and in 1983, the United States established the Naval Spaceflight Command. In 1985, the two commands and affiliated army commands were combined to form the U.S. Spaceflight Command. Not long after the United States had established the Air Force Spaceflight Command (1982), the Soviet Union appointed Lt. Gen. Sadaluofu as the "Aeronavigation Forces Commander." Some reports have said that "it is possible that the Soviet Union had already established a military spaceflight command like the U.S. Air Force Spaceflight Command and that the aeronavigation force was nothing but a subforce of that command." Various evidence has shown that the growth of the militarization of space has brought about the birth of the "Space Forces." With the advancements made in microelectronics, computers, and artificial intelligence technology, multipurpose robots could soon be used more and more in military applications and in those work areas where the labour is heavy and environmentally dangerous; thus a "robot force" would have to be deployed. The influence of weapons development on military administrative systems and deployment and on the overall structure can be easily seen. At present, the strategic course for overall military development is: a reduction in the overall personnel strength, a rise in the proportion of technical military personnel in the overall structure, a decrease in the proportion of personnel directly involved in combat, and a different scale for the increase in the proportion of logistic personnel (including technical support personnel).

The impact of modern weapons on military theory has been profound and extensive. The various sophisticated tools, means and methods of modern policy decision studies, projection studies, and futures studies have scientifically given impetus to and provided directions for military theories and strategic growth. It has allowed the military to grow scientifically so that it can completely anticipate conflicts and play a better leadership role.

Weapons and Equipment Development Strategy Research

The weapons development strategy is dictated by the realpolitik of politics, economics, national defence and science and technology. These situations suggest comprehensive ideas for the development of weapons. Weapons development hinges between the needs of combat and military construction, and what is possible economically and in science and technology. At the same time it is also determined by a country's political system, its national defence strategic policies, and its fundamental appraisal of the international condition. Thus, different countries have different weapons development strategies.

China is a socialist country and a part of the Third World. This is the political basis from which China formulates its national defence development strategy. China espouses a foreign policy of independence and self-determination. It is against all expansionism and aggression. It supports all struggles and movements for justice. China, together with the rest of the Third World, is a major force for the preservation of world peace. This demands that China have the necessary military strength and an appropriate weapons development program to defend itself against outside aggression. It also demands that it have the ability to completely protect its territory and rights, to protect its country's unity, legitimate rights, interests and self-respect, to prevent the breakout of world wars and to protect world peace. China is a country that is still economically, scientifically, and technologically undeveloped. This in itself imposes a limit on the amount of money it can possibly commit to weapons development and makes it even more impossible for it to be involved in an arms race. Thus, the development of China's weaponry must be based on the needs of national defence and military construction and economic strength, the level of potential in construction and its economic strength, the level of potential in the development of its science and technology, and the independent, self-determining and self-reliant road it takes toward developing weaponry. In the near future, our actions must be firmly directed toward transforming our present weaponry, so that our military weapons will be improved by the end of the century and they will have the ability to meet the demands of a localized conflict. We must also face the future by developing weapons systems for our country, striving to reach world advanced standards in weapons in the next century and carrying out the modernization of our weapons. In order to realize the objectives of the above-mentioned weapons development strategy, our military must develop suitable strategic nuclear weapons and tactical nuclear weapons, strengthen its research for precision-guided weapons and electronic and technological equipment, and work even more toward modifying various conventional weapons.

10

Civil-Military Relation in Today's China

CIVIL-MILITARY RELATIONS

Lines between civilian and military leadership and institutions in China have been indistinct.

All high-ranking military leaders have high-level party positions, and many high-ranking party officials have some military experience. When military leaders participate in national policy making, therefore, it is not clear whether their positions reflect PLA corporate interests or the interests of groups that cut across institutional lines.

In general, in times where there was national leadership consensus on national policy, such as in the 1950s, the PLA was politically quiescent. Once the PLA was drawn into civilian politics during the Cultural Revolution, the military became divided along the lines of civilian factions. As long as the national leadership remained divided on a number of policy issues, the PLA, fearing factional struggles and political instability, was reluctant to leave the political scene. When Deng Xiaoping was rehabilitated in 1977, however, the stage was set for the withdrawal of the military from politics and a partial return to the PLA's previous political passivity.

POLITICAL ROLE OF THE PLA

Deng Xiaoping's efforts in the 1980s to reduce the political role of the military stemmed from his desire to reassert civilian control over the military and to promote military modernization. To accomplish his objectives, Deng revitalized the civilian party apparatus and leadership and built a consensus on the direction of national policy. He also established personal control over the military through personnel changes, and he reduced the scope of the PLA's domestic political, economic, and social roles. Finally, he strengthened party control over the military through institutional reforms and political and ideological education. The revitalization of the party and the establishment of a consensus on national policy assured top military leaders of political stability and a vigorous party capable of handling national and regional affairs without extensive military participation.

Deng's personal political control was established over the military through his assumption of the position of chairman of the party Central Military Commission in June 1981 and through his appointment of his supporters to key positions in the party Central Military Commission, Ministry of National Defense, and the PLA's General Staff Department, General Political Department, and General Logistics Department. Occasional replacement of military region and military district commanders also strengthened Deng's hand. Military leaders who objected to Deng's policies were replaced with more amenable personnel.

The creation of the state Central Military Commission in 1982 aimed to further strengthen civilian control over the military by stressing the PLA's role as defender of the state and by establishing another layer of supervision parallel to party supervision. The civilianization of several PLA corps and internal security units reduced the size of the PLA and the scope of its involvement in civilian affairs. The placement of defense industries under civilian control and the transfer or opening up of military facilities, such as airports and ports, to civilian authorities also limited the PLA's influence in economic and political matters. Propaganda using the PLA as a model for society also diminished, and emphasis was placed on the PLA's military rather than political role.

Party control

In addition to making personnel changes, Deng revitalized party control over the PLA and diffused the military's political power by designating provincial-level, municipal, district, and county party committee secretaries to serve concurrently as the first political commissars of their equivalent-level units in the regional PLA. The percentage of PLA personnel permitted to join the party was limited by restricting party membership to military academy graduates.

Political and ideological training stressed the military rather than the social, ideological, or economic role of the PLA. Special effort was made to discredit the PLA's role in the Cultural Revolution; the PLA's support for the left was described as incorrect because it caused factionalism within the military. While emphasizing the necessity and appropriateness of reforms to modernize the military, political education also sought to guarantee military support for Deng's reform agenda. Beginning in 1983 a rectification campaign (part of the party-wide rectification campaign aimed primarily at leftists) reinforced this kind of political and ideological training (see History of the People's Republic of China (1976–1989)).

Beginning in the late 1970s, Deng Xiaoping succeeded in decreasing military participation in national-level political bodies. Military representation on the Political Bureau fell from 52 percent in 1978 to 30 percent in 1982, and military membership in the party Central Committee declined from 30 percent in 1978 to 22 percent in 1982. Most professional military officers shared common views with the Deng leadership over military modernization and the fundamental direction of national policy, and they willingly limited their concerns to military matters. Nonetheless, some elements in the PLA continued to voice their opinions on non-defense matters and criticized the Deng reform program.

Dissent centered on prestigious military leaders, notably Ye Jianying, who feared that ideological de-Maoification, cultural liberalization, and certain agricultural and industrial reforms deviated from Marxist values and ideals. The Deng leadership contained these criticisms with the help of the personnel changes, political education, and the rectification campaign just mentioned. In this way it was able to keep military dissent within bounds that did not adversely affect civil-military relations.

Popular Attitudes toward the PLA

Starting in the late 1970s, popular attitudes toward the PLA also underwent considerable changes. In the 1950s and 1960s, the military's prestige was very high because of its wartime exploits, because it was held up as a role model for society, and because of its participation in civilian construction projects. But the power gained by the PLA during the Cultural Revolution reawakened civilian resentment of military privileges and abuses of power. By the early 1980s, with the restriction of the PLA's domestic role and the implementation of agricultural reforms offering greater opportunities for rural youth, the PLA's reputation as a prestigious, elite, Marxist-model organization and a promising channel for social mobility was severely tarnished. Society's perception of the military appeared to be returning to the traditional viewpoint that "one doesn't make nails out of good iron; one doesn't make soldiers out of good men." To restore this damaged image in the late 1980s, the media extolled the PLA's martial virtues and the great strides made in military modernization in recent years.

MILITARY ORGANIZATION

By 1987 changes in military organization indicated the importance Chinese leaders attached to structural reform in building military forces capable of waging modern, combined-arms warfare. These reforms included the creation of the state Central Military Commission parallel to the party Central Military Commission, reduction in force, reorganization of military regions, formation of group armies, enactment of the new Military Service Law, and reorganization of defense industries.

State and Party Central Military Commissions

At the apex of Chinese military organization stood two bodies—the state and party Central Military Commissions. The 1982 state Constitution created the state Central Military Commission as the state organ subordinate to the National People's Congress responsible for "directing the country's armed forces". The state Central Military Commission was the state's decision-making body in military affairs and directed and commanded the armed forces. The state Central Military Commission consisted of the chairman, who was commander in chief of the armed forces, an executive vice chairman, two vice chairmen, and four other members.

The party Central Military Commission, elected by the party Central Committee, exercised de facto, authoritative policy-making and operational control over the military. In addition to the chairman, the party Central Military Commission in 1987 included a permanent vice chairman who was concurrently secretary general, two vice chairmen, and four deputy secretaries general. The leadership of the state and party Central Military Commissions was identical, but the membership of the party Central Military Commission below the top leadership was thought to include regional commanders and service chiefs. Because the PLA has been under party control since its inception, the leadership of the party over the military did not change with the establishment of the state Central Military Commission. Although parallel leadership blurred the distinction between the two groups, the party Central Military Commission retained its traditional, preeminent position in charge of military affairs.

Ministry of National Defense and NDSTIC

Beneath the two Central Military Commissions were the Ministry of National Defense and the National Defense Science, Technology, and Industry Commission (NDSTIC), which separately took orders from the two Central Military Commissions but had no operational control over the PLA. The Ministry of National Defense was responsible for military modernization and provided administrative support for the PLA. It was responsible for planning, manpower, budget, foreign liaison, and training materials, but it possessed no policy-making or implementation authority. The NDSTIC—formed in August 1982 by merging the National Defense Science and Technology Commission, National Defense Industries Office, and Office of the Science, Technology, and Armaments Commission of the party Central Military Commission—was responsible for military research and development, weapons procurement, and coordination of the defense and civilian economic sectors.

Operational Control

In 1987 operational control of the PLA ran from the two Central Military Commissions to the PLA's three general departments: General Staff Department, General Political Department, and General Logistics Department. Below the department level ran parallel chains of command for operational, political, and logistical matters, each with its own separate communications facilities. Military policy originated in the party Political Bureau or the party Central Military Commission, became an operational order at the General Staff Department level, flowed through the military regions, and arrived at a main-force unit. Orders to regional forces also passed through the military district (provincial) level.

General Staff Department

The General Staff Department carried out staff and operational functions for the PLA and had major responsibility for implementing military modernization plans.

Headed by the chief of general staff, the department served as the headquarters for the ground forces and contained directorates for the three other armed services: Air Force, Navy, and Strategic Missile Force. The General Staff Department included functionally organized subdepartments for artillery, armored units, engineering, operations, training, intelligence, mobilization, surveying, communications, quartermaster services, and politics. Navy Headquarters controlled the North Sea Fleet, East Sea Fleet, and South Sea Fleet.

Air Force Headquarters generally exercised control through the commanders of the seven military regions. Nuclear forces were directly subordinate to the General Staff Department. Conventional main, regional, and militia units were controlled administratively by the military region commanders, but the General Staff Department in Beijing could assume direct operational control of any main-force unit at will. Thus, broadly speaking, the General Staff Department exercised operational control of the main forces, and the military region commanders controlled the regional forces and, indirectly, the militia.

General Political Department

The General Political Department was responsible for ideological indoctrination, political loyalty, morale, personnel records, cultural activities, discipline, and military justice, and it provided the party structure for the PLA. It also published *Jiefangjun Bao* (Liberation Army Daily), the PLA's influential newspaper. The General Political Department director was at the head of a system of political commissars assigned to each echelon in the PLA. One of the primary tasks of the political commissar was the supervision of the party organization through party committees at the battalion level and above or through party branches in companies. Virtually all high-ranking officers in the military were party members. Until the early 1980s, when party membership in the PLA was restricted, an effort was made to have a party or Communist Youth League member in every unit down to the smallest maneuver element. Political commissars were equal in rank and authority to the commander of their echelon in peacetime but theoretically deferred to the commander during war. Commissars assumed many time-consuming chores, such as personnel problems, relations with civilians, and troop entertainment.

General Logistics Department

The General Logistics Department, headed by a director, was responsible for production, supply, transportation, housing, pay, and medical services. Historically, much of this support came from the civilian populace, and before the establishment of the General Logistics Department it was organized most often by commissars. PLA logistical resources in 1980 were far fewer than those of Western or Soviet forces; in the event of war the Chinese military would be heavily dependent upon the militia and civilians. In 1985 the General Logistics Department was reorganized, its staff cut by 50 percent, and some of its facilities turned over to the civilian sector.

Streamlining and Reduction in Force

Efforts began in the 1980s to streamline the PLA and organize it into a modern fighting force. The first step in reducing the 4.5-million-member PLA in the early 1980s was to relieve the PLA of some of its nonmilitary duties. The Railway Engineering Corps and the Capital Construction Engineering Corps were civilianized, and in 1983 the PLA internal security and border patrol units were transferred to the People's Armed Police Force.

In 1985 China reorganized its 11 military regions into 7 and began a 2-year program to reduce the force by 1 million. Eight military regions were merged into four—Chengdu, Jinan, Lanzhou, and Nanjing—and three key regions—Beijing, Guangzhou, and Shenyang—remained intact. The PLA accomplished its 1-million-troop cut by streamlining the headquarters staffs of the three general departments, the military regions, and the military districts; reducing the size of the Air Force and the Navy; retiring older, undereducated, or incompetent officers; and transferring county- and city-level people's armed forces departments, which controlled the militia, to local civil authorities.

The PLA also reorganized its field armies (main-force armies) into group armies to increase its capability to wage combined-arms warfare. Breaking with the previously triangular organization of military units, the group armies combined formerly independent arms or services into a comprehensive combat unit. Group armies consisted of infantry and mechanized infantry divisions, tank divisions or brigades, and a number of artillery, antichemical, air defense, engineer, signal, reconnaissance, electronic countermeasure, and logistics troops. In the late 1980s, some group armies also had helicopter, air support, or naval units.

In 1987 PLA strength was about 3 million. Ground forces numbered about 2.1 million—the world's largest standing army; the Navy about 350,000—including those assigned to Naval Aviation, Coastal Defense Forces, and Marine Corps; the Air Force about 390,000; and the Strategic Missile Force about 100,000. The PLA was supported by an estimated 4.3 million basic (armed and trained) militia and 6 million ordinary (poorly armed and trained) militia.

According to the 1984 Military Service Law, the militia, which was being combined with a newly developed reserve system, and the People's Armed Police Force also formed part of the Chinese armed forces. In 1986 reserve forces were included officially in the organizational system.

Doctrine, Strategy, and Tactics

From the early 1950s until the mid-1970s, people's war remained China's military doctrine. The PLA's force structure, however, which came to include nuclear weapons as well as artillery, combat aircraft, and tanks, did not reflect the concept of people's war. In the late 1970s, Chinese military leaders began to modify PLA doctrine, strategy, and tactics under the rubric of "people's war under modern conditions."

This updated version of people's war lacked a systematic definition, but it permitted Chinese military leaders to pay tribute to Mao's military and revolutionary legacy while adapting military strategy and tactics to the needs of modern conventional and nuclear warfare.

Elaborating on Mao's concept of active defense—tactically offensive action with a defensive strategy—Chinese strategy was designed to defeat a Soviet invasion before it could penetrate deeply into China.

Chinese strategists envisaged a forward defense, that is, near the border, to prevent attack on Chinese cities and industrial facilities, particularly in north and northeast China. Such a defense-in-depth would require more positional warfare, much closer to the border, in the initial stages of a conflict. This strategy downplayed the people's war strategy of "luring in deep" in a protracted war, and it took into account the adaptations in strategy and tactics necessitated by technological advances in weaponry. The PLA emphasized military operations using modernized, combined arms tactics for the dual purpose of making the most effective use of current force structure and of preparing the armed forces for more advanced weaponry in the future.

The doctrine of "people's war under modern conditions" also incorporated the use of strategic and tactical nuclear weapons. China's own nuclear forces, which developed a second-strike capability in the early 1980s, provided Beijing with a credible, if minimum, deterrent against Soviet or United States nuclear attack. China repeatedly has vowed never to use nuclear weapons first, but it has promised retaliation against a nuclear attack. Chinese strategists also evinced an interest in tactical nuclear weapons, and the PLA has simulated battlefield use of such weapons in offensive and defensive exercises.

Education and Training

Reforms in training and education constituted an important part of the military modernization program in the 1980s. Senior officials recognized that improving the military skills and raising the education levels of both officers and troops were necessary prerequisites for the utilization of more advanced weaponry and the conduct of combined-arms operations. The PLA leadership focused education reforms on the military academy system and altered training to emphasize the officer corps, mechanized warfare, and combined arms operations.

Revitalization of the Military Academy System

Beginning in 1978, the PLA began to revive the military academy system, which the Cultural Revolution had devastated. By 1984 the system had over 100 institutions and consisted of two kinds of schools: command schools and specialized technical training centers. The PLA increased funding for military education, incorporated the study of foreign military experiences into the curriculum, and expanded contacts with foreign military academies. The rejuvenation of the military academies highlighted the emphasis placed on officer training. The PLA stipulated that most new officers should be military academy graduates, set minimum education levels for all officers, and established special classes to help officers meet those standards. Education and military academy training thus became criteria for promotion, in addition to seniority, performance, and experience.

In 1986 the PLA introduced three measures that further strengthened the military academy system. First, at the top level the PLA's Military Academy, Political Academy, and Logistics Academy merged to form the National Defense University, China's senior military training and research institution. Second, a new, three-level training system for command officers was announced, whereby command officers would receive regular training at junior, middle, and higher military command academies. Third, noncommissioned officer (NCO) training entered the military academy system with the establishment of a naval academy for petty officers and an air force NCO academy and the creation of NCO classes in over forty ground force academies.

Training Reforms

Before the military modernization program began, PLA training was highly politicized and emphasized single-unit infantry troop training. Training reforms started with the depoliticization of training, whereby troops spent 80 percent of their time on military activities and 20 percent on political training. The scope of training then changed to concentrate on training officers capable of directing combined-arms warfare. Improved military education in the rejuvenated military academies provided some of this officer training. In addition, large-scale combined-arms exercises, which served to raise officer capabilities in commanding and coordinating combined-arms operations under combat conditions, occurred on a regular basis. These exercises stressed defense against attacking tanks, paratroopers, and aircraft and on occasion involved the simulated use of tactical nuclear weapons. The PLA also began using simulation equipment in training and in 1985 held its first completely simulated combat exercise. In 1986 the PLA training system underwent further reforms that complemented changes in military organization. A combined-arms tactical training center was created for training the newly formed group armies (former field armies) on a rotational basis. The training center coordinated group army exercises and utilized laser devices and simulation equipment in its training. The PLA also established a systematic training program for new recruits, replacing the old system in which inductees received basic training in their units. Under the new system, before new recruits were assigned to PLA units, they completed four months of training by a training regiment attached to a group army. The training regiments also trained squad leaders.

Personnel

Defense modernization brought changes to military personnel policies and practices. Personnel reforms emphasized upgrading the quality of recruits, improving conditions of service, altering promotion practices to stress professional competence over seniority or political loyalty, and providing new uniforms and insignia. The 1984 Military Service Law codified some of the changes in personnel policies and set the stage for further changes, such as the restoration of ranks.

Recruitment

The Military Service Law provided the legal basis for conscription, and it combined compulsory and voluntary service. All citizens between eighteen and twenty-two, regardless of sex, nationality, profession, family background, religion, or level of education, were obliged to perform military service. Almost 10 million men reached conscription age each year, but the PLA chose less than 10 percent of those eligible. A very small number of women were inducted annually. In the 1980s the PLA attempted to upgrade the quality of its inductees by changing recruiting practices. The PLA previously drew its recruits from rural youth of politically acceptable families. But the Military Service Law, the introduction of rural reforms offering greater economic opportunities for rural youth, and the PLA's requirements for higher educational levels caused recruitment to draw more recruits from better educated urban youth. Officers were drawn from military academy graduates; enlisted men and women who completed officer training in officially designated institutions and passed officer fitness tests; graduates of universities and special technical secondary schools; and civilian cadres and technical personnel recruited by nonmilitary units in the PLA. As a result of the new conscription and officer recruitment practices, the level of education in the PLA was much higher than that of the general population.

Conditions of Service

The Military Service Law stipulated changes in conditions of service. Compulsory terms of service were three years for the ground forces and four for the Air Force and Navy. Soldiers could elect another term of one or two years in the ground forces and one year in the Navy and Air Force. After completing five years of compulsory service, a soldier could switch to voluntary service and could serve an eight- to twelve-year term until the age of thirty five. The conscription law also made provisions for limited preferential treatment of service personnel and their families. However, military service was regarded by some as a hardship because of low pay, poor food, lowered marriage prospects, and difficulties in finding jobs after demobilization. To alleviate the unattractive aspects of military service and to help local economic development, the PLA instituted a program of dual-use training, whereby soldiers learned skills useful in civilian life in addition to military training.

Promotion

In the late 1970s, the PLA began altering its promotion practices to reflect the new emphasis on professional competence. Previously, there had been no retirement system in effect, and junior and field-grade officers had remained at their posts for many years with little opportunity for advancement. When promotion occurred, it was based on seniority, political rectitude, or a patron-client relationship. Officers advanced up a single chain of command, remaining in the same branch or service for life. In 1978 the PLA reinstituted the retirement system established by the 1955 Military Service Law and promulgated officer service regulations, which set retirement ages for military officers. Thus the PLA began a two-pronged effort to retire older officers and to promote younger, better educated, professionally competent officers. Older officers, including many over seventy years of age, were offered generous retirement packages as inducements to retire. The PLA also formulated new promotion standards that set minimum education levels for officers and emphasized education in military academies as a criterion for promotion. Officers below the age of forty had to acquire a secondary-school education by 1990 or face demotion. Furthermore, past promotion practices were to be discarded in favor of greater emphasis on formal training, higher education levels, and selection of more officers from technical and noncombat units. With the reduction in force begun in 1985, professional competence, education, and age became criteria for demobilization as well as promotion. By 1987 the PLA's promotion practices were based more on merit than they had been a decade earlier; nevertheless, political rectitude and *guanxi* (personal connections) continued to play an important role in promotion, and no centralized personnel system had been established.

Ranks, Uniforms, and Insignia

The 1984 Military Service Law also stipulated that military ranks would be reintroduced to the PLA. Military leaders justified the restoration of ranks as improving organization, discipline, and morale and facilitating coordinated operations among different arms and services, thus serving to modernize and regularize the military. The PLA's experience in the 1979 Sino-Vietnamese border war, in which the absence of ranks led to confusion on the battlefield, was another factor leading to the restoration of ranks. However, the rank system was not immediately implemented because "preparatory work" still needed to be done. Implementation was delayed by disputes in higher echelons in the PLA over who would receive what rank and by the long process of reducing the size of the military. In mid-1987 the PLA still had not restored its system of ranks. The ranks for officers reportedly were to be based on the 1955 rank system, which included one supreme marshal and ten marshals at the very top. Ground force and Air Force ranks were to be senior general, general, lieutenant general, major general, senior colonel, colonel, lieutenant colonel, major, senior captain, captain, first lieutenant, and second lieutenant. Naval officer ranks were to be senior admiral, admiral, vice admiral, rear admiral, senior captain, captain, commander, lieutenant commander, senior lieutenant, junior lieutenant, and ensign.

Although the restoration of ranks was delayed, in 1985 PLA personnel were issued new uniforms and service insignia. Officers at and above regimental level wore woolen and blended woolen uniforms; officers at battalion level and below and soldiers wore cotton uniforms. All personnel wore visored military caps, new collar insignia, and shoulder boards. The cap emblem was round with a design of five stars and the ideographs *bayi* (August 1st, the anniversary of the 1927 Nanchang Uprising) surrounded by wheat ears and cog wheels. Uniform colors were olive green for the ground forces; dark blue in winter, and a white jacket and dark blue trousers in summer for the Navy; and an olive green jacket and dark blue trousers for the Air Force. Officer jackets had epaulets and golden buttons with the five-star and August 1st design. Collar badges were red for the ground forces, black for the Navy, and blue for the Air Force. Personnel of the intraservice Strategic Missile Force wore distinctive patches but otherwise retained the uniform of their parent service. The new uniforms replaced the baggy, green fatigue uniforms that had made it hard to distinguish between officers and soldiers. The change in uniforms served the needs of military modernization by raising morale, strengthening discipline, and facilitating command and organization.

CIVIL-MILITARY RELATIONS IN THE EARLY DENGIST YEARS: 1979–1989

The Third Plenum of Eleventh Central Committee in December 1978 marked a major turning point in the Chinese political system and the beginning of wide-ranging economic, social, political, and military reform. It also marked an end to Mao's emphasis on "continued revolution" and a repudiation of the radical policies of the Cultural Revolution in favour of an emphasis on rapid economic development, pragmatism, and opening to the West. In terms of military reform, the coalition around Deng wanted a more modern and technically qualified military, signaling a return to the professionalization of the 1950s and a reduction in the PLA's extra-military roles. The political environment was relatively benign to military reform and by the end of the 1980s the PLA was more modernized and professionally oriented than at any previous time in its history. The political environment was also very much shaped by the remaining revolutionary elders in the Party and civil-military relations in China have to be understood against that background.

For most of the 1980s, debate on the study of Chinese civil-military relations was dominated by two basic approaches: factionalism and professionalization (also sometimes referred to as the interest group model). Both approaches pre-date military reform. Each approach has its merits and the role of factions and the degree of military professionalization continue to be important points of debate down to the present. It will be useful, therefore, to begin this discussion with a brief summary of the two approaches.

Factional models have long been popular among some China watchers, especially in Hong Kong and Taiwan. This approach stresses the existence of personal networks and cliques in the PLA as the primary locus of civil-military relations. It is an approach that assumes a high degree of politicization, as personal networks determine the rise and fall of individuals, policy outcomes, and interactions between the Party and the military. There have been a number of different types of factional models. Nelson, for example, based his factional model on the cleavages between regional and main force units. Another variant was a factional model based on generations. Advocates of this approach argued that it was possible to identify groupings based on generational experiences. Each generation was posited as having its own specific experiences that defined its outlook and unified its members. The standard version of this argument divided the current officer corps into rough groupings, including the Korean War generation, the Cultural Revolution generation, the revolutionary war generation, and so forth.

Most of this type of analysis, however, centered on the field army hypothesis, of which the best (and oldest) U.S. exposition is Whitson's *Chinese High Command.* Briefly put, the field army thesis argues that during the course of the Chinese revolution, military factions emerged that centered on the five separate field armies. These military factions were forged as a result of shared dangers and experiences, with years of close personal contact among each faction's members. Advocates of the field army thesis claim that these factions continue to this day and military involvement in politics is read primarily in the context of these military groups, particularly how they balance each other, form coalitions with other groups in the Party, and so forth. During the Cultural Revolution, this dynamic was believed to explain who sided with Lin Biao in his 1971 coup attempt (fellow Fourth Field Army men). In the 1980s, Deng Xiaoping's hold over the military was judged to be the result of his cramming the military leadership with Second Field Army men who served with him during the Chinese Revolution.

These factional analyses of the PLA included non-military elements as well. As many of the civilians in the Chinese leadership served in the field armies before 1949, factional behaviour is seen as crossing the military-civilian line, thus bringing the military into politics and politics into the military. This was further facilitated by the fact that many Chinese Communist Party leaders held both military and non-military positions and that all high-ranking PLA officers were members of the CCP. Several of those who wrote about factions in the 1980s saw a complex web of field army and other factions connecting civilian and military cadres and argued that the distinction between military and civilian elites was artificial and that civil-military relations should be seen as a "process of coalition politics among factions." In this regard, some of the factional analyses are not unlike the "symbiosis" argument put forth by David Shambaugh and others in that both argue there is no clear line of distinction between Party and army in the Chinese Leninist regime and that the system is one of a dual elite.

In contrast to the field army thesis and other factions is the professionalization approach. This approach derives from Huntington's work on military professionalism and argues that the Chinese military is essentially professional in its outlook. The main writers here have been Ellis Joffe, Harlan Jencks, and Paul Godwin. Huntington makes a distinction between those who pursue a career for monetary gain and those who, as professionals, "pursue a 'higher calling' in the service of society." Simply wearing a uniform does not make an officer a professional. Military professionalism, as with other types of professionalism, is made up of three components: expertise, responsibility, and corporateness. Expertise refers to the central skill of the military officer in "the management of violence." Competence in this requires lengthy training, and the resulting expertise is fundamentally different from the expertise of other professions, though universal in that ideology, place, or time do not alter this qualification. What makes a good officer in the United States also makes a good officer in Japan, or Great Britain, in the nineteenth century or in the twentieth.

This special expertise, according to Huntington, engenders a special sense of social responsibility. This responsibility takes three forms. First, the professional officer represents the claims of military security of the state. It is he who informs the authorities about what is necessary to guarantee the safety of the state in a potentially hostile international environment. Second, he has an advisory capacity, reporting to the state on the implications of alternative courses of action from the military perspective. Third, the professional officer is responsible for the implementation of state decisions requiring his particular expertise. The military, unlike other professions, has but one client, the state. Above all else *this is an apolitical arrangement, since the professional officer is the servant of the state and not an individual, a political organization, or an ideology*. Furthermore, the professional officer does not serve for personal gain or because of a temporary emergency such as a war, which may invoke intense but temporary feelings of patriotism or duty. A professional serves out of a "technical love for his craft" and a desire to use his knowledge for the benefit of society. He is thus different from the mercenary, the temporary citizen-soldier, or those who see the military as a mere occupation.

The third characteristic of the military profession is that of corporateness. The officer corps is a public bureaucracy, though the legal right to belong is carefully defined. Entrance to this bureaucracy is restricted to those with the necessary skills and training. Levels of competence are distinguished by rank, reflecting professional achievement in terms of experience, ability, education, and seniority. Ranks are normally awarded within the profession itself based on its own internal criteria. The specialized knowledge of the military helps give it a special sense of identity. It is the military professional who defines the boundaries of that profession by excluding others, such as reserve officers, mercenaries, police, and so forth, who lack similar training and expertise, from the profession.

According to Huntington, the nature of the military profession means that its members are largely isolated from the rest of society. For him, and for most other writers on civil-military relations, professionalism means a very sharp distinction between civilian and military, dividing the two into fundamentally separate and inherently conflictual groups. What keeps this conflict under control is military subordination to civilian rule. Huntington further argues that there are two types of civilian control: subjective control and objective control. Subjective control is a way of maximizing civilian control either by social class (Junkers, Samurai), by government institution (such as supervision by parliament), or by constitutional means. As van Doorn has argued, subjective control usually implies political indoctrination. In other words, getting the military to share the norms and values of the civilian elite. The problem with this form of civilian control, according to Huntington, is that civilians are not a cohesive group; therefore, maximizing civilian control usually means maximizing one group's control over the military at the expense of others.

To Huntington a much better means is objective control over the military which arises from recognizing the autonomy of the military as a profession. By letting the military professionals be military professionals, control is achieved because the military has control over its own institution and is by nature the loyal servant of the state. Its professional responsibility does not make it loyal to any individual or group in society. Subjective control, by contrast, injects the military into politics by embroiling it in competition among civilian groups.

In the Chinese case, of course, the military cannot be truly apolitical. In Leninist regimes the military must be subordinate and loyal to the Party. A truly autonomous military that is loyal to the state would go against Leninist organizing principles. Jencks therefore modifies Huntington's original conception by arguing that rather than becoming apolitical the trend of professionalization in China is toward "political quiescence," meaning that professional officers seek to withdraw from politics and concentrate on military affairs while accepting the principle of civilian rule, reinforced by political indoctrination and other party controls. In other words, in China and other Leninist regimes, civilian control is subjective rather than objective and this is made manageable by the common values held within the Communist Party by military and civilian elites.

Jencks and Joffe admit that not all PLA officers are professional and that many of the revolutionary war veterans were highly political, but they also assert that the trend is toward professionalism as the Chinese military becomes more modernized. That is, as the PLA becomes more professional it will seek greater autonomy in institutional affairs and become less politically active, though never to the point that it becomes separate from the Party. Jencks presses the link between professionalization and modernization quite strongly, arguing (based partly on Kolkowicz's work on the Soviet armed forces) that just as technology produced military professionals in the Soviet Union, so it would in China. As with Huntington above, the authors agree that the demands of modern warfare are universal in their nature, producing the need for the same kind of military organization, training, and outlook regardless of political system. China needed a military capable of meeting the needs of modern high-tech warfare and this would create the conditions for a professional military elite to emerge. Jencks' argument, therefore, is highly teleological, linking military modernization with professionalism in a linear fashion.

How useful have the factionalism and professionalism models been in helping us to understand civil-military relations in China? There are several reasons why the field army hypothesis and other factional models are worth considering. First and foremost is the obvious fact that personalistic ties (*guanxi*) are pervasive in Chinese society. There are a number of studies on personalistic politics and factions in China. Lucien Pye, Lowell Dittmer, Andrew Nathan, Tang Tsou, and several other scholars have provided extensive discussion on the role of factions in Chinese politics and almost everyone agrees that personalism continues to exist. Michael Swaine has provided considerable evidence that even in the 1990s, the PLA high command remained highly personalized. Moreover, fear of factional activity has been a consistent theme within the Chinese political system, lending further credence to the factional approach. The real question is, how much of what we see can be explained by these factions?

A second argument in support of the salience of factional models notes that factionalism has been a feature in the civil-military relations of many other countries and, therefore, there is no a priori reason for not considering a factional approach to Chinese civil-military relations as well. Third, before the 1980s both military units and military personnel remained in the same areas for decades, strengthening the notion that the field army elites remained cohesive groups over time. Rotations in command, a common practice in many armies, were extremely rare in the PLA during the Maoist years. Most officers spent their entire careers in the same unit and units were seldom moved around the country. A classic example is Xu Shiyou, who remained commander of the Nanjing Military Region for 27 years. Li Desheng was associated with the Shenyang Military Region for over 12 years. As most of the top PLA commanders in the 1980s began their careers in the 1930s, we see cases of PLA leaders serving together for decades, during which time it was assumed that extremely tight bonds were formed between them. Presumably these factions were reinforced through recruitment of new members to the factions, as responsibility for promotion depended in part on patronage of those at the upper levels of the military regions.

However, factional models in general and the field army thesis in particular proved rather unsatisfactory in trying to analyze civil-military relations in the period 1979 to 1989. To begin with, it is extremely difficult to link factions with specific policies. In part, this is because we simply lack sufficient information on decisionmaking to know precisely how key groups and individuals behaved. But it is also the case that these factions are clearly not interest groups with specific policy agendas. The case simply cannot be made that, say, officers who served in the Third Field Army believe in rapprochement with the Soviets or that former members of the Second Field Army were more in favour of the reintroduction of ranks than other factions.

Nor were these groupings a good predictor of actual behaviour. In many cases individuals did not side with their alleged factions. Wei Guoqing, for example, was a member of the Second Field Army yet he opposed many of the economic, military, and social reforms associated with fellow Second Field Army veteran Deng Xiaoping. As Monte Bullard has argued, organizational interests can cause a "conservative" factional member to be very "liberal" on some issues and vice versa. In other cases, issues are supported across the old field armies. Supporters of military modernization in the 1950s can be found among members of all the old field armies. Even Lin Biao supported some military modernization.

Thus, was Deng able to initiate military reform in the 1980s because of support from members of his old Second Field Army or because of support from officers desiring modernization irrespective of their personalistic affiliations? Political outcomes attributed to factional behaviour can just as easily be explained by other means, as Parish's classic critique points out. There is no credible evidence that members of other field armies were opposed to modernization purely on a factional basis. There certainly are non-factional reasons for supporting military modernization, for example, combat experience in Korean, Sino-Indian border, and the 1979 Vietnam conflicts. In fact, we now know that interest in modernization can be found across the field armies, as well as resistance to change. William Ting's 1979 attempt to mathematically model factional behaviour in the PLA anticipated this observation. As factions are officially banned in China, they are far more informal and fluid than in more open political systems, thus creating more opportunity for cross-factional alliances. That is, individuals and groups should cross factional boundaries in pursuit of goals of common interest.

This leads to a second problem with factional analysis. It disaggregates the military into distinct units and for this reason fails to focus on issues of common interest. This is important because there are many factors which promote corporate identity and interests in the PLA. The greater the extent of corporate identity and interests, the less room for factionalism and the more the nature of civil-military relations changes. For example, security issues such as the Soviet threat, the status of Taiwan, and the 1979 invasion of Vietnam unite the PLA around its primary mission of national defense. How to deal with these threats more effectively becomes an issue which transcends domestic factional concerns and gives most of the PLA a stake in supporting military reform and modernization. Some scholars in the 1980s, following the logic of factions, argued that "Maoists" in the PLA made alliances with Party conservatives to block reforms. As Bullard and O'Dowd correctly argue, however, this ignores the PLA's obvious interests in change. Most of the PLA supported reform because it was in their corporate interest to do so. This is not to argue that factions were not a factor at all. Alastair Johnston has argued that the rectification campaign of 1979 through 1984 was in part aimed at reducing opposition to reform in the PLA though he does admit that resistance to reform during this period was a losing cause. What this suggests is that focusing on factions is revealing only part of the story and perhaps not even the most important part.

A third problem with factional approaches, especially the field army thesis, is that they are overly static. The field armies were formed before 1949. If nothing else, death and retirement were thinning out the ranks by the 1980s. Younger officers may be recruited into these factions, but they were recruited under different circumstances and therefore there is no reason to believe that their bonds will be as tight as those of the original members. This leaves the door open to other possible factions, with personalistic ties becoming more important. Overemphasis on field army loyalties initially blinded observers to the possibility of new personal associations emerging, though this oversight has since been addressed in the post-1989 literature.

Even more important, the static nature of the field army hypothesis diverts attention away from change. The field army thesis and other factional models are essentially a product of the Maoist period and the factional politics of the Cultural Revolution. Thus many of the basic assumptions in this kind of approach to civil-military relations are based on a political context rather different from the one that emerged in the 1980s. The dominant characteristic of Chinese politics over the past 20 years is change, but as Bullard noted, methodological approaches based on factions cannot explain change or offer predictions. Too often, such analyses took factions as a given. Too little thought was given as to what conditions would encourage or discourage factional behaviour and what developments could and would restrict and curtail factional behaviour. This omission is glaring in the context of the 1980s because many of the military reforms launched in this period should have reduced the level of personalistic politics. These measures included, but are not limited to: mandatory retirement ages for officers, the beginning of a system rotation among regional commands, the reintroduction of military academies, the introduction of a military service law and other regulations, the reintroduction of a system of ranks, and promotion based on merit and technical accomplishments.

There is one final problem with stressing personalistic and factional ties. The literature on civil-military relations in Southeast Asia, the Middle East, and Latin America (especially nineteenth century Latin America) abounds with studies on factions, personal cliques, cabals, and the like. Yet outside of Chinese studies, factionalism and personalistic politics are often associated with frequent military coups. This is clearly not the case with China and is further evidence that factional analyses are providing only part of the explanation.

We do not wish to argue that factions and personalistic politics are not a factor in China; clearly that is not the case. Nor do I want to argue that they should not be considered in analyzing the PLA. My point is that the field army and other factional models represent a seriously flawed approach to understanding civil-military relations in the 1980s. Factional politics represents only one aspect of civil-military relations, and does not sufficiently take into account political and organizational changes taking place at this time. Factional analyses are most valuable when looking at periods of very low institutionalization and high levels of political uncertainty. The field army approach does not offer a superior explanation for why Deng initiated military reform or how he was able to implement those policies, though the existence of personal ties may have made implementation easier. Factional analysis is also a poor guide in trying to anticipate the likely impact of military reforms on civil-military reforms, as it is ill suited to analyzing important and fundamental changes in the system. In this regard, the professionalism model is far more useful as an analytical and theoretical tool.

Many aspects of the professionalization approach proved to be an accurate indicator of how civil-military relations developed in China in the decade prior to Tiananmen. The leadership that centered on Deng Xiaoping had as its goal a stronger, more economically developed China. They were interested in modernization, better expertise, skill and education in cadres, more regularization and legalization of the political system, trade, and political stability. They knew that China needed a more modern military to meet its security needs, to protect increasingly important trade, to take advantage of new military technologies, and so forth. Professionalism, unlike factional analyses, predicts what sort of changes needs to take place to achieve military modernization and predicts the consequences of that modernization. That is, the military should become more withdrawn from political life and be more insistent on autonomy for its own affairs, restricting its influence to issues directly related to national security. Unlike factions, the professionalization model offers something concrete to measure: the degree to which military reforms conform to the expectations of the professionalization model. The model can also easily explain why the military supports reform.

Many of the developments in the Chinese military seem to bear out the assumptions made by Jencks, Joffe, and Godwin. To begin with, the 1980s saw a renewed emphasis on professional military education. The National Defense University was reopened in 1986 and many other military academies were established or revived during the 1980s. Officers were no longer recruited from the ranks as during the Cultural Revolution but were expected to be trained in military academies. Merit and technical skill became more important than ideology as criteria for promotion. Attempts to retire older officers led to a general trend toward lower age and better education among officers at all levels of the military hierarchy. Military officers spent less time studying political content and more time perfecting their military craft. Interestingly enough, this education included exposure to Western military theorists and their theories of professionalization. These new ideas were also introduced in the course of increased exchanges with Western military personnel. Deng and others also called for changes in the content of training, requiring, among other things, political officers to increase the amount of time spent acquiring professional, rather than political, skills.

Training became more important, reflecting changes in equipment, military doctrine, and the need to coordinate combined arms operations. Much of the writing on military professionalism carefully documents the increasingly larger military exercises and other improvements in training and their implications for instilling a professional ethos among the PLA officer corps. Political work also changed, stressing the importance of being professionally qualified as well as revolutionary. Ideological models of virtue, such as Lei Feng, temporarily disappeared from the scene. Political commissars seemed to be moving more in the direction of becoming morale officers rather than indoctrinators. There was a clear trend toward the importance of expertise in the PLA in this decade.

Another development of special importance was the reintroduction of ranks in 1988 (abolished in 1965), regulations on promotion, and new uniforms. Ranks and regulations are obviously important in developing a hierarchy of professionals based on impersonal rules of merit. The greater the degree to which officers are chosen on merit and expertise, the greater the ethos of professionalism, and the less important personalism becomes as an explanatory factor in military politics. New uniforms and military decorations have the effect of reinforcing the distinctiveness between military and civilian, reinforcing professional pride among military personnel, and helping to build a sense of corporate identity.

Just as important was the shedding of many of the PLA's non-military roles and apparent retreat from politics. In September of 1985, six of the nine military men on the Politburo resigned and the decade as a whole witnessed a reduction in the number of military personnel serving on the Central Committee as well as the Politburo. This change was particularly noteworthy, as the PLA had long been noted for having more officers in these bodies than the militaries of any other Communist regime. Even more dramatic was the separation of military and civilian personnel at the regional level. There is no longer an interlocking directorate at the regional level with Provincial First Secretaries serving as political commissars of military districts and military commanders serving on provincial party committees. This split between regional civilian and military elites was further enhanced by the beginning of a system of rotation among the military region commanders.

In addition to its political roles, the PLA shed many other non-military activities. The railway engineer troops were transferred over to civilian control in 1983. In 1985, the last of the Production and Construction Corps, the Xinjiang PCC, was also civilianized. Many internal security duties were turned over to the revived People's Armed Police, which had been partially formed from units transferred from the PLA. While this was not a complete separation and the PLA continues to have some internal security role, it did mark a renewed emphasis on the primary duty of any professional armed force—national defense.

In sum, there were many trends in the 1980s that tended to support the hypothesis that the PLA would become more professional. Furthermore, there was considerable evidence that these and other changes, such as force reductions and doctrinal change, could be implemented because many officers within the PLA supported these reforms from a professional standpoint. Those who stressed professionalism clearly got many things right. But in focusing on these positive developments, writers within the professionalism paradigm did not always look sufficiently at other issues and this led to errors in their analysis.

In looking at many developments leading to greater professionalization, scholars sometimes fell into the trap of overestimating the extent of reform actually achieved. For example, ranks were originally to be introduced in 1985. They were in fact not introduced until 1988. Many other structural reforms were also slow in being implemented. The military law promulgated in China since 1978, for example, 12 were not enacted until after 1988. In point of fact, most of the military laws and regulations currently in existence did not come into being until the 1990s. While the PLA was becoming more professionalized, it still was a long way from being professional. Many gaps remained to be filled in.

A case in point was the long-term impact of PLA economic enterprises, which hurt efforts at regularization and training, encouraged officers to disobey superiors in order to hide profits, and most of all increased the degree of military corruption to new levels. All of these developments seriously undermined the process of professionalization, recommitting the PLA to a whole range of non-military activities at a time when it was shedding many of its other traditional non-military roles. In the long run, analysts such as Jencks, Godwin, and Cheung were correct in their predictions that the PLA would eventually shed many of its entrepreneurial activities. However, the task of getting the PLA out of business was far more problematic than was anticipated. The transition to a fully professionalized PLA (assuming it is ever fully realized) will take far longer than originally predicted.

Part of this can simply be explained as underestimating the amount of time it would require to overcome the damage of the Cultural Revolution. But there was also considerable resistance to many of the military reforms. While most of the PLA supported reform in principle, some felt threatened by changes and new standards and were in a position to block or slow down changes. Others had genuine ideological concerns about the long-term impact of some aspects of reform and/or were loath to see the ending of traditions they had helped create. PLA commercial activities, which grew rapidly in the 1980s, were a counter to professionalism. Yet commercial activities were accepted as legitimate in part because the PLA had a well-entrenched tradition of economic activity. The revolutionary elders dominated the leadership in the 1980s and this shaped which aspects of military reform were acceptable and which were not. Not all reforms were equally supported.

The case of China's parallel Central Military Commissions (CMC) is a good illustrative example. The Party's CMC has always been the organization directly responsible for running the PLA. When a state CMC was founded in 1982, it immediately attracted attention and speculation that this represented a major step in separating Party from state and, therefore, Party from army. In reality it was nothing of the kind. The state CMC has the exact same membership as the Party CMC with no separate existence except as a legal fiction. Nor, in hindsight, should there have been any expectation the case would be otherwise. Communist parties have always been very careful to maintain that the Party, not the state, controls the gun. To this end, the client of the military always must be the Party and only the Party. Putting the state CMC on the same level as the Party CMC would be a fundamental redefinition of the nature of the Party-state relationship in China. Such a redefinition would go against the beliefs of many of the top leadership within the People's Republic of China (PRC). Whatever the real reasons behind the establishment of the state CMC, a genuine separation of party and state was not acceptable to Deng and other elders who saw them as essentially identical.

Another analytical trap centered on the fact that the professionalization of the PLA is very much a political process. This is recognized by many writers on the subject, but their interpretations are open to dispute. Joffe argued that the PLA willingly accepted their subordination and that by 1985 the PLA was out of politics. This is somewhat misleading and the actual situation was far more complex. Joffe and others are correct, for instance, in asserting that the PLA has withdrawn from many aspects of politics, but it has never withdrawn entirely. Reducing the number of Politburo members who are military men reduces the formal lines of influence, but informal ties remain. As Michael Swaine has demonstrated, retired elders were still able to exercise varying degrees of influence even after retirement.

The irony is that military reform left the higher levels of civil-military relations still very much political and personal. The real demarcation was at the lower levels of civil-military relations, where there is a more definitive split between civilian and military elites. This created the unusual situation of a split between the functioning of civil-military relations at the top and the grassroots levels.

Another problem relates to the nature of professional expertise. As the PLA becomes more professional it should withdraw from many non-military roles, in a process of de-politicization. Yet as the synopsis of Huntington above indicates, the expertise of the officer qualifies him (or her) to give advice on security and other related matters. In a Leninist regime, where military leaders are also Party members, this expertise could translate into the military seeking a greater political role in foreign policy and other areas close to its corporate interests. This possibility has received a lot of attention outside the China field. Among PLA scholars, however, very little attention was paid to this possibility in the 1980s.

Finally, while it is easy to measure reforms that should encourage professionalism, actually measuring professionalism itself is rather difficult. All too often there is a tendency to assume that there was an automatic correlation between military modernization and professionalization. However, as Fang Zhu has argued, it is possible to have military modernization without professionalization. Both Joffe and Jencks recognize that the PLA's officer corps is not entirely professional in outlook and have argued that what really matters is that most of the officer corps is professionally oriented. In his study of praetorianism, Perlmutter argued that only about 5 percent of an officer corps need be politicized in order for the military to behave in a praetorian manner.

How many officers must be professional in order for the PLA to behave as a professional force? The longer the PLA remains a semi-professional force in transition, the more important this question becomes.

CIVIL-MILITARY RELATIONS: 1992 TO TODAY

In the aftermath of Tiananmen there is a greater diversity of opinion on how to approach Chinese civil-military relations. Some scholars have focused on the top of the military and Party hierarchy, where politics remains highly personalized. Others have continued to argue that professionalism still offers the best framework for thinking about Chinese civil-military relations. Still others have argued for a "symbiotic" framework as an alternative to professionalism. Finally, some PLA scholars are now suggesting that new patterns in civil-military relations are emerging in the post-Deng era.

Factional Analysis in the 1990s

The role of factions has continued to be a point of debate since Tiananmen, though the terms of that debate have shifted in many important ways since the 1980s. There is little discussion of factionalism at the regional level, reflecting a growing consensus that promotions, regular rotations, and other policies have largely reduced the basis for regional factions. Current discussions of personalistic politics focus almost exclusively on the highest echelons of the PLA. Few Western scholars continue to discuss field armies, though the subject remains popular with observers in Mainland China, Hong Kong, and Taiwan. In place of field armies, scholars have discussed factions based on followers of the Yangs, provincial origins, even school ties. Most important, perhaps, in the 1990s factions are seldom regarded as a primary causal explanation in civil-military relations. They are considered of importance in promotion or "latent personnel relationships" that matter during a time of crisis such as an uncertain succession.

The most extensive and ambitious attempt to look at factions in the post-Tiananmen era is in the work of Michael Swaine. Unlike many of his predecessors, his approach has tried to identify those factors in the Chinese political system that encourage and sustain personalistic politics. These include the absence of an institutionalized structure to determine leadership succession, an unstable domestic environment with high levels of social and economic discontent, and uncertainty about the transition from the remaining elders of the revolution to a much younger generation that is more specialized and lacks the breadth and experience of their predecessors. Under such conditions leaders in the Party can maintain their positions only by having networks of support within the military, and military personnel can really influence decisionmaking only by maintaining ties with civilians. It is important to stress here that Swaine feels that these factions are most important during times of crisis, when political and military leaders rely heavily on those personal ties that they can trust. One important aspect of Swaine's study, and perhaps his most useful contribution, is the evidence he presents about the high degree of control exerted by a few individuals over the military. Only Deng or his personal representative could give certain orders, and military commanders are highly restricted as to how many troops may be moved without permission from the centre. This has provided us with a much better understanding of the highly personalized nature of politics at the top of the politico-military command, as well as giving us a better appreciation of how control can be maintained in such a highly personalized system.

A different approach to understanding how personal ties might affect the post-Deng succession was proposed by Li Cheng and Lynn White, who predicted that as the process of modernization proceeds and Chinese elites become more technocratic, school ties will become more important as a basis of personal ties and the field armies will become less important as a source of factional behaviour.

There is a certain irony here in that Li and White are looking for evidence of affective ties based on military education, a product of the professionalization of the 1980s. In the end they provided some very good evidence that the officer corps was becoming better educated and professionalized, but were much less successful in demonstrating that a by-product of officer education was a new form of personal ties. It is not that the logic was faulty. Educational ties have been shown to matter in other developing countries. The problem is that it is not clear whether educational cliques have an impact outside promotion.

In the end, these and less well articulated discussions on factions and the post-Deng succession were largely moot, as Jiang's succession was relatively uneventful. The proposition that personalistic alliances might become very important in the event of another crisis remains untested. The post-Deng succession went smoothly in part because the PLA is loyal to the Party and there was no obvious alternative.

But writings on Jiang's succession also indicate that Jiang's "courtship" of the PLA was an important aspect of his consolidation of power. This tends to reinforce Swaine's central contention that the uppermost levels of decisionmaking civil-military relations remain highly personalized and even members of the professionalism school accept this argument. This serves to remind us that though there has been a transition to a post-revolutionary elite, the Chinese political system is not yet sufficiently institutionalized to end personalistic politics.

That said, assessing the role of factions in the 1990s remains highly problematic. All the limitations on factional approaches remain valid, especially in terms of linking perceived groups to causation. The "Shandong Faction" represents a case in point.

Officers from Shandong province are very prominent in the upper levels of the PLA. In 1994 both the People's Liberation Army Navy (PLAN) commander and the political commissar were from Shandong, as were one-third of the CMC's membership. Overall, Shandongnese make up about a quarter of PLA senior officers. It may very well be that this "faction" has an impact on promotion and other decisions within the PLA. It also may be the case that the high proportion of Shandongnese simply reflects where the PLA did much of its recruiting in the late-1940s and early-1950s. The literature is also divided on the Yangs, with some scholars arguing that the end of the "Yang family village" increased factionalism at the top. Others argue that the Yangs inadvertently helped restrict the role of factions. Factions exist in Chinese politics, but how we should think about them in civil-military relations remains a point of contention. Perhaps the only thing that can be said with any certainty is that personalism remains and its persistence allows us to measure the limits of institutionalization within the Chinese political system.

Professionalism After 1992

For those writing within the professionalism paradigm, the essential arguments remain largely unchanged. They continue to view the PLA as a basically professional force within a Leninist state, with few substantively new ideas in the professionalization literature of the 1990s. As both the 1991 Gulf War and the recent NATO bombing of Yugoslavia aptly demonstrate, China's security lies in developing a modern, technically proficient force. Therefore, China will need to continue to upgrade the skill and expertise of its officer corps, thereby strengthening the trend toward professionalization. The political campaigns that followed Tiananmen have subsided and are now viewed as a temporary manifestation of the normal tensions between a professional force and the

Party's desire to maintain control, a process that goes back to the 1950s. The transition to a post-revolutionary elite should, in theory, further encourage trends toward professionalism. For the first time there will be distinct civilian and military elites. Unlike their predecessors, the new military elite ought to be more inwardly oriented toward professional concerns and less involved in political matters. Barring a major conflict among civilian elites, the PLA should become even more like the Soviet military, which many observers regard as highly professional.

Much of the writings that come under this category between 1992 and 1998 largely consist of new evidence that the PLA is acquiring more of the aspects of a professional force and in many respects is more professional now than in the 1980s. Reflecting vastly improved sources of information and some path-breaking work in statistical analysis, a number of studies have been published in the last few years on officer education that indicate a trend toward greater professionalization. It is not just that the data indicate that officers are better educated than before. The data also indicate that the content of that education has also changed, emphasizing technical knowledge and military theory over ideological issues. Technical specialization is increasing within the PLA. Contacts with foreign militaries and exposure to the professional norms of Western armies have steadily increased.

Trends in officer education are reinforced by other developments in the 1990s. Since Tiananmen, the pace of regularization has picked up. Twelve of the thirteen sections of military law were enacted in just the past ten years. The year 1999 saw major steps toward greater regularization with the introduction of new combat regulations, as well as changes in logistics, military education, and training. Studies of promotions indicate that professional qualifications are more important than ever. The retirement system too seems to be more effective than in the 1980s when it was first introduced. The trend toward a reduction in domestic affairs (except commercial activity) increased through most of the decade. Whereas there were many at the beginning of the 1980s who claimed that the PLA was involved in making domestic policy, few would make that argument now. The preponderance of the empirical data presented in the literature of the mid- to late-1990s indicate an irreversible trend toward a more professional officer corps. Perhaps the best indication of the strength of the evidence is that virtually all scholars writing on the PLA now acknowledge that at least some professionalism has taken place since the 1980s.

It is, therefore, rather ironic that at a time when the evidence for the arguments of Joffe and Jencks is stronger than ever, there should also be a considerable body of evidence that runs counter to those arguments.

Two areas stand out: commercial activity by PLA-owned enterprises and growing evidence that the PLA is increasingly active in the foreign policy arena. The existence of PLA enterprises was a result of historical legacies. The decision to use them to generate funds for the PLA was in part because historical and ideological legacies meant both PLA and civilian Party leaders felt they were legitimate. Historical legacies still affect the PLA despite two decades of growing professionalism. PLA enterprises became highly dysfunctional in part because of social, political, and economic forces that are outside the military. Thus, PLA commercial activities have had an extremely negative impact on the PLA and even though the PLA was ordered to divest itself of these enterprises in July 1998, it will be years before the damage is repaired.

The point I want to make here is that the issue is not just the damage that PLA commercial activity has done to the military. Jencks and Joffe are well aware of the extent to which "PLA Inc." undermined professionalism. But professionalism focuses attention as much on what is happening inside the military itself as it does on the issue of civilian control. This is often a weakness of the approach because there are often many social, political, and economic developments in the society as a whole that can affect professionalism. Officers may be *distinct* from citizens, but the military is seldom truly *separate* from society. PLA commercial activity is not just about the military being involved in the economy. It is also about bringing the larger society into the PLA, exposing officers and enlisted personnel to a whole range of norms and values that are at odds with professional norms and the political message of the Communist Party. By focusing on the military itself and not the military's relationship to the entire political system, analysts may be missing trends that may help or hinder professionalization. Given the enormous amount of change going on in China, this is an important omission in how we think about civil-military relations. Those using the professional approach need to think more about how the developments in society may impact the PLA.

Turning to national security policy, there is increasing evidence of a substantial military role in this policy area. This stands in remarkable contrast to the past, when there was little evidence to suggest that the PLA had any role in foreign policy. Not only has the passing of the old revolutionary elite meant a new political role in national security policy, available evidence indicates that the PLA's involvement is growing. The emergence of a new generation of separate civilian and military elites helps make this possible. Not only do the new civilian elites lack the stature and military experience to set security policy, new military elites are more expert and have a stronger sense of the PLA's corporate interests in security policy. To a certain extent this does not pose a problem for the professionalism argument. As the synopsis of Huntington at the beginning of this paper shows, one of the responsibilities of a professional officer is advice on defense-related issues. The problems start when generals start giving more than advice. That opens the door to bargaining, coalitional behaviour between the PLA and civilian groups, political influence, perhaps even directives to civilians by military personnel. All these types of behaviour pose problems for the image of a politically quiescent PLA. It may very well be that professionalization of the PLA will lead to a narrowing of the PLA's political role, but with the countervailing effect of intensifying the PLA's political influence in those areas that it remains active.

In sum, while the 1990s has been a good decade for many aspects of the professionalism argument, there are also many issues that do not fit well with the expectations of the argument, and this leads to the possibility that the professionals do not have the full story.

New Trends and Developments in the Literature: Symbiosis and Beyond

The post-Tiananmen period also sees some new trends and developments in how PLA scholars think about their subject. The writers who will be considered in this section are rather heterogeneous in their work, but they all have at least one of the following aspects in common. First, in the wake of Tiananmen and the subsequent and intense political campaign in the PLA, many observers began to look for an alternative conceptual approach to professionalism. Second, in the 1990s some PLA scholars started to take more interest in the literature on civil-military relations in other Leninist regimes. Third, many PLA scholars began to think seriously that post-Deng civil-military relations might be different from the past. In the early 1990s, both Cheng Hsiao-shih and Nan Li drew on the work of Soviet specialists in developing their analyses of the PLA's political work system. Cheng agreed with the work of William Odom, especially the latter's argument that the divide between military and civilian was an artificial one in Leninist regimes. Rather, Party and army should be regarded as a whole and civil-military relations are really relations within the party. While providing some valuable insights into the work of the GPD and making a valuable contribution by comparing the PLA to Taiwan's ruling Guomindang Party, Cheng did not really develop his ideas about civil-military fusion. Nor did he carry his analysis past the mid-1980s, when professionalism became more prominent within the PLA. Nan Li, on the other hand, drew on the work of Timothy Colton to create an alternative argument about the political work system. While Li's work provides some good arguments as to why the factional approach will become less useful as the political system bureaucratizes, he is less convincing in his argument that changes in the political work system invalidate the assumption that the PLA acts as a professional interest group.

Another study on the political work system that has had a wider impact on the debate on Chinese civil-military relations is that of David Shambaugh. Shambaugh has drawn on the work of Odom, Perlmutter, and LeoGrande to develop what he calls the "symbiosis" model. Briefly stated, Shambaugh accepts that the PLA displays many of the aspects of a professional force, particularly in terms of skill, expertise, and obedience to civil (Party) authority. Unlike Jencks and Joffe, however, Shambaugh contends that the PLA has historically been "inextricably intertwined" with the Party-state and is therefore very political as well as professional. This apparent contradiction is resolved by understanding that the PLA and the Party have evolved together in a symbiotic relationship, each affecting the other. Indeed, the long period of revolution guaranteed that this symbiotic nature would last long after the founding of the PRC. Symbiosis, however, is not static. Shambaugh's analysis of the political work system within the PLA indicates that the relationship between Party and PLA changes over time and that there have been periods where the Party has been more dominant and sought control. In some respects this argument is not new. Several writers in the 1980s argued that the PLA and the Party formed a dual elite. What is new is the emphasis on the professional aspects of the PLA and the idea that symbiosis can evolve.

The strength of Shambaugh's approach is that it reconciles the problem of professional military behaviour (loyalty to the Party) with the obvious fact the civilian in the Soviet Union, but neither does he find such a boundary as conflict ridden as Kolkowicz does. Rather, the military participates in Soviet politics, bargaining and interacting with civilian elites. Neither side tends to dominate the other, but the military accepts the party's ultimate authority. Colton's model also allows for alliances and political support to crisscross the boundary between civilians and the military. In the end, though, he admits that the Soviet military does not participate as much in politics as it could. The Soviet military does not involve itself in societal choices.

PLA does indeed participate in politics, albeit in a subordinate role. The symbiotic argument is also in many ways more appropriate to the Maoist and early Dengist period than the professionalism approach. The level of professionalization is so much higher in the 1980s and 1990s compared to the 1950s through 1970s that one wonders how much of Maoist civil-military relations can be explained by professionalism. Shambaugh's argument allows for the possibility of evolution from symbiosis to professionalism. I would agree with Shambaugh that the PLA is best thought of as being symbiotic before reform. There really was a dual elite and symbiosis reflects well the revolutionary legacies of the PRC. Professionalism in the PLA was at best partial before the 1980s. However, there is no denying that there has been considerable professionalization of the PLA since 1979 and no one could argue that the PLA has been moving away from symbiosis. To this extent, symbiosis and professionalism are not alternatives but complementary. Joffe is correct in arguing that each describes part of what is a multi-faceted problem.

Shambaugh has recently suggested that there have been subtle changes going on in the relationship between Party, state, and PLA in the 1990s. In this respect Shambaugh touches base with Paltiel. Paltiel also sees the Party-army connection as being symbiotic and argues that there are tensions in the constitutional framework of the Party-state-military relationship. He too sees the potential for important changes in the nature of this relationship. Exactly where these subtle changes may ultimately lead is far from clear. However, Shambaugh does provide some evidence that the state may be (stress on may) developing more direct controls over the armed forces, even to the point of the Party allowing the PLA more relative autonomy. Such a development, if it occurs, would be a logical result of the trend toward professionalism. It is known that some PLA officers desire a state-centered army. A new generation of professionally oriented civilians may also be open to the idea of a clear division of labour between state and Party that gives some control of the PLA to the state.

However, considerable caution is needed here. Leninist regimes are not known for their tolerance of state-centered armies, the Chinese Party especially so. Even minor changes in the relationship between Party, state, and military would have a major impact on civil-military relations. William Odom is adamant in his new study that altering the link between Communist Party and military was very detrimental to the Soviet political system under Gorbachev. There is a real problem in determining how far one can go in reforming the Party-state relationship without undermining the Party-state itself.

James Mulvenon offers a rather different argument about where the PLA is going in the post-Deng era. He argues that civil-military relations are now essentially a balance of power with intense bargaining going on between civilian and military leaders over policy and distribution of resources.

Mulvenon also argues that civil-military relations have moved from symbiosis to professionalism. However, he also argues that in a Leninist context, Huntington's notions of responsibility, corporateness, and expertise lead not to political quiescence but to political involvement. Expertise, he argues, may be a double-edged sword that makes it easier to intervene in domestic politics. Responsibility means that the PLA is very nationalistic in defending China's strategic interests, but he argues that the PLA has yet to grasp the other half of the equation, which is responsibility to society or to state. Corporate identity, when combined with the Party's demands that the PLA remain a political force, creates the potential for praetorianism. In making this argument, Mulvenon is one of few people within PLA studies who has noted that many scholars in the study of civil-military relations have argued that professionalism is a two-edged sword. It can lead to a withdrawal from politics and it can lead to intervention in politics. As evidence for his argument, Mulvenon cites the growing influence of the PLA on national security policy and bargaining surrounding the divestiture of the PLA's enterprises. It is an interesting argument and Mulvenon deserves credit for expanding the terms of debate on professionalism. However, it remains to be seen whether the bargaining and balance of power he describes are a temporary manifestation of the transition to a post-Deng China or if they are a more permanent state of affairs.

So we return to the opening argument of this paper. Twenty years ago there was greater clarity in the study of Chinese civil-military relations. Either civil-military relations would continue to be shaped by the politics of the Cultural Revolution era or reforms would take hold and move civil-military relations in a new direction.

The PLA has been in transition for 20 years. Some of the concepts we use to analyze civil-military relations pre-date that transition. China is still a Party-state, but it is not the same Party-state it was 20 years ago. In the year 2000 we understand less about civil-military relations than in the past. The literature of the past ten years offers a variety of contradictory interpretations.

Factional politics remain important, or it may be declining, or the basis for factions may be changing. The PLA is showing signs of being more professional, yet there are also many factors that serve to undermine that trend. The PLA may be moving, however uncertainly, to a more state-centered army. The PLA may be becoming more active in political bargaining with the Party. There may very well be some important trends that we are not yet aware of simply because we are not asking the right questions. In many respects all the main themes described here are looking at different parts of what is a multifaceted relationship between the PLA and the Party that created it. They point to the need to step back and try to integrate the various elements of that relationship to better understand how it has evolved over the years.

We would argue that we have taken current arguments as far as we can, using China alone as our model. One of the most striking features of PLA studies is how little comparative work has been done. To a certain extent that is natural. Many aspects of Chinese politics are highly unusual, if not unique. However, Chinese civil-military relations, like the rest of its politics, are becoming more like those of other countries and PLA scholars need to look to other countries to help us form ideas and questions, especially suggestions about paths for future research.

11

China, India, and Pakistan—Growing Nuclear Capabilities With No End in Sight

CHALLENGES TO INDIA'S CURRENT DEFENCE PRODUCTION AND RESEARCH AND DEVELOPMENT CAPABILITY

India's experience of developing its defence industry and research and development capability over the past decade has been mixed.

Ordnance Factories and PSUs

Outwardly, both the ordnance factories and the PSUs can be considered successful enterprises. The country's ordnance factories are capable of providing the Indian military with a significant proportion of their ammunition and low level material needs. In the period 1992/93-1997/98, for example, India only imported 11 per cent of its total ammunition needs. India is also planning to open a 40th Ordnance factory in the near future. Furthermore, speaking in the Indian Parliament, the *Lok Sabha*, on 4 July 2000, George Fernandes, the Indian Defence Minister, stated that the country's ordnance factories recorded a surplus of Rs 780 crores (a crore is ten million rupees) during the period 1999-2000. In addition to this, Fennandes stated that due to last year's Kargil conflict, output increased from 33 per cent to 900 per cent for ammunition items; 20 per cent to 108 per cent for clothing items; and 76 to 233 per cent for cables. More generally, an overall increase in output value of 34.6 per cent in 1999-2000, as compared to the value of issue in 1998/99. The picture for the PSUs is similar. Output in the sector has been rising rapidly since the 1980s, and all the companies have started to move into profitability. According to the latest MOD, moreover, the value of production in 1998-1999 (Rs 7205.55 crore) registered growth of 15.57 per cent over that in 1997-1998 (Rs 6234.75 crore). In addition to this all the defence PSUs reportedly earned a profit in 1998-1999.

Set against that is the fact that these two elements of India's defence industrial base continue to receive large amounts of money from the government in the form of government loans. Between them they also employ in the region of 300000 people. The picture is further complicated by the fact that almost half the production of the PSUs goes to the civil sector; a small proportion of the Ordnance factory production also goes this way. (Put another way if is arguable that, certainly in the case of the PSUs, it is the production of equipment for civil use rather than for military use that is actually making money). Against this backdrop, questions have been raised about their efficiency and ability to meet production targets, as underscored by the fact that it has taken Garden Reach Shipbuilders 12 years to build the Indian Naval Ship (INS) Brhamaputra; three times longer than it would take Russia's cash strapped shipbuilders to do. Traditionally, the price of purchasing systems and platforms from the PSUs has also worked out more expensive than purchasing them from abroad. For example, back in 1956 it was estimated that the cost of independently producing under license the HS-78 plane would be in the region of US$320000; come the end of the 1970s it stood at $1.5 million per unit.

Indigenous R&D

The success of India's indigenous R&D efforts is even more questionable: despite considerable investment through the 1990s nearly all major programmes implemented in the 1980s are experiencing time and cost over-runs.

The IGMDP: Covering the Prithvi and Agni short and medium/ long range ballistic missiles, the Nag anti tank missile, and the Akash and Trishul surface to air missile, this programme has scored a number of notable and high profile successes. For example, the Prithvi has been tested regularly since 1988 and three versions of the missile (150km, 250km, and 350km ranges) are now believed to be in (or close to) production. The Agni was first tested in 1994 and in a 1998 missile test the missile flew close to 2500km. According to some reports, moreover, the missile is now operational. The Aksah, Nag and Trishul, meanwhile, are expected to enter service soon. However, none of these missiles are entirely indigenous. Some reports suggest, for instance, that five to ten per cent of the technologies used in the Prithvi are imported from abroad.

The Arjun: India's experience of designing an indigenous tank has been less successful.

Take the example of the Arjun tank. Originally, expected to be in operation service by 1985 the tank has suffered from continued problems, such as problems with the engine overheating. Limited production of the tank has now started; however the Indian Army has cut back on the number of tanks that it is ordering. *The LCA* The story of the LCA is almost identical to that of the Arjun tank. The programme has experienced delays since its inception in 1983 for a variety of reasons. And the first flight-test, originally scheduled for 1996, is now not expected to take place until some time in 2002. The cost of the programme, in the meantime, has increased from Rs 560 crores. This increased to Rs 2188 crores in 1993, when approval was given to enter the Full Scale Engineering Development Phase-1.

Other Programmes: The picture is much the same for a number of other less high profile programmes, such as the Pinaka, MBRL. This was initiated in 1986 with a budget of Rs 25.6 crores. This was subsequently increased to 49 crores. The system underwent troop trials in October 1999, moreover, but is still waiting for acceptance by the Army before entering full production. A similar story emerges for products such as the Indian Small Arms System (ISAS). The only product deemed to have been a complete success is arguably the ALH. The failure of many of India's R&D programmes and its reliance on the outside world for key technologies is confirmed by a number of by external assessments, such as the United States government Military Critical Technologies List (MCTL). For example, India's capability to manufacture, gas turbine engines, and human crew systems (aeronautic systems technology) is not even considered worthy of a mention in the MCTL. Likewise, its ability to manufacture the systems necessary to ensure that a combat vehicle is superior to the technology that it is confronting. India scores a little better in the area of Marine Systems Technology, where it is rated to have limited Sub-surface and Deep Submergence Vehicle Capability. One area where India is deemed to have been successful is in the area of Means of Delivery Technology for nuclear and other non-conventional weapons, where it is rated as having a sufficient Theatre Ballistic Missile Capability (TBMC), some ICBM capability; and a sufficient Cruise Missile capability. By way of a comparison, outside the core-areas of competency that it has developed, India's defence production and R&D capabilities do not compare that favourably with other developing countries such as China, which has managed to develop its defence industry across a broader spectrum.

Consequences and Responses

India's inability to meet its top end defence needs have been compounded by the approaching obsolescence of a number of platform and systems; a problem that has been made even worse by the fact that Indian has not made any major defence purchases for the past ten years. Last year's crisis in Kargil has also impressed the need to introduce new equipment on the armed forces-according to the reports, for example, the Indian military assessed Pakistan's Ukranian T-80s as being 'almost a generation ahead of what we had'. In response, as far as major systems and high-technology products are concerned, the government has reversed the pattern of the 1990s and shifted the balance of procurement funding away from its home grown programmes and back towards external procurement. This re-evaluation started in the late 1990s and has progressed since there. Thus in 1996-97 and 1997-98 the DRDO's share of the defence budget decreased in real terms for the first time in that decade. At the same time, India announced its decision to purchase 40 SU-30MK fighter/bombers from Russia in India's largest ever defence deal. Likewise, even though India announced that it would increase its defence budget by 28 per cent to $13.94 billion (2.5 per cent of GDP) in 2000-2001 this March, funding for domestic R&D was only raised by 5.2 per cent; the percentage of the defence budget allocated to defence R&D has also slipped to 4.4 per cent of the total budget. At the same time, while this year's defence budget has seen the amount of money for R&D fall in relative terms, the funds for the purchase of defence equipment from abroad have been steadily increased since 1998.

Reviving the Russian Link

Despite the challenge to their defence relationship that occurred following the end of the Cold War and the economic crisis in India, Russia and India still managed to maintain close defence ties throughout the latter part of the 1990s. For example, the two countries signed a long-term defence co-operation programme in 1994; a number of agreements for the upgradation of Indian defence equipment were initialled; India also agreed to buy 40 SU-30MKs in 1997; and according to the Russian Vice Premier Liya Klebarov, defence sales to India account for between 20 and 25 per cent of the annual total export of Russian military goods, making it India's largest arms supplier. It comes as little surprise to find, therefore, that much of the money allocated for procurement will be spent in Russia.

Although many of the deals have been under negotiation for some time, the October visit of the Russian president, Vladimir Putin, appears to have broken the logjam. Thus, although the details still have to be finalised, India and Russia officially agreed to extend their defence co-operation programme until 2010. Furthermore, India announced its intention to buy Russian arms worth more than $2 billion. Intended purchases include, additional Su-30 long range fighter bombers, a number of which will be made under license in India, more than 300 T-90 Main Battle Tanks (MBTS), one third of which will also be made in India, the ageing Soviet-era aircraft carrier, the Admiral Gorshkov, which will be provided for free but would cost $500 million to refurbish; an, as yet, unspecified number of MiG-29s for the ship; and a number of Smersh MRBLs.

European and Other Suppliers

India has also looked to solidify its links with European suppliers. For example, although the details of the deal have yet to be finalised the British based company BAE SYTEMS is also believed to have secured the deal to provide India with the Hawk advanced jet trainer aircraft. (India has been negotiating this purchase for over a decade). France has also been particularly successful, recently concluding an.agreement to sell India additional Mirage 2000 fighters. Outside Europe, India has established a close defence procurement relationship with Israel, which is thought to have provided it, among other things, with equipment suitable for border surveillance. Furthermore, reliable sources have suggested that the Phalcon early warning plane (AEW) that Israel was building for China but recently agreed not to sell to Beijing after pressure from the United States will be delivered to India. South African arms exports have also managed to carve out a small niche for themselves in the country. A number of Eastern European nations are also looking to provide India with new equipment and to help it upgrade its existing inventory. Quite simply, these purchases will fill those gaps that have appeared in India's armed forces in recent years.

The Fourth Phase-All Change in Indian Defence

In hindsight it appears that India, along with other LDCs, has learnt the lesson that while it is one thing to produce equipment such as ammunition and manufacture other people's platforms under license, it is another all-together to be able to locally design and build high-technology weapons systems, particularly in an environment in which the R&D programmes of the developing countries are producing increasingly sophisticated and indeed expensive weapons systems. At this stage, however, nobody is talking about getting rid of defence production and R&D-India is still officially committed to purchasing 70 per cent of its defence needs from indigenous sources by 2010. Rather, a growing number of military officials and businessmen are now calling for a radical shake up in the way in which India approaches defence procurement and indigenisation, largely by allowing greater private sector and possibly foreign participation.

Promoting Privatisation

Of course, interest in promoting greater private sector participation in defence is not new: as stated earlier the law was changed in 1991 to allow the private sector to provide components as well as assembly and sub-assembly to the military. Likewise, in 1994 the country's former Prime Minster Narashima Rao gave a speech in which he noted that 'the domestic arms industry must be opened up to private investment and competition'.

However, in a sign of growing convergence between the government and the private sector on the need for change the Confederation of Indian Industry (CII) and the Ministry of Defence (MOD) agreed in 1998 to establish six task forces to look at the subject. They recommended 1) reviewing the existing partnership between the MOD, industry and the military; 2) evolving strategies for long-term partnerships between these group; 3) studying the existing capacity of the defence PSUs and ordnance factories; 4) exploring the possibility of joint ventures; 5) developing joint marketing arms for exports; and 6) leveraging India's strengths in information technology in the defence sector.

Both the government and the military appear to be embracing these suggestions. For example, in July this year the Defence Minister, George Fernandes, called for greater co-operation and interaction between the Ordnance factories, the PSUs, and the DRDO. Speaking at a September conference organised by the Confederation of Indian Industries (CII) and the Indian Airforce (IAF), meanwhile, the Chief of the Airforce, Air Marshal A.Y. Tipinis, called for much greater participation from private manufacturers in the production of aircraft and weapons support systems. At the same conference, Vijay Kapur, Chairman of the CII National Committee on Communications, stated that: 1) the private sector should be allowed to manufacture arms and armaments and that the government should review its industrial policy accordingly; 2) that foreign collaboration should be allowed;

3) that arms and armaments currently in the 'reserved' category should be moved to the licensed category; 4) that industry should come forward as a partner with the services and not as contractors; and 5) that the government should fund private sector R&D. He concluded that if these steps were followed India would be able to soon meet its defence requirements indigenously. In an interesting development, at an earlier CII conference, George Fernandes, also welcomed the suggestion that the private sector be allowed to play a larger role in defence research and development (R&D) by calling on the private sector to compliment the role of the DRDO. The main advantage of private sector participation in defence R&D and/or increased government funding for private companies engaged in defence R&D is that the government can tap into the private sector's recent success at IT R&D. Private sector involvement should also serve to reduce costs as these firms operate on free-market principles.

Drivers of Change

Interestingly, this willingness to consider a change of direction is not only the result of the failure of India's ambitious R&D programme, but also due to a number of domestic and international factors. *The End of the Cold War:* In addition to the defence production issues and problems with Russia, the end of the Cold War has had a number of often contradictory impacts for Indian defence planners. On the one hand, India, like China was shocked by the quick success that the Allies scored over the Iraqis during the Gulf War. Particularly, the sight of a large army equipped with much Soviet equipment struggling to compete with European and North American technology was not lost on the Indians, convincing the country's senior military officials of the needs to introduce high-technology equipment. Likewise, India was disturbed by NATO intervention in Kosovo on the basis of support for human rights. America's desire to deploy a National Missile Defence (NMD) system has also been opposed in India. (Its opposition is partly related to the fear that advances in technology in this area will undermine the limited advances that India has made in its own nuclear and missile capabilities). On the other hand, thanks to its emergence as a major IT power, India's decision to fly in the face of international convention and conduct nuclear tests in May 1998 has been largely forgotten by the international community and particularly the United States. The crumbling of the traditionally strong bonds between Pakistan and America in the wake of Pakistan's decision to test nuclear weapons shortly after India; the Kargil crisis and the October military coup have helped this process of rapprochement. In response, India has attempted to maintain and build on its existing relationship with Russia, particularly in the area of defence sales, while establishing new ties with the United States in both the economic and diplomatic spheres.

Global Defence Industry Restructuring: Since the end of the Cold War global defence spending has decreased by 28.6 per cent between 1990 and 1999. Over the same period there has been a rash of consolidation among major arms producing companies in the United States and Europe. The decreasing size of the major producers' home markets has encouraged them to look abroad to new markets, in which defence spending is still growing. The impact of this process on India has been two-fold. Firstly, as the process of globalisation continues there is growing scope for partnerships to be established between Indian defence producers looking for access to new technology, and foreign defence manufacturers keen to tap the sales potential in the Indian market and also its strengths in areas such as IT. They may also wish to use the country as a platform from which to launch its products into other markets. Domestically, meanwhile, those civil servants and bureaucrats at the heart of the Indian government are unlikely to have missed the fact that process of privatisation and consolidation in defence was a reaction to declining defence budgets after the Cold War. And that these new companies are often leaner and more competitive than their predecessors; while strategic alliances and joint ventures are now the rule rather than the exception in the sector due to the rising costs of designing and producing the next generation of defence equipment.

The Election of the Bharatiya Janta Party (BJP). The BJP led coalition government is more committed to tackling defence issues than its predecessors. Examples abound: in May 1988, shortly after first coming to power, it presided over India's first nuclear tests since 1974; while March 2000 saw the government reverse the downward trend in defence spending established in the 1990s. From the start the BJP government has also made an effort to articulate what the country's defence and security policy was, in opposition to the previous government, which according to the BJP was merely to assure Indians and indeed the world that India actually had such a policy.

Economic Reform. India's economic reform programme has gained momentum since it was introduced in 1991. Crucially, it now has support from across the political spectrum. As the government slowly retreats from the 'commanding heights' of the economy, moreover, greater attention is starting to be focused on the benefits to be gained from allowing greater private participation in defence, which to a large degree explains the involvement of the CII. India's moves towards privatisation, however, have not been plain sailing. Despite moving away from its policy of 'Swadeshi' or self-reliance, there remain elements of the BJP who still oppose the process; the same is true of many of the country's citizens. Efforts to dismantle the so-called 'Permit Raj' through a process of 'dis-investment' have also progressed more slowly than many had hoped, due largely to bureaucratic opposition and inertia.

Information Technology: India is quickly becoming a major player in the field of information technology (IT). For example, there are currently 340000 software professionals employed in the country-in 1996 there were only 180000-while India's technology schools are producing 100000 software professionals a year. The country has also developed its own super-computing capability, the Paran, which it has exported to Russia. India's strength in IT having a major impact on India's economy: total exports of IT related products amounted to about $9 billion in 1999. This sector of the economy has also managed to attract significant amounts of foreign investment, much of it into the cities of Bangalore and Hyderebad. The emergence of India as a major IT power is interesting for a number of reasons. For instance, although the principle of IT development was supported by the late Prime Minister Rajiv Ghandi in the 1980s, the sector has grown up outside the normal regulation and red tape associated with the Indian economy.

Dominated as it is by private sector companies it has also proved to be rather more innovative and flexible than other industries. Additionally, information technology has been India's bridge with outside world: its technicians and programmers are at the forefront of the IT revolution in the United States and are being courted by Japan, Germany and the United States. Attracted by the loosening of government control over the economy, moreover, many of these people are now returning to India, thereby breathing new energy into the economy.

CHINA

Unlike India and Pakistan, China is formally a nuclear weapon state under the nuclear Non-Proliferation Treaty (NPT). China is also a major nuclear power possessing advanced, repeatedly tested, and diverse nuclear weapons designs, diverse delivery systems, and a centralized command and control network that is intended to ensure that the leadership of the Chinese Communist Party can exercise effective command of the country's nuclear weaponry.

In contrast to the United States and the former Soviet Union, China historically maintained a small nuclear force consisting primarily of land-based missiles whose warheads were stored separately, with the delivery vehicles maintained routinely in un-alerted status in silos or caves. This relatively relaxed posture was viewed as sufficient to protect Chinese security during the Cold War because Beijing believed that the positive externalities of mutual U.S.-Soviet nuclear deterrence bestowed on China sufficient protection. Because even a small number of survivable nuclear weapons capable of reaching an adversary's homeland could wreak unacceptable damage, Chinese leaders sought to maintain relatively modest forces that through a combination of opacity, sheltering, and sometimes limited mobility, could survive the remote contingencies of direct nuclear attack at a time when these dangers were limited principally by the political constraints of strong bipolar competition.

With the ending of the Cold War and with the progressive rise of Chinese power, Beijing—whether it publicly admits it or not—has come to view the United States as its principal strategic competitor. Given China's recognition of the sophistication of U.S. nuclear and conventional forces in the face of Beijing's desire to reclaim the strategic primacy it once enjoyed in Asia, Chinese nuclear modernization became inevitable. This modernization, which consists principally of efforts to increase the survivability of its nuclear deterrent in the face of what it perceives to be a formidable U.S. nuclear threat supplemented by other major regional dangers from Russia, India, and other prospective nuclear powers, has taken the following form: the deployment of new land-based solid-fueled ballistic missiles of varying ranges (to include intercontinental-range ballistic missiles); ballistic missile submarines with weapons capable of reaching the continental United States; new highly survivable nuclear weapon storage sites; and a robust national command and control system that incorporates a resilient, dedicated nuclear command and control segment.

The number of nuclear warheads in the Chinese arsenal has also progressively increased as the nuclear delivery systems have been augmented, but there still significant uncertainties about the existence and the number of nuclear gravity bombs and tactical nuclear weapons in the Chinese arsenal. The total size of the Chinese nuclear weapons inventory today is widely believed to consist of some 250 nuclear warheads, but the accuracy of these or any other numbers is debatable. China has a substantial fissile material stockpile consisting of some 16 metric tons of highly enriched uranium and some 1.8 metric tons of weapon-grade plutonium, so there are no practical constraints on its ability to produce an arsenal of any size it chooses. Given the choices China makes in regard to delivery systems, it could deploy anywhere up to an additional 150 warheads over the next ten years.

At arsenal levels of such size, the Chinese nuclear force will be oriented fundamentally towards deterring nuclear use (or the threat of use) against China by maintaining a survivable retaliatory capacity during conflicts with any nuclear-armed state and by maintaining the capacity for escalation dominance vis-à-vis weaker nuclear adversaries. Toward these ends, China will continue to reiterate its "no first use" nuclear policy, though what that doctrine means precisely is unclear.

China today views the United States as its principal active nuclear and conventional threat, followed by India in the nuclear realm. Russia remains a latent nuclear threat and although it was historically an important driver of Chinese nuclear planning, Russia has receded considerably in Chinese calculations today. North Korea, Taiwan, and Japan remain longer-term sources of strategic uncertainty for Beijing, with nuclear threats remaining a current or prospective challenge in all three cases. The most pressing practical contingencies involving Chinese nuclear use in the prospective future, however, involve employment against U.S. forces to forestall defeat or signal a willingness to risk further escalation in the context of a successful U.S. intervention in a Taiwan crisis or in another crisis of similar magnitude in East Asia (for example, on behalf of Japan), and the use of tactical (or other) nuclear weapons in a conflict with India.

INDIA

The rivalry between China and India since their birth as modern states after the Second World War created the preconditions for a nuclear rivalry between them—a competition that was inflamed when China first tested nuclear weapons in 1964 driven by its antagonism to the United States and its emerging split with the Soviet Union. The first Chinese nuclear test, coming two years after India's defeat in the 1962 Sino-Indian conflict, precipitated the Indian nuclear weapons program, which in turn first demonstrated its capacity in 1974. Despite the supposed Chinese disdain of India, Beijing began to systematically target India with nuclear weapons after the latter's first nuclear test, and sometime in the late-1980s transferred a nuclear weapon design and fissile material to Pakistan, at least in part as a strategy of containing India. New Delhi responded to the Chinese challenge with additional nuclear tests in 1998, declared itself to be a nuclear weapon state, and began to overtly develop its nuclear deterrent since—aimed at both China and Pakistan.

India today is believed to possess an arsenal of some 100 nuclear weapons, though this figure is highly uncertain. The country is thought to have produced close to 600 kilograms of weapons-grade plutonium, though it is unclear whether all this material has been machined into warheads. India can produce extremely large quantities of weapons-grade plutonium, should it chose to use its power reactors currently outside of safeguards for this purpose. To date, however, there is no evidence that India has embarked on any crash program to enlarge its nuclear arsenal, despite its having the technical capacity to do so. If India persists in producing about 5-6 nuclear weapons annually (as it is believed to have done since 1998), the India nuclear deterrent would consist of some less than 200 nuclear weapons by 2025—assuming the public assessments of its current inventory are correct. These weapons will be deployed aboard primarily mobile, solid-fueled, ballistic missiles of up to intermediate range, though these will be supplemented by a limited number of legacy gravity weapons and a small but growing number of sea-launched ballistic missiles. All Indian nuclear weapons currently are maintained routinely in de-mated condition, though whether this posture will persist after the four ballistic missile submarines are eventually inducted into its arsenal is unclear.

The heart of India's current nuclear modernization program, which is centered on developing and inducting mobile, sold-fueled intermediate-range ballistic missiles, deploying ballistic missile submarines, developing a ballistic missile defense system, building weapon storage and integration sites, and completing its command and control network, is aimed principally at refurbishing its deterrence capability vis-à-vis China. The threats emerging from Pakistan are significant, but Indian policy makers judge that their current deterrent against Islamabad as generally adequate. The deterrence gap versus China, however, is considerable and it will not be bridged until India acquires the capacity to range the Chinese heartland with missiles of adequate reach.

Even when the effort to reach this goal is completed—an endeavor that will continue well beyond 2025—it is likely that New Delhi will persist with its currently relaxed nuclear posture so long as current trends in Sino-Indian and Indo-Pakistani relations persist. This posture is predicated on the requirement of a "minimum" deterrent (whose numerical size is not publicly known) and a strict "no first use" policy (which is likely to subsist durably because of India's general conventional military superiority over Pakistan and its still substantial, though decaying, operational military superiority over China along their disputed border). As long as these conditions obtain, there is little incentive for India to violate its "no first use" policy, which is oriented fundamentally towards deterring nuclear attack (or threats of attack) emerging from Pakistan and China.

PAKISTAN

The contrast between India and Pakistan on "no first use" could not be greater. Unlike India, which is both stronger than Pakistan and no pushover where China is concerned, Pakistan is a weak state that is unfortunately growing even weaker as a result of its awful strategic choices. Pakistan's security competition with India, which dates back to the creation of the two countries as independent states, is multi-dimensional in nature and involves territorial, religious, and power-political dimensions. These grievances have combined in unhelpful ways to make Pakistan the anti-status quo power in the Indian subcontinent. Having fought four unsuccessful wars with India in an effort to secure its strategic aims, Pakistan switched to a dangerous and provocative strategy in the last decades of the 20th century—a strategy of supporting terrorist groups aimed at enervating India through "a thousand cuts," even as Pakistan began to feverishly expand its nuclear arsenal in an effort to prevent New Delhi from retaliating with conventional forces.

The post-2001-02 shift in Indian policy, which holds out the threat of conventional retaliation to Pakistani-supported terrorist attacks (despite the overarching presence of nuclear weapons in the subcontinent), has only deepened Pakistan's dependence on nuclear weapons further, resulting in an acceleration of its weapons program. Today, the Pakistan arsenal includes both gravity weapons and ballistic missiles of up to medium range as well as cruise missiles, glide bombs, and a plethora of new and diverse tactical nuclear weapons. The Pakistani nuclear arsenal is judged by many reputable scholars to consist of some 90-110 weapons, though at the current pace of growth the force could easily expand to over three times that number within a decade.

Pakistan's strategic weaponry is believed to be deployed in de-mated condition routinely in peacetime. Whether that posture will apply to the newer tactical systems is unclear. Pakistan's nuclear doctrine, unlike India or China's, is centered fundamentally on first use, and it is oriented primarily towards defeating India's conventional superiority in the event of conflict. Although Pakistan's nuclear forces are intended, strictly speaking, for deterrence and not war fighting, Islamabad's emerging tactical capabilities could inadvertently push Pakistan towards the latter.

The external dangers of deterrence breakdown, which could precipitate the catastrophe of Pakistani nuclear use against India, are complemented by internal dangers as well. Pakistan's internal fissures, it is often feared, could bleed into its armed forces, resulting in risks to the security of its nuclear weaponry. Although the Pakistani military has made enormous investments in enhancing nuclear security (aided by the United States) in recent years, fears about the loss or compromise of its nuclear weaponry because of domestic dangers still persist—and not unreasonably so.

TAKING STOCK

When all three states are synoptically considered, therefore, the following contingencies remain the most pressing from the viewpoint of U.S. strategic interests for the reasons adduced below:

1) Chinese use or threats of use of nuclear weaponry to deter U.S. military intervention on behalf or Taiwan or other American allies in Asia. Of the three nuclear weapons states that are the subject of this testimony, only China conceives of its nuclear arsenal as having direct utility for deterring U.S. military operations directed against its interests at various locations along the Asian rimland. Any contingency that brings U.S. forces in confrontation with China would represent a dangerous predicament and would require both local conventional and overall nuclear superiority for political and military success. Any failure on this score could not only precipitate immediate

operational reverses that would frustrate the realization of U.S. political aims, but it could lead over time to the erosion of the U.S. alliance system in East Asia, the future acquisition of nuclear weapons by current American allies, and the eventual loss of American primacy in the Indo-Pacific. For all these reasons, preparing seriously to ensure success in this contingency should remain at the top of American strategic priorities. The recent innovations centered on the "AirSea Battle" concept indicate that the Pentagon has taken the emerging Chinese threats to the U.S. ability to aid its East Asian allies seriously, though it is unclear whether force planning for nuclear escalation vis-à-vis China has been adequately integrated into the current war plans. If this lacuna is real, it could prove costly in the context of a conflict—and could undermine the confidence of the allies in the viability of the U.S. nuclear umbrella.

2) Pakistani "use" of nuclear weapons as cover to support continued terrorist attacks against India. Although this contingency derives from Pakistan's ability to exploit the deterrence capability inherent in its nuclear reserves for revisionist ends—and represents the dominant threat levied by the Pakistani military against India now for some three decades—it embodies the most likely route to nuclear deterrence breakdown in South Asia. Neither Indian nor U.S. nuclear capabilities are directly useful in defeating this threat, but U.S. and international political pressure on Pakistan, which has been employed episodically, might offer a means of mitigating its worst dangers. The most likely antidote that could alter such Pakistani behavior, however, would be the rising costs of terrorist blowback within Pakistan—which is, unfortunately, an expensive way of getting Pakistan to change course.

3) Pakistani nuclear use against India or against Indian military forces in the context of Indian retaliation against Pakistani-supported terrorist attacks against India. This contingency arises if India decides to retaliate against Pakistan through the large scale use of military force for

punitive purposes. Any significant employment of Indian military force obviously carries the risk of a Pakistani nuclear response, which is why Indian leaders have shied away from exercising major conventional war options that require especially the large scale use of land forces. Should India contemplate major military operations, however, it is likely that the United States would intervene, but mainly through energetic diplomacy as it did in 2001-02 and again in 2008. It is unlikely that the United States would choose to intervene militarily to prevent either conflict escalation or nuclear weapons employment for a host of operational reasons, though some kinds of trans- or post-conflict assistance might be feasible: in such circumstances, the most important U.S. capabilities that would be relevant would be intelligence, surveillance and reconnaissance (ISR) assets, capabilities required for noncombatant evacuation operations, and Nuclear Emergency and Support Teams (NEST) and other assets essential for post-detonation assistance and recovery (if nuclear use has occurred). Because of the large numbers of U.S. citizens normally resident or traveling in India, and the complexity of evacuation operations in a nuclear environment, this scenario can be more stressing than is commonly realized. The most useful U.S. contribution towards preventing a Pakistani use of nuclear weapons in such a scenario—and the Indian nuclear retribution that would result thereafter—would be to press Pakistan to exit the terrorism business or risk being left alone (or, even worse, the object of international sanction) if a major Indian military response ensues in the aftermath of any pernicious terrorist attack. Other than this, there is little that the United States can do to preserve deterrence stability between two asymmetrically-sized states where the gap in power promises to become even wider tomorrow than it is today.

4) Pakistani loss of control over nuclear assets in the context of conventional military operations against India OR a compromise of nuclear security in peacetime in Pakistan. This scenario, which has been discussed considerably in

recent years both in India and in the United States, would also be highly complex in the demands it places on the U.S. military, depending on the details of the contingency. U.S. ISR elements, special operations forces, and other quick reaction capabilities would be highly relevant in such a contingency—as would close coordination with the government of Pakistan and its armed forces. The United States has already aided Pakistan significantly in regards to nuclear weapons protection, but there are obvious limits to further assistance beyond a point, not least because of the deep-rooted Pakistani fears about the United States seeking access and information about the location of Pakistan's nuclear weaponry.

5) Chinese or Indian nuclear coercion against the other in the context of a border crisis OR in the limiting case, the actual use of nuclear weapons to stave off battlefield defeat. This last contingency, admittedly remote today, would put a high premium on U.S. ISR assets as well as, obviously, active U.S. diplomacy. At the present, it is unlikely that the United States would find itself involved in such a conflict except as a concerned bystander, but if this situation were to change as U.S.-Indian ties grow deeper over time, U.S. conventional and nuclear forces might acquire new roles for extended deterrence and reassurance with respect to India. Until then, however, U.S. ISR capabilities and diplomacy would represent the instruments most relevant to coping with such a scenario.

Implications for the United States

The broad range of nuclear challenges arising from a consideration of the problems involving China, India and Pakistan suggest several important conclusions as far as U.S. strategic forces are concerned.

First, U.S. nuclear forces will continue to remain the ultimate backstop where American national security is concerned. The notion that these forces will become irrelevant any time soon, or that their abolition can be contemplated, is a dangerous fantasy. Eliminating nuclear weapons globally must instead take a backseat to protecting U.S. nuclear dominance and maintaining the effectiveness of the U.S. nuclear deterrent over the long term.

Second, the progressive growth of Chinese, Indian, and Pakistani nuclear forces over the next ten years—and the likelihood of further proliferation elsewhere in years to come--implies that any further reduction of U.S. nuclear forces beyond the New Start treaty ought to be eschewed. Given the complexity of the emerging nuclear environment—a world that is best described as asymmetric nuclear multipolarity—the United States must seek to maintain the requisite superiority of the total force that permits it to achieve conventional success in regional contingencies while preserving the advantages currently enjoyed by U.S. nuclear forces. Given the onerous U.S. extended deterrence commitments in Europe and Asia, American nuclear parity with Russia must not diminish to a point where parity with China slinks into reach.

Third, the United States must think seriously about the threat of nuclear deterrence breakdown in Asia as a time when the continent will host many nuclear powers whose arsenals vary in capacity, architecture and doctrine. The desire to reduce the salience of nuclear weaponry in global politics is estimable. That means that U.S. nuclear weapons ought not to be brandished unnecessarily. However, it does not imply forgetting that U.S. nuclear weapons are still essential for deterring not only nuclear attacks (or the threats thereof) on the United States and its allies but also major conventional attacks as well, while still remaining useful as tactical warfighting instruments in certain specific, admittedly limited, contingencies where conventional weapons currently remain ineffective. As a general rule, therefore, the desire to reduce the salience of nuclear weapons in world politics should not extend to devaluing the utility of nuclear weapons for deterrence because these instruments will continue to remain the ultima ratio in an environment that only promises more, not less, proliferation.

NUCLEAR WEAPONS ARE NOT FOR WARFIGHTING

In the 1950s, the US made extensive efforts to develop, produce and deploy, tactical nuclear weapons in the European and the

Pacific theatres. By the mid-1960s, approximately 7,000 warheads had been deployed in Europe and an undisclosed number in the Pacific. The Soviet and Warsaw Pact forces soon followed suit and are known to have deployed about 3,500 of these weapons.8 However, unlike the surfeit of intellectual debate and discussion on the strategic nuclear issue, tactical nuclear weapons generated only limited interest. Explicit doctrinal criteria for tactical nuclear forces were not formulated. Employment policies were initially hazy and for long training to fight in a nuclear environment was almost completely neglected.

Even the US Department of Defence, on whose insistence NATO's flexible response strategy centred around the first use of nuclear weapons despite the misgivings of some allies, by and large had a decided aversion to using tactical nuclear weapons and an ambivalent and muddled policy embracing their role. William R. Van Cleave and S. T. Cohen write that the 1977-78 doctrinal manual The Army in the Field stated:

"Unless the enemy uses them first, nuclear weapons will not be authorised before conventional defences have been severely tested and found inadequate. The situation facing corps at the time nuclear weapons are requested must therefore be grave – under sustained attack by superior forces, own forces becoming fully committed and not likely to hold, reinforcements not available, insufficient combat support and combat service support available to sustain the defence, and the survivability of the force in question."

Proponents of tactical nuclear weapons justified their requirement on the following grounds:

- They deter the use of tactical nuclear weapons by the enemy.
- They provide flexible response over the whole range of possible military threats.
- They offer nuclear military options below the strategic level.
- They help to defeat large-scale conventional attacks.
- And, they serve the political purpose of demonstrating to the European allies the US' commitment.

Throughout the 1970s and 1980s, the NATO allies of the US were never happy with the manner in which tactical nuclear weapons were stored in a limited number of storage sites where these were highly vulnerable to a pre-emptive attack and destruction. Exacerbating the problem were the vintage, lack of technological sophistication and, consequently, the questionable effectiveness of most of the warheads and some of the delivery systems. The only new warhead to be introduced into service was the so-called 'clean' enhanced radiation 'neutron' bomb, but its production was slow and not enough numbers reached the NATO theatre. Opponents of tactical nuclear weapons asserted that such 'more usable' weapons would lower the nuclear threshold and make nuclear war more likely. Before the INF treaty came into force in 1988, the Honest John rocket was over 30 years old, the Sergeant missile had mostly been retired and the F-4 aircraft which carried the bulk of NATO's tactical atomic bombs during the 1960s and 1970s was designed in the late 1950s. Fears of collateral damage in the extensively populated and developed NATO heartland also spurred European opposition to tactical nuclear weapons. Many European political and military leaders convincingly argued that NATO would be better off without tactical nuclear weapons. Alain Enthoven wrote: "Tactical nuclear weapons cannot defend Western Europe; they can only destroy it there is no such thing as tactical nuclear war in the sense of sustained purposive military operations "

In the US too there was a lack of unanimity about the usefulness of tactical nuclear weapons and lack of coherence in policy. The 1975 US Department of Defence annual report left considerable doubt about the possibility of the use of tactical nuclear weapons: "...as a practical matter, the initiation of a nuclear engagement would involve many uncertainties. Acceptable boundaries on such a conflict would be very difficult to establish. A nuclear engagement in the theatre could produce much higher military and civilian casualties and more widespread collateral damage than its non-nuclear counterpart

"What is more, it is not clear under what conditions the United States and its allies would possess a comparative military advantage in a tactical nuclear exchange.

"...We must recognise in our planning that the decision to initiate the use of nuclear weapons—however small, clean, and precisely used they might be—would be the most agonising that could face any national leader."

While the West was debating the merits and demerits of tactical nuclear weapons, Soviet military doctrine was predicated on the selective use of nuclear weapons in consonance with well-defined political and military objectives. The Soviets emphasised the increased effectiveness of nuclear weapons for warfighting purposes and it was their expectation that large-scale military conflicts, such as a NATO-Warsaw pact confrontation, would involve the use of nuclear weapons. Marshal Grechko wrote:12

"The art of conducting military operations with the use of nuclear weapons and that of employing conventional forces have many fundamental differences. But they are not in opposition, are not mutually exclusive, and are not isolated one from the other; on the contrary, they are closely correlated and are developing as a single body

"Nuclear missiles will be the decisive means of armed combat. Along with this, conventional weapons will also find use, and under certain conditions, the units and subunits can conduct actions solely with conventional means."

The use of tactical nuclear weapons can be a rational option only if it does not finally lead to irrational, more destructive levels of warfare. Gradually, but inexorably, it dawned on the military planners on both the sides of the Iron Curtain that the first use of tactical nuclear weapons was bound to lead to uncontrollable larger nuclear exchanges. After protracted negotiations, the Intermediate-range Nuclear Forces (INF) Treaty between the US and the Soviet Union, was signed in Washington on December 8, 1987 by President Reagan and General Secretary Gorbachev. The treaty proposed the elimination of all INF missiles and practically outlawed the use of tactical and theatre nuclear weapons in Europe.13 Since then, all tactical nuclear weapons have been removed from Europe. It is now universally accepted that nuclear weapons are political weapons and are no longer weapons of 'warfighting'. By extension, 'tactical' or battlefield nuclear weapons should now have no role to play in combat.

Tactical Targets and Yields

Strategic nuclear targets are either counter-value or counter-force targets. Counter-value targets include major enemy cities and industrial centres and these are the ones that generate the 'terror' of the 'balance of terror' through the threat of causing millions of civilian casualties. Counter-force targets primarily comprise the nuclear assets of the adversary including delivery means, bases, nuclear warheads and missile storage sites, command and control elements and early warning and targeting infrastructure. While the aim of selecting counter-value targets has generally been to maximise deterrence, counter-force targets aim to degrade the enemy's capability to make optimum use of his nuclear forces. Military planning for the use of nuclear weapons, in the eventuality that deterrence fails, includes a judicious mix of both counter-value and counter-force targets in first use as well as retaliatory strikes.

Bibliography

Anil, K.C.: *Military and Democracy in South Asia : Challenges, Politics and Power*, Sumit Enterprises, Delhi, 2009.

Arend, A.: *International Law and the Use of Force*, London, Routledge, 1993.

Ashton, S.R.: *British Policy Towards the Indian States, 1905-1939*, London, Curzon, 1982.

Atar Singh Jadoan: *Military Geography of South East Asia*, Anmol, Delhi, 2001.

Barua, Pradeep: *Gentlemen of the Raj: The Indian Army Officer Corps, 1817–1949*, 2003.

Bhaskara Rao: *Military Conversion : Impact on Science and Technology*, Discovery, Delhi, 2003.

Boubel, Richard W.: *Fundamentals of Air Power*, San Diego, Academic Press, 1994

Cathy Solheim: *Military Economics: Issues, Policies, and Solutions*, Washington, D.C., Island Press, 1995.

Chakravarty, B C Dr.: *Indian Armed Forces - Official History of the 1965 Indo-Pak War*. Ministry of Defence.

Darwin: *A Study of the Aerospace Industry*, North Carolina, Amalie, 1964.

Dixit, A.K. : *Military Wars and Rescue Techniques*, Cyber Tech Pub, Delhi, 2010.

Goel, Suresh : *Military, Security and Intelligence Agencies*, MD Publications, Delhi, 2009.

Gupta, P. S. and Anirudh Deshpande: *The British Raj and its Indian Armed Forces, 1857–1939*, New Delhi: Oxford University Press, 2002.

Heathcote, T. A.: *The Indian Army – The Garrison of British Imperial India, 1822–1922*. David & Charles. Newton Abbot, Devon. 1974.

Huntington, S.P.: *The China Modernisation Military and the State*, N.Y., Vintage Books, 1964.

Jackson, Major Donovan: *India's Army*. Sampson Low. London, 1940.

Janowitz, M.: *The Professional Soldier: A Social and Political Portrait,* N.Y., The Free Press, 1960.

Mary, W.: *Asian Power and Politics: the Cultural Dimensions of Authority,* Cambridge, Belknap Press, 1985.

Nininger, Robert D. *Minerals for Atomic Energy*. New York: D. Van Nostrand Company, Inc., 1954.

Noorani, A.G. : *Indian Political Trials : 1775-1947,* New Delhi, Oxford University Press, 2005.

Peter Lambron Wilson : *Traditional Modes of Contemplation and Action,* University Press, Tehran, 1977.

Radhakrishna: *Military Ethics: Guidelines for Peace and War,* Sumit Enterprises, Delhi, 2009.

Rosen, P.: *Societies and Military Power: India and its Armies,* Ithaca, Cornell University Press, 1996.

Seth, Vijay: *The Flying Machines - Indian Air Force 1933-99*. Seth Communications, Delhi, 2000.

Simon, D. : *Societies and Military Power,* Ithaca, Cornell University Press, 1996.

Tanham, George K.: *The Indian Air Force: Trends & prospects*. Rand, Santa Monica, Delhi, 1995.

Weeks, John: *World War II Small Arms,* New York: Galahad Books (1979).

Winkler, Allan M. *Life Under A Cloud: American Anxiety About the Atom.* New York: Oxford University Press, 1993.

Index

◆◆◆